Right from the Start

A Guide to Nonsexist Child Rearing

Right from the Start

A Guide to Nonsexist Child Rearing

Selma Greenberg

HOUGHTON MIFFLIN COMPANY BOSTON 1979

Library of Congress Cataloging in Publication Data

Greenberg, Selma Betty.
    Right from the start.
        1. Children—Management.   2. Sex role.
3. Parent and child.   4. Sexism.   I. Title.
HQ769.G744   649'.1   77–20000
ISBN 0–395–25714–X   ISBN 0–395–27817–1 pbk.

Printed in the United States of America

p 10 9 8 7 6 5 4 3 2 1

The lines quoted on page 57 are from the song
"Tea for Two," © 1924 by Warner Bros. Inc.;
copyright renewed; all rights reserved;
used by permission.

For Arlene and Lee Weisman
Special People, Special Parents, Special Friends

Acknowledgments

ALTHOUGH MANY PEOPLE have assisted me during the book's preparation, I am particularly grateful to the following people.

Linda Nadel and Sheldon Miller from the very outset helped me to clarify the direction the book was to take. Lisa Serbin has not only made her own work readily accessible to me, but she has been enormously helpful in directing me to other pertinent research, sharing with me her interpretation of past and current research findings. She has been my research "fairy godparent." Beverly Fagot's discussions with me of her own work and the work of others helped to deepen my understanding of research issues. Patricia Lynch, Audrey Kurland, and Patia Prowtin were among the many who typed various versions of the manuscript and contributed valuable criticisms and insights. Audrey Kurland has been the person most responsible for the notes. Anita Gurian, Flavia Stutz, and Van Angelo read the developing manuscript and made important suggestions that were incorporated in later revisions.

The final version of the manuscript was read by Florence Howe, Lisa Serbin, and Barbara Sprung. Their comments and suggestions have been invaluable. Frances Tenenbaum is truly a working editor. She labored long and hard to bring order, organization, and clarity to the final version of the manuscript. As always, I received help, support, encouragement, and nurturing from my family. I owe Lisa, Andrew, Ellen, Bill, and my mother, Anna Weintraub, a lot.

S.G.

Contents

1. Right from the Start   1

2. Redefining Motherhood   12

3. The Pink and Blue Blues   29

4. Creating the Myth of the Opposite Sex   40

5. A Girl for You, a Boy for Me   57

6. Redefining Fatherhood   71

7. The Inside-Out Family   83

8. Breaking the Housework Connection   99

9. Family Power Plays   123

10. Talking Straight and Speaking Equal   154

11. "Good" Girls — "Bad" Boys   164

12. The Toy Curriculum   175

13. Dolls, Dolls, Dolls   187

14. Co-Ed. Phys. Ed.   194

15. What Will You Be When You Grow Up?   201

16. Subliminal Sex Education   209

17. Parent Support Systems   219

18. The Problem with Myths   227

Notes   235

Right from the Start

A Guide to Nonsexist Child Rearing

CHAPTER 1

Right from the Start

FOR MORE THAN a decade, women have been working to free themselves from the early programming that has limited their growth, narrowed their choices, and inhibited their power. They have been meeting, talking, reading, analyzing, writing, struggling, and fighting their way to liberation. Some men, too, understanding that their lives have also been lessened by sexism, have joined their sisters in attempting to get clear of the ideas, ideals, and behaviors that limit their own lives. At some point it occurs to all of us who have been engaged in this process to wonder how different our lives might have been had our parents refused to conform to the societal press to raise us as "proper" girls and "proper" boys. How much easier we might have pursued the liberated life had we led it right from the start. That is just what many young parents wish to do today: raise their children right — right from the start.

But if women are correct in asserting that all established social structures operate to press females and males into two distinct roles, one lesser, one greater, from where are the new ways to raise children to come? Surely not from the traditional child-rearing theorists who have helped create the very sexist society we now seek to dismantle. Surely not from members of the legal, medical, psychiatric, and psychological establishment. They are only now beginning to show the faintest signs that they are willing to recognize their own institutionalized and personalized sexism. The professionals and professional establishments that have delivered twentieth-century sexism to us are hardly likely to be suitable guides for raising tomorrow's liberated children. Similarly, the information and theories derived from these establishments are often no more reliable for present child rearers than the people who have produced them.

Many of our most widely circulated child-rearing theories assume overtly or covertly a patriarchal family structure and a fixed, unchanging child-rearing environment. Women today challenge both these assumptions.

The patriarchal family structure firmly embedded in our child-rearing theories pictures papa as either a good boss or a bad boss, just as he is either a good provider or a bad one. Mama is either a satisfied or dissatisfied dependent, a willing or unwilling supplier of care. Female children dress up, play house, and dream or fantasize a rescue that will permit them to keep their own houses. Male children, too, try to get free from their family, not by rescue but through plotting revolutions or rebellions.

Child-rearing theories that embody these patriarchal notions, no matter how subliminally, are no help at all to contemporary parents. Patriarchy is sexism. A patriarchal family, like the patriarchal society that it mirrors, is just what women have been declaring they will no longer tolerate. As women work to remove all vestiges of sexism from the larger society, it would be the ultimate irony if they continue, inadvertently, to transmit sexism to their own children.

Child-rearing theories that are based on descriptions of present-day realities are similarly useless for parents who envision changed family relations. These descriptive theories are worse than useless if they lead people to relax their efforts to correct inequitable, harmful, or unjust social conditions.

Descriptive theories may begin harmlessly enough with observations, often casual and unsystematic, of present-day realities. The descriptions then become explanations, the explanations, predictions, the predictions, prescriptions, and the status quo becomes hallowed. For instance, many children are observed to be "negative" at two. They often do not follow orders well; indeed, they reject them. That simple observation becomes its own explanation. Children are not only negative when they are two, but *because* they are two, as if negativeness at two was part of their genetic inheritance. We then move to prediction: Children when two will be negative. Finally, we end with prescription: If children are negative because they are two, then children *need* to be negative at two and failure to pass through a negative stage may cause later trauma.

When I visited Williamsburg recently, I was struck again with how small the community was, how isolated, how far from major libraries and established centers of learning it was. How could revolutionary theorists like Thomas Jefferson have produced their works so far, so removed from the sources of knowledge of their day? Then I began to see the virtues in distance and isolation. Perhaps it was just these conditions that made a revolutionary view and a revolutionary perspective possible. The most revolutionary aspect of Jefferson's ideas was the notion that the future was accessible to human influence, that the future need not repeat the past. Jeffersonian ideas and ideals not only directed our own nation's founding, but stimulated and excited the imagination of people all over the world. Yet the Jeffersonian notion of an open future, a future rich with possibilities, continues to be at odds with an ancient academic tradition that suggests that future conditions can be little different from past and present ones.

Even the relatively young academic disciplines of psychology and sociology, from which much of our knowledge of child and family life derives, carry within them the seeds of conservative and reactionary thought. "What is" is held in this way of thinking to be "what must be." Attempts to provide equity and freedom are viewed as tinkering with an acceptable status quo and risking personal, familial, and social peace. The fear of what is new often results in a tradition-bound academic community. Often the best trained minds cling to falsehoods longer and with more tenacity than those with less vested interests in sustaining current knowledge and theoretical systems. When the issue is the need to dismantle the public and private structure of sexism, normal conservative thought is strengthened and sharpened by the academic community's own sexism.

That democracy is always tied to a positive view of the future was also the perception of those who, in the early twentieth century, called themselves progressive educators. They recognized that if our early personal experiences were characterized by equity and justice, we would be more likely to grow into adults who would be comfortable in a democratic society. Concentrating on children's experience in schools, the progressive educators insisted that the school setting and curriculum reflect our commitment to democracy by fostering equity and egalitarianism. As women have worked to end patriarchy and extend democracy, they too have concentrated much energy on reforming the school setting and curriculum.

But what of children's earlier experiences, their experiences long before they come to school, their experiences within the family? Can they grow to adulthood freed from notions of patriarchy if their earliest experiences are overtly or covertly sexist? To raise children right from the start, the family setting and curriculum, no less than the school's, must reflect a positive view of the future: a commitment to democracy, to equity, and to justice.

A view of the future that reflects our athletic tradition

rather than our academic one will be more useful to women. In the world of athletic competition, the basic material is always the human body. Yet, it is always anticipated that people will find a way to make this same body more swift, more strong, more agile, and more graceful in the future than it was in the past. Current records are simply seen as quite temporary limits, which will yield to those better-fed, better-trained, more highly motivated, and better-spirited athletes of the future.

Feminists, too, anticipate a future where present limiting conditions are overcome. A future that includes a more democratic, nonsexist society and a more democratic, non-sexist family — a family in which two equal adults hold a continually diminishing trusteeship over their young. The present day-to-day realities of those who live in this kind of structure, as well as the stages children, mothers, and fathers go through, will differ from those experienced within a sexist family structure.

If women and men lived similar lives, experienced similar interpersonal relations, had similar access to power, money, and influence, and discharged similar responsibilities in the world, they could, with some logic, speak for and on behalf of each other. Unhappily, that is not the case now. It is the mark of women's oppression that while they are held to be vastly different from men, and held to be the only ones legitimately responsible for baby and child care, they are also held to be insufficiently worthy to instruct each other in just how babies and children are reared. Males who have never raised children, who feel themselves to be totally different persons from females, and who profit personally from the undermining of women's strength, instruct mothers on how to care for and manage their young and how to care for and manage their husbands. As women work to break free of an imposed personal and social perspective, they can no longer accept male child-rearing ideas or ideals.

Because of my conviction that child-rearing theories that derive from a commitment to patriarchy and the status quo are of little use, I have chosen to explore these issues myself, to see where the feminist perspective leads, and what child-rearing issues it helps illuminate. In doing so, I have experienced many surprises. The feminist perspective leads to challenges and issues far beyond what one might have expected. Not only is it immediately clear how limiting theories like "proper" sex-role identification and penis or womb envy are, but even less clearly sexist theories — Oedipal conflict, sibling rivalry, adolescent rebellion — begin to give way once one assumes the family structure is democratic rather than patriarchal. More astounding still is how different even the old dependable parent-child problems, like sleeping, feeding, and disciplining, appear when one's perspective changes.

Sexist child rearing has not only given us a host of personal and familial psychological and social problems, it has resulted in enormous learning deficiencies for individual children. The deficiencies boys experience with early schooling, particularly in the areas of reading and writing, and the difficulties girls experience in later schooling, particularly in math and science, are part of the negative legacy of a sexist upbringing.

I find it amusing to see how common is the observation, in books directed at parents, that child-development knowledge and theories are unnecessary for parents. Is this because the parent role is envisaged as simply following orders, or because the particular child-development theories that are around are singularly useless in helping parents develop a joyful, supportive family? I suspect both are true. Since I believe parents should be child-rearing decision makers as well as child-rearing technicians and workers, I have attempted to focus on the issues that I have found central to family life, issues that make a difference in how children grow and grow up. In doing so, I have often found the knowledge, skills, and strategies of the early childhood educator much more applicable to the joyful and healthy structuring of family life than the knowledge, skills, and strategies of therapists. Since I was my own three children's principal child rearer, since the issues central to young women today were issues central in my own life, since my husband and I were feminists long before we knew it, and our family life reflected this commitment, and since my three grown children approve, I feel comfortable in offering new parents my perspective on child rearing.

There is, alas, no shortage of books written about child rearing. What is different about this book is that it makes the immodest claim of reflecting a feminist perspective. While I believe I understand a great deal of what aware women have been saying about the world, themselves, and their children, I cannot possibly incorporate all the different ideas women have forged and are in the process of developing. So while I owe much to the feminist movement, the responsibility for the ideas is my own. I have taken some ideas common to feminist consciousness, mixed them with what I know about teaching, learning, and children, and have achieved what I hope is a useful, democratic, and optimistic child-rearing perspective. I hope this perspective serves to stimulate thoughts and actions that liberate women and children where it counts the most; in the home and in the family.

My notions of child rearing include three general themes. The first is the constantly recurring insistence that we re-design the parent role so that it liberates rather than oppresses women. The second theme stresses the need to think about and act toward our infants and children in ways that allow them to develop vigorous and sound bodies, spirits, intellects, and emotions and permit them the broadest possible life options. Third, I believe parents are entitled to an added profit from the child-rearing experience. Not only should the parents profit by being liberated by the experience of child rearing, not only should the children profit by growing to adulthood healthy and sound, but the experience should also include a happy ending.

A happy ending to the child-rearing experience is a positive adult relationship between oneself and one's children: a relationship characterized by mutual affection, respect, and pride. But I believe this happy ending occurs most often if it has been built into the parent-child relationship from the beginning; for patterns of behavior once established are difficult to change. Adults who deal joyfully, flexibly, and equitably with each other, who initiate actions characterized by those qualities with their children, even in infancy, will find that these same qualities define their relationship with their children when grown. Happy endings, like the liberated life, are most easily achieved when begun right at the start!

•   •   •

I've had to make two basic decisions about definitions in writing this book. The first was what to call the process that takes place between parents and children; the second was what to call the adult who is engaged in this process. In deciding to return to the older terms of "child rearing" or "child raising," I consciously rejected "care-taking," or the more au courant "care-giving," as I also rejected the more prevalent "nurturing." I believe all three terms trivialize the process as well as those engaged in it. "Care-taking," "care-giving," and "nurturing" are terms that conjure up the providing of food, clothing, shelter, cleanliness, affection, and affiliation. Clearly, these needs are the central needs of infants but are not all the needs that children have. "Child rearing," or "raising" includes nurturing and care-giving, but is a process both deeper and broader. It is a term that more clearly than others includes the teaching of values, attitudes, knowledge, and strategies for present and future growth and development. While the nurturing aspects of parenting are most apparent when the child is young, the other rearing tasks are more obvious responsibilities as children grow older. Moreover, it is folly to believe infants are not simultaneously developing in all areas just because parents are focused on only a few of them.

Focusing parents on infants' bodily care encourages parents to view their children as beings who are either getting ready to be serviced, being serviced, or finished being serviced. Thus the baby is often described as "just fed," "just changed," or needing or wanting to be fed or changed. In between times, the baby is viewed as either doing nothing or "playing," a word used in our culture as the opposite of work.

If babies and their actions, interactions, and activities are trivialized by describing what they are experiencing as the "getting of care" or "nurture," mothers are even more trivialized when what they do with their babies is summed up as giving care or nurturing, which allows mothers to be pictured as soft-food delivery systems.

The decision to write of "mothers" and "mothering" rather than the more "in" terms, "parent" and "parenting," follows from similar reasoning. While I believe men can and should rear children, I fear that moving too swiftly away from a concentration on mothers may mute the issues that so clearly affect the woman parent only. I shall therefore move between discussions of "mothers," "fathers," "female parents," "male parents," and "parents." For example, when I discuss the need to break the housework–child-rearing connection, it is clearly one in which only female parents have been caught. When I talk of equal access to money opportunities and experience within the family, again this access has been denied to mothers, not fathers. Conversely, when I speak of inexperience in giving care, this is more likely to apply to the father.

It is simplistic and unhelpful to discuss mothering and fathering as if women and men's relation to each other, to the world, and to their children are the same. It is, I believe, nonproductive to write about equal child-caring independent of the inequality that exists in two-parent families because one is female and one is male.

Liberation will not come to family life through proclamation. In general, to speak of parenting before one speaks of two equal people in a relationship of equality misdirects our efforts. We are only now at the beginning of a process that will move us toward a concept of equal parenting. It is a process and goal that is inevitable because the traditional concept of mother is no longer acceptable to free and equal women: For the emerging, aware women of today as well as their liberated male contemporaries are demanding private lives as satisfying, empowering, and joyful as their unfettered hearts, minds, and bodies can establish. Should today's women and men choose to rear children, new sets of relationships must characterize their relations to each other, their children, and their world. Women will refuse to accept the definition of motherhood that a male-dominated society has fashioned. Men will reject the notion that the role of father can only be played as hero or villain. Men, like women, will wish to explore the limitless range of possible relations they can enjoy with their children. Both will wish to share in building a home based on equality of opportunity and responsibility. Female and male infants will only grow as equals in an environment where equality between the sexes is daily modeled by all who care for them.

•   •   •

Babies and children, like their parents, have certain basic needs that transcend time, space, class, and race. These needs are for food, clothing, shelter, and protection, and, less obvious but no less important, for affection, affiliation, language, culture, stimulation, relaxation, and novelty. However, at different times and in different places, these needs are expressed and provided for in different ways. Readers whose backgrounds and experiences are dissimilar to my own may find that some of the material presented here does not correspond to the world they know. This problem is the result of my determination to present issues that I have actually lived and dealt with. My decision to speak only about what I have intimately known grows from my conviction that for too long mothers have been instructed by people who have shared nothing of the lives they lead.

CHAPTER 2

Redefining Motherhood

SEVERAL YEARS AGO, a very special gorilla who lives in the San Diego Zoo gave birth. After observing her mothering attitudes and abilities, the humans in charge decided she was a rotten mother. So rotten, in fact, that the infant gorilla was removed from her care and raised elsewhere.

Sometime later, the gorilla again became pregnant. The question, of course, was what to do about the soon-to-be born baby gorilla. Among the options that might have been considered, but probably wasn't, was to encourage the gorilla father to raise the baby. After all, he could have had a "natural" child-rearing talent, and God knows he wasn't out pursuing a career, defending his country, or in the attic composing a magnum opus. The actual decision, however, was both more traditional and in a sense more revolutionary: This time the gorilla would keep her child. But this time she would be taught to be a good mother.

How do you change a "bad" mother into a good one? You can't simply tell her to relax and do what comes naturally because she has already demonstrated that mothering does not come naturally to her. Since the client was a gorilla, the techniques of intimidation so often invoked when human mothers are the clients would clearly not do here — and might prove downright dangerous. Gorilla mothers have to be treated with respect. So a creative approach was decided upon, which was to teach the gorilla what mothering was all about. Because they couldn't talk motherhood to her, they had to show her what they meant. So they showed her movies of gorilla mothers and infants — and guess what? It worked. Oh, she probably thought, *that's* what you do with those little ones. Why didn't someone let me know sooner?

•　　•　　•

The reason mothers don't receive education is because mothering has been declared a natural function for women. Like most assumptions concerning women, especially those in the area of their natural functionings, innate roles, responsibilities, and obligations, it is men who make the declarations, which is undoubtedly why they often turn out to be inaccurate and wrong-headed. Perhaps no notion is more wrong-headed than that which suggests the innateness of child-rearing abilities to women. Let's look a bit at the reluctance of society to provide information and teaching to mothers.

The fact that some women in nonindustrial, and tribal societies bear and raise babies without formal education is repeatedly presented as proof that mothering does not have to be taught. Other societies raise food without formal education, but almost one hundred years ago, our large state universities were publicly funded to provide agriculture with the research and theoretical base thought necessary in a modern society. Other societies have waged war with only an "intuitive" understanding of conflict, yet we have three large military academies, ROTC, and basic training. While other societies create music, art, and dance seemingly untutored, we have music, dancing, and art schools.

Just because some societies don't give formal instruction in intellectual and practical skills does not mean that those skills are not taught. Neither does it prove that formal education is unnecessary in a society such as ours. In small, slowly changing societies, all early life is a preparation for a generally predictable, unchanging future. From birth on, one is socialized through a continuous process of observation, investigation, and participation. The infant sees, the child investigates, the adolescent participates and understands. The parents-to-be, since their earliest years, would have observed the process of animal and human pregnancy, animals and perhaps humans being born and "claimed," parents and others caring for infant needs, early infant difficulties, and infants learning to stand, walk, and talk. As young people grow up, they also participate with increasing responsibility in these activities. Child care in nonindustrial and tribal societies is taught through a continuous, uninterrupted life process. In addition, there are on-site, respected, experienced people to assist a new mother and father.

At the same time that we tell women how easy it is to mother "naturally," we encourage them to reject their most natural sources of mothering information and assistance — their own mothers, grandmothers, and other older female relatives and friends who are considered old-fashioned, unsophisticated, even superstitious. From them you don't get helpful time-tested advice, but old wives' tales. So we leave young mothers to their "intuition," offer them some simple and often simplistic advice from some friendly male experts — pediatricians, ministers, psychiatrists — and expect them to make it as parents. A Hollywood story tells of a Hungarian director whose first American movie was a disaster. When asked about this many successful years later, he replied, "Oh, that first picture was made after I had forgotten Hungarian but before I learned English." We've spent about a hundred years forgetting the old ways and have not as yet learned any new ones.

While experts are generous to a fault in accepting limited parenting abilities, most mothers and fathers would prefer to be good at what they do. As primary care-givers, they would rather not be exhausted in day-to-day struggles with children. Their preference would be for a relationship that enriches and empowers their lives rather than one that depletes and exhausts them.

The female child abuser is said to see herself as isolated, powerless, and without control over her life (just like a gorilla in captivity might!). These feelings are often precisely why the woman wanted to have a baby in the first place. She hoped that the act of having a child and becoming a parent would provide her with the love, power, and control so absent in her life. Instead, she finds that her baby makes her more vulnerable to internal and external forces and thus leaves her even less powerful and more oppressed. Without the resources to understand and combat the real sources of her victimization, the mother identifies the infant as responsible for her powerlessness. She vents her hostility, frustration, and anger on the one person in her environment who is actually incapable of oppressing her. However poorly she manages her life and copes with her infant, though, this woman is not entirely inaccurate in her estimation of the mother role. Somewhere hidden, masked and disguised, there exists a potential for power and control ("the hand that rocks the cradle rules the world"). Indeed, the fear of actualizing the power inherent in the mother role has made necessary much of women's oppression.

Primary care givers, as a group, could restructure a society's political, economic, moral, intellectual, physical, and emotional values by radically altering its child-rearing practices. The undermining and destruction of the power potential within the mother role has taken two related directions: One has minimized the importance of mothers and the early years of life; the other has completely divorced discussions of what makes the good person (typically presented as what makes the good man) from how to care for babies and infants. The discussion of what makes the good person has always been seen as proper speculation for the most learned folk of a society: philosophers, religious leaders, psychiatrists, almost always male. Any speculation on how to care for infants and babies, however, is seen as a fit subject for housewives, nursemaids, home economics teachers, and others whose designations are usually preceded by "only a" — all of them female.

While women engage in the day-to-day work of child rearing, they do not make child-rearing policy. This is one reason why raising children is often offensive to women of trained intelligence. They sense correctly that their minds are not welcomed in the process. And, indeed, their minds are not, for someone else's mind got there first. Women's intelligence is all right as a tool for developing their children's intelligence by reading to them, talking to them, and providing them with people who will engage them in stimulating activities; but women are not supposed to analyze child rearing, their role and responsibility in it, or the direction they wish it to take. Knowledge is power and the power component of parenting is what women are not encouraged to claim.

Even a woman with a professional reputation and intellectual credentials is dismissed as "only a mother" when it comes to raising her children. Mary Anne Raywid, a colleague of mine, is one of America's leading philosophers of education. Since her only child is considerably younger than my three children, she often discusses mothering with me and another colleague, Ruth Formanek, a psychologist who is also the mother of three grown children. One day Mary Anne came to my office upset and worried because her son, Scott, needed a tonsillectomy. Ruth and I talked to her about her own worries and how to get Scott prepared. Since he would have to stay overnight in the hospital, we said we thought it was important for her or her husband to stay with him.

"He'll be anxious, you'll be anxious, and he may need

help." We warned her that the pediatrician might try to talk her out of it.

Sure enough, when she told the doctor that she wanted to stay with her son, he said, "Scott's a big boy now, he's seven." When she stood fast, the doctor escalated his response. "I hope you'll let Scott get married one day." Since Mary Anne is a woman of considerable strength, she didn't cave in, which, as it turned out, was lucky. The night after the operation, Scott woke up vomiting blood and was very scared. The nurse was some distance away, but Mary Anne was right there.

Often the same doctor who frowns on paid, employed mothers because they are absent from perfectly healthy, perfectly cared-for children, feels no self-consciousness dismissing these same mothers from situations where the children desperately need them.

When parents express their need to remain close to ill children, not to be separated, this need is not only ignored by professionals, it is twisted and derided. Here is an example of the doublethink we constantly come upon when we explore mothering: First, women are told how natural, how intuitive and innate mothering is for them. Then anytime they make moves that do reflect their strong intuitive feelings, their actions are ignored or derided, especially if they threaten professional decisions. Since neither a mother's feelings nor her intelligence is given credence, the result is a mother without confidence, unable to make demands on those whose business it is to serve her. She is the perfect bureaucratic foil.

There is perhaps no greater concern to new mothers than the newborn's well-being and no greater need than to feel the baby as her own. There is an overwhelming need to see the baby, to check the baby out as soon after birth as possible, and through that experience, to build the mother-child bond. This process, which all mammal mothers go through, is called "claiming" ("Yes, sir, that's my baby!"). In the animal kingdom, mothers follow quite patterned procedures to "check out" the baby. Human mothers seem to have a pattern also. They check extremities first, counting fingers and toes before moving to the trunk. If hospital policy forbids a mother from seeing her infant for the first twelve to twenty-four hours, the mother's anxiety level will rise to almost unbearable heights. Under natural childbirth conditions, the mother can be satisfied immediately after the birth that the child is well. The child will be given to her, she can touch the child, speak to the child, and examine the child. She can go through the claiming procedure. Many childbirth methods prevent claiming from occurring immediately after birth. Any further delay occasioned by the hospital's own regimen is unconscionable. The mother's anxiety is due only in part to her weakened condition and the strangeness of the experience. It is also common knowledge that no deformed or unhealthy baby will be brought to the mother without preparing her for the experience. Thus, the continued delay in seeing the baby will tend to build the belief that something is wrong.

This situation, like Scott's tonsillectomy, not only illustrates how insensitive establishment structures are to the needs of mothers, but how necessary it is for women to defend themselves against this insensitivity. Women who question issues concerned with motherhood and raising children are dangerous because their doubts about established practices may lead them to make some changes of their own, rather than to simply accept the periodic changes in direction that are imposed upon them. Male experts seem to prefer rather hapless, nonintellectual, malleable, good-natured mother types. Preferably, they should have enough day-to-day difficulties to keep them preoccupied with the details of child raising and in constant need of expert advice.

Dr. Benjamin Spock, in his latest edition of *Baby and Child Care,* written, so we are told, to be responsive to the new feminism, specifically warns mothers against choosing as care-takers women who have "too many" child-rearing theories. While thinking and theorizing are apparently perfectly all right for a male expert like Dr. Spock — some of whose past theories have been so outrageously defamatory to women that he has had to recant publicly — they are not fit practice for women who take care of children. No wonder women of trained intelligence often find child rearing unappealing.

One of Spock's new theories suggests the notion of womb envy, to replace penis envy. It's hard to know whether that is one theory too many or two. And even in his new edition, Spock continues to defame and de-power women. He advises women when arguing with their mothers about child-care techniques, to settle the argument by saying, "My pediatrician advised me to do it this way." Presumably, the mother's own decision doesn't carry sufficient authority. Since it took the women's movement to educate Spock to his past errors, one would think he would encourage women child rearers to be up to their eyeballs in theory, building and communicating new ones, and analyzing and evaluating old ones. But perhaps it was just his own experience that taught him how dangerous intelligent women can be to theoretical imperialists.

If Spock is suspicious of women with too many child-raising theories, Dr. T. Berry Brazelton, another pediatrician, extends his suspicion to women who are capable child-carers. In his book *Toddlers and Parents* he describes a woman who manages a group of children efficiently and happily. The children play well together, eat enjoyably, and sleep without fussing — a situation that causes Brazelton to fuss. He wonders if this kind of atmosphere gives the children enough opportunity to be negative! Like most competent pediatricians, Spock's and Brazelton's instructions on medical issues are worth having as they doubtless reflect the best of present medical thinking. On other child-rearing issues, they carry as much authority as any intelligent, non-experienced child rearer; but they are less modest. Over the years, the emphasis in child-care advice has changed from the physical to the emotional and, about ten years ago, to the intellectual development of children. Now we hear about the need to develop the "competent" child. Surely all of these needs have always existed and always will.

Today we are experiencing something entirely new in the world of mothering as a result of the rise of the active, assertive, and authoritative woman as mother. In all areas, women are rejecting the role of knowledge and value consumer. They are casting off the silent, passive role they have played in the formulation of public policy and opinion. And they are demonstrating particular concern over the practice of developing and promoting ideas about themselves and their children in which they have played no part. They will no longer accept the notion that their intelligence and critical faculties are unnecessary when they mother. What this means is that women will decide what kinds of assistance, education, and support are necessary to the mothering experience. Women will decide what priorities they will set in their own and their children's lives. Women will also decide without outside direction and interference when they need help, when they don't, when they are troubled, and when they are not. Perhaps nothing will be more liberating for mothers than to be able to holler "Help — I need help," "I don't know what I'm doing," freed from the fear that this will mark them as dumb, unsuited, or what's worse, unnatural.

If women are to liberate themselves through mothering by being honest, active, and critical, what of their infants? How can these women make sure that their children will be raised so that they emerge from the process free and equal beings?

Now there is a new focus for parents' attention, one that

derives from women's perceptions of what is significant. This focus, which is the focus of this book, is on the development of liberated girls and boys as free and equal beings. That this is an appropriate focus from the earliest days of life becomes daily more clear as our research on sex-role socialization develops. Sex-role socialization is the process by which girls become "proper" socially approved girls, and boys become "proper" socially approved boys. Our evidence tells us that by three, four, five, at the latest, most boys and girls clearly perceive that their lives are different, now and in the near and distant future. We are only now beginning to understand that the lives of infants, babies, and children anticipate their future. How this comes to be and how this can be changed are what we are just starting to uncover.

Wordsworth's notion, "The Child is father of the Man," while couched, like our whole literary tradition, in male terms, expresses the truths we must confront if we are to understand how we grow to "fit" the preconceptions of our parents and the wider society. The circular relation of parent to child, child to parent, derives in part from one of the basic tasks of parents: the raising of children who will grow up to be acceptable members of the particular society or culture into which they were born. Thus parents always have somewhere in their minds a kind of mental picture of the adult their infant will one day become. This picture, or perhaps more accurately these sets of pictures, influences the parents' interaction with their children from their earliest moments of life. It is the existence of these mental pictures that accounts for the fact that infants in different times and places have been quite successfully, and with little conscious effort, raised to be proper slaves, masters, serfs, subjects, girls and boys, women and men.

We are only now beginning to realize the extent to which parental mental pictures and expectations are dependent on their infants' gender. How differently they perceive their infants' futures will depend on whether the infant is female or male. We are only now beginning to uncover the means and methods — the subliminal structure — by which most parents have insured that their offspring will fit society's designation of appropriate female or male behavior. These societal views are today being vigorously challenged, as at other times similarly limiting designations were challenged. The challenge is a double one. The first is a challenge to the whole theory of "appropriate" female/male behavior, of sex-role designations, because this narrows and depresses human growth and potential. The idea of sex roles, like any other designation made before children are born as to the paths their lives must take, limits their individual lives, liberty, and yes, even their opportunities to pursue happiness. Much more serious is the second charge, which is that the "appropriate" behavior assigned to females and males is never equal: the behavior and role of females is invariably viewed as inferior to the behavior and role of males.

One of the most powerful ways mothers and fathers transmit to children their ideas on what kind of adults they should grow up to be is through the parents' own behavior. By looking, by listening, by observing, children also learn a lot about their place, their station in life. In the past, by observing those older children and adults closest to them, children of serfs, slaves, and subjects learned behavior considered appropriate for them, while the children of masters, gentry, and royalty learned behavior considered appropriate for them. Indeed, so easily and so early are behaviors learned, that it often led the most sophisticated to conclude how naturally the one fit the designation of slave, the other the designation of master. Thus it was once concluded that these differences must be in the blood, or, to be more modern, in the genes.

So, too, has it been with female and male attitudes and behaviors. So quickly are the differences learned, so easily

equal participation in interdependent relationships than this one?

Although single mothers may believe they have much more direct child-rearing responsibility than married mothers, this is rarely the case. Most mothers, single or married, are the only child-rearing adult in their households. Single mothers do have very difficult problems, but these are, more often than not, the result of women's second-class social and political status. Lack of money, limited access to power, difficulties in finding a community of people who welcome and support them are the harsh realities with which single mothers must deal. Of course it is a very real possibility that the single mother's own insecurity and vulnerability makes it difficult for her to create a secure environment for her children. On the other hand, in spite of inequities, many single women do not find severe difficulties in raising their children. Indeed, women who have brought up children both when married and when single, have found that their homes were more egalitarian, more democratic, and therefore happier when they lived alone with their children.

To suggest that mothering and parenting problems are tied to women's second-class status is not to imply that equality for women will make parenting problem-free. Rather, it is to suggest that our problems are often not what we think they are, and that issues of which we have long been ignorant are more crucial to us and our children than we have been allowed to believe. Consider the issues others will force upon the mother: cloth versus disposable diapers; whether to "allow" the baby a demand schedule or not; or whether to buy a playpen or not. While mothers' energies are directed to issues such as "Is a crib bumper bad because it inhibits environmental observations, or is it good because it protects the baby from bumping?" others will be deciding more important issues for her and her children.

Women are not encouraged to view themselves as having a larger stake in the world because they are mothers; men have been quite content to represent children in the world, and women as well. Women have been discouraged both by social restrictions and law from seeing themselves as their children's guardians in the world. Discouraging women from recognizing their greater stake in the world when they become mothers is but one way in which motherhood has been shorn of a rightful dimension of power, authority, and intelligence. Raised to be distrustful of their decision-making ability, untrained in the most elementary knowledge of child development and techniques of child care, women have only rarely seized the opportunity to make the basic value decisions for their children that our society clearly permits. For up till now, while formal permission to set means and ends for child rearing is given, informal social pressures, often demanding the most rigid conformity to one set of socially approved means and ends, have effectively limited the socially tuned-in mothers' and fathers' ability to parent creatively in a style that reflects their own sense of what is moral, what is joyful, and what is appropriate. In the past, religious leaders, with their "spare the rod and spoil the child" precepts, had great influence on child rearing. As the authority of religion waned and one could not be frightened into conforming through the threat of going to hell, psychiatrists and psychologists replaced the fear of an outer hell with the fear of an inner hell composed of anxiety, neurosis, or even psychosis.

When power to raise one's children any way one wishes is so clearly available, why do parents find it so difficult to exercise it? It may be that only powerful people can see the positive aspects of power, freedom, and opportunity. For uncertain adults, power opportunities are often more of a burden than a bonus. When my youngest daughter was in high school, she was in a special program. When she graduated, she received two diplomas: a regulation one, and a hand-lettered, hand-decorated one from the special program. Each year the special program has a motto, inscribed on the diploma. The motto of her year was: "We shall find the path or we shall make one." It is a view of the world for confident, powerful people only.

The undermining of the mother's intelligence reduces her authority with her children and thus their ability to feel secure and confident in the care of a person who is not respected by others. Mothers suffer even more than the children from the widely held belief that mothering is a task in which intelligence and intellect play no part. One of the most depressing research findings on women has to do with the effect of the mothering experience. Women who engage in child rearing suffer a loss of self-esteem. This is not a natural consequence of mothering, but due to the definition of mothering as a narrow optionless activity, whose continuous focus is the servicing of infants', babies', and children's bodily needs, and the tying of child care to housework. More depressing still is the degree of equanimity with which society accepts the mother's loss of self-esteem, as it accepts almost any cost to women that motherhood entails. The idea that the mothering experience more often than not drains, depletes, and/or depresses mothers seems to be quite socially acceptable.

While in the past, few voices have been raised to protest the wasting of women in exchange for the production of children (often read as sons), all that is changing now. Women are no longer willing to buy into the Service Station model of motherhood and child-rearing. The Service Station model is one in which mother gives, child receives; mother grows less important, child is made more important. In this respect, mothers have been not unlike serfs and peasants. For serfs and peasants too were once viewed as appropriately spent in service to others, to their betters. Women, particularly in their roles as mothers, have been seen as appropriately used-up in what has been at various times announced as: their service to the race, the destiny of their biology, and the demands of nature. Just as all sections of society profited when serfs and peasants no longer accepted their "superiors'" definition of their destiny, so society will benefit when women refuse to accept a destiny established by others, hallowed by tradition, but formed without their individual or collective consent. Not only will women profit from a refusal to accept mothering traditional-style, but their children will profit as well. Girls will not grow up to believe their own lives limited and narrowed by constant, mindless activities. Boys will not grow up to believe their own lives automatically come equipped with a mind, body, and ego-support system.

My own militant opposition to this Service Station model of mothering is reflected throughout the book, but particularly in its structure. I do not focus on the baby's needs alone, but on the interaction of the baby's needs with the needs of others. I do not suggest what mothers and other adults can do for the baby, or even what the baby can do for them, but what they can do for each other. For the mothering, child-rearing experience, when seen as anything other than an evolving mutual relationship, quickly becomes oppressive either for the mother, the child, or both.

As soon as mothers are freed from the idea that there is one single "right" set of means with one single corresponding "right" set of ends for child rearing, they can begin to see mothering as a process that requires the constant making of decisions and choices. Once women can identify and make their own decisions in child-rearing means and ends, they will begin to experience mothering as an activity in which intelligence plays a crucial role. The making of careful, rational, intelligent decisions that reflect parents' own value commitments will help to build mothers' authentic authority.

For a long time, we lived in a society with a stable set of

child-rearing ends. The aim of child rearing was to produce God-fearing, flag-loving, obedient girls and masterful boys. Recently, we've been through some rapid changes. The aims have changed from the well-adjusted child to the creative child to the high-performing child, and now, to the competent child. (All with suitable directions for their production.)

The decision to move away from one right way to reach one right end will be liberating for both adults and children. The notion of different strokes for different folks is nowhere as true as in the parenting, child-rearing enterprise. It is obvious that children flourish in vastly different child-rearing environments. Equally clear, though, is the fact that it is difficult for both parents and children to flourish in environments where they are out of step with societal rules. It is hard to remain mentally healthy when you are the focus of a great deal of societal disapproval. One way to be healthy is to conform to social demands, but in order to be both healthy and liberated you have to withhold your own approval from those social demands whose net effect is to limit human opportunity and potential. Success depends on joining with others to resist the press to believe in one socially approved way.

The current determination of women to be heard on all issues of public policy and national goals is extremely positive for women who choose to mother. Indeed, one consequence of the development of powerful mothers will be the increasing ease with which they ask self-proclaimed experts, "On the basis of what evidence do you urge me to take your advice?" "What data support your theories?" "Do you share my assumptions?" "What alternative assumptions and goals have been formulated?" or, "Is there another way to go?" Finally, "Thanks for the advice; I'll think it over."

CHAPTER 3

The Pink and Blue Blues

"IT'S A GIRL!" or "It's a boy!" With one or the other of these sex-labeling announcements, the obstetrician, the nurse, the parents, and the grandparents herald the arrival of the newborn infant. In the average hospital nursery, too, sex-labeling has a high priority. Although each basinette contains a card with the infant's name, generally a clear indication of the baby's gender, the words "It's a boy!" or "It's a girl!" are printed at the top of the card. Just to make everything perfectly clear, the name cards — and of course, the blankets — are often color-coded, pink for girls and blue for boys. Yes, from birth on the babies are divided in two, and the message is perfectly clear. Either you are a boy or you are a girl.

Even before the baby's birth, the parents have been divided into two groups because of their own gender. Typically, the expectant mother has been readying herself for a far different role from that of the expectant father. Yet, still a further division will take place at the child's birth, and those parents naive enough just to want to parent a healthy normal child will be in for a surprise. Now the separate roles of mother and father are subdivided into the roles of mother-of-a-girl or mother-of-a-boy and father-of-a-girl and father-of-a-boy. Not only will doctors, relatives, and friends beam different parenting expectations at the mother and father, depending on the offspring's sex, the business community, too, will enter the act.

If you order flowers for the mother-of-a-girl, the florist will tuck a plastic parasol, ballerina, or bow among the blossoms. The mother-of-a-boy will find boxing gloves, a football helmet, or a hockey puck in her flowers, which may also have been dyed blue. The custom whereby fathers announce the birth of their children to other men with a cigar, an act one would think sufficiently sexist, has been commercially refined even further. Instead of cigars with labels that say El Producto or La Corona Corona you can now get ones that proclaim: "It's a boy!" or "It's a girl!" Or you can be very chic and hand out cigarettes wrapped in pink or blue paper. Some enterprising hospitals have a lapel pin the father can wear identifying his child's sex and thus himself as the father-of-a-boy or the father-of-a-girl. Jokes will be directed at him about the difficulty of making button holes (girls) or buttons (boys). Parents who wanted a child of a particular sex and got what they wanted will be offered congratulations. Those who "got" a child of an unwanted sex may even be offered condolences: "Maybe you can try again." And now everyone is suitably launched on the traditional venture of producing either a socially approved boy or a socially approved girl.

The sex labeling that is begun so insistently at birth is only the beginning, just one theme in the creation of "opposite sexes," an important sexist myth. Once the infant is announced to be a boy or a girl, a host of expectations, attitudes, events, and objects will be directed toward the baby or away from the baby. It is the parents, primarily, who will insure that girls experience only those aspects of life appropriate to girls, while boys experience only those appropriate to boys. However, parents get a lot of help, whether they want it or not. Try to buy a gift for a newborn without mentioning the infant's sex. It's close to impossible, for, ignorant of the infant's sex, the salesperson may offer something "inappropriate." And a sex-inappropriate gift will cause, it is believed, great embarrassment and discomfort.

But what could be a sex-inappropriate gift? Well, it could be the wrong color. Pink, while suitable for a girl, would be an insensitive choice for a boy. Blue, while suitable for a boy, would be less so for a girl. We shall see much of this inexact match between girls' and boys' things as we consider our sexist ways of raising children. Girls' things are good for girls and only girls. Boys' things are best for boys but may be good or okay for girls. Thus, dresses are good for girls and only girls (though once baby boys wore dresses too). Pants are best for boys but all right for girls.

A newborn's gift might also be thought inappropriate because it was the wrong style. The wrong style might suggest an unsuitable direction for the infant's taste. Ruffles and frills are nice for a girl, who from birth will be taught to include decor and decoration as proper interests. Infant boys' presents should show restraint and classic tailoring, for boys are to be focused, beginning at birth, on utility and action. Other gifts, too, will point to proper future directions and interests. Dolls, dolls, and more dolls are appropriate for the little girl. If boys receive something to cuddle, it will be shaped like an animal. While boys can be directed to care for and nurture animals, to suggest that a boy's future might include the care of humans is to commit a social gaffe. In the days, weeks, and months following their birth, babies will live in a world of boys' clothes, girls' clothes, boys' toys and girls' toys. They will live in girls' rooms or boys' rooms, where the paint, paper, lamps, furniture and decoration will announce not only which sex the child is, but also which sex the child is not.

As infants, girls are less subject to negative environmental effects: more of them live and fewer are subject to disease and handicap. Yet, it is to the infant boy that we address such phrases as "Hello, there, you big bruiser," "Feel that grip." We are focused and thus focus the male infant on his potential, his strength, and his power. Through words, through gestures, through play, we focus boys on their future, on their developing power. When we look at a baby of the same size who happens to be a girl, we coo and wonder at her tiny hands, her tiny feet. We compare the girl baby to a doll (a decorative object of total passivity and maximum malleability). We are focused and thus we focus the female child on her present perfect state of inactivity and fragility. In *My Fair Lady* Eliza Doolittle explains to Higgins that being a proper lady is not the result of acting like one, but in being treated like one. Being a proper female and being a proper male are also the results of having been treated in such a manner. Thus the reason for color-coding babies: pink for girls, blue for boys. We simply have no words, no gestures, no approaches to a baby independent of its sex.

The sex-labeling process, so total, so intense, carried out with such contagious enthusiasm is a barely conscious series of actions. It is very difficult to raise it to a conscious level. It is more difficult still to see the sex-labeling process as a series of separate and distinct controllable events: Events that trigger other events and produce particular effects on infants and children. If seeing these sex-labeling events clearly is difficult, attempting to analyze or evaluate them is practically subversive.

To hint that there is something amiss behind all the high good humor (vive la différence!), celebration, or consterna-tion, to suggest that a price is paid for these finely developed sex initiation rites, is to bring unwelcome news. Feminists are repeatedly told they have no sense of humor because they fail to find the vast repertoire of verbal sexism enter-taining. However, while high spirits and good humor attend our society's sex-labeling processes, they are entirely absent in the harsher sex discrimination activities of many other societies. Indeed, the manner in which sex labeling is done offers us a clue as to the expected future tone and quality of the relation between women and men within a society. In societies that practice female infanticide or the total lifelong physical, emotional, and intellectual subjugation of women, sex labeling is done ruthlessly, quickly, and with no hint of sentiment or humor. In these societies, parents and infants alike accept as "natural" how unlucky they were to bear, or to be born, a female.

Our style of sex labeling, more benign, less damaging, accompanied by joking and good humor, typifies our lifelong attitude toward this issue: "My wife oppressed? I should have it so good!" "What's a beautiful girl like you want to be a doctor for?" Our style fits better with our democratic ideals. Our style is more useful in a society requiring a relatively high-functioning woman. Our style also permits us to be unconscious of what we do. Now that women are actually seeking abortions for a "wrong-sex fetus" — not an unwanted child but an unwanted girl or an unwanted boy — we are forced to recognize that the high spirits that often accompany the earliest acts of sex identification mask harsh social discrimination.

Our "cute" and "cunning" boxing gloves and parasols, football helmets and ballerinas are visual aids in a continuing instructional process. The object of that process is to teach the idea that the one great difference that separates people is their sex. Genitals are usually quite distinctive at birth, and sex identity is most often the clearest, least ambiguous bit of information one ever gets. Why, then, is there such extraordinary societal effort to persuade one of a fact more obvious than most? The effort is made so that no one can avoid understanding the importance of this difference. That is what the whole act of early sex labeling is about: the focusing of everyone's attention on the crucial nature of the sex difference.

This decision to declare the difference between female and male crucial and of primary significance in the lives of both is what feminists challenge. For even today, living as we are in a world of heightened awareness, it is still possible for child-development experts to report that they see no differences between the way boys and girls are raised. This reminds me of Marshall McLuhan's comments about fish. McLuhan said that fish don't know they swim in water, they think that's all there is. Only we can see that it is water. We place our infants in an environment that relentlessly labels them by sex and then we cannot see the process of discrimination while it is happening. We may not be able to see it but the babies surely can.

Traditionally, in our society, it has been important that the sex labeling begun at birth and fostered with such insistence throughout the child's entire development appears to arise naturally. A female is supposed to emerge from this sex-discrimination process as a lover of men, or at least as a lover of one man, and to be sympathetic to men's needs and demands. She must accept that the male role includes access to money, power, and sex, while her own consists of subservience and service. She is to accept with equanimity that her role is to be a member of the Ladies Aid or Sancho Panza to another's Don Quixote. The belief that this course of female development unfolds "naturally" lends it acceptability and a superficial sweetness. This sweetness sours with the realization that it did not all happen "naturally," and, in fact, that it all might have been different.

That it not only might be different but indeed is already different under particular and unusual circumstances can be seen if we return for a moment to the baby's first minutes of life. The sex of the newborn, typically so crucial, rapidly diminishes in importance under several circumstances. Let us look at a few. When a multiple birth occurs, sex labeling immediately becomes of secondary importance. Then the information presented centers on the unusual number of births rather than the gender, and the announcement is "It's twins, triplets, quads, or quints!" The number is also a signal to the parents that their parental role will be different. Mother-of-twins, father-of-twins, is seen as a whole special category. Parents of twins are recognized as having other than normal needs, problems, and opportunities, while the parents of one-at-a-time children are involved in a fiction that holds they need no education or support to successfully rear their young. The acknowledgment that twins present a difficulty focuses adults away from sex labeling and onto the solving of day-to-day problems.

Another fact that tends to minimize sex labeling in multiparous births is that twins, triplets, quads, and quints often have more troubled births than do singletons because their birth weights are too low. Thus the significant people in their environment concentrate on the crucial question of the infants' survival rather than on their sex. Survival needs always reduce sex-labeling and sex-discrimination activities to low priority events. As we shall see repeatedly, sex labeling and discrimination are luxuries, so that when the mother's or baby's survival is in question, sex labeling becomes muted. Then the primary questions switch from "Is it a girl?" or "Is it a boy?" to "Will mother and baby be all right?"

Babies born with serious birth defects or health problems, who require and will require special care and special facilities, receive the close attention of adults who will also ask questions other than "Is it a girl?" or "Is it a boy?" These adults ask other questions directly or indirectly: How can we minimize the baby's problems? How can we maximize all the baby's strengths so that the problem is manageable?

The questions that substitute for the sex-labeling one in the case of unusual births might very well be the focus of our continuing interest in the baby born without difficulty or problems. Will the mother be all right? Will the baby be all right? How can we minimize any problems the baby may have? How can we maximize the baby's strengths so that any problems can be managed?

•   •   •

When we move beyond "pink" and "blue" thinking, we can ask ourselves new questions about the baby's environment, dress, and play opportunities; questions that focus on the baby's needs rather than our own. Items for babies are designed not only to help adults to discriminate between girls and boys but to please the adult sense of what is attractive or good for the baby. For a long time adults were convinced that very small children did best with tiny objects and playthings. Although it seemed logical to place children in a child-sized or Lilliputian world, further investigation has indicated this to be not always true. Obviously, scaled-down clothing and often furniture makes sense. However, when toddlers actually handle or manipulate items, they are more successful with adult or jumbo-sized objects. The fine motor coordination necessary to manage teeny, tiny scissors, crayons, spoons, and toothbrushes is simply beyond the development ability of very young children. The world of young children, when furnished in ways that best reflect their own needs, is Alice-in-Wonderland-like, that is, one of mixed scale. Young children enjoy small chairs, swings, sleeping places, and of course clothing that fits. They do quite well with regular-sized spoons, cups, and toothbrushes. They enjoy outsized pencils, pieces of paper, crayons, blocks, balls, and toy trucks.

Just as adults have, in the past, thought small in relation to children, they still continue to think pale or pastel, as the pink and blue choices indicate. Whether babies see or are interested in color at all when they are quite young is questionable. That pale colors would be pleasing is more questionable still. Strong lines are thought to attract them more. So dressing babies and furnishing their rooms in checks, plaids, and patterns might be potentially more interesting to children than the traditional solid pastel. But is interest what adults wish to provide for young children? The answer is, probably, maybe. The tendency of baby dress and decor to be done in muted or quiet colors doubtlessly is related to the adult notion that if babies aren't sleeping they ought to be, and muted color may help by not being stimulating. In any case, the color or pattern of whatever is put on the walls near where the baby spends a lot of time is less important than placing the baby near a nondrafty window with a good view. A large mirror on a wall as the baby gets older is often fascinating. Try putting large pieces of cork on the walls and then putting up all kinds of pictures and patterns. This will help you discover what your baby finds interesting and not overly stimulating.

Conscientious parents who wish to avoid stereotypic child rearing with its pink and blue thinking are often most bedeviled by the issue of dress. Obviously you should first provide children with comfortable clothing that can help them be active in an unrestrained manner. You should also talk to the babies and young children about this kind of clothing. The virtues of sturdy, well-cut, long-wearing clothes should be discussed: "Those pants have sure been useful for climbing," or "This is a good shirt to keep you cool on a hot day." Next, it's nice when children have a range of choice in clothes: things that flow, like robes; things that hug the body like bathing suits; short things; long things; and fabrics that are rough, smooth, and nubbly. It's also nice when children hear positive talk about old clothes: "I've had this sweater since I was a kid," "This used to be Grandpa's coat." By talking of clothing in dimensions other than "pretty," or "new," you help children understand clothing as protection, as an aesthetic experience, and as a link with the past. This helps both boys and girls to get more out of clothing and also helps to move it beyond being a sex-discrimination signal. Indeed, daily we witness the breaking down of the stereotype that suggests that clothing is an interest females and only females *must* have and an interest inappropriate to males.

Since, however, it is the girls whose appearance has received the most continuous and continued focus, it is often the issue of girls' appearance, and thus girls' clothes, that worries parents most. Let's consider some ways for parents to analyze this issue. To compliment or not to compliment, that is often the first question. Girls receive a lot more adult criticism and compliments than boys when very young and perhaps dropping comments on appearance altogether is one way to move. Another suggestion is to make general family or group statements: "Everyone looks terrific today," or, "You all look as if you slept well." Another way to respond is to insure that appearance comments are not inevitably directed at your female children but are also directed at male children. Yet another way to deal with appearance is to be positive toward children when they are dressed for action: "You can sure stay out long in such a warm snow suit," "It looks like you can run fast in those shoes." But perhaps most liberating is to let children tell you about their clothes, once they can speak. "What would you like to wear today?" "What tops do you find most comfortable?" "Do you like these big buttons?"

I don't think liberation should minimize dress opportunities unless those opportunities are dangerous to your health. Mothers who wear slacks and jeans should not feel threatened by daughters who want to wear dresses — any more than mothers who wear dresses should be upset by daughters who prefer jeans. Only if choice of clothing inhibits activity, participation and outdoor play should it become a problem.

Perhaps more of a problem than what is worn by a girl is what lies behind the girl's relation to clothes. If a girl receives compliments from the adults around her only when she's in dresses, and then becomes hooked into compliments, puts energy and effort into receiving them, and feels cheated and disappointed when they are not offered, she's in trouble. Her self-image depends upon the approval of others, and this dependency is a much more significant mark of an oppressed woman than the wearing of dresses. Some parents deal with this issue by finding as many opportunities as possible to compliment their daughters on their work, their effort, and their diligence. Others prefer just to cool the compliment issue and encourage other adults to do the same. If to be indifferent to other people's likes and dislikes is to be uncivil and boorish, to be in constant need of other people's approval is to be forever insecure.

CHAPTER 4

Creating the Myth of the Opposite Sex

BABIES WHO are the continued target of sex-labeling announcements get the message and they get it quickly.
Children grow to believe that sex labeling is a necessary and
vital aspect of life and one that they must make haste to
practice. Indeed, by the time they are two or three years
old, they insist on sex labeling when it is entirely inappropriate. We recognize this phenomenon in the insistence of
young children that cats are female, dogs male. Look at the
evidence from the young child's point of view, keeping in
mind the sex-stereotypic messages received since birth. The
dog is usually larger, deeper voiced, fights more, and is more
threatening than the cat. The cat is more often around the
house, likes to play with wool, does a lot of washing, never
runs away. Ergo, the dog is male, the cat female.

Although erroneous, the childish reasoning demonstrates
how well the lesson in sex stereotyping has been taught and
learned. We, too, can learn a lot from children's mistaken
notions of cats and dogs. Their confusion indicates how
little connection we make between sex labeling and actual
sex functioning and real sexuality. We do not feel any need
to give our young children real information about sexual
differences, differences we will only teach children "when
it's time." While European children have been playing with
anatomically correct female and male dolls for years, this is
the first year such a male doll has been made for American

children by an American manufacturer. No anatomically correct female doll exists for our children's play. American parents are not quite ready for that. It seems that they are hardly ready for the boy doll with a penis: Some stores that stock this doll have been picketed; the doll has suffered castration at the hands of irate parents eager to demonstrate how strongly they object to making children aware of real sexual differences. Indeed, we are able to be positively puritanical about anatomical sexual differences while simultaneously totally committed to the notion of differential sex roles. While giving children little or no sex information, we overload them with our notions of sex-role differences, mostly always overgeneralized, often totally inaccurate.

By the time they are three, children often wish to play with and be with only the people and things they have been taught to consider appropriate to their sex. When children hardly beyond the toddler stage are introduced to new clothing, toys, activities, and events, their first question is often, "Is it for a girl?" "Is it for a boy?" Translated, the question means, "Is it for me?" "Can I try it?" "May I use it without fear of embarrassment or humiliation?" A four-year-old Japanese child brought a fan to the class my son was teaching. One of the youngsters asked, "Is it for a girl or a boy?" My son said, "Oh, it's for anyone who's hot!"

By the time they are three, children have already learned to inhibit curiosity and exploration when presented with material and activities linked to the other sex. This avoidance behavior doesn't develop out of choice, but through fear, as the following research project indicates. Lisa Serbin and Jane Connor, research psychologists, placed toys, some typically associated with girls, some typically associated with boys, in a room. Young children were brought in and invited to play with whatever toys interested them. They were told that the investigators were watching to see what toys children most enjoy. When a single child entered and remained in the room, the child played with toys linked to both sexes. However, when another child was very casually placed in the same room, the child being observed primarily chose to play with "sex-appropriate" toys. Just having another child sitting at a table in a corner of the room altered the behavior of the observed child, stilled the child's curiosity, and inhibited exploration. Peer pressure so subtly applied served to remind the child of what was off-limits play.

So-called boy-toys and so-called girl-toys are not simply colored or styled differently; they develop, train, and enhance different skills and abilities. When children avoid a whole area of toys and play, there are serious developmental consequences, as we shall explore later. Here we might pause to consider just one issue raised by this study. The study indicates that the child, if left alone, is uninhibitedly curious and interested in trying out things irrespective of their labels. It is others who teach the child to exhibit only sex-appropriate curiosity and interest and to inhibit inappropriate curiosity and interest. In short, children are taught not only what to try and what to learn, but what not to try and what not to learn.

Adult investigators are amazed at the young age at which children practice sex labeling and can divide the world into sex-stereotyped activities. My own work, done in 1971 with Lucy Peck, indicates that by three children not only identify males and only males as appropriately doctors, mechanics, and television announcers and females and only females as teachers and nurses, but they also already expect that only boys will grow up to be doctors and mechanics and only girls will grow up to be teachers and nurses. The ability of adults to be impressed by the children's sex-labeling discrimination ability is itself surprising. Nothing is easier to learn than a simple two-group discrimination. Yes-no, good-bad, black-white, right-wrong, enemy-friend, those kinds of two-group discriminations have plagued adult thinking simply because they are so easy and so efficient. It is the complex discrimination — the grey areas — that are difficult to comprehend, not the clear either-it-is-or-it-isn't distinction. From the amazingly competent pigeons of B. F. Skinner to the precocity of computers, the simple effectiveness of the single two-part discrimination is easily demonstrated. Indeed, racism and sexism both owe their incredible tenacity to the ease with which they can be taught and learned and to the corresponding difficulty in teaching more complex, truer notions about people.

In addition to the ease with which simple discriminations can be made, children have had sex labeling and sex discrimination constantly, consistently, and dramatically demonstrated to them since birth. Only our heroic efforts to remain unaware of our persistent sex-identifying behaviors allow us to be surprised at what we choose to see as precocity in the children. But our determination to be unaware of our own behavior serves a useful purpose. It permits us to see the children's behavior as evidence of the "naturalness" with which the young choose sex-stereotyped playmates, toys, and activities. It allows nursery school teachers to explain the lack of female and male involvement in certain activities as a normal phenomenon that just seems to repeat itself naturally and automatically.

Again and again we hear how natural and normal the phenomenon is: How naturally girls choose to play with dolls, how naturally boys choose to play with trucks. The pressure to believe that the children's choice derives from a "natural" instinct takes a nasty turn right at this point. (Nor will we find this the only nasty turn as we make our way through the many twists and bends that sexist child development takes.) The decision to call that which is carefully taught to children, trained in children, and practiced with children an inevitable natural emerging development not only has grave societal consequences, but also often a dismal and disastrous individual consequence. Those who flunk sex labeling or sex discrimination are not seen as slow learners, or poorly taught children; they are seen as abnormal and unnatural. By the time children reach the ages of two, three, four, and five, adults are already evaluating them. One evaluation will center on whether or not the child appears to be developing "normally" from a psychological point of view. Those children who, through some fluke, have reached three years of age without having learned with whom to play, with what to play, and how to play with what they may play, will often be done real mischief by adults. The mischief will, however, be unequally distributed. Girls, typically, will be less harmed if they engage in "boy only" play than will boys who engage in "girl only" play. Girls who do not play appropriately, if they are even moderately lucky, will be dubbed tomboys. This name doesn't worry people because they are confident that tomboys will "grow out of it" in time. Indeed, many children's books directed at young girls have this necessity to grow out of tomboyhood as the central crisis of the book. Only lately has this need to grow out of tomboyhood been challenged, as feminists urge women to see the growing out as a "selling out." In the past it was only when girls remained tomboys too long that parents and others began to worry.

Boys are generally not so lucky. Role demands on boys are harsher, more rigid, and less compromising. Unlike girls, boys are not offered a period when they may without risk of ridicule "try on" the female role. For, as is true in much sex-designated language, there is no exact male corollary for the rather benign female tomboy. Thus the boy who chooses activities thought appropriate only to girls will at best be called "sissy," not a benign label. Just how malignant the sissy label will be very much depends, as always, on the adults and children who surround him. If he lives among people who accept more quiet, less active traits as a sign of future artistic or scholarly bent, he will be viewed as unusual but not unacceptable. His behavior may even gain him a certain distinction.

Unfortunately, most boys who exhibit so-called sissy behavior live among those who define both female and male roles narrowly. A boy's failure during his childhood to give proper signals of his intention to mature as an aggressive, assertive, and active man will panic the people around him. If these people also believe that boyhood sissy behavior leads inevitably to adult homosexual behavior, and if homosexuality is greatly dreaded, he will suffer incredible mental and physical punishment from the adults in his life. For now the adults become victims of their own fiction. If one believes that children choose actions, attitudes, and activities naturally, then children who choose incorrectly choose unnaturally. It is not, unfortunately, difficult to move from that conclusion to the conclusion that there is something unnatural about the child. The real victims of adult fictions are young children.

After the passage of the Freedom of Information Law granting parents the right to inspect children's school records, parents and school officials alike were shocked to see "homosexual tendencies" written in a diagnosis of an elementary school child. This was not because the child was having sexual relations with a child of the same sex, but because the child's walk, talk, play, and behavioral preferences did not match the adult's sexual stereotype. Actually, it is unusual for a child not to meet the adult stereotype. Most often, children by the age of three will meet enough of the adult's demands to pass as developing normally. If a boy casually drapes his mother's beads around his neck, the mother's quick response reminds him that beads are not for him. Sometimes boys will, by three, become furtive about their interest in "girl only" play and hold a doll when no one looks or push a doll carriage roughly, so that they can have the experience, but in a way that will cause no reproof.

The idea that children who fail to meet rigid sex-role requirements will become homosexual as adults is often subtly and not-so-subtly communicated to parents. It would be foolish for parents to accept this idea, for homosexuality has been an honored relationship in societies that have had almost total sex segregation — ancient Greece is an obvious example. Indeed, one might argue that homosexual behavior is more likely to be related to the presence of rigid sex segregation than to its absence. For, if sex roles are so narrowly defined that they allow little room for diversity, one might view nonconforming females and males as literally being forced into sex-role switching. The derivation of homosexual behavior in adults is a subject upon which there has been little investigation, but much emotional speculation. The little data we have suggests that male homosexuals are the sons of cold, bullying, distant fathers. Fathers whose relations are positive, warm, and nurturing do not tend to have sons who grow up to be adult homosexuals. Little research has been done on the early childhood of lesbian women.

Children become, as we saw earlier, expert self-censors; however, the child's success at selecting only sex-appropriate actions, activities, and attitudes has serious consequences. Not only do these self-censoring activities limit participation, but they consume an enormous amount of the young child's focused attention. Sexist, like racist, child rearing serves to limit and to waste children's potential and energy. First, there are whole areas of participation they, especially boys, must scrupulously avoid. Next, there are numerous sexist rules that children must concentrate on and absorb in order to demonstrate how normally and naturally they are developing. As we have seen, we indulge in the luxury of pursuing this kind of behavior only when we are convinced we have human potential to spare: when children are born undamaged and in good health.

Similarly, it is only during times of disaster, such as wars, that the strict sex-appropriate behavior among adults is suspended. Then women are encouraged, even conscripted, into doing work normally considered "men's" and are supported and praised for attempting it. In underground, guerrilla, and revolutionary movements, when anybody will do, women are always conspicuous by their presence. When conditions become normal, women are again seen to have "natural" liabilities that prevent their participation in many human endeavors. It is as if we seek to maximize human potential only during social and personal catastrophes. Under normal social and personal conditions, we minimize human potential by limiting access on the basis of sex.

Creative teachers and therapists constantly demonstrate how we maximize abilities under conditions of personal difficulty. One semester when I was giving a course to teachers in which sex stereotyping was discussed, a member of the class commented that she never had any difficulty getting the boys in her class interested in sewing. I asked how she had brought this about and was quite surprised to hear that she had made no particular effort — the boys chose sewing quite spontaneously. Although I had recently heard of a junior high school where boys and girls were fighting to get at the sewing machine during spare hours to sew their jeans, ski jackets, and sleeping bags, that feverish sewing activity was the result of a very carefully designed curriculum. This teacher, though, reported that the boys in her class just chose to sew in a completely natural, unprompted fashion.

"Well," I said, "tell us about your class — the children's ages, your curriculum — just talk and maybe we'll figure it out." (I am apparently so much a victim of my own belief in sex-role stereotyping that I could not believe all the males in the class had escaped the process.) This is what we learned as the teacher described her class.

She taught a class of seven-year-old second grade children diagnosed as "learning disabled." At the beginning of the

semester she had an interview with each child to discusss
the child's problems and what could be done to reduce or
eliminate them. Each child was given a list of activities that
would always be available when the assigned work was
completed. Together the teacher and pupil starred those
activities that might help the youngster develop needed
skills and abilities. A common disability in small boys is
poorly developed small-muscle coordination. (Girls do not
as a group suffer from small-muscle deficiencies because
many activities socially designated as appropriate for them
help develop that ability.) Well-developed small muscles
are what we need for such activities as writing, cutting, and
delicate mechanical work. Sewing is a small-muscle activity
par excellence. So sewing was an activity starred on many
young boys' lists. When time permitted, they chose sewing
just as frequently as they chose any other starred activity.
The teacher had performed a great service for the children.
By removing the sex label from sewing and recategorizing it
as an activity good for development, she had freed it for the
un-self-conscious participation of all children. But notice
that this was a class where the children were identified not
primarily by sex but by their disability, and the focus was on
overcoming their handicaps.

Just as boys are denied participation in small-muscle activities because these are frequently identified as female,
girls are denied participation in large-muscle activities because these are frequently characterized as male ones. Well-
developed large muscles are needed for swinging, lifting,
running, and jumping. In the special environments established for children with cerebral palsy, for example, both
girls and boys are encouraged to develop as much strength
and agility as their bodies will permit. Here the question is
also: "What will help me overcome my difficulty?" not, "Is
this appropriate for a girl?"

Do we really wish to continue to develop the kind of society in which a child must have a handicap to be encouraged to participate freely and un-self-consciously in all activities? One can certainly hope that in the future egalitarian environments will not be reserved only for children with troubles and for adults in times of trouble.

Happily, there is already evidence that some "normal" children not confined by sex stereotyping already dwell among us. Geneva Woodruff, an early childhood educator, studied children of traditional mothers and children of feminist mothers to see if, and to what extent, the children were affected by the differences in their mothers' — and, presumably, their fathers' — beliefs and behaviors. Dr. Woodruff designed a series of tests to determine differences in children's sex-labeling behaviors. One test contained pictures of common objects, such as ladders, pliers, scissors, a wrench, and an iron. As each picture was presented, the children, who were about five years old, were asked, "Who uses this, a man or a woman or both?" Both sets of children responded with sex-stereotyped answers: Fathers climb ladders, mothers iron. (When doing research in this field one always wonders, not without cause, whether the research itself does not teach or at least suggest stereotyping.) However, while no differences appeared in answer to that first question, the one that followed identified a great deal of difference between the two groups of children. The second question, which tapped what Woodruff calls the commitment level, asked whether a person of the other sex might use the object also. For example, if a child shown a picture of a wrench was asked, "Who uses this — a man, a woman, or both?" and responded, "a man," the interviewer would then ask, "Could a woman use it also?" In general, the children of traditional women said, "No, of course not." The children of feminist mothers, while also perceiving these objects to be sex labeled, generally answered the second question with, "Maybe," "Oh sure," or, "I guess so."

Two explanations quickly suggest themselves for the difference between these children's responses. One explanation centers on children's direct observations of adult behavior. The alternative or additional explanation focuses on the direct instruction children have received from parents on this issue. That is, in traditional homes children may have observed a strict division of activities and expressed interests between men and women. Children watch women, and only women, doing certain things, and men, and only men, doing certain other things. In homes like these children would probably conclude that it is impossible, improper, or unlikely that women or men might do tasks typically done by the other sex. In nontraditional homes children might have observed occasions when both men and women used objects or expressed interest in activities usually associated with the other sex. Children raised in homes like these might conclude that it is possible, proper, and likely for women or men to choose activities and interests that are not always associated with their own sex. Also, sex-stereotyping activities might have a high priority in traditional homes: mommy baking, cooking, shopping; daddy working, fishing, fixing. Children raised in these homes would thus be more conscious of sex-labeled activities than children from nontraditional homes. While parents in nontraditional homes might continue to divide activities by their stereotyped sex roles, they might not sell it as important, proper, and necessary. Thus the children would not judge it to be a significant or crucial aspect of behavior.

In working on a nursery school project, I had a clear example of a child with a low-level commitment to stereotyping and a child with a high-level commitment. I placed pictures of three males and three females in front of a little girl and said, "One of these people fixes cars. Guess who?" The child pointed to a woman. Her classmate, who was watching, said, "I never saw a woman fix a car." His response was immediate to what he believed to be the wrong sex for the job. I said, "Well, I'm sure there are women who fix cars." The boy said, "Yeah? I never heard about it before." Although he had neither seen nor heard of it before he was willing to accept the idea that it could be true. Women could fix cars.

The other incident involved a five year old with a high level of commitment to sex-role stereotyping. This boy was at play with a five-year-old girl, who announced her intention to be an astronaut when she grew up. The little boy said she couldn't be an astronaut because she was a girl. The children went to the teacher to have her settle the dispute. (This is a classic situation for children between the ages of four and six. The children disagree on an aspect of the adult world and find the most convenient adult to act as arbitrator! That is why enlightened parents and teachers are so crucial.) The teacher's response went something like this — "Well, by the time you grow up I'm sure there will be women astronauts." A good answer from the feminist perspective. Too often teachers say, "Perhaps you'll get to marry an astronaut," or, "Wouldn't you rather be a stewardess?" The teacher continued, "One of the first people launched into space was a Russian woman." The little boy looked at the teacher and at his female classmate, and then said flatly, "Maybe in Russia, but not here!" At five he was a committed sexist! Moreover, his answer suggests that he was already not only aware of the greater privileges of the male role, but also prepared to defend them.

Until the early environment of infants is freed of its heavy emphasis on sex identification, it is a safe assumption that young children will have absorbed and will continue to absorb these notions at a very early age. Young children need adult assistance in overcoming these limitations. When a wide range of normal activities are sex linked, they are then effectively rendered unavailable to half of all children.

Serbin, and her associates, pursued an investigation into this issue with some illuminating results. She began by giving three playthings to each member of a group of nursery school teachers. The first item had no typical sex identification, the second was commonly male identified, and the third was commonly female identified. The first was a neutral manipulative toy, the second a fishing pole, and the third a sewing or lace-up card.

The teachers were simply instructed to gather the children around them and introduce the three new objects. They were not told how to do it. The teachers introduced the sex-identified objects in a way that signaled to the children which sex might appropriately use the objects. How did they do it? First, by association: a teacher would show the children the fishing pole and say, "Anyone ever gone fishing with their father?" or "Does your father enjoy fishing?" or "Do you know any men who like to fish?" Teachers tended to sex type the sewing or lace-up card as well. After identifying the object either as male or female by associating its use with the children's mothers or fathers, or with other adult female or male users, the teacher further emphasized its sex-linked nature by choosing a child of the "expected" sex to model its use.

A complete introduction to a new item of play, which carried with it sex association in the teacher's mind, would go like this: "Here is a fishing pole. How many of you have daddies who like to fish? Sam, would you come up and show us how to use the fishing pole?" or "Here is a sewing card. How many of you have mommies who like to sew? Sally, would you come up and show us how to use the sewing card?" Following those introductions the items would be effectively unavailable to the "wrong sex" child. All this could be observed, coded, and analyzed, and yet the teachers were convinced that in the days following, the boys naturally selected the fishing pole, and the girls naturally selected the sewing cards.

Serbin, convinced that she understood some of the ways in which sex labeling and sex discrimination came about, decided to see if one could unhook these same items by altering the way in which the teachers introduced this material. She selected a new group of nursery school teachers and developed ways in which they were to present this same material. This time, in presenting the fishing pole the teacher said, "This is a fishing pole," or "Anyone know what this is?" She then said, "It is used to catch fish," or "Anyone know what it is used for?" The teacher was then instructed to choose both a girl and a boy to demonstrate or to serve as models: "Sam and Sally, will you come up and show us how to hold it?" And, when the items were introduced in this manner sex linking was reduced and children participated more freely.

Mothers — even more than teachers — have the ability to liberate activities for their daughters. Fathers, too, can liberate an activity for sons that has been previously labeled "for females only." When my son, Andrew, was nine, he used to hitchhike to a place where a young woman gave exercise and modern dance classes. He became wildly enthusiastic about modern dance and used to follow the teacher, Kathy Joyce, around whenever he could and wherever she was. From the library he took out books about the ballet to read when he wasn't busy practicing. I was somewhat taken aback by Andrew's enthusiasm at first, but drove him to his appointments when he couldn't hitch, and controlled any sexist remarks that might in those olden days have crossed my mind. His uncle called to express his concern for what we both, at the time, regarded as an awkward situation. His concern was mild, expressed jokingly, naturally, but was happily not contagious. It was Andrew's father's attitude and behavior that made this interest and many of my son's future interests possible and positive. Each time Andrew would begin his warmup exercises, his father, if he were near, would take off his shoes, get on the floor with him, and do the exercises Andrew had learned. Andrew would show his father how to do the work, and together they did floor exercises and leaped and danced all through the house. As is the case with many enthusiasms, this passed — but not before I had become positively excited about my future as a "stage mother," and somewhat disappointed when Andrew gave up dancing. Ten years later, in one of his first psychology courses, Andrew saw a movie called *Men's Lives.* The saddest vignette concerned a young man who wished to dance but whose family, particularly his father, could not accept his interest. Andrew had been luckier!

•   •   •

Sad as it is that perfectly normal children, by two or three years of age, are limited in what they may do by their socialization, it is pretty exciting news that the process may be undone. However, the ability of creative teachers and researchers to free both children and activities from sex stereotyping reveals just how subject to environmental manipulation all those "natural" tendencies really are. The work Serbin and others have done must challenge us to rethink our whole notion of the spontaneity of children's actions and of the extent to which there is real freedom in "free play." The advocates of free play hold that children's play is most satisfying and most developmentally sound when adult direction is absent. These ideas have been so attractive and so acceptable to parents and teachers of young children alike that to suggest they embody shaky assumptions takes people by surprise. But how free can free play be when by three or four, at the latest, a bright child has already learned that most objects and events are associated with one sex and one sex only? How spontaneous can choices of actions and activities be when the making of correct sex-linked decisions is taught in the cradle?

Fortunately, in spite of the convincing evidence that children are socialized into sex-discriminatory patterns of behavior by the time they are three, all is not lost if a child is more than three years old. Children's minds develop in a way that permits them to reformulate their notions of the world radically during adolescence. This inability of young children to envision a world substantially different from their own experience is the basis of my earlier interpretation of Woodruff's work. Young children who accept the idea that women and men might do things generally associated with the other sex must either have experienced such exchanges or have lived in an environment where not much emphasis was given to sex labeling. Young children are very reality-bound. Not so the adolescent. While it is impossible for young children to consider a world different from the one they have known, at adolescence young people can begin to consider a whole world of possible alternatives. The adolescent mind is capable of analyzing society and considering a host of alternatives. That is why the phenomenon of the teen-age radical is so common. It is from the work of the great Swiss cognitive psychologist, Jean Piaget, that we have come to understand the dynamic nature of the human brain. The child's mind does not just acquire new facts and information with age, but undergoes dramatic structural shifts allowing for new kinds of thought processes. Thus while young children believe what they see, and sometimes even see what they believe, older children can see visions and envision new possibilities.

The ability of young children to see what they believe is not unlike that of adults who allow bias and prejudice to affect perceptions. Since children have been so thoroughly trained to perceive the world as split in two, if the world doesn't split as expected, the evidence of their senses is ignored. One nursery school teacher told me a story that illustrates this phenomenon. Their school bus is driven each day by a woman and so the teacher was surprised when the children in her room insisted that only men could be bus drivers.

"But," the teacher said, "the person who drives your bus is a woman." "No" said the children, "it's a man." The bus driver had to be invited to class so that the children could see she was a woman.

The adolescent and adult are capable of thinking new thoughts, considering new possibilities, and attempting alternative actions and behaviors. In fact, it is only because we are capable of rethinking, reevaluating and revising old and earlier held notions that liberation movements are possible at all. All liberation movements have as one important goal the overcoming of early oppressive programming, the mitigating of the effects of negative early childhood practices. Even after having been raised as a sexist or as a racist, as an adult one can become more egalitarian if one chooses. But it's hard. One has to simultaneously catch up on all the opportunities missed, practice new behaviors, and overcome notions conveyed too early and accepted too quickly and too easily. As we find out more and more about how systematically, how persuasively, and how universally, early sexist training is pushed, we can better appreciate how great a task it is for adults to resocialize themselves. That is why there is such strong support among aware people for raising children as egalitarian and nonsexist right from the start. One hopes that parents as well will benefit from engaging in a liberating child-rearing enterprise.

CHAPTER 5

A Girl for You, a Boy for Me

LET'S RETURN again to the moment of birth and pick up another theme in the sex-identification chorus. This is the theory that the child must identify with the parent of the same sex: a son with the father, a daughter with the mother.

Did you ever hear the old 1920s song hit, "Tea for Two" (" . . . and two for tea/A boy for you/A girl for me")? We take that boy-for-father, girl-for-mother idea to mean that a child is similar to the parent of the same sex and different from the parent of the other sex. So girls are supposed to grow up to be like their mothers and boys are supposed to grow up to be like their fathers. As a child-rearing theory, this is a particularly limiting notion of how personality development should take place. In large families children grow to adulthood in the midst of many older children. Rose Kennedy once wrote that it was less difficult than it appeared to raise a large family. You only had to worry about the older ones and the younger ones simply learned from their siblings.

Similarly, in times past, when many adults lived together in close relationships, children could identify with a whole host of adults. As children grew, they would watch older children as well as a circle of adults. They would then choose, most often unconsciously or semiconsciously, but sometimes consciously, to mimic, and finally to incorporate some traits, some mannerisms, and some behaviors from the thousands enacted before them. These children lived in a world rich with models who provided various possibilities. I have often recognized postures in my son that vividly remind me of one of my brothers — a brother my son rarely sees. I could never figure out how it could be until I realized I too must exhibit these same mannerisms. But I only recognized them to be family traits when they are "played back" through my son. There is a marvelous line in Updike's *A Month of Sundays* when the hero says heredity works both ways. We learn who and what we are from watching our children.

Today most middle-class babies and infants live in a world particularly barren of human material. It is made even more barren because our sexist notions of identification — that is, who may grow up to be like whom — are set in the post-World War II small, nuclear family form. Although sex labeling, sex identification, and sex discrimination predate recorded history, some sexist notions are amazingly resistant to change, while others are quite transitory. Some sexist ideas disappear because they cannot fit the particular family or societal form of the day. Others, however, often arise tailor-made to fit changes in individual and family life-style. Many of our particular notions of sex differences are no more than thirty years old, coincident with the development of our pattern of nuclear family life. Thus they are only now affecting the second generation. Let us take some time to carefully consider some of the particular sexist ideas that gained wide currency among post-World War II middle-class American families and are now seeping into all levels of society.

The family form we now live with has many permutations and combinations, but basically the form preferred by society consists of two married adults, one male employed outside the home, paid, one female employed inside the home, unpaid, and their 2.3 children. The family often lives at a distance from both parents' families and from their childhood friends and neighbors. The more prestigious the family, the larger the house, the larger the piece of land that surrounds it, and the greater the isolation. Prestige will cause everything to grow larger except the family size. That the rich get richer and the poor get children is a relatively new development. Large families were, till only about seventy-five years ago, very much a part of the "rich life."

Today's family is seen at its best if there are two children, one of each sex, with the male child older. It has been reported that women who seek abortions for the wrong-sex child do not necessarily do so because they don't want a child of that sex but rather because the girl or boy must come into the family in the correct order. A girl first is "out of order." Like a perpetual remake of the biblical story of creation, Adam is to come before Eve forever and ever. Thus the son will always be taller, older, and stronger, with a little sister over whom he can practice superiority. The daughter will be shorter, younger, and weaker, needing the protection of the big brother. The incredible need to make life follow the artful fictions of stereotyping is just one more example of the lengths to which sex identification can go. Since we in our society are most comfortable when fathers are taller, older, stronger, richer, and more intelligent than mothers, in short, superior, why not arrange so far as possible to have male and female children live out the same relative power relationship? If by chance nature discourages such well-ordered superordinate and subordinate arrangements, one can keep having abortions until nature cooperates. For those of us who have worked, fought, and campaigned for abortion laws that give women freedom of choice, it is both revolting and ironic to find abortions being used to aid the most profound of all sexist notions. On the other hand, the lengths people will go to reflect society's

demands for a male-superior, female-inferior family structure demonstrate the grim reality of sex discrimination.

The idea that children should be like parents of the same
sex, chips off the old blocks, is not new. What is new is the
sexualizing of what it means to be a real woman and a real
man. To be a real woman was for Freud to resemble female
genitalia — soft, passive (the biology is a little off but it
was formulated in the nineteenth century) — incorporating,
yielding, and flexible. The real woman awaits filling, refill-
ing, fulfillment. To be a real male is to resemble the characteristics of a penis, but only when erect. Taut, active,
hard, striving, thrusting, impatient. The true male searches
and researches, he goes into things in depth.

What is also new is the extraordinary emphasis on sex
identification and the particularly unwholesome direction it
has taken. It is part of the Freudian and neo-Freudian
legacy that holds that the completion of the sex identification process is a result of the resolution of the Oedipal conflict. In Sophocles' play *Oedipus Rex,* Oedipus unknowingly
kills his father, the king, and through a series of "fateful"
occurrences, marries his mother, the queen. Freud inter-
preted the play as a metaphor for generational conflict and
saw the conflict as being basically sexual.

Freud saw all little boys as Oedipus and all little girls as
Electra — a character from another Greek tragedy, *Electra,*
identified by Freud as the female parallel. As Freud saw it,
by about age three, each child is in love with the parent of
the other sex. Not in love as anyone might love the people
who care, comfort, and love them, but in love in the same
way as presumably the parent of the same sex is with her or
his spouse, only in a junior version. The theory goes on to
explain that this is the root of the conflict between parent
and child. Since the child wants sole sexual possession of
the parent of the other sex, the child is in conflict with the
parent of the same sex. The child cannot live with the con-

flict because of fear that the parent of the same sex will learn of the child's sexual desires. Thus the young child gives up the idea of sexual possession of the other-sex parent and decides to become like the same-sex parent. Why? So that *one day* or *someday* the child will "get" someone just like dear old dad or dear old mom. Thus, this theory suggests that what fuels the sex-identification process is the sexual desire to claim a person of the other sex in adulthood. It is a theory with an extraordinary view of the world and one that has profound and distressing consequences for children.

It is difficult to imagine why a three-year-old-child would have sexual longings requiring sole sexual possession of the other-sex parent if the process of sex identification had not already been completed. It would be more logical to see being in love with the other-sex parent as the consequence of sex identification rather than its cause. Freud was quite accurate in his view that children are born sensual, sentient, sexual human beings, an idea quite revolutionary in his time. Freud's determination to see them as monogamous and heterosexual by three is rather much, as was his ability to endow the child with such a precocious capacity for delayed gratification! Remember, these kids can't wait two weeks for their birthday party! Yet we are asked to believe they are capable of renouncing their sexual longing for the sole possession of the other-sex parent (whatever that means for a three-year-old) and resolving their conflict with their same-sex parent for the promise that someday they will meet and marry a junior version of dad or mom. Incredible as the theory seems, it has great popularity. Its popularity is due to its quite conservative and ego-satisfying notions. Satisfying, that is, to adults. Just as what satisfies men's egos is what men believe about women, adults' ideas on children satisfy adult egos.

Thus the first critical conservative idea underlying the Oedipal and Electra conflicts is that family struggles are

inevitable. Conflict will occur independent of parental behavior and attitudes. The conflict is not only inevitable, it is
tied to sexual competition and parental power and, moreover, is absolutely necessary for proper growth and development. For Freud, the family structure of the two ancient
legendary Greek royal houses was the proper metaphor for
all families across time and space.

The second critical conservative idea imbedded in the
Oedipal and Electra conflicts gives us not only innate monogamous, heterosexual longings at three, it gives us also
innate competition, conflict, and desire for individual ownership. Freudians rarely notice how neatly these ideas com-
plement our social and political ones. In China, child-development theorists see children as born "naturally" sharing.
Since the "natural order" suggests that more than one child
will be born to the same parents, it would be unnatural for a
child even to consider the possibility of sole possession of a
parent. In any case, the Chinese have concluded that competition and individual ownership are not innate traits, but
capitalistic notions that only exist if they are stimulated and
developed.

It is easy for us to see how Chinese child-rearing theories
reflect their political ideas. It is not so easy for us to see how
our child-rearing theories reflect our political and economic
notions. But think how marvelously these ideas fit our free
enterprise, capitalistic beliefs! The Freudian notions are not
only conservative and satisfying in the public realm, but
they are equally so in the private sphere. Consider for a
moment the same-sex child dedicated to being just like mom
or just like dad. Unchanged and unchanging, this younger
version of the parent extends the parent into the future,
granting the parent immortality (a hint at least!). The other-
sex child first gives the parent a hint of romance by foolishly
and unwisely loving and idolizing that parent and then offering the promise of an unchanged and unchanging future by

wanting to marry only someone exactly like mommy or daddy.

One result of this theory is the stimulation of a great deal of provocative sexual behavior by adults toward children. Adults have been encouraged to project onto children notions of warped adult sexuality entirely absent in children. Three-year-old girls are described as engaging in "precourtship" behavior if they comb their hair in a way adults code as "seductive." Two-, three-, and four-year-old children are referred to by adults as "tease," "coquette," and "ladykiller."

To adults obsessed with sin, children were once seen as giving off signs of being inhabited by the devil. Recently, repressed adults obsessed with sex see children as giving off signs of mature distorted sexuality. Since World War II plain old sex identification has taken on an all-important sexual dimension, which has been made even worse by the Freudian theory that completion of the Oedipal conflict, ending with "proper" sexual identification, is the primary job of childhood. "Proper" sexual identification is not only primary in the sense of being most significant, but primary in the sense of being first. In this view, all other development follows, and depends on, a "proper" sexual identification. Although all areas of a child's development take place simultaneously, this building block or layer cake notion of development was and is widely held.

Now let's put all the pieces together, to see what happened to the mother in post-World War II America when Freudian and neo-Freudian notions swept the country. Take the definition of the mother as the womb and the father as the penis, add a belief in the sexual longings of the child for the other-sex parent, throw in a decision to be like the same-sex parent as a means toward a romantic end, top it all off with a belief that nothing so enhances childhood as the successive stimulation and repression of incestuous desires, and what do you get? Let's first look at what you lose! The pioneer model mother — strong, enduring, capable, and, above all, adult in mind, body, and spirit — which had served frontier and immigrant Americans so well, went out of style in 1945. Until the end of World War II, most Americans lived on farms or in small towns, and most children were raised closely or loosely supervised by at least two and often by many more adults. With the wholesale switch to suburban and urban centers where families lived far from paid work, a dramatic change occurred. Women were and are left entirely alone for ten or more hours to do child rearing day after day, month after month, year after year. Just as the individual mother's responsibility in child rearing increased, the model that would have been most helpful for her to identify with has disappeared. While one talented, interested adult can quite capably raise children, an infantile adult cannot. If one parent is properly passive, docile, and hapless, characterized by an underdeveloped mind, body, and spirit, and the other parent is properly active, assertive, competent, swift of mind and body, and ethically sound, which parent is deemed to be the proper child rearer? Which parent is left alone to raise the children?

The nuclear family design for living makes the child's human environment sparse indeed. When only two adults, at the very most, live with three children, at the very most, there are very few models of behavior a child can draw on in becoming a person. Other aspects of our picture of the ideal family life make the young child's human environment more arid still. Our insistence that the mother and only the mother be the constant child rearer is one such confining notion. The child during its critical learning years then has just one major source from which to glean notions of human behavior. Child-rearing "experts" of the last thirty years view all mother substitutes with suspicion. They are never thought positive and are considered necessary only in times of life-and-death crises. The presence of a mother substitute, this view holds, is a signal that something is amiss. Yet for centuries, and in all parts of the world, persons other than the mother have raised or helped to raise young children. Indeed, in some instances the care of infants and young children is thought so burdensome and unpleasant a task that no person, woman or man, with alternative occupational choices, would undertake to pursue it. This view is growing increasingly popular today, unfortunately. In other cases the care of infants and young children is considered so specialized a task that baby nurses, nannies, mammies, governesses, and the like, are the only ones thought capable of pursuing it.

In many societies only accessibility or cost limits the amount of infant and child rearing done by the specialist. Why then has other than mother care been viewed so negatively in American middle-class society in the past thirty years? Why has the natural mother been identified as the principal, primary, and only child rearer? The answers are both sexual and sexist. In the Freudian view, woman would want no other occupation than the care of the visible symbol of her mature, adult, highly prized sexuality. The other reason is based on the popular psychological idea of the one-to-one relationship. This theory goes as follows: If infancy and early childhood are primarily a training for adult sexual intimacy, then it is reasoned with some logic that the best training for intimacy is intimacy. Thus a close, uninterrupted relationship with the mother would prepare the baby for later life intimacy. Here's where we get the first hint of a sexual twist. Typically, notions of sexual identity and sexual stages are quite rigidly heterosexual. But mothering, although clearly seen as the only true feminine occupation, gets to be something more complex when we consider the consequences of the one-to-one relationshp. The one-to-one relationship can be significant for the child in one of two ways. Either the relationship between mother and child is a manifestation of future heterosexual activity, a "warm-up," or it is a demonstration of how female or male intimacy takes place and thus a part of sex identification. If the one-to-one relationship is seen as a warm-up for the real thing, it would be appropriate for sons to do so with their mothers but should not daughters then be warming-up with their fathers? On the other hand, if the object of the one-to-one relationship is to demonstrate female intimate behavior and thus form a part of sex identification, it serves the needs of daughters, but from whom should sons learn male intimate behavior? If identification is the goal, don't young males have to learn adult male intimate behavior?

But no one has ever dealt with the differing implications of the one-to-one relationship for sons and daughters because no child-rearing expert would dare suggest that fathers should stay home and develop such ties with the daughter or son.

Now let's take one more look at the ramifications of these widely held psychological theories as they affect developing female and male infants. Think of "proper" female and "proper" male behavior and the gulf that separates them. Think how impossible it is for boys to identify and learn from women if we insist that women have none of the characteristics adult men shall embody. Think how impossible it is for girls to identify with and learn from their fathers if adult women and adult men are to be so very different from each other. The particular problem this raises for girls is that in being discouraged from identifying with fathers, the world of knowledge, skills, and opportunities that greater social access and preferential social treatment have given him is denied to his daughters.

Think of the boy at home with one adult whom he is neither to walk like, talk like, think like, or act like. But stop for a moment and think too of the little girl who may be three, four, or five years old and is unwilling to play out the script. She may not be a Freudian. She may simply be rejecting the idea of growing up to be just like her mother. She may like her mother without wishing to emulate her. If she is fortunate, she will not be seen as a rebellious, disturbed child, and rushed to a psychiatrist to be made into a "real female." If her decision to march to the sound of a different drummer is respected, she will often have a harder time hearing the drummer than will the boy left at home with no model at all. Here is another interesting twist: While the boy in our system appears to be more deprived under certain conditions, he really is less so. For boys continuously scan the outside world and are able to find male models to answer the question "If I am a male and can only do male things, what is it that males do?" But when girls wish a different model from their mothers or actually suffer the loss of a mother, they are in much greater difficulties than the boys. As they scan the environment to seek an answer to the question "What do women do?" they find few clues in books, magazines, and movies. Indeed, the power television holds for children may in part derive from a generation of children hungry for information as to what makes a human being human. It is rather frightening to think this information is coming to children from the one-dimensional, stylized, mechanistic characters of television, but are there any alternatives?

If children have suffered from the lack of human resources, from our notions of female and male as "opposite" sexes, and from the idea of mother as combination body servant, house cleaner, and pinup, so too have the mothers. Having convinced women and men alike that they are creatures quite different from each other, women are then placed in charge of raising both kinds of humans: the one she believes to be very much like herself, the other she holds to be very unlike. Tragedy lurks for both mothers and children in these two notions. At the lunatic fringe, the tragedy is the decision to abort a "wrong sex" child. If we have convinced women and men that parenting a boy and parenting a girl are two entirely different experiences, it seems logical not to wish for a child but for the particular experience of raising a girl or a boy. For other, saner parents, the idea of opposite sex will stimulate great anxiety as well.

A woman's anxieties are usually focused on raising sons, only one half of her problem. Since she believes that in raising a daughter she is simply making an updated model of herself, she generally has little anxiety about her daughter in the early years. As mother-of-a-son, however, she believes she is raising an "alien." Left alone to raise sons, women worry lest the sons overidentify with them. They are often desperate for a male presence, not only so that their sons can identify with the male, but so that they themselves can devine some clues to "maleness." A "busy" father will be cajoled by his wife into doing things with their son. Little League, scouts, father-son banquets will all be set as traps for interaction. Women worry not only for their son's welfare, but for their own well-being. Although they know only daddy or some male can supply the model for identification, they believe they will be held responsible if something "goes wrong." Mothers of sons are often paralyzed in their behavior with them. They are afraid to show affection, lest they seduce; give direction, lest they castrate; show concern, lest they overprotect.

Earlier, we spoke of the luxury of de-powering people, that one can only waste human resources when one believes, always wrongly, that one has a lot of human resources to spare. As Thorstein Veblen pointed out more than seventy-five years ago, the decision to render women useless, fit only as decorations, is made only under conditions of affluence. We have come through just such a period in America. Post-World War II society, reflected in its notions of family life and proper male-female roles much of what English society was like in the Victorian era. In the Victorian middle class the husband-father was busy outside the home doing important, executive, organizational work while the wife-mother remained at home with the children, the visible proof of her husband's success. Yet, in that society, the wife-mother was not viewed as the appropriate child rearer, the nanny was. The delicate Victorian woman, swooning and fragile, was characteristically believed to lack the qualities needed for day-to-day interaction with developing minds, bodies, and spirits. The tougher, more sensible nanny type was, therefore, essential in the Victorian household. American women were perhaps the first required to combine the subordinate attitudes of a geisha with the tough good-natured common sense of Mary Poppins. It is an impossible combination! A principal task of childhood is to negotiate the rocky road from total dependence to independence and interdependence. How can a person whose own dependence is so highlighted assist the child's move to adulthood? She simply cannot.

The feminist ideal stresses the notion of good human traits and moves us from such silly formulations as opposite sex to mothering, fathering, and child rearing invested with both sense and sensitivity. Not only opposite sex but theories like sex identification and one-to-one relationship must be looked at critically. These theories have rendered child rearing not only sexist but senseless and insensitive as well. Would not a better ideal of child rearing include maximizing all areas of development, empowering all who participate, encouraging the participation and influence of all kinds of adults and older children, and hold both good and virtuous behavior to be independent of sex? But this kind of child rearing requires that adults let go of their children's futures. Whatever satisfaction the promise of immortality through one's children may have brought, it is not possible with child rearing that is open to the influence of many people and dedicated to the stimulation of all kinds of development. Adults who are unable to bring up children without the promise of reproducing miniature versions of themselves will find that the future is bright indeed: They can always wait for cloning!

CHAPTER 6

Redefining Fatherhood

WHEN I WAS PREGNANT with Lisa, my oldest child, I took a course in child care given by the Red Cross. In addition to child-care information, which was generally factual, interesting, and helpful, we received advice on managing our lives as mothers. One particular bit of wisdom was so startling that I have remembered it for almost a quarter of a century. We were told to be sure to be extra careful of our husbands' needs following the birth of the baby, lest he feel "left out" and become jealous of the baby. We were given a schedule which, at least on paper, would make it possible to provide high-level service to both baby and husband separately, with little need for interaction between them. It was perhaps at this moment that the seeds of my rebellion to the system were sown. I knew with instant clarity that all the pregnant women in the room were being indoctrinated into considering ourselves, our husbands, and our soon-to-be-born infants in a way that was both oppressive and obscene. Just how oppressive and obscene would take me years to discover. Embedded in that advice lay many evils that plague men, women, and their children: the isolation and emotional poverty of many men; the oppression and neuroses of many women; and the misery of their children, which is expressed in self-destructive rebellions, alienation, and joylessness. At the heart of the advice given to all those young pregnant women, in case growing up in a sexist society had not sufficiently hammered home the message, was: It is a woman's and only a woman's job to provide care; a man's job is to absorb it.

Thus, immediately after the birth of a child, when the father's health is vigorous and unimpaired, the wife's strength diminished, and the infant's needs all encompassing it is held that the father's needs are equal to the infant's. Moreover, they must be attended to, or fathers will become jealous of their own children. This jealousy amazingly enough, is seen not as the father's problem, or even the baby's problem, but another problem for the mother, and one that she has brought on herself. And this is only the beginning. Once a woman accepts the idea that a mother is to be the perpetual, perennial, private service station, all family life has no place to go but downhill. While the idea of a new mother zipping around the house balancing her time, attention, and care-giving between a totally helpless infant and a totally healthy husband borders on insanity, like most wrong-headed notions it carries within its convoluted folds a kernel of truth. The truth is that the husband *will* suffer if the wife centers all her attention on the infant, just as this baby will suffer later if another infant is born and all of the mother's attention shifts from baby number one to baby number two. This suffering is the consequence of a system that creates a single source of care (mother) with many care-absorbers and care-spectators.

If the father's role at the infant's birth is to be primarily a spectator, he will be left outside a central family event. He will be offered unnecessary care symbolically to show he is still "important," but will be deprived of participation in a vital family drama and of great new opportunities: opportunities to deepen his relationship with his wife; to learn and explore aspects of himself and his environment previously unknown; and, perhaps most important at the moment, to begin building a warm, loving relationship with his child.

Although many individual men have built close, complex, and meaningful relationships with their children, this is not the inevitable outcome of fatherhood. To father a child often has no meaning beyond the basic biological one. In order to know his child and to have his child know him, it is vital that the relationship begins with physical care right at the start. There are just very few other ways to begin. Recall the biblical notion of "knowing" as sexual congress, as physical intimacy. Physical intimacy is also the way to know one's child when an infant and, perhaps, it is the only way. For in the baby's earliest days and weeks, all needs are typically satisfied as the physical ones are. It is in the earliest days, when the baby's physical needs are greatest, that the father as well as the mother should get "to know" the baby.

Bonnie Klein, a filmmaker, told me of her experiences some years ago when she was planning a film on fathering. She interviewed many fathers of grown children and asked them to speak of their early experiences with their children. Most of them simply could not recount any significant incidents. Similarly, in newly developed courses on child rearing now given to high-school and college students, participants have little memory of father as a figure in their childhood. Young children also often experience difficulty in giving more than a two-word description in answer to the question, "What does father do?" I experienced one delightful exception to the usually low-keyed father-child relationship when I asked one three-year-old "What do fathers do?" "Well," said the child, sitting back and making himself comfortable, "He takes you on adventures, he helps you with lots of things, he gives you a bath and reads you a story before you go to sleep." He had a lot to say about fathers, all positive. His father had built a close, deeply involved relationship with him.

One of the problems many new fathers face is their feelings of inadequacy and awkwardness in dealing with their newborn infants. Although many women are frightened by the overwhelming responsiblity of being the life-support system for a seven-pound newborn, many other mothers, after a brief period of nervousness, feel quite at home. The fact that most fathers don't as easily feel comfortable with infant care is one consequence of the different childhood experiences of girls and boys. Unless the baby is colicky, or in any other respect unwell or disabled, it is during the first weeks and months of birth that the infant most resembles the baby doll the typical young girl always believed her baby would be. Women who were early socialized into their roles find that the first few months are often quite serene; they now seem to receive confirmation of the idea that they were born to mother. The baby's father, however, rarely has any experience, real or in play, to call upon when his first baby needs care.

How the father deals with his inexperience and with his more experienced wife, just as how the mother deals with her husband's inexperience, will have enormously positive or negative effects on their relationship and on the relationship they are able to develop with their children. Perhaps the first step is for the father to accept that he is liable to be considerably more clumsy than his wife. That is one cost of having been raised in a sexist society. Clumsy behavior is better than no behavior at all, and it also passes amazingly quickly. Asking his often more adept wife to show him how to hold, diaper, feed, change, and soothe the baby will minimize his inexperience. But how will his wife deal with her husband as the father? Will she be supportive of his beginning child-rearing attempts, his breaking of stereotyped conventions, as he must be toward hers? In the earliest days, it is often the mother who has the power to help or to hinder a willing husband establish a fine relationship with his child. If he chooses to learn what she chooses to teach, it will be good for all of them.

What is crucially important for both parents to understand is that the quick, efficient, silent processing of the baby's needs is not particularly good for the baby. Indeed, there is evidence that it is quite detrimental. Better slow, more inefficient handling, which includes soothing, talking, rocking, huddling, and cuddling. Since babies have to get it all together in the early weeks of life, they generally are exhausted from the sheer effort of sucking, burping, and defecating. Because most babies sleep a lot, it is only when they're being fed, cleaned, and changed that there is time for them to get their love, affection, and human contact. Although it is believed the parents can communicate great fear and anxiety to infants by becoming tense and rigid, slow, bumbling handling is just as healthy for the baby as quick, knowing, and graceful handling. After all, the babies are pretty bumbling and awkward too, at first. They are also pretty good sports about the whole thing and help their parents along by signaling with crying and sleeping that things are either awry or okay.

In the first days of the baby's life, it is usually the mother who has the power to decide whether or not to make father an equal partner in the baby's care. Some women want to be the major if not the only significant figure in their child's life. For them the desire to be in charge in the home and with their children is quite strong, not only because other areas of control are closed to them, but because they have been raised to believe that these two areas are truly theirs. Having carried and delivered a baby from her own body, it is not difficult for a mother to believe the baby is hers alone. Also, when husbands exhibit inadequacies, many women believe that it is better for the infant to have the superior care they alone can give. But is that so? Babies need people deeply involved with them, as they will need to be deeply involved with many people. Babies, we have seen, become close to people through touch and care. This is an important idea to understand, not only because it allows mothers to be relaxed about fathers' first fumbling efforts, but more important, it permits mothers to be comfortable about their own first attempts at baby care, should they be fumbling, too. The one advantage the fumbling new father has over the fumbling new mother is that a fumbling father is more expected and therefore more acceptable. Indeed, his awkwardness is downright reassuring to those who believe men unsuited to child care.

Yet clumsy fathers derive from the same source as clumsy mothers — lack of experience. Not all new mothers played with dolls when young, not all new mothers helped care for younger siblings, not all young mothers were baby sitters as teen-agers. They, just like many new fathers, come to parenthood without experience, so often they will be clumsy at first. So what? If they were nontraditional little girls, they probably were sent a great many messages suggesting motherhood was not for them. In any event, it is reassuring to note that opinions on child care change every twenty years or so. Sometimes what was once considered excellent appears to be less so in retrospect.

In sum, we know that infants and children, like adults, need food, clothing, shelter, protection from disease, disasters, and temperature extremes, language, culture, stimulation, novelty, and lots and lots of action, attention, and affection. Our knowledge of these specific needs, however, is only now beginning to grow. There is no need for new parents, especially fathers, to feel particularly ignorant about the details of child care; ignorance is about the only thing that we all share.

Perhaps the most important thing to remember is that fair, good, or excellent fatherhood, like fair, good, or excellent motherhood, is not defined by how exquisitely the baby is dressed or how many cooked meals the baby is provided each day. This elementary aspect of care passes very quickly while others remain for a lifetime. So if you're good, kind, noble, intelligent, witty, charming, and creative, your time will come shortly. Just hang in for a few months till the baby gets a chance to know what a find you are!

A far more common problem than the fears of ignorance and incompetence, however, is the reluctance of many fathers to share child and household care. It was (and perhaps in some places still is) quite common for people to say to the woman who hires a substitute to care for her children, "If you didn't want to raise them, you shouldn't have had them." This kind of remark has never been directed to men. Men are thought to be making their contribution to the children by doing just what some women want to do — engaging in paid employment in order to pay the baby's bills. While it seems obvious that working women are not mothering during the time they are away from home, why is it that fathers are assumed to be fulfilling their fathering role when they are away at work? The reason is that the father role, like the husband role, is totally undefined beyond its sexual and financial support aspects.

Men who believe that providing money for the family relieves them of other kinds of duties have been taught that they have no obligations to care for themselves or others because they are men — not because they make another kind of contribution and are exhausted from the efforts. Similarly, women are taught to believe themselves to have total care obligations for themselves and others because they are women, no matter how exhausted they may be from other contributions they make to the family. When the newspapers report that Betty Ford doesn't want Jerry to come home for lunch, everyone smiles and understands this bit of family byplay. For should Jerry come home after a hard day on the golf course, the understanding is that Betty, cancer and arthritis notwithstanding, will have to provide his lunch. Like Jerry Ford, retired, unemployed, or vacationing husband-fathers often take on no more responsibility for their own and other family members' care than do employed ones. In an entirely opposite fashion, it is the rare employed wife-mother who believes her outside-the-home work is an excuse not to take care of her children and home during her "free" time.

In discussing the father role, it has been common to hear people say that a baby doesn't need two mothers, a child needs one parent of each sex. A foolish statement, but one that points out the consequences of sexist role division and readies us to transmit this division to a new generation. If you accept a sexist notion of appropriate human behavior, a notion that posits human traits dependably and persistently divided in half — a nurturing female, a detached male; a subordinate female, a superordinate male; a weak female, a strong male; an emotional female, an analytic male; a passive female, an active male — then it follows quite logically that a child needs two parents, one of each sex, to get a picture of one whole human being. If, however, you believe human behavior is wide ranging, not limited to role definition, varying and changing, then you can begin to think of babies as needing as many humane adults to help them grow as they can attract into their service (a skill babies are often quite good at: "May I hold the baby?" "Is it all right if I give the baby a bottle?" baby enthusiasts shyly ask the parent).

When you move beyond the narrow limits of sex role, you can then put first things first. The first thing is not what roles the parents should or should not play but what does the baby need? Immediately after birth, a baby needs a great deal of loving, physical care. One person can raise a baby well and lovingly; indeed, one person often does. However, if babies have two parents, the babies' lives, and the parents' lives are enriched by the active participation of both parents. When father and mother give up playing roles and emerge as complex, strong, independent, and interdependent persons, they will both be able to respond to their child's changing needs. Fathers will then develop their own loving relationships with their children. Fathers who form their own strong bonds of affection with their young children need not depend on their wives to package and sell daddy to his own children: "Daddy really loves you"; "Daddy works hard all day so we can have nice things"; "Say, 'thank you' to Daddy." Public relations must have been invented by women left alone to raise children. They have to "sell" an invisible, inaccessible, distant daddy as a vital, attractive item. Nor will fathers who actively father have to accept as real love the stylized affection that children offer fathers who for an excessively short time hold power over their lives. If daddy waits in the wings for his moment, a time when he feels comfortable with the children or a time when they can profit from his advice and counsel, he will often find his children have no time for him. The life of the family will have passed him by.

•   •   •

When fathers are partners in care, it becomes both natural and normal for the children to grow to be care-givers as well as care-takers. When children, like fathers, share care giving, they feel as rewarded giving care as receiving it. For it is said of everyone that it is more blessed to give than to receive. When adults and sometimes even children speak of spoiled children, they are often speaking of the care-spectator. Like spectators everywhere, care-spectators find it quite easy to carp, complain, and criticize when things are not quite right. One husband plus one, two, or three children, sitting around a table awaiting the wife-mother's service, have little difficulty finding her service inadequate, particularly when it is not directly focused on themselves. It is not unusual to hear such care-absorbers complain about the food: "The meat is fatty," "You know how I hate broccoli," "I hate boiled eggs," "You know I like my meat well done!"

"Yich — who can eat that mush!" "The steak looks like shoe leather," "Can't I have something else?" These scenes simply do not occur when shopping, cooking, serving, and cleanup are chores shared by all. When parents and children share care, criticisms and jealousies are muted or do not arise at all because everyone is part of the action.

Adults who walk into a home where all members of the family cooperate in maintaining the house, find the environment admirable and enviable. What they may not understand is that children find it equally so. Homes based on equality and cooperation make everyone feel good about themselves because it is basically right, and being right, it is also empowering. I once read some interesting advice on children and housework that I have found to be quite accurate and that helps explain the enormous success some parents have in achieving shared household responsibilities. The advice suggests that the way to initiate children into housework is to make it, in a sense, too hard for them, rather than too easy. It is a mistake to make requests for help that are beneath the interest level of the child. When very little children are eager to help with tasks such as carrying dishes and putting them away, they should be enthusiastically encouraged rather than discouraged because parents think them too young. If you wait till children are seven or eight years old to ask them to set a table and put things away, unless it is part of a more complex task, it will be experienced as trivial and annoying. Not that this means it shouldn't be done — but just that those tasks could have been handled by a sturdy three-year-old. So the way to deal with less than enthusiastic children is to escalate the level of their participation, rather than to minimize it. When participation is begun right at the start, however, and is modeled by everyone in the house, there are few complaints from the children.

The absence of any emphasis on helping young children

to become competent care-givers derives in part from stylized thinking about family life. Despite the ever increasing numbers of women who work outside the home, divorced parents, and single mother households, each young child is presumed to come automatically equipped with an at-home mother who services all the bodily needs of the children and with an employed father who pays the family bills. Russian and Chinese societies do not share our presumptions and in those countries great stress is placed on helping quite young children to become skillful in self-care. Even when our young children begin to care for themselves, eating on their own, brushing their teeth, washing and dressing themselves, mother is still assumed to be managing those events: "Don't eat so fast," "Go upstairs and really wash your hands," "Did you forget to brush your teeth?"

Maria Montessori, a giant in the early education movement, viewed children who grew up incapable of self-care as passive and dependent. Montessori worked with lower-class children whose mothers had many obligations to fulfill if their families were to survive. The mothers of the children Montessori worked with in the slums of Rome, circa 1910, simply could not be considered as likely candidates for the role of continual child servant. Here, as in all other areas of sexist upbringing, one literally has to be able to afford the luxury of incapacitating children.

I know one family with six children that has practiced maximum participation in household responsibilities with great enthusiasm and one might say conspicuous bravery. At six, each child becomes responsible for one dinner a week. They decide what they want to eat, they do the shopping with their parents, they cook (if they need help, a parent or older sibling joins in), and everyone helps serve and clean up. Now in practice, it comes to a lot of peanut butter and jelly sandwiches, spaghetti, hot dogs, and hamburgers, but I'm told it irons out in a few years and you have quite an achievement — a family of shoppers, cookers, servers, and cleaners. More important, you have a family that not only shares and cares, but is learning and growing as well.

This kind of child rearing is much more demanding on the parents at first. Teaching children to care for themselves and others, like teachng anything to anyone well, requires time and effort, but mostly time — time for errors, time for false starts, time to get things all together. It is what mothers not overburdened with house care have time to do: teach and learn. Parents who claim it's easier to do things themselves than to help their children become partners are both quite right and quite wrong. They are right in that an inexperienced child can accomplish little and the time for teaching could be spent elsewhere. Well-taught, powerful children, however, become more and more helpful and easier to live with as they grow older, just as inexperienced, de-powered children become increasingly burdensome over time. While mothers may find servicing three-, four-, and five-year-old children a not terribly unpleasant task, cleaning up after children twice your size gets awfully hard to take. When chores are dispatched with efficiency (no matter what system is used), each member of the family has time to do enjoyable, interesting things alone and together, freed from drudgery or guilt.

CHAPTER 7

The Inside-Out Family

MOMMY HOLDING baby at the window as daddy leaves for work. Mommy with baby in her arms opening the door for the returning daddy. These pictures are familiar to us all — a common scene in fiction as well as in fact, in pictures as well as in words.

> *Bye, baby bunting,*
> *Daddy's gone a-hunting,*
> *Gone to get a rabbit skin*
> *To wrap the baby bunting in.*

The very familiarity of this scene dulls us to its significance, its ordinariness blinds us to its consequences. Just as good cheer and high spirits attend the early acts of sex identification of infants, here too a great deal of the good cheer and happiness is visible. As daddy comes and goes and mommy and children remain fixed in place, the "typical" American family is pictured smiling and waving. Everyone is happy. To view this picture with misgivings appears small-minded and carping, for the glowing, radiant faces present the picture's message in an aura of rightness, goodness, and acceptability. What then is the message? One of the oldest sexist notions extant: It's a man's world, and woman's place is in the home! Men are unbounded and free, women constrained and confined. Mary Wollstonecraft observed nearly two hundred years ago that the only women who grew up undamaged were the ones who, by accident, had been permitted to run wild as little girls. But, alas, most young girls are raised properly, and properly raised young girls are not permitted to run wild.

Research evidence gives us some interesting clues as to how children develop different space patterns. In the earliest months of life, until babies are six months old, boys are observed to receive more attention than girls. Dr. Michael Lewis is one researcher who has detailed these different responses in mothers. More recently, Sarah Sternglantz documented similar responses in nurses who care for infants immediately after birth. After six months a switch occurs, and girls receive greater amounts of attention. They will be spoken to more, checked up on more. This attention switch takes place then when children begin to move around. Because parents make more contact with girls than boys after the first six months, girls are more apt to be within parents' range, boys more apt to be out of parents' range. By twelve months girls give evidence of staying close to parents; by eighteen months girls are rewarded by parental attention, especially from fathers, for staying close.

Lisa Serbin has observed variations on this theme of different responses to girls' and boys' spatial explorations in her studies of nursery school teachers. In nursery school, when boys or girls become upset, they approch the teacher for comfort; they come close. The teacher comforts the girls and boys in the same manner. After comforting the female child, however, the teacher moves to another activity, keeping the child by her side. After comforting the male child, the teacher, before moving on to another activity, sees that he goes back to his work. Thus the male child does not remain close by. Serbin also documented that little boys receive the teacher's attention whether close or far, but that girls attract this attention primarily when they are close; that is, the teacher scans the room with her eyes to see that everything is all right. When both boys and girls are distant she directs positive remarks only to the boys: "Nice building, Joe," "Good sharing, Henry!" Girls only get praise when they are close to the teacher.

In studying the research that indicates boys are allowed greater spatial exploration than girls, one begins to understand how quickly the ideas of the boy as roamer or wanderer and the girl as clinger or homebody are taught. More surprising is that the difference in allowable space that girls and boys may explore increases as the children get older. The space boys are permitted to roam continuously enlarges relative to their sisters. One consequence is that males, and often females, from their earliest years, believe that distant space, and thus public space, is male and male only. The idea that male space should be free of females is reinforced for children by television shows, stories, and "good" children's books in which the exclusion of girls is viewed as an appropriate male prerogative.

How clearly males possess space has been demonstrated by studies of the so-called open classroom, which indicate that little girls move through only five sixths of the space. Boys exhibit no similar spatial inhibition, they move through the entire classroom. These early spatial messages allow boys when they become men to feel un-self-consciously hostile to the notion of a woman on the floor of the Senate, a woman on the floor of the stock market, or a woman on the bench, whether it be a Little League or the Supreme Court one.

By the time children are nine or ten, the difference between the amount of space girls and boys are permitted to explore may be calculated in miles. But this is not the only difference researchers observe between them. Although the girls are allowed much less spatial freedom, they generally accept their restrictions, they don't attempt to negotiate any extension of the restrictions, nor do they attempt to circumvent the spatial rules. Boys, on the other hand, who are formally permitted more spatial freedom to begin with, either negotiate for still more or simply ignore the restrictions. They not only ignore them, they believe that their mothers know that they are ignoring these restrictions and will do nothing about their disobedience. After all, boys will be boys! Boys learn quite early that they may take liberties with imposed limits. The difference between the restriction girls and boys will accept is thus even greater than the difference formal limits suggest.

Besides controlling children's space when they are quite young, adults further insure differential spatial exploration by buying children the kinds of toys that will stimulate what they believe to be sex-appropriate play. Boys receive toys that stress the management of space and relations in space: blocks, erector sets, Lincoln Logs. Boys also get playthings that encourage them to explore outdoors: balls, bats, cars, fishing poles.

If boys' toys position them outside and encourage their understanding of space, girls' toys typically place them inside. The only toy young girls receive that they can use outside — the doll carriage — inhibits rather than stimulates movement, just as many real baby carriages will inhibit the speed and easy movement of the mother who is tied to it.

Perhaps one of the most serious corollaries of these spatial restrictions on little girls is that they rarely develop their large muscles fully and are therefore not as agile and quick as they could be. They can never run away. Boys who run poorly or who cannot catch or throw a ball are said to do so like a girl. The truth is that untrained runners, catchers, and throwers do resemble girls because girls, as a group, are untrained and inexperienced. If clinging and a fear of distance is taught to girls in their earliest years, how can they develop the desire to run, to jump, to climb, and to chase? If girls retain the desire to run, jump, and climb, they are apt to be criticized by their parents for engaging in such activities. Think of one of the few good large-muscle activities girls often play — jump rope. It is played by standing in one place. How about hopscotch? A fine game, but a game distinguished by its narrow use of space where spatial precision or accuracy, rather than speed or distance, makes one a winner. Not a bad spatial skill, but surely not the only one to develop.

The well-advertised inappropriateness of athletic activities for girls is only now receding as women demand their fair share of the playing fields for themselves and their daughters. But it is during the earliest months and years of life that girls will get positive or negative messages about moving through space. The Olympic motto "Higher, Stronger, Faster" has meaning only for people free to enjoy speed, distance, and height.

The intellectual development of girls, too, is thought to be adversely affected by their lack of experience in exploring physical space. Their ability to understand and manipulate spatial relationships and spatial reasoning lags behind their male peers. Girls generally receive dolls, tea sets, dolls, play furniture, dollhouses, toy vacuums, or dolls — toys that encourage them to imitate and to practice physical child care and repetitive housework but do not foster exploration, problem solving, or creativity. The mix of miniature stoves, pots, pans, washers, couches, brooms with dolls, dolls, dolls, forces the coupling in little girls' minds of physical child care and housework, a connection both arbitrary and artificial. But because women are to be confined and both women and children are to be excluded from worldly and intellectual activities, their place is appropriately seen by both men and women as inside and at home.

It has been a common inference by people who do research with young children that girls are socialized more easily than boys. They learn to obey societal rules more quickly, more thoroughly, and more regularly than do boys. Evidence of girls' acceptance of greater spatial restrictions and boys' rejection of much looser restrictions, as detailed earlier, is used to support the conclusion that the socialization of girls is achieved earlier and more dependably than that of boys. While the evidence clearly allows for that conclusion, it is one that beclouds more than it illuminates. Like many conclusions about female-male differences, it implies inevitability, permanence, and virtue where no inevitability, permanence, and certainly no virtue exist. Conclusions like these permit the drawing of a further and quite questionable conclusion: girls and women are inherently law-abiding and boys and men are inherently lawless; while girls and women are inherently compliant, boys and men are inherently defiant.

It would be better, and more helpful, especially to child rearers, to use the evidence of current research on female-male differences as a beginning, rather than as a conclusion. The evidence might better motivate questions than preclude them. Why? How? How come? are the questions feminists ask when presented with the evidence of different patterns of female-male behavior. More cynically, they also frequently ask the question detectives always ask when a crime has been committed, "Qui bono?" ("Who benefits?"). Take the statement "Girls are socialized earlier than boys." The language suggests that the girls have achieved something positive more quickly than their brothers. But is this the case? Is early, regular, dependable compliance to barely understood restrictive rules and regulations a virtue? Is the inability to negotiate with parents good? Suppose we changed the word "socialized" to "tamed," as in the taming of lions, or broken in, as in the breaking in of horses. Would we still believe girls to be ahead if we called their experience early taming or early breaking in?

The very fact that little girls don't seek to modify rules or to negotiate or to circumvent them, indicates that their socialization has been quite different from their brothers'. While boys are only casually controlled, and often not even casually, girls are indeed broken in. The rules girls learn are embedded in such concern for their ultimate physical or social well-being that negotiation, like experimentation, is simply unattractive. If you have been clearly, continually, and consistently taught that space and distance are unsafe, you eventually find it unattractive. You will avoid experiences that require you to roam distant spaces. Confinement taught to you as your only safety will be attractive and sought. Girls are simply frightened into "good behavior." When Nadia Comaneci burst onto the world's consciousness at the 1976 Summer Olympics, great interest was expressed in her development as a gymnast since she was only fourteen at the time of her triumph. It was reported that she had been selected at age five by experts who had observed her on the playground. "She exhibited," they said, "no fear." That was her most outstanding quality. By fourteen she could move through space as if it were her natural environment.

• • •

In general, we believe an extended childhood and adolescence is good for children. If they are forced to assume adult behaviors, roles, and responsibilities too early, they are thought to be denied opportunities for growth and development that are necessary in order to live a rich and complex life. If a long period of exploration and learning is agreed to be a virtue, why then is it that limited or limiting behavior is declared to be laudable for young girls? Feminists identify the adult admiration and enthusiasm for the tamed little girl who is a "real little mother" at ten as the surest sign of oppressive child-rearing patterns. (Indeed, even today in some societies the little ten-year-old girl will soon mother a child.)

Taming girls is what society is into and this taming is

neither easy nor automatic. It requires the most diligent, consistent, and persistent efforts. These kinds of efforts are simply not invested in the socialization of boys. Parents are quite ambivalent about how much limitation they really want to place on a boy, for they are quite ambivalent about how much limitation they wish him to internalize. After all, he may want to be an explorer, an astronaut, or a sea captain. He may have to climb high, dig deep, travel far. He may have to lead others (lead and follow, here too we see the metaphorical use of space). Parents don't want him too inhibited, too tame, too much of a sissy. Yet they don't want him out of control either. This ambivalence toward the boy but not the girl is what causes many parents to feel it is much tougher to raise the male child — they can't figure out their task clearly. Mothers will leave a male child unsupervised for a much longer period than a female child before checking up. Parents' verbal behavior, too, is tied to this process. Mothers talk more to girls, with both positive and negative consequences. On the positive side, little girls become more verbally facile and better prepared for the world of reading. The negative consequence has to do with the content of the mother's talk. Generally, she directs a great deal of praise and criticism at her daughter, and, most of all, she delivers instructions in behavior. In contrast, by the time children are observed in school, almost all of the comments designed to control behavior are directed at the boys. The mother and father have already effectively — too effectively — brought the girls' behavior into control. In school the effects of grossly different child-rearing practices are quite observable. The girls are "too good" and the boys "too bad." The fact is that children who are successful in school are neither the super-good girls nor the super-bad boys.

It is not only the parents' behavior and example that restrain little girls; the messages beamed at them from society convey the same kind of expectations. When feminists began looking at children's books they were shocked to observe with what regularity females were pictured confined in space while males roamed free. Like the princesses locked in the innumerable towers of countless fairy tales, the more modern books placed young girls and women inside more modest modern establishments where girls and women appear to remain willingly. No need for a key to lock up these modern docile creatures. Fairy tales are also excellent sources for the notion that "bad things" happen to young girls who wander unprotected. Many a wolf is pictured waiting to attack all the Little Red Riding Hoods, even those who, like her, venture out for the most socially approved purposes. Analysis of the children's reading material substantiated still another sexist space theme: the notion that certain places are off-limits to little girls; that boys without any self-consciousness can bar girls from their play spaces, just as later, as men, they will bar them from hunting lodges, fishing trips, and places to work. Although easily as tough and as strong as their brothers, little girls are taught to think of themselves as frail and in need of protection if they venture "out."

In the "in-out" issue we get another glimpse of a continuing theme in sexist child rearing. That is the simultaneous focus on the predicted future "weakness" and "vulnerability" of all little girls and the future "strength" and "invincibility" of all little boys. Now we must ask ourselves the question that the people who study self-fulfilling prophecies always ask: Do we expect little girls to grow up weak because they do, or do they grow up weak because we expect it? Conversely, do we expect little boys to grow up strong because they do, or do they grow up strong because we expect it? We not only expect it, we invest almost all of our money, effort, and time to see that our expectations will not be disappointed.

Mothers and fathers who are members of oppressed racial,

religious, and ethnic groups, like mothers and fathers of daughters, act to limit their children's freedom in space, but there are often important differences in how this is done. When parents must limit both daughters' and sons' spatial freedom because of an identifiable enemy "out there," their behavior is often conscious, well thought out, and communicated to the children in a straightforward manner. When children are raised to understand that there is a realistic danger out there, and the danger is caused by people who wish them harm, even though confinement is difficult and painful, it can be managed by the children. But when minority parents try to pass off these spatial restrictions as legitimate, they have to twist reality and twist their children's minds as well. Unfortunately, this is exactly the technique that traditional mothers and fathers use in dealing with little girls' spatial limitations.

The theme that one sex is appropriately "out" while the other only safe when "in" runs through all of society's fictional messages as well as through parental behavior and attitudes. But other aspects of our life-style transmit this space-distinction message too.

One of these is the nature of our housing patterns. If children lived in heterogeneous neighborhoods in which some women worked outside the home and some men worked at home, their view of their own family's structure would be modified as they grew older. Children living in extended-family households often have an opportunity to observe adults with varied life patterns. Unfortunately, the result of much of our suburban developments is to place together in the closest proximity nuclear families whose daily life patterns are quite similar and whose very structure excludes adults whose life-styles might be different. We have a growing population of older people whose life patterns change as these women and men retire from paid employment. Their segregation from families with young children makes this large group of older people unavailable as models for young children.

The separation of housing from work, a development that became complete for most American families after World War II, further complicated the men "out," women "in," sexual division with unfortunate consequences for womens' reputation for knowledge of worldly things as well as their actual knowledge. Until approximately thirty years ago, most women and men lived quite close to where they worked. If they lived on farms or in small towns, their work was clearly observable and often women and children were integrated into farm and small-town manufacturing and merchandising efforts. When paid employment was removed and became distant from home, many women and almost all children became totally estranged from "worldly" work. This strangeness and isolation from what men were becoming increasingly involved in led to a loss of understanding by women of the way the "outside" world operated. But the loss of understanding was never as great as the women's loss of standing and status as participating members of their community.

The social world of middle-class adults, as observed by children, further strengthens the "in-out" sexual distinction. Many women design their entire social life so that it takes place only when in the company of a man. If the women are not "taken out" by their husbands, they remain in. Young children learn much just from observing the phenomenon of adult men being needed to take adult women out. Children are often taught by their mothers to anticipate excursions with daddy rather than mommy, so daddy is viewed not only as sponsoring mother in the world but as sponsoring the children as well. It is daddy, the "outside" one, who organizes outings and takes the children out. A more oppressive refinement of this notion encourages fathers to take sons out more than daughters, for that is part of the identifying routine. On those father-son outings, adventurous trips are often suggested — hiking, fishing, camping — while the womenfolk (one- to one-hundred-year-olds) stay at home. The observation and direct experience children have with mother and father on this in-out issue encourages children to view mothers as unwilling or incapable of organizing ventures and adventures. This aspect of family life, like mother being separated and isolated from worldly effort, and hundreds of other seemingly unrelated ones, helps build a picture of mother as slightly hapless, weak and incapable. This is the future woman the young daughter is taught to want to become, or, perhaps what's worse, will become.

When daddy, as is frequently the case, only participates in household work as the outsider, still other lessons are taught and learned. Many men will do plumbing, carpentry, or electric work. Often daddy will do the unusual, special, or "fix-it" tasks assigned the paid outsider if daddy cannot or will not do them. The fix-it daddy is thus associated with jobs for which money is paid, while mommy is usually associated with efforts for which typically no money is paid. When engaged in these fix-it enterprises, the father will often encourage his son, but not his wife or daughter, to assist and thus to learn. Daddy thus produces yet another family handyman.

Middle-class men, particularly, will also do regular tasks cheerfully if those tasks are outside ones. Fathers will mow lawns, wash the car, and cook on grills. But watch what happens when the "outside" moves "inside." Since dad has not been integrated into family functions, he simply remains an outsider even when inside his own home.

When daddy is a "good guy," he often assumes the posture and status of being a special guest in relation to the stay-at-home mother and children. He is company, they are everyday. The nonintegrated beloved daddy has something of the aura that grown-up children away at college or in the services, or married with homes of their own, achieve on their return to the old homestead. When daddy is feared or disliked, his homecomings are viewed with misgivings and are seen as unwanted and unwarranted disturbances of the peace.

In some homes daddy's expected return is anticipated by personal primping and house straightening to make home and family appear more ordered than they actually are. It is as if the rules of a many-servanted household apply to normal family life. In the Victorian age those few homes that had many servants had strict rules concerning what the master might see and not see in the household. Servants caught cleaning in sight of the master might be discharged. Although logic might suggest that one would wish to view those in one's employ engaged in the task for which they were hired, this does not seem to be the case. Housework is apparently so mundane and unattractive that it must be completed out of the master's and daddy's sight. Or perhaps daddies, like the masters of stately homes, do not wish to be reminded that in living they incur maintenance obligations that others discharge for them. Perhaps in the case of families there is even a simpler explanation. Daddy's schedule is the schedule with which all other time schedules must mesh. If daddy has finished his work, mommy is supposed to be finished with hers, and the children finished with their private activities.

Daddy's time is special and even inside the house so is his space. Daddy, in pursuing his outside or guestlike status in his own home, develops strategies for the use of inside space that further assure that no one will think him just one of the family. Daddy will often have a special chair, a special place at the table, and a special place to work or pursue his interests. Sometimes males' special places are quite elaborate: offices, dens, studios, or shops.

Consider for a moment the family car. Here too, mommy

and daddy have different spaces, and the result is a different relation to the children. Even within the confines of a Volkswagen, daddy is able to be alienated. When the family is together in the car, daddy's special seat is the driver's seat. Mother acts to protect daddy from the children: "Shush, your father is trying to concentrate on the road." If her attitude is positive, she will sing, joke, and help them and herself pass the time. But when mother drives, and as family chauffeur she is more apt to do the driving alone with the children than the father, she also interacts with the children. If she is negative she will shush them, hush them, and threaten them. If positive, she will sing, tell jokes, and point out interesting things on the road. To this day when I see a train I say to the empty car, "Look at the choo-choo." Daddies drive when they drive. Mothers drive and child rear.

In choosing or in accepting this special status, father pays a heavy price. Daddy does not really belong. The superficial and shallow nature of his relations to his home is often evident when, through calamitous or fortuitous circumstances, he must be at home for an extended period of time. He walks aimlessly about, his wife and often even his children find him in the way. He now becomes a problem for his wife who has not expected to share her inside territory with an outside person. There is an old sexist statement that no kitchen is big enough for two women. I have always found women do quite well together in kitchens for they've had a lot of training. Remember those hilarious group cooking experiences in junior high school? When my mother reminisces about her school days, circa 1910, it is those slapstick comedy-type cooking classes that remain most vivid in her mind; however, to a grown, skilled woman, having an inexperienced demanding man in the kitchen can be a source of great dismay unless she is willing to teach and he is willing to learn. But because the work and space divisions have been so rigid in the past, there rarely can be a reciprocal teaching-learning relationship. Thus, when the outside daddy comes home to roost, he has no idea how to roost, how to plan varied periods of stimulation and relaxation, excitement and rest, creation and recreation. He has had no practice in distilling joy, pleasure, and satisfaction from inside.

The woman who maintains a tight grip on "her" home also deprives her husband and children, especially boys, by preventing them from developing the skills, abilities, and knowledge that would enable them to enjoy their homes, the present one and the future one as well. On the other hand, if men and boys are brought into the home, women, too, will have to change their attitudes. Accustomed to at least one arena where their knowledge, their taste, and their power are evident, some women are reluctant to let the outsiders in. This is often why the notion of a special place for daddy does not offend, for then mommy may fool herself that the rest of the house is hers. I believe women who wish to remain sovereign in the home make a great error. Even though this decision does give them an identifiable area of expertise and decision making, it confines and confirms them, and them alone, as the homebodies. Furthermore, this decision can limit whatever else they may aspire to be in the future. It is depressing that managing a home, unlike managing a factory, a labor union, a farm, a school, or a business, is seen as a poor set of credentials for public service. The description "just a housewife" does not deliver messages of experience as a decision maker, priority setter, risk taker, or critical evaluator — which of course is untrue.

Women's notions of home often clash in other ways with those of men. While women *think* their houses are theirs, men *know* their houses are really theirs. Legally, the house belongs to whomever's name is on the deed, and that name is more often than not, the husband's. So "her kitchen," "her bathroom," "her house," are often actually "his," wherein she is free to work. Few other workers make the same kind of mistake! Women are often unaware of their legal position in marriage; unaware of how shaky their relationships are to real estate. Although in the popular mind, mother goes with the house, the house doesn't necessarily go with mother. But many women do indeed believe that a kind of reciprocal relationship exists between themselves and their houses — that is, if they are tied to the house, the house is also tied to them.

If, by leaving a special place for daddy, women believe the rest of the house is theirs, they may set the tone for making the children feel like intruders in what in any fair arrangement would be public space — kitchens, dining rooms, living rooms, halls, and dens. In any case, few women seek, receive, or achieve any house space that is really their own. In believing that they have the whole house, they really, in effect, have no particular space of their very own. There is no place where they and only they can drop in to drop out: a place where no other person can come without permission. Privacy should not be as it often is, a prerogative of dad's, a status symbol. Of course it has been dad rather than mom who has received an early training in space and in exclusive space use: especially exclusive of females. Privacy — especially in a family that typically interacts a good deal and where most house space is willingly shared — is a helpful and desirable goal for each family member.

CHAPTER 8

Breaking the Housework Connection

THE IDEA THAT "tamed" behavior coupled with an interest in homemaking is a sure indication of a talent for mothering is not only untrue, it negatively affects almost all women, though in different ways. Little girls who are neat, clean, helpful, quiet little homebodies are continually led to believe they have all the characteristics necessary for effective mothering. What happens, then, when it turns out that these are not the assets one needs for a job that is to assist an unformed being to become a humane, human one, sound of mind, body, spirit, and soul?

Since we have convinced these mothers that they are right for the job, then the fault must lie with the babies; the baby is a bad eater, or a poor sleeper, or difficult to deal with, or maybe just plain bad. And what of the girls who were not easily inhibited — the tomboys? They often assume they will not be good mothers because they know they have none of the societally approved signs. They don't think sleeping infants are cute, they don't find buying or knitting things a particular pleasure, dressing a girl is not their notion of fun. But these women may be outgoing, adventurous, inventive, well-disciplined, and great copers — characteristics absolutely essential for successful child rearers. So women who have had the least opportunities for self-development often enter child rearing with great confidence, while women with great inner resources enter not at all, or with many misgivings. The first group is bewildered by their difficulties, the second, if brave enough to have babies in the first place, continues to mother beset by the conviction that they are in the wrong business.

When women are at their most vulnerable right after the baby's birth, when their awkwardness and inexperience is evident, those old messages are activated. Doubts as to their ability to mother assail them. The baby begins to personify what they believe is their failure not only to be proper mothers, but proper women as well. It's enough to make someone feel unfriendly to the baby! It's enough to give someone a postpartum depression! Mothers with this particular difficulty should try to remember that they are only inexperienced, not unnatural. Inexperience doesn't mean much to a baby, who has never had a more experienced mother. You can stay a chapter ahead of the baby by reading up on food, clothing, and diapering.

The belief that tamed women are somehow good for and with children is easily observable in teacher-training institutions, to which shy, diffident, fearful young women and men are often directed by people who know nothing about the rigors of the classroom. Their very timidity releases in poorly controlled youngsters behavior with which neither they nor the children can cope. Successful teachers are people of spirit, verve, and vitality. (It is the youngest students, incidentally, who become most disorganized when the adults are inadequate.) In any event, the real needs of children are ignored when we sell motherhood and teaching as appropriate occupations for the tamed woman.

When aware women reject motherhood it is not because they can't appreciate how terrific it might be to participate in the rearing of a new human being, but because it is difficult to get child rearing cut loose from the brambles, thorns, and undergrowth of its oppressive associations. Nowhere is the difficulty greater and clearer than on the time-space issue. To see child rearing as possibly free from past oppressive patterns and associations, let's begin by making no automatic or unnecessary assumptions of how, when, where, and with what other activities child rearing must go forward. Instead, let's examine past child-rearing practices in terms of the kinds of space and time demands they make on women, men, and children. Once we have separated what is crucial to the well-being of mother, father, and child from what is either secondary or inimical, we can make space-time decisions that make sense to parents who intend to live free, rich, complex lives while rearing their children and who also wish to rear children who will have an opportunity to do the same.

There is a new vogue among big corporations called zero-based budgeting. It does not assume that just because an item has always been in the budget it must necessarily be there now, nor does it assume that just because money has always been spent in a certain way, or for certain things, that it necessarily has to be that way again. Every item placed in the budget, therefore, has to be justified in terms of present needs and priorities. Parents are wise to approach child rearing with a similar view, a zero base. Staying clear of the assumptions and behavior of the past is a good way for parents to free their resources to promote goals they believe to be worthwhile. Space and time are two of parents' major resources, as well as two of the major factors they must be aware of in making child-rearing decisions. Now, once we keep in mind the generally agreed upon basic human needs of infants and commit ourselves to provide them, all attending aspects of typical family life are up for review. First, though, we will concentrate on time and space issues.

Let's begin by suggesting that there is nothing necessarily normal or natural about babies being inside. There are baby nomads, there always have been, and before the dawn of agriculture all babies must have been nomads. Babies must be protected against exposure, for they simply cannot survive without warmth in winter and protection from the direct rays of the sun in summer. But that hardly accounts for the incredible amount of time most infants spend inside the house in good weather and bad. We have blankets and clothing that make it possible for babies to be protected outside in quite cold weather. In some parts of Russia (as was supposed to have been the case in ancient Sparta) the progressive exposure of babies to colder and colder weather was thought to be a sound way to make infants and babies hardy, build resistance, and allow them to be comfortable in the cold with a minimum of clothing to inhibit movement. Healthy babies and young children can enjoy an enormous range of temperatures and weather conditions especially if some care is taken with their clothing.

Once while I was visiting St. Mary's College, the public relations director, a young mother, told me of her concern with her three-year-old daughter's nursery school teachers. She was bothered because when the weather was cold and snowy, the boys remained outside playing while the girls were kept inside with their female teachers. This is not an uncommon observation of girl, boy, and teacher behavior in the nursery school. In Barbara Sprung's book, *Non-Sexist Education for Young Children,* she writes that the young girls in one nursery school engaged in vigorous outdoor play only after their female teacher had made a special effort to participate in outdoor play herself. The power of the female teacher to broaden young girls' opportunities may also be related to the absence of people other than the mother in the young girls' environment. The nursery school or kindergarten teacher is often her only alternative model. But by the time they are old enough for nursery school, little girls have already learned to confine themselves spatially and to be timid about "stepping out."

Babies and young children do not have to spend their time inside. They are marvelously portable. But children are inside because mothers are inside, and mothers are inside because they are doing housework and they have been trained to feel more comfortable bringing up babies and children inside. Assuming that child rearing is a task that necessarily needs to be associated with another activity, there is certainly nothing normal and natural about the association of housework and child rearing. Indeed, most aspects of housework fit less naturally with child-rearing activities than most other adult enterprises. The warning on many household cleaners reads, "Keep out of the reach of children." Cleaning with those poisoned substances is hardly an activity in which mother and child can happily and jointly participate. One can scarcely imagine a situation in which parents would voluntarily bring their infant or young child into an environment in which poisonous substances were being freely used. Yet that is what happens inside their home where chlorines, oven cleaners, and disinfectants are casually used in close proximity to the children if "normal" housework is being done. What about pails of hot soapy water? What kind of environment do these provide for infants and children? Are hot irons, hot pots, and hot stoves any better? Electric cords in outlets provide another kind of hazard, as do the highly waxed floors we have all been taught to admire. Just the sound of vacuum cleaners in action causes some infants stress. It is no wonder that homes are the scene of more accidents than any other single environment. Look what's going on there! Indeed, cooking, cleaning, and ironing are among the most hazardous of all the activities in which adults are typically engaged. Just compare this environment to a store, a school, an office, a park, a courtroom. Where is there more danger?

It doesn't make sense to try to dissuade mothers from placing toddlers in playpens and using television as a useful distraction when the housework demands that mothers be engaged in activities dangerous to the child. Playpens do indeed teach poor spatial and interpersonal messages. They may teach babies that exploration is dangerous and to be avoided, that good behavior is restricted behavior, and that private, individual play is preferred by mothers to playing together. Playpens, however, will be used for young children as long as mothers continue to pen themselves in their homes busy with activities that enhance the house but neither themselves nor their children. For if babies are in playpens to prevent their getting into things, we can think of homes as mothers' playpens used to prevent mothers from getting into things. A mother's exploration of the outer world and her inner needs are, like children's exploratory needs, prevented from finding expression by the home's spatial restrictions and the using up of her time with repetitive, monotonous household tasks.

I've often thought how bizarre it would seem to parents if they visited their children's nursery school and observed the following scene: Some children wandering aimlessly around; others watching television; some tugging at the teachers; and teachers ignoring the children's requests for attention. The teachers (in a good nursery school there would be at least two) would be busy, one scrubbing the floor, the other arranging the shelves in the closet or scrubbing the rings from some shirt collar. But why is this scene, so obviously unacceptable in the group setting, so acceptable at home? Are the needs of the children so different when at school than when at home? It is simply that our expectations are different as to what may properly take place in school and at home. At school we expect children to be provided with activities that interest them and engage their attention; we expect the teachers to be focused on the child, promoting the child's well-being, growth, and development. Why do we have no similar expectation for the toddler and parent at home?

Because child care is only considered a total occupation when one gets paid for it. When carried out by mothers, it is expected that child care will be discharged between other more observable efforts. Although motherhood is often presented as a primary occupation for women, in most cases it is at best a semi, demi, or mini one. While inside looking after the child, she is simultaneously the family's cook, cleaner, and laundress. Women who are hired as infant nurses, governesses, and tutors, wiser than young mothers, realize the trap that awaits women who accept the child-care role. Professional child rearers clearly delineate before accepting a position, how much, or rather how little, how frequently, or rather how infrequently, they will discharge any task other than direct, focused infant and child care. Baby nurses may prepare an infant's meals or may rinse out some particularly precious item of infant apparel. All other cooking, cleaning, shopping, and washing are not only de-clared beyond their responsibility, but their own personal food, clothing, and housekeeping needs are often provided by others. Similarly, people paid to cook or clean rarely accept, or are expected to accept, the responsibility for infant and child care. Mothers, however, have been programmed into the combination of housework and child care.

Twenty years earlier when these mothers were young girls in nursery school and kindergarten, they were provided with a "housekeeping play corner" (surely a contradiction in terms) sometimes called a "doll corner." This corner, in which they spent a great deal of their time, contained and continues to contain a toy refrigerator, stove, sink, table, chairs, and dolls, dolls, dolls. Dolls in high chairs, dolls in cradles, and dolls in carriages. This combination of little girl toys along with her observation of her own mother's and other mothers' activities convinced her and her male peers that the child-rearing–house-keeping activities are not only linked but are almost the same thing. In fact, through some incredibly wrong-headed associations, many mothers think housekeeping *is* child rearing. That is, they come to believe they are engaged in child-rearing activities when they wash clothes, clean toilets, shop, and cook food. This confusion derives only partly from the artificial grafting of housework to child rearing. It is also the result of a particularly narrow notion of child rearing, which fixes the mother's attention on the baby's physical care. Being a parent, particularly a mother, has been presented as an exercise in feeding, changing, and bathing babies. When children learn to feed, toilet, and wash themselves, the mother often translates child care to cooking the family food, cleaning the family bathrooms, and washing the family's clothes. In doing this the mother believes she continues to mother. This is simply not the case! She has exchanged mothering for housework. When we nurse a baby, change a baby, and wash a baby, we are interacting with the baby. When we shop and cook, clean bathrooms, and wash clothes, we interact with storekeepers, stoves, cleaning products, washers, and dryers.

Let's consider the actual changes in the way mothers budget time and space when their infants are first born and as the infants become independent. When babies are first born, their total helplessness demands the physical presence of an adult at clothing, feeding, diapering, and dressing times. Since the conscientious parent is then often in close contact with the infant, she has little difficulty in talking, singing, cooing, and snuggling the baby. Now if both parents are energetically devoted to changing, bathing, and dressing as well as feeding, the infant receives a large amount of positive talk, touch, and tenderness during those first months of life. Sylvia Brody has calculated that a thousand hours are spent during the first year of life just in feeding the baby. Indeed, so much time is spent between adult and baby just in feeding that Brody believes the quality of interaction that characterizes the feeding relationships greatly affects the baby's development. Now if all loving language, caressing, and touching time is associated with infant dependency, trouble may occur between baby and mother as the baby reaches two years of age. The mother often has no idea how rich the care experience is for the baby, how meaningful beyond the servicing of physical needs (although this is not a small or unimportant aspect). Indeed she often doesn't realize how meaningful that inter-action has been for her and how deprived she is if tender-ness, talk, and touch end as baby grows older.

A mother's lack of awareness results from the absence of information about the totality of what she does and the fix-ing of her attention on physical care. The use by parents of pediatricians as child-rearing guides accentuates this focus because it is basically medical. Thus a mother thinks about the formulas, shots, bath temperatures, disposable versus nondisposable diapers, one blanket or two, instead of the more complex needs — which she has been unconsciously satisfying all along — that the baby has for affection, lan-guage, and thus culture, stimulation, and novelty. The con-sequences of the mother's ignorance is painful, for in con-tinuing to offer cooked food, clean clothes, and bathrooms, mothers think they are maintaining their level of mothering. But, if they are not providing other opportunities for the exchange of affection, attention, language, stimulation, and novelty, they have drastically reduced the quality of their interaction with their children. The mother's continued ex-clusive servicing of the physical needs of her babies and children is depressing for her own development, the child's development, and for their developing relationship. Burton White has said that mothers who respond to the baby's de-mand for attention with food raise children who are less intelligent than others. If all the mother can think of is food when the baby is looking for intellectual and emotional stimulation they're both in bad shape. (Responding with food may also indicate that the mother was in the kitchen too busy playing the proper mommy role to play with the baby.)

The baby who just a few months earlier was the focus of much adult-initiated joyful play, talk, and activity tries to initiate some when the adult slacks off. Often the infant will crawl, creep, or walk to the mother, yank at her, pull at her, or grab her leg in an attempt to get some action going. If the baby's overture is responded to enthusiastically, with some talk, some touch, some play, the baby will try with ever-increasing success also to be entertaining. If the mother engaged in household tasks, believing she is already fully occupied with baby-related needs, responds in anger, frustration, and annoyance, then there is trouble between them. Unfairly, in some ways, the more conscientious the mother was in the first few months, the more painful the withdrawal of contact and the more baffled the baby. Now the baffled baby can do just a very few things to signal pain: cry, howl, and tug some more. If the mother reads this behavior as the baby's escalation of a vast plot to prevent her getting her work done, or, worse, a fiendish attempt to annoy her, she will often move to punishment, and it will work! That is, the baby will learn that this once playful, entertaining, stimulating, and affectionate person can inflict pain. It will be awhile before the baby again tries to initiate contact.

Let's consider a day in the second year of a baby's life in a not unusual family. Mother arises and serves her family, including the baby, breakfast. Daddy goes to work, everyone waves good-bye, and what happens next? Mother begins to work at some household task, first providing the baby with a toy or toys. Often baby and mother do not speak, do not interact. If the baby makes some attempt to get mother involved, she will often ignore or be hostile to those attempts. The baby will be alone a lot. Occasionally the mother will check to see that the baby is "all right," that is, the baby is in no physical danger. The morning will pass; lunch will be prepared by the mother alone and served to the child.

Now the mother is ready for the baby to have a nap. The baby might legitimately wonder why a nap is needed since one generally rests up from something rather than nothing, so there is a struggle, a little negative interaction, and the baby does or does not sleep. When the baby awakes and if the weather is good and if a conscientious housekeeping mother has completed all her self-assigned chores, she will take the baby outside. Now, except for the breakfast and lunch meals, this is often the first bit of interaction the baby experiences in the day. The outing may be rather stylized, but sometimes the baby sees other people, other places, seasonal changes. The mother is more relaxed and may have a pleasant talk with the baby and squeeze and hug the child. But before you know it, it's almost dinner time, and mother and baby return home to repeat much of the morning's actions.

If the weather, however, was "bad," then the two- or three-hour outing is omitted. Mothers in cold climates go mad during the winter months from their feelings of isolation and seclusion — what they do not understand is, so do the babies. That is where the evening sleep problem begins. If the mother has been waiting to talk, to laugh, to be stimulated by the return of the husband, the baby is hardly going to want to sleep when finally there is a chance to participate in a little animation. What self-respecting family member would go to bed just when the day begins to get interesting? More seriously, what self-respecting family member would not think of father as special, interesting, and enlivening when the whole focus of the household is upon his return? What baby will not get the message that fun things, interesting, and stimulating things come from dads and, by association, men, while the boring, monotonous, everyday day-time world is mother's and, by extension, women's?

This whole development takes one year: in one year the mother can go from being powerful, stimulating, affectionate, and fascinating to drudge, nag, and punisher. Only the mother thinks the change is in the baby. It is, but not in the way the mother perceives it. Think of this situation from the baby's point of view. For the newborn, just being alive provides a powerful amount of stimulation. Newborns sleep a lot because they are weak, and the amount of energy they need to get their systems going independently, to observe, to get to know what it's all about, is enormous. Watch a baby sucking, moving its bowels, crying; the whole body gets a workout. It's an engrossing, involving affair, getting to know places, peoples, things, learning to act, react, to signal, to respond. Those babies put in a rough day for all the sleeping time they get. Infants have almost too much stimulation. Being bored is not a typical infant problem. But children by the middle and end of the second year have learned a lot; they are stronger and do not use up all their available energy in eating, bathing, or defecating. These children need a new kind of action. The mother doesn't see this because she's not been taught to see babies in that way; in part, because of those idiotic dolls that she's been taught to believe, since her own babyhood, in some way represent a baby. One of the interesting things about dolls is that they in no way deliver the essence of baby or infant. Dolls do not move, need no physical care, nor do they seek, require, or appreciate novelty, stimulation, or culture. Why in heaven's name is rehearsal for child rearing thought to be legitimately enacted on a piece of attractive, well-dressed, mute plastic? Perhaps dolls are appropriate as props for little girls to re-enact mothering as they have experienced it themselves. Thus they learn nothing of its reality and cannot practice new ways. A plant, a gerbil, an avocado pit teach more about nature and nurture, the effects of good care (especially now that we are being urged to talk and sing to our plants) than a hundred beautiful dolls.

• • •

How can we take these issues, turn them around, and make them work for the liberation rather than oppression of mothers and babies? Let's consider the issues: in-out, time-space, breaking the housework–child care connection, and responding to babies' and mothers' need for action, interaction, and reactions.

Many parents believe that routine is good for a baby and it may be; however, it also may be that it is the parents whose need for routine is greatest. Especially when mothers do almost all of the child rearing and housework themselves, a strict routine is often the only way they can balance all the incredible demands on their time. But the baby is often assumed to profit by this routine; one can only wonder if it is so. Of course, if the only choice is between the baby having regularly scheduled times with mother or a few rushed and harried moments, clearly the former is preferable. But if we could think of mothers freed from total household responsibility, sharing them with other family members, then baby-care possibilities and opportunities broaden immeasurably. For the baby-raising adventure really allows for a great deal of temporal as well as spatial freedom. First, you have to gain it, but you also have to be comfortable with this freedom. If a mother has been trained from early years to oppressive patterns, time and space freedom, like all other freedoms, will be experienced as a burden. The circularity of this issue often prevents a truly fresh beginning even for the next generation: The baby's opportunities for choice and freedom depend quite heavily on the mother's behavior. The mother's ability to free herself from traditional oppressive family structures often depends on her own early upbringing. But mothers must get clear of those early and later structures that constrain them.

The efforts women must make vary depending on whether they live with people who wish to help in this liberation or who prefer to profit from maintaining oppressive traditional family structures. If women have to battle both their early conditioning and an adult oppressive environment, their task is truly monumental and for many women an impossible one. If women only have to fight their own early conditioning, one that has linked baby care to housework and linked both to her, she will have problems enough breaking free. Studies show that women do not do less housework when "time-saving appliances" are introduced into their houses; they simply raise their standard of cleanliness. Most women, like most men, are unprepared to deal creatively with "free" time. Only the most well-adjusted, best educated people seem to be able to experience nonstructured time as other than burdensome. Mothers who are their children's primary care-takers often feel more satisfaction discharging the concrete tasks of housework, repetitive and boring though they may be, than initiating activities or responding to the overtures of their children. It is only assertive, creative, and powerful people who feel challenged and free when a day stretches before them and they must consider how to spend it in a way best for them and their young ones.

The need for strict routine in a young child's life, like the need for playpens, is more a reflection of the oppressive demands placed on the adults who rear them than a reflection of the baby's needs. While we generally assume a chaotic environment to be a destructive environment, a totally routinized one is probably quite as damaging. It is certainly difficult to imagine flexibility and adaptability growing in such an environment, or spontaneity or enthusiasm. Children fed, slept, bathed, and played with on a tight schedule will often be patterned into behavior that at first promises adults more freedom. If babies are on a strict schedule, adults then can plan their other activities knowing what time the baby will "take up." This makes it an attractive notion to parents who are hard pressed for time for many reasons. On the other hand, flexible, easily adaptive children offer freedom to adults in a different way. Children who can sleep in varying surroundings, at different times, under varying conditions, who can eat a wide range of foods, who can vary active and passive behaviors allow the people who care for them a very valuable kind of freedom. Although the strictly scheduled baby at first appears to offer adults a great deal of control, after a time the parents often find they are as tied to the schedule as are the children.

Life with children is easiest when a decision has been made to live with simple furnishings that require minimal maintenance. The more simple the physical surroundings, the more space and time there are for play projects, dancing, and physical activity. As housework is both minimized and shared, time, space, and energy are released for activities in which children can become involved. It would be a welcome change to have people regard as bizarre a home where home development receives maximal adult attention and child development receives little. Let us for a moment consider concepts like "development," "enhancement," and "extension" and contrast these with the notion of "maintenance." Development, enhancement, extension all suggest increasing, adding on, improving, or bettering. Generally, maintenance suggests keeping the status quo; not allowing things to grow worse, not losing ground. It is at best a nongrowth enterprise. If parents are spending their time in child maintenance and home improvement, they have things backward. The time children are young is very short (it feels very long when you're in the middle of day-to-day care, things aren't going too well, and no one's there to help). Parents' opportunities for easy, pleasant, satisfying interactions are at their peak when babies are young. Take advantage of those opportunities. Experiences of caring, sharing, enjoying, and supporting build bonds between people that serve them all emotionally. Casual, superficial interchanges between parents and children do not produce deep bonding. For that you need time; time to gain a knowledge of each other's needs, wishes, hopes, fears, and time to share experiences. But the enormous pressure on young women to get "into" housework distracts them from their own and their children's development.

An incredible amount of household enhancement is stimulated by television commercials. Nonspotted glasses, nonringed collars, nonyellowed whites are set as important, desirable, and crucial goals. Not for the whole family, of course, just for the wife-mother. It's not pure sexism, it is sexism well mixed with greed. If there was a way to show a profit selling good relations between mother and child, someone would. In the meantime, what is sold mother is soap — cakes of it, flakes of it, liquid, and solid. Its constant use will keep mother and child isolated and inside, so forget it. Strip care to a minimum, share care, and get set to go out.

Remaining inside with children separates children and women from contact with other adults, other children, and many possible experiences. Much of the negative effects continuous child rearing can have on the adults involved results not from single traumatic incidents but from the minute-to-minute, day-to-day experience that often continues without variation or change over an extended period of time. Lack of interest, excitement, and change make the time seem endless and eventually unendurable. Staying in, which begins as the seemingly "normal" response to infant care, becomes a serious and totally unexpected burden. The tendency of women to remain inside when they mother is what I call the First Law of Child-Rearing Inertia. Staying inside is especially burdensome in climates where winters are long and children are often sick. In a household of more than one young child, where for weeks at a time illness seems to pass from one to the other, the inability of the at-home parent to get out is a difficult experience to endure and a difficult experience to manage positively. Outside help and support are needed, but developing strategies for maximizing your own ability to handle this situation is important too. There are some ways of preventing the negative aspect of the "locked in" experience from mounting and becoming overwhelming.

First, try to be outside as much and as often as possible. Only stay in for the most extreme kinds of weather and illness. Even during really inclement weather, there is often a time of day when a very short excursion outside can be managed. The effort of dressing, undressing, and venturing out is all worthwhile — it is an adventure, something to talk about — do it! Have infants receive all their shots quickly so that taking them out is not dangerous. Maybe they want to see a football, basketball, or baseball game or a tennis match or neighborhood Little League or stickball game. Infants who are breast-fed are particularly portable and are also believed to have greater immunity to illness (children literally absorb immunity with their mothers' milk). Yet, while children and their mothers make quite attractive additions to any gathering, they are often not welcomed in either private or public spaces. Nursing mothers who go public should either be very comfortable about their own feelings of its rightness or psych out the situation to insure a good welcome — or take a supportive friend along.

Feeding babies on the go, whether breast-fed or not, is not hard, and neither is changing them. Once babies are protected by shots, have warm clothes and blankets, they are ready to go. Infants and children are usually better set for poor weather than the adults who are with them. Both girl and boy babies have equal access to warm clothes in the first months of life. Only as children get older are girls often put in clothes that give them less warmth (dresses and tights), which encourage their indoor positioning.

Whether the adult is a parent, grandparent, or teacher, it is the adult who is apt to become uncomfortable outdoors first and who projects this discomfort onto the child. Parents who live in climates where winters are cold and who've never learned to make peace with it, might use the pregnancy period to start getting ready. One way to get ready is by getting winter clothing. Not the sort of clothing that makes it possible to run from a heated car to a heated house, but clothing that permits long outdoor hikes, excursions, and exertions. Few other investments will insure so much pleasure and sanity as the proper parental clothing investment. If you are not a winter sports freak, you will be amazed at what's available in lightweight cold weather gear: from battery-heated socks and mittens to crushed aluminum liners for socks and gloves, to padded thermal underwear, companies are working overtime to keep you warm through and through in the cold. Thermal underwear, lined boots, foot and hand liners (either silk, cotton, or aluminum) inside woolen or down-filled gloves or mittens (mittens are warmer than gloves but more clumsy), woolen slacks under waterproof pants, wool sweaters over shirts, all under a waterproof down- or fiber-filled jacket will enable the parent to roam the outdoors with pleasure. Warm hands and feet are an absolute necessity because extremities get cold first. Heads should be kept warm, because 35 percent of the body heat is lost through an uncovered head. Masks over faces, unless you wear glasses, are also a good idea. Former skiers are a good source for second-hand warm clothes, as are thrift shops, Army-Navy stores, and end-of-season ski sales. If you have hesitated about becoming involved in winter sports, a decision to have a baby should increase your motivation for winter activities, since you'll want to model good physical practices and large-muscle activity. This is one of the many instances where one can see the baby as encouraging worldly involvement rather than enforcing confinement.

In warm weather and warm climates also, active sports clothes are the kind of clothing parents of young children should own. Good rain gear encourages greater outdoor activities as well. I always experience mixed feelings in recommending purchase of items at considerable cost. On the one hand, I feel that the real absence of spending money should be dealt with as a serious issue and ways of gathering needed items at low or no cost developed. However, I also wish to avoid the trap of suggesting that the clothing needs of child rearers are somehow less serious than the clothing needs of wage earners. It is often suggested that the larger society does not wish to spend money on young children or on child-rearing needs. This is often matched by the belief that they should require little if any familial resources as well. (It is interesting that when one discusses the issue of women working outside the home, the expenses associated with that effort are often mentioned — clothing, travel, and lunches among them — as if non-wage-earning women are not expected to have these needs.)

A common error mothers make is to place infants and young children outside to receive the benefits of outdoor fresh air, while they remain indoors. It is not only unfortunate because it models the female parent as the insider-homebody for the children, but it is poor policy for the parent. The typical non-wage-earning mother will spend many hours of her day inside her home, taking a short respite outside the home. When that short respite is removed, as it often is during very severe weather and during periods of severe illness, the parent feels a sense of loss that can be appreciated only by those persons who have had the same experience. So for prevention's sake, the principal child rearer should normally spend great amounts of time outside the home. If you find it difficult to spend large amounts of time outdoors, build it up slowly by extending outdoor time each day by five-minute intervals. Reverse what has become normal female parenting behavior by routinely beginning the day with a large breakfast produced cooperatively, packing food for one's own and infant's snack or lunch, dressing for an extended outdoor period, and having all members of the family leave together.

Taking long walks exploring your environment assisted by field and bird guides, or books on architecture and city life if your environment is urban, a call on the local library, local construction sites, parks, and ponds are fine ways to spend a day or morning. The important aspect of these activities is to demonstrate ease and familiarity with the outside world, to awaken interest — your own, and your child's — in your surroundings, to develop greater depth of knowledge about your environment. In watching the effects of seasonal changes upon the trees, the animals, the weather, mothers and children are rewarded by a sounder knowledge of and relation to their environment. Holding infants so that tree barks, leaves, and flowers can be touched and felt gives pleasure, stimulates the senses, and focuses attention. As the infant grows and moves around with growing independence on these excursions, both parent and child experience the kind of positive physical exertion that makes later eating more enjoyable and resting and naps more appreciated.

Mothers should also make plans for the times when they must spend extended periods of time indoors. Since these periods are usually in the winter, each spring begin to collect loads of paperbacks, arts and crafts materials, puzzles, and other materials for the long winter days ahead. Start storing things like a squirrel — but good things you'd like to do — and try to avoid those you hate when you might feel low. They will get done when you're feeling higher, and in a much shorter time. A special adult's winter box as well as a special children's winter box will help make the otherwise difficult days pass. Important, too, is a reliable baby sitter who will give you time to rest, or work, or pursue some desired activity. The use of baby sitters or parent exchanges is often reserved by the woman-parent for times when she goes "out" with the man-parent. But it is often in the long dark afternoons of winter when a succession of illnesses have confined a parent to the point of distraction that the sitter is most needed. Parents who pursue projects at home not only are happier staying at home than those who do not, they break the conviction that suggests home work is housework and is thus repetitive, boring, and dull. They also teach their children that doing, making, and creating are enjoyable, self-engendered worthwhile activities. There is no sense inveighing against television as children's nemesis if the only leisure-time activity exhibited in the homes is television watching.

• • •

Simple furnishings, comfortable and appropriate clothing are all ingredients that will make the task of child rearing easier and more joyful. But few decisions will be as important to promoting the joy of child rearing as where you choose to live, if choice is possible. The younger the children, the more important the kind of place you live will be. In deciding where to raise a family, it is far more helpful to choose a neighborhood, a particular apartment house, or an area, than to search for a dream house or an ideal apartment. To make child rearing a liberating experience, it has to be structured in a liberating fashion and whether you will be supported or undermined in your child-rearing decisions will be greatly influenced by where you live. Only the strongest and most secure among us can sustain a continued feeling of self-confidence when acting in an environment hostile to our aspirations, attitudes, and behavior. If you have the choice, find yourself a permissive, friendly, prochild environment. While some people are comfortable only if they are totally surrounded by people who conform to the same standards as they do, most of us can manage if there is a mix of people, some who share our attitudes, some who do not. However, an environment in which people are openly hostile to us is quite burdensome and oppressive.

The impact neighbors will have on your life as a parent eventually will be constant, pervasive, and satisfying or unsatisfying. One of the potential advantages, and potential disadvantages of having children is their ability to link you to people, places, and things, as well as to goals, principles, and ideals. One of your best shots at having some influence on what kinds of people, places, and things you will be involved with for the next decade is where you choose to live; again presuming you have a choice. Much is made of parents who force children to conform; little is mentioned of the efforts of children to force their parents to conform to the common neighborhood ethic. Young children have great difficulty in accepting parents different from everybody else. It is possible of course, but it is less of a strain on parents to live among "live and let live" families, or families who share their own life-style and values. If one is "odd parent out" in a neighborhood, it is likely that all the public services, schools, hospitals, clubs, activities, and libraries will reflect the notions of the neighbors.

Of first importance in choosing a place to live is the presence of other children — the more the better. Those of us who grew up with great mobs of children experienced terrific opportunities to choose friends, lose friends, make new friends, and to return to former friendships. Easy access to other children, in the same large building, down the block, or around the corner, is urgent for mother, father, and children. The constant walking or chauffeuring children to find companions for them is among the most persistent and trivially oppressive tasks for parents. Also, when arrangements must be made for children's play, parents will have to participate. Often parents who are poor at casual, informal talk find friend-making personally difficult and dread the need to become party to their children's first friendships. Again, one can move at least in one of two ways. Choose a place to live close to other children so that your own involvement is limited, or use the early years of your child's life as a particularly golden opportunity to get into the friend-making business. One can very quickly become involved with people who raise children at the same time and in ways similar to your own. The experience of closely watching children other than your own grow and develop is also very positive. Fortunately, you often find yourself, twenty years later, the friend of both the parents and the children with whom you and your children were young together. Thus young children can often help broaden your opportunities to meet and know in a close and meaningful way people different from your ordinary associates.

Equally as important as an apartment or neighborhood with many children is an area where people arrange their lives in many different patterns. Suburbs are increasingly drawing from a diverse community of people. Whether or not both parents of young children have paid employment, it is important to live in a neighborhood where at least *some* parents do. Living among people who live the way you may choose to live one day will allow you to change and develop new life-styles with ease.

Some neighborhoods also develop a tone particularly their own. One sometimes hears of areas where people are enormously helpful to each other. This is attractive to some people, unattractive to others. However, parents of babies usually benefit from neighborhoods with a great deal of house-to-house sharing and visiting. Perhaps, one of the most important facts to remember if you select a place to live when your child is an infant is how rapidly that infant will become a school-age child. If, as parents, you hope to live a happily balanced, independent-interdependent life with your children, choose an area that allows for the gradual development of the child's own independence. The location that permits a walk to schools, libraries, stores, movies, trains, or buses is best. The greater the freedom the location of your house permits the developing child, the greater will be both the parents' and the children's freedom.

So if you have a choice of where to live with a growing family, try to find a place where there are (a) lots of children, (b) adults with various life-styles, (c) easy access to meaningful places for you and the children, (d) warm interaction among the neighbors, and, if you are very lucky, (e) a place where others share some of your important values.

CHAPTER 9

Family Power Plays

THE BOSS YELLS at his employee, who stands there and takes it. When the employee returns home that evening, he yells at his wife, who stands there and takes it. When the wife catches sight of her children, she yells at them. They stand there and take it. Finally, the children turn on the household pet and yell at the pet, who stands there and takes it.

You'll recognize this scenario if you've had a beginning course in psychology. It's a great favorite, for it's considered an amusing way to introduce the psychological phenomenon of "displacement." In case you never took the course, or have mercifully forgotten its contents, displacement is the phenomenon that results in your hitting or yelling at something or someone other than the person responsible for your anguish or pain. Displacement is a valid psychological idea, and there are certainly occasions when it grants insights. But this isn't one of them. This series of progressively bullying, threatening events simply cannot be summed up in the term "displacement." Studied closely, however, it can tell us much about power — its use and misuse — a subject basic to any attempt to create an egalitarian environment in the home and for children.

Consider, first, that this sequence of events is looked at as an amusing way to grab the attention of first-year psych students with eight o'clock classes. Since it is served up as entertaining, we are encouraged to see this as a "slice of life," and respond to it with tolerance as one more bit of "only human" behavior. Because it is only human and presented without negative comment, social permission is given to act out what the sociologists would term — with full negative comment — "scapegoating." Scapegoating, though, is what "bigots" do to outsiders, to ethnics, to blacks, to foreigners. When bosses scapegoat workers, when men scapegoat women, and women scapegoat children, when it's all in the family, the psychologists take over and tolerantly explain it away as an example of personal dynamics.

In truth, what that Psych I scenario illustrates is unequal power and the consequences of unequal power relationships between adults, adults and children, and even children and animals. It is the illustration par excellence, not of the psychological relationship between people, but of the political relationship. If we will only "see" it we can gain insight into the political realities of work, marriage, and child rearing. Once we achieve this insight we will gain some clues as to what, how, and even why things go wrong in marriage and, more particularly, child rearing. Our scenario encourages us to recognize the parallel relationships between boss and worker, husband and wife, wife and children, humans and animals. It is uncanny, for this is the feminist perception, except that the feminists set it in political terms and urge women to recognize their "stay-at-home-wife role" as playing worker to their husbands "boss" role. While psychologists are amused by what they identify as a personal strategy for dealing with frustration, feminists are enraged by what they identify as a system of oppressive power relationships.

This brings us to the core of the child-rearing issue: Are problems related to child rearing the result of adults' (particularly mothers') neuroses and character disorders, or is the system that relegates parenting and child rearing to a stay-at-home mother, responsible for the problem? Do neurotics make "bad mothers" or does the currently designed parenting experience make mothers "bad"?

Since I will concentrate on exploring the second position, a few disclaimers are in order before beginning. First, it is obvious that if disturbed people rear children, there will be problems. These people and their children need help of every kind to survive. Just as having a baby doesn't cure a damaged marital relationship, it certainly is no cure for a disturbed person. While child rearing is no cure for what ails people, however, it certainly should not harm either parent or the relationship between them. Rather, it should liberate each parent and enhance their relationship.

While the child-rearing experience has been analyzed and directed in recent years only from a psychological or psychoanalytic perspective, it was previously analyzed and directed only from a religious perspective. From "the devil made me do it," to "my subconscious made me do it," took only one generation. The fact that our insights come only from psychologists and psychoanalysts is no reflection on their discipline, but rather a comment on how little the world of women and children attract the attention of learned folk. The only other academic discipline with a record of serious interest in child rearing is anthropology.

Historically, the sociologist's interest in families is kindled only after they are designated as different or troubled. As a result, the only child-rearing perspective middle-class parents have is the psychological one, unless they have retained a religious perspective. The psychological perspectives that dominate child rearing derive from the ages-and-stages developmental crowd or the Freudian and neo-Freudian one and therefore offer an even more limited framework. These two groups represent only part of the psychological establishment. The social psychologists, cognitive psychologists, learning theorists, and group-dynamics specialists all have much information that would help us to understand and enjoy child rearing more, but the public only gets whispers and murmurs from them.

Although the feminist perspective is a complex interdisciplinary approach, depending on the particular feminist's skill and training, there is one basic similarity: In all cases feminists believe that the hard core of sexism is the unequal access to power and the use and misuse of power between women and men. Thus my fascination for the Psych I scenario.

Feminists believe that women's troubles are not usually the suggested ones: premenstrual cramps, postpartum depression, and hot flashes. Women's trouble is basically one trouble. They remain second class in a world where they have never been first class. Though all that has been presented so far grows from this basic feminist perspective that we do indeed have two kinds of people — one more powerful, the other less powerful — here I would like to explore the way their second-class status affects women as mothers and the corresponding effect on the children she, primarily, rears — half of them destined for first-class citizenship, the other half for second class.

In speaking with mothers, I often begin by saying that child rearing can be joyous, self-enhancing, and give enormous satisfaction, whether done full or part time, but only if it is done in a prepared environment. One aspect of that preparation, and perhaps its most important aspect, concerns the mother's ability to come to terms with her own power first. There is no way that motherhood will be anything other than oppressive if the power relationships a mother has with husband, parents, doctors, repair people, and school personnel are not equalized. For children learn to treat their mother exactly as they observe others treat her. Just as children learn to treat with great respect people who receive respect from others, children learn to demean and put down those who are treated with disrespect by others. This truth helps us to understand why the children of socially powerful families are often raised by women belonging to groups their parents defame and despise. These parents intuitively understand that their children, when adults, will have no problems continuing their parents' patterns of discrimination.

Perhaps there is no more disheartening and depressing news to give women than that loving, caring for, and cherishing children does not guarantee a reciprocal loving, caring, and cherishing response. It is perhaps the most depressing truth about motherhood. Once recognized, however, it can be a powerful insight. It can help to unravel a whole host of inexplicable child-rearing realities. Once these realities are understood, mothers can take actions to achieve the measure of dignity, self-confidence, and ego strength necessary to enhance their own and their children's mental health.

To understand this truth, let's explore another "slice of life." Within one week's time a young mother has the following experiences, all carefully observed by her three- or four-year-old child. Her father and mother come to visit. In discussing an upcoming election, her father, the child's grandfather, comments, "Women never see the larger picture." Later in the day, her mother, eyeing the bookshelf, inquires, "When is the last time you read a good book?" The next day she brings her youngster to the pediatrician. As the child is being examined, she confides to the pediatrician that she is concerned about her child's slow growth rate. The pediatrician replies, "Now listen, mother, don't be like all the other new mothers. Don't be hyperanxious."

Toward the end of the week the mother and father discuss the purchase of a new car. In the course of that discussion the mother may be told by her husband that (a) she knows nothing about credit and time payments, or (b) she knows nothing about cars, or even (c) she needn't worry because he has already made the decision, knowing how the whole subject bores her. In some instances she will be "lucky" and get away with only one put-down. In the most destructive unequal power relations, every household decision or, worse, every communication will be an occasion for a barrage of slight and not so slight acts of defamation. Typically after each barrage, the mother will just stand there and take it. And remember, I am not talking here about a fight, but about a belittling environment: "A lot you know," "When I need your advice I'll ask for it," "You never were very good at figures."

Remember these incidents can occur in the space of one week. Multiply them and you will get some picture of how many times young children will have observed this belittling behavior directed at their mothers. If there are enough such instances to observe, to study, to *learn,* inevitably someday it will be mimicked. One day when the mother tells her child to do something, the child will turn to her and say (take your choice), "What do you know?" "Who says you're so smart?" or "I don't have to listen to you." Sometimes the line will be accompanied by a smile of triumph not unlike the breakthrough smile children wear when they stand alone or take a step unaided. The smile, as well as the mocking statement, will be misunderstood. Now, for the first time, the mother should just stand there and calmly take it. Usually, however, it will be just this time when she chooses not to. She may hit, she may yell, she may threaten. But if she was shocked at her child's taunts, her child will be stunned by her reaction. What went wrong? While the child was simply following the script, the mother blew it. The child had never observed her show any sign of displeasure at that kind of behavior in the past — why now? It seems hardly fair. Congratulations at acquiring a new skill would have been more expected. Her anger is truly incomprehensible. Unfortunately, it is often incomprehensible to the mother herself. She just knows in her guts that she doesn't have to take that from any four-year-old.

Remember our opening displacement scenario? The

mother, having internalized that power hierarchy, knows she may bully her young kids, but she'll be damned if she's going to allow them to bully her! The kids, however, don't know the power game yet. All they know is that they have always received approval for effectively mimicking adult behavior. The kids don't know this game is different. Since they have not as yet internalized the power hierarchy, they don't know that in the minds of adults they are only one up from the dachshund. The mother will be incapable of understanding that the child, in taunting her, is simply copying the behavior of beloved relatives, is simply treating her in a way she has always accepted and, perhaps what's worse, expected. The mother will be incapable of understanding this because to understand the dynamics of this situation would be too painful, would give her a clearer picture of her own status than she can often tolerate. So when she yells: "You can't talk that way to me!" or "How dare *you* use that tone of voice to me!" she is not only yelling at the kid, she is yelling for all the times she was silent and just stood there and took it.

Yes, she is displacing, yes, she is scapegoating, but she is also truly angered or perhaps horrified by the child. For in this, as in her marital relationship, she had hoped things might be different. This child whom she carried for nine months, fed, bathed, diapered, taught to walk, to talk, to eat, this child whom she rocked, sang to and protected, not only belittles her, but smiles while doing so. It is more than a body can stand! Indeed, one of her motivations in having a baby was her need to build a loving, caring relationship that would be mutually satisfying. Now it seems it's hopeless. But she is wrong. What she has received from her child is a signal, a very clear signal of how she is observed to be treated in the world. What she does with that signal is up to her. If a mother believes her child's initial attempt at "putting her down" indicates another oppressor has come into her life she makes a great mistake. (But the pain she experiences is real and she should acknowledge it rather than minimize it. When parents speak of their kids being "spoiled rotten," or "fresh brats," they are masking great unhappiness that often begins with just such an incident as this.) If the mother chooses to retaliate, she makes an even greater mistake, for then their relationship will begin to spiral downward, insuring that parent and child will indeed be busy oppressing each other for many years to come.

Unhappily, once the relationship begins to spiral downward it takes an enormous amount of energy to reverse direction. I call this my Second Law of Child-Rearing Inertia. (Remember, the First Law of Child-Rearing Inertia applies to that built-in resistance to move out and around with infants and children.) The second law asserts the tendency of good parent-child relations to remain good and sometimes to get better, and the converse tendency of bad parent-child relations to remain bad and sometimes to worsen. There are those who argue with this formulation. Their position is that certain ages and stages are more difficult for some parents to negotiate than others. Thus, if parents have difficulty with very young children they sometimes do "better" as the children get older. My response is that those parents still must make a stronger effort to turn the situation around than would have been needed to maintain an already good one. As you can see, I don't quit so easily.

If retaliation is bad and will make the situation worse, what options are there? If retaliation is a strategy doomed from the start, what should the mother do immediately? If she is not terribly annoyed, she might just say in a firm, quiet voice, "I do not like to be spoken to that way." But if she is angry, she might say, "I get angry when I am spoken to that way." If she is very angry she should say, "I am very angry, I do not like to be spoken to in that way. I shall go to my room [or outside, or to sit in the car] till I am calmer."

Before we continue to explore specific responses, treatments and cures, let's take some more time to diagnose mothers', fathers', relatives', strangers' and children's power plays. Think back to our opening scenario and freeze the series of events at the point where mother yells at the children. For it is the dynamics of this situation we wish to explore. Just what happens when mother either elects to "displace" or "scapegoat" the children or to retaliate when they have actually provoked her, or when, as we have just seen, her anger is heightened because her child's taunts echo the taunts of the more powerful people who surround her? The decision of mother to yell, that is, to do unto another what was done to her, may give immediate relief but it will cause her troubles to multiply. Although she has been encouraged to see herself in the power hierarchy as having the same power relative to her child as her husband might have toward her and a boss might have to a worker, a mother's situation *is* entirely different for two enormously significant reasons. Consider the first: Unlike a "real" boss (one whose workers are unorganized) and unlike her relationship to her husband, her power relationship to her children constantly changes. Although she literally has life and death power over the child from the moment of conception through the earliest months and years of life — a baby can indeed die of neglect — the relationship is in constant flux and all in one direction. When she reaches her ninetieth year the power situation will be completely reversed: Very old people also die of neglect. While only technology, bankruptcy, revolution, and unionization overturn the real "bosses," while only the most energetic in-house revolution or divorce restructures an oppressive wife-husband relationship, children simply grow up!

The second difference has to do with how adults can handle other adults' anger, and how children experience the same hostility. Children who continually experience a full load of adult anger are literally frightened witless. They are damaged in all areas of development and sometimes irrevocably so. Milder doses of adult anger delivered at stronger children have lesser effects. These help produce frightened, nervous, and jumpy children whose movements are jerky, whose speech is halting, and whose thinking is clouded. They live in fear and pain or learn to escape into an inner world of pretense and fantasy. It is important here to observe that it is often the father rather than the mother who is responsible for the most outrageous displays of anger in the household. For unlike the Psych I displacement scenario, father often returns home and yells not only at mother, but at everyone in sight, and not only does he holler, but he often hits.

Several years ago when I was working with Lucy Peck on a study of young children's perceptions of adult roles and their own aspirations, two questions asked of the one-hundred and fifty nursery school children were, "What does a mother do?" and "What does a father do?" To the question, "What does a mother do?" their responses were "Takes care of you," "Cleans," "Cooks," and so on. (Two children gave rather surprising answers. One said, "She swims," the other said, "She puts rollers in her hair".) Many of the answers to, "What does a father do?" were more surprising or shocking. While most children answered, "He works," a significant number replied, "He hits you."

Since all the children were assumed to be from a middle-class background, as our work was done in two private nursery schools whose fees were pretty steep, we in our innocence were shocked by the number of children who responded, "He hits." At that time we still believed the middle-class myth that associates brutish behavior toward children with lower-class louts. That this is a myth is confirmed by the people who work in the area of child abuse, who report that the physical and emotional abuse of children occurs at every level of society. But whether father yells or mother yells, young children are scared out of their wits by their parents and for good reasons. The first is an obvious one: Children are literally completely in their parents' power. Parents control all the goodies: food, clothing, shelter, care, love. But what's more, young children simply cannot get out from under their parents. They're stuck! Before society will intervene to remove a child from a parent's custody there must be evidence of the most monumental kinds of child abuse. But if the power seems obvious and its consequence awesome, parents are often totally unconscious of that aspect of their relationship to their children. Mothers particularly find considerations of the power scene so difficult that they are unsure of when and where they do have power, when and where they don't have power, and when and where they lose it. Fathers are often a bit more sophisticated about power in general, but they too tend to make gross errors in relation to their children.

Young children are also terrified by manifestations of adult anger because they have no strategies for defending themselves against it. Perhaps the biggest single difference between the child's circumstance and the adult's is that the child cannot say, "I quit," can't even leave the scene, for an adult can hold a child in place. Indeed, a screaming adult often will hold a frightened child in place, shaking or hitting the child. A young child simply cannot interpret, see behind, or write it off. While it is often terribly difficult for adults to experience another's out-of-control anger without pain, it is impossible for children to be the object of adult anger without great, great pain.

Children who do survive large doses of adult anger relatively intact will soon find a way to gain a measure of control over their bullying parents. They will simply tune out and turn them off. Once that happens, communications of all kinds will be crippled. Parents' ability to rear their children will be damaged. To teach, to counsel, to advise requires that parents have not been shut out. Remember: Once things are bad they tend to remain bad; or, more pessimistically, once things are bad they tend to get worse. Once a parent is tuned out, those channels will remain closed unless the most tireless efforts are made to open them again. Yelling, screaming, and shouting will not be the only parental power abuse that will result in a child learning to turn off communication. The turn off is often a response to other kinds of parental verbal abuse — sarcasm, insult, and nagging.

But let's think about yelling and consider how tied it is to authority. One can think of it as an attempt to make oneself bigger than one is, to take up more than one's fair share of the environment, with the corollary effect of reducing the listener or the listener's space. Think a minute of how blustering, yelling people are depicted in a cartoon. They are pictured as increasing in size until finally they are so inflated with their own hot air that they explode; only in real life they tend not to.

I happen to know a lot about yelling as a result of a study I ran last spring, with my youngest daughter, then a high-school senior, doing the leg work. The study was begun because in preparing to write this book I believed a little consumer research might be helpful. I decided the child-rearing consumer might have some interesting thoughts on parenting. Since my daughter Ellen had been assisting in an "open classroom" composed of eighty-five students in grades four, five, and six with four teachers, it seemed a good place to gain some first-hand information. Together we worked up the questionnaire, and she then interviewed each child. As she was young and knew the children quite well, I thought Ellen would get good cooperation and perhaps more candid responses than an adult interviewer who was also a stranger. To the question, "What do parents do that children like least?" two answers were given repeatedly: "Yell," and "Overprotect." "Yelling," however, outscored any other response. These children too, were generally middle-class ones, and I guess if one compares their responses to that of the nursery school group, it might suggest that aggressive parents move from hitting to yelling as children grow older.

I had promised to discuss the findings with the children, teachers, and parents. In presenting our results, I began by saying that in general the children's view of parenting was quite positive. When the children were asked the last question, "Would you like to be a parent?" almost all of them said, "Yes." (One more cautious student said she'd like to try it and if it didn't work out, get someone else to do it! Another child thought it would be great to be a parent because then you could go to all the places you wanted to and say you were doing it for the children. One child rather cryptically replied that it would be nice to have a child because then you could have grandchildren.) When asked, "What do parents feel they should do for their children?" most children replied, "Care for them," "Help them," or, "Teach them right from wrong." These kinds of answers, I said, indicated a positive view toward parenting in general and reflected a positive view toward their own parents in particular.

This information was accepted without question and with satisfaction by the parents. The mood changed quite drastically when I presented the results of the question that asked, "What do parents do that children like least?" First, I told the group that "overprotection" was a common response to that question. One parent quickly spoke up and requested that the children "define their terms." Since the children were between the ages of nine and twelve I thought that a rather inappropriate request. The children, however, were quite eager to respond. Although they did not — or more accurately, could not — "define their terms," they were quite deft at giving examples of what they believed to be overprotection. While they produced example after example, the children simultaneously exhibited great sensitivity to their parents and recognized the parents' concern for their well-being. Finally, I said that while overprotection was a common response to the question, the most frequent response was "yelling." After presenting that fact I went on to say that I thought children experience yelling negatively because it is painful, nonaesthetic, and especially, frightening. It is frightening to children because it is an extension of parents' already enormous power.

On this issue, the parents had a great deal to say. But unlike the discussion on overprotection, in which the children had enthusiastically joined in, this time they sat silent. The parents who spoke said some surprising and some expected things. Strangely, no one denied that yelling went on, nor did anyone suggest the children were making too much of it. Rather, over and over, the accusation was made that the parents' yelling was either caused by the child or resulted from outside pressures, a situation they fully expected the nine-, ten-, eleven-, or twelve-year-old-child to appreciate. It seems the parents also believed in displacement and in accepting one's role in the yelling hierarchy. Now let's think about the first point they made, that is, that the behavior of the children caused their parents to yell. While chicken-egg arguments are often futile, in this case, I believe the parents have to take the responsibility for communication gone wrong. After all, for at least two years their children can't talk at all! Surely, with a two-year lead on a two-year-old, parents have an opportunity to set the pattern of how the verbal flow will go.

Next, we went on to the parents' notion that the children should understand their need to yell, to appreciate their parents' difficulties and frustrations. That response really astounded me! It seemed to me they wanted to yell at their children to discharge angers developed elsewhere and they wanted their children to accept and appreciate their need to be used or abused in this way. Several parents and children came to me at the conclusion of the night's meeting to make personal comments. One mother, repeating what was said frequently during the evening, said, "My children don't listen unless I yell." "Well," I said, rather casually, "what do you say?" She began to laugh (it was one of the few obvious consciousness-raising moments of the evening) and said: "I guess I nag a lot."

Another woman said, "Look, it's very clear — the kids don't want them to yell, and they don't want to stop!" I guess she summed up the evening — it was a draw. The parents who choose to yell at their children for release accept the power hierarchy and expect their children to accept it and recognize their lowly place within its structure. Yelling at kids is obviously seen as a fringe benefit of being a parent, and many will not give it up. It always seems a lot easier to parents than dealing with the true sources of their anger. It is easier, but only at the start.

As long as parents continue to perceive themselves as powerless, they will continue to use abusive strategies toward children. This is true of male and female parents alike. The consequence to the female parent, however, of buying into the idea of the power hierarchy and selling it by precept and example to her children is the most self-damaging act in which she can engage. For if her children are one up from a gerbil, she is only one up from her children, and only temporarily so. Especially if her children include sons her embracing of the power hierarchy will come home to oppress her, for young boys quickly observe that those with the power to oppress mothers are often men. Mothers must learn quite quickly that power hierarchies are dangerous for women and children.

Women are encouraged to play boss in relation to their

young children, and mothers are encouraged to get angry when their little children sass them or mimic the adults who oppress them. Mothers are not encouraged to evaluate the cost of their very brief stint of bullying. I cannot emphasize enough that because the role of the mother to her young children does not enjoy a terribly long season, how she plays out this short season will often determine her lifelong relationship with her children. If she wishes it to be a rewarding one, it is within her power to establish it this way, but she holds that power for only a short time. Even at the height of their power, mothers will be prepared by folk and professional wisdom to expect little future reward from their relationships to their children. Thus they will hear the old saying, "One young mother can care for six small children, but six grown children can't care for one old mother!" Child-rearing experts will urge her not to have children if she expects "gratitude." Well, she may not exactly expect gratitude, but she would like a warm, close, friendly, and loving relationship with her children, both when young and when grown. Should only women who wish to raise ingrates bear children?

Work done by myself and others on young children's aspiration levels generally indicate that girls, from the time they are quite young, have limited aspirations. Their aspirations are limited both as to number and the amount of power or degree of adventure. So girls are said to have a low level of aspiration in the world of work. What is often not recognized is that they are taught a low level of aspiration in their mother role as well. They are psyched to expect few rewards and little satisfaction and to minimize and hide from children the pain they feel in relationships gone sour.

Once, in discussing the issue of power with a class of high-school students, I asked them whether they believed the desire to have power over other people was innate or learned. "Did," I asked, "people come down the birth canal planning to seize power?" One senior, Mark Reibstein, replied, "No, you didn't come down the birth canal wanting power, but once the doctor slapped you, you understood what it was all about!" Quite soon after that incident I began reading the work of the French obstetrician Frédérick Leboyer, and I thought of Mark. Both he and Leboyer had identified a new dimension in the birth process — the teaching and learning one. But if the obstetrician's slap (done, as everything is always done for children, for their own good) is one power play we are trying to end, what about the countless others exerted on both mothers and children?

Since one of the principal ways women are put and kept in their place is through humor, few women are as yet, or ever will be, ready to take a sexist joke. Humor between un-equals is often characterized by embarrassment, shame, and annoyance rather than fun. That's why making fun of women and children is not so funny. Nor is it very good motivation and stimulation for the development of the child's own wit and humor. Even very young children love fun and fooling around, striking poses, and making faces that start adults smiling, grinning, and laughing. Young children enjoy verbal humor but not if it is laced with deri-sion and masks hostility. Soon after children learn to speak they often find certain words funny and certain phrases make them smile, just as certain people and things amuse them. They will want to share their amusement with others. One of the great joys of being in touch with young children is the opportunity to gain a fresh perception of reality by sharing the child's view. This fresh perception comes through most strongly in their wit and humor, traits that will develop if verbal play is truly good, clean fun.

Neither children nor parents can live happily in a lan-guage environment that oppresses them. Although people defend themselves against defamation by blocking the words of others and pretending they don't hurt, a price is still paid.

Having hateful words said about you or the group to which
you belong poisons your environment and undermines your
ego. In the past, people have been amazingly unconcerned
with the ego needs of women and children, while they have
invested huge amounts of energy in selling the needs of the
male ego. Respect and psychic support has gone to people
who already wield power and control the purse strings, leaving little for the others. It is sufficiently bizarre to characterize motherhood as a job for which little ego strength is
required, and childhood as a period where ego support is
unnecessary, but in some cases, in addition, the husband-
father's ego is fed by consuming the ego of others; that is, he
feels stronger as he makes others feel weaker.

Unfortunately for many mothers, husbands are not the
only source of put-downs. Often the most undermining remarks come from their own parents who may still be building their own egos at their daughters' expense, or who may
be locked into poorly developed patterns that they can't
break. Nor is family the only source of outrageous behavior;
doctors, lawyers, and even total strangers often join in. If
women in general often stimulate condescension from many
men, women with babies or with young children seem to call
forth more than their fair share of denigrating behavior and
comment. It is as if women lose thirty IQ points as soon as
they hold a baby in their arms. I suspect it goes back to the
disdain boys were stimulated to feel toward anyone who
played with dolls. Many women feel vulnerable when they
hold young babies or are with young children, and the often
cold, negative, rejecting public reception they receive
strengthens their feelings of defenselessness.

A nursery school teacher told a group I was addressing the
following story: There is a three-year-old boy in her class
who hugs a doll whenever he gets nervous. He brings the
doll to school with him and puts it in his cubby (if nursery
school is new to you, a cubby is a cubbyhole, a kid's version

of a doorless locker). When something happens that un-nerves him, he gets the doll and holds it. When he calms down, he puts the doll away. The teacher and children never make any comment about his behavior. One day, his mother asked for a conference with the nursery school teacher and told her the following story.

The child was scheduled for a visit to the pediatrician. Figuring this might be a time of stress, he took his doll with him. When it was his turn to be examined, he walked into the office with the doll. The male doctor seized the doll, threw it on the floor, and lashed out at the mother, "How dare you let him play with that! Do you want him to grow up to be a homosexual?" The mother did not kick the doctor in the shins, did not threaten to send a letter to the county medical society; she came to the child's nursery school instead. Why? To see if the teacher had noted any signs of homosexual behavior!

The only trouble with that story is that it's true. If it were a consciousness-raising fiction, as one is tempted to believe it is, designed to sensitize us to the fate of passive women, it would be more bearable. How can we have so badly taught ourselves that women will just stand there and "take it" no matter what the provocation and no matter how stupid and inappropriate the behavior?

What happens to the child who shares this experience? What has the child learned? That the doctor is the boss? That his mother can't (or won't) protect herself? That his mother can't or won't protect her child's interest? That dolls are bad? That for him to play with dolls will cause both him and his mother embarrassment and shame? Or perhaps, what is worse, that the person who screams and yells controls the field? I find it interesting that when women cry they are thought to be "out of control," and that when men yell and bang tables with their fists or shoes, they're thought to be "in control." Actually, it is more correct to see the woman or man who cries as "losing control," and the man or woman who yells as "gaining control." For it is often the people yelled at who leave the field to the loudest voice. Rarely does anyone feel they are being "cried at." In spite of all the fiction about women gaining their ends through tears, they rarely gain little more than better surrender terms.

What might the mother have done? No matter how limited her combat ability, in all situations like that, her first move should be to the child. In a well-modulated, controlled voice, she should say, "The doctor (substitute the name of the appropriate villain) is out of control. He (or she) is behaving badly." If she can only make it through one move, that should be it. She should then pick up the doll, hand it to her son, and get out! Why is that so important? She must always indicate to her child that she remembers the child is there and that she understands that the incident was a disturbing one. It does no harm to suggest to the doctor and to the child that she, at least, has not lost her head. Perhaps, more impotrant, she must label this behavior as bad and unacceptable. It is not only unacceptable behavior that should be labeled as such for the child. When a particularly kind or generous act is observed, the mother should say to the child, in whatever language she is comfortable with, "That's a very good thing to do," or, "That's very helpful." Although generally children are only instructed to say "please" when they want something, and "thank you" when they get something, it is more important for them to learn which behaviors are good and which are unacceptable.

There is a whole style of positive authority that a mother must be able to summon in relation to strangers because infants and young children out in the world must be able to see her as their protector. Having been fed from childhood dreams that cast her and all females as the victim, the de-

fenseless one in need of protection, it is not difficult to understand why a mother finds it hard to assume the role of
defender or rescuer herself. Thus when outsiders try to
bully her and her young, she often stands there and takes it,
waiting for someone else to come and save her. Do we need
any further indication of how far into absurdity our strained
notions of artificial differences between females and males
have taken us? Feminists are always accused of trying to
build an unnatural unisex society. Presumably, then, we are
now thought to live in a more natural state! But what female lion, tiger, cougar, or elephant needs lessons in her role
as protector of her young?

Some mothers, however, are quite good at dealing with
the outside world. A friend of mine went to a conference at
her children's nursery school. She was told by the teacher
that her son rarely played with children other than his one
close friend. He often was happiest being alone. When the
conference was over, my friend went home quite upset
about her child. She pictured him going through his life
friendless, unloved, and unloving. Finally, she picked up the
phone, called the nursery school, and asked to speak to the
teacher. The gist of what she told the teacher was: "If I
came to the conference feeling good about my child and left
feeling badly, perhaps there was something wrong with the
conference." This mother can express her feelings clearly
and without hostility, and reset a situation so that it can be
rationally discussed without anyone being bullied. This
mother happens to be a physician. Is she a physician because one of her personality traits is her capacity to cope?
Or does her training give her more authority in all situations? Or do people respond to her differently because they
know she is a physician? Or all of the above? How do the
children of "copers" and "noncopers" experience tense situations?

The young children of noncopers simply can't relax in any

situation of even slightly heightened tension. They simply cannot rely on their mother's protection. Long ago, when I was an undergraduate, I heard a professor say that the difference between a professional and a rank amateur was that a professional can relax an audience and an amateur cannot. When one listens to Beverly Sills sing, one only wonders how good she will be; one does not worry if she's going to get through the selection. A mistake made by a professional is just a mistake. It does not cause further worry to the audience. Another way of putting it is that the audience can allow the professionals to worry about themselves, but the amateurs export their own tensions and anxieties to the audience. This is perhaps the phenomenon that explains the success of the overly strict teacher. While the best disciplinarians are those who model good discipline, support good behavior, and encourage the development of inner control, the worst disciplinarians are not their opposites. The worst disciplinarians are not the authoritarian people who bully children into externally imposed rules but the ones who can't handle situations of tension and disorder; the ones who can't cope. They add an adult-size load of uncertainty and tension to that with which the children are already struggling.

A major source of women's oppression derives from the myth that the jobs traditionally reserved for them require little physical, mental, or psychic strength and can be discharged without a sense of authority. This mythical thinking accounts for the obvious societal concern for the male ego and the obvious societal indifference to the female ego. Men, the myth suggests, must be "built up," "empowered," because they go out into the "cold, cruel world" to earn a living (writing jingles, working on the assembly line, filling prescriptions, fixing zippers, reporting the news). Women, it is presumed, need less strength because they deal with the young, the old, and the infirm. Only when women enter the "man's world" are they thought to need the qualities of personal strength that all males are assumed to require and the same dimension of authority as men. Indeed, the concern is often expressed that women will grow hard and tough "out in the world" instead of remaining soft and tender, as life with the kids presumably permits.

No one is more taken in by this mythology than women. Middle-class women especially have bought into this nonauthoritative pattern. As we have already discussed, the tame girls often look forward to mothering, to teaching, to nursing, for they have been urged to believe that these activities are just for them. The untamed women often stay away from these activities for they feel these occupations lack adventure and cannot engage the soul of a free spirit. The thrusting of tamed women into motherhood often results in one of two sets of responses. The first is flight. Simple flight, or running away, is something that mothers are doing with increasing frequency. Another kind of flight is one that allows the mother to remain home but to take flight from the child-rearing role that she at first thought she wanted. If these women and their children are lucky, someone else will be found, better able to cope. Unluckier women will take flight through alcohol, pills, and mental illness.

Flight of all kinds is not the only set of responses possible. Another frequent response is for the tame woman to adopt the role of bully. Unfortunately, she only adopts this role toward her children's out-of-control behavior. In every other case, like our mother with the pediatrician, or our mother in the displacement scenario, she accepts the bullying behavior of others. She enthusiastically enters the power hierarchy, treating her children with the same abuse, denigration, and defamation she has had to absorb from those in her environment who hold power over her. In sociopsychological terms, it is called identifying with the aggressor. She thus cooperates in the socialization process that insures another generation of the bullies and the bullied. Since she has had little opportunity to build her own rational authority as a mother, she is at a loss to know how to deal with power other than in the form she has always known it. A sad fact is that tamed women are not alone in feeling a lack of authority in the mother role. Women of great energy, spirit, and intelligence, who are generally more sure of themselves than are their sisters, often suffer their greatest pangs of insecurity when they become mothers. Believing they are without "natural ability," they know they have neither experience nor training. Thus it is often impossible for them to feel confidence in themselves and fill the role with authority.

Mothers' self-images fail to develop as they mother because it is difficult for women to build authority in any typical women's role. They are not intended to have it or want it, or even expected to need it. Where do you think, "Just wait till your father gets home!" came from?

If the young mother needs a whole host of strategies in dealing with bullying strangers, she certainly has to clarify her relationship with her immediate family, quickly, clearly, and thoroughly. Many young parents find that this is the hardest thing to do. But they are wrong! A far harder thing will be to try to straighten a parent-child relationship that has gone wrong. Remember, it is only when the baby is young that it seems easier to negotiate with the baby than with the adults who surround you.

The most persistent efforts to offer and accept only good, considerate behavior in your home is the greatest gift you can give your child. It is worth all the effort it requires. At some point a mother-to-be or a mother must sit down with her near and dear ones and lay down the law. Language in her home will be considerate, direct, and straightforward. She will not tolerate sarcasm, nagging, put-downs, and belittling and biting language in the environment in which she is raising her children. It's important to say it! It's important to mean it! If you fail to clean up the verbal environment, your children will learn how to bully and how to be bullied, and they will specifically learn how to bully you. Don't kid yourself that you have no enforcement power. You control access to the child or children. Simply do not grant it to people who cannot behave. All the other adults who regularly surround a young child gain significance because the principal child rearer or rearers sponsor them. They not only permit them access to the children, they often act as press agents. "Well, isn't it great, today Grandma is coming." "Look at the nice present Grandpa brought you!" "Grandma really loves you." A mother often builds father's role also, by promising the children good times when daddy comes home.

While mother is everyone's press agent, she rarely has one of her own. (Ironically, only when children have nurses or governesses do their mothers get the same kind of star build-up that fathers and other relatives regularly get.) Since mother builds up all the other relatives, is it any wonder the children consider it perfectly acceptable to mimic their behavior? Have they not been told repeatedly how great dad and the grandparents are? Although it hardly seems unreasonable that mothers demand respect from those she builds up and permits to have access to her children, many women find it hard to make this demand. But the mother must be an authoritative person in her relations with all the people who surround her and the child.

• • •

Of all the unequal relationships between husband and wife the one that requires the most strenuous clean-up is the conflict over money. An egalitarian relationship often requires major shifts in thinking about money: mine, yours, and ours. I always urge parents to complete the power clean-up before the first baby is born. The financial relationship in a marriage, however, is often more egalitarian before the first baby is born. Many women who leave paid employment to rear their children full time find their relationship to their husbands does experience a major shift in the wrong direction. As women leave a world of work in which their husbands remain, housework becomes less shared, and conversation is less equal and more of the "Did you have a good day at the office, dear?" variety. When the husband becomes the single wage earner instead of one of two, an enormous power shift occurs. How that is handled will constitute a major factor in how egalitarian their marriage will be and, therefore, how egalitarian it will be possible for their children to be. It will also determine how at ease the mother will be as a child rearer.

Many feminists believe the role of full-time child rearer is inherently oppressive because it is a role that prevents direct access to money. They might be right. Most of us live in a world that has become amazingly controlled by money. So accustomed are we to exchanging money for food, clothing, shelter, and care that we have forgotten how novel this situation is that now engulfs us. Before World War II most of us lived on farms or in small towns, and we were not yet a nation of high consumers. At that time most of one's food, clothing, and shelter were produced or processed by family members or secured through barter. On farms, money was rare, and the cash crop was often controlled by women. Selling eggs, the marketing of vegetables, as well as the production of goods and services were often activities women engaged in. The role of the men as wage earners and the corollary role of the women as consumers are recent developments. This development has enormously reduced the power of the female child rearer.

Let me review how the financial relationship of wife to husband, wife to children, and husband to children is typically viewed. The money earned by the husband, except in four states, is viewed as his. The wife who does not earn money is viewed by law as his dependent and she often feels this dependency for her basic human needs. Because she often is the family shopper she is viewed as the "spender." (In a discussion with a group of young mothers on the need for them to get out, to move out into the world with their infants and young children, one mother said she felt unwelcome in most places. Shopping malls were the only places she could comfortably go with her infant.) In any event, if this is how the money relationship is viewed — as husband and only husband gaining, acquiring, and owning this precious stuff upon which almost all basic material needs depend, and wife as losing or spending money that is not her own — their power positions are totally unequal. For until the marriage is a true fifty-fifty partnership, one that includes joint ownership of all assets acquired after marriage as well as joint responsibility for all liabilities, incredible inequalities will spin off from the very important economic one. The children will quickly perceive these differences because their parents will constantly broadcast their feelings about money.

In a family where both stay-at-home mother and paid-employed father view the family money resources as his, one can identify two different sets of money-power plays. One is the Sugar Daddy one; the other is Scrooge. In the first set of plays, husband-father gives gifts and presents. He buys the children toys, he "gives" his wife a rotisserie — he is very magnanimous. The children are told to ask daddy if they want a treat. Everyone is very good to daddy, and daddy is very good to them. Sugar Daddy or Sugar Mommy or Sugar Kid or Sugar Person is a nice role to play, and everyone should get a chance at it. Otherwise, mommy is just one of the kids who gets gifts from a generous daddy, and clearly is unable to provide for her children as daddy can. Kids, too, need practice in giving as well as taking. When daddy plays

Scrooge, then pain is added to inequality. The purchases mother makes are carefully scrutinized; she is grilled over the prices she has paid; she is constantly asked what happened to all the money she was given a week ago.

When one purchases for groups other than one's family, one is seen as having a profession or occupation that is appropriately rewarded with varying amounts of money, status, and prestige. Consider the buyers, the quartermasters, the decorators, and procurement agents. Money spending on behalf of a family (because women often do it) is considered frivolous, humorous, and unnecessary. Women shoppers are the focus of jokes, cartoons, and not-so-funny stories.

When daddy plays Scrooge, everyone in this kind of family must beg for money and they are frequently reminded how much is sacrificed for their comforts, how little they appreciate it, and how little respect the "man of the house gets." Here too, mommy is just one of the kids, and the kids are constantly reminded that she, like the woman married to Sugar Daddy, could never provide for herself, let alone for her children. When mommy is one of the kids in relation to big-spending or tight-wad daddy, the children don't have a chance of building a rational approach to money with their parents and perhaps with others as well. If a sound adult method of dealing with money is absent in the parents' relationship with each other, young children have no opportunity to observe the making of rational money decisions; when they are older they will have no opportunity to learn by participating in these decisions.

In one child-rearing book recently published, we are told that mothers who work often buy their children lots of presents because they are guilty about being absent from home. How absurd! Why do some fathers buy their children lots of presents? Are they guilty too? I doubt it. (My colleague Bruce Grossman told his class that he bought his two young children so many toys, they thought shopping or toy hunting was his occupation.) It is more likely that working mothers buy their children lots of presents because they enjoy it, because they enjoy a chance at the Sugar-Mommy role, because they enjoy being generous, because they finally feel at ease with money. A situation unfortunate as it is necessary!

An interesting incident occurred some years back when Lucy Peck and I were working on a nonsexist curriculum with young nursery school children. The curriculum we developed was called the Basic Human Needs Curriculum, and during each two-week period the children would study a basic human need and some of the jobs, occupations, and professions associated with each. During our first two-week period we studied clothing. At the beginning of the unit a "factory" was organized, where the children drew patterns, cut, traced, sewed, or, if too young, stapled material together. After several days, during which time several items were produced, a clothing store was set up, and the children "reached a consensus" on who could be the sales personnel. Anyone who wanted to buy and would be willing to wait in line could be the customers. The salespeople were quite competent getting the store ready and then opening it for business. There was an eager line-up of customers, but the action couldn't continue. The salespeople simply would not allow any items to leave the store because the customers had come with no money. They were quite adamant: no money — no sale.

Although we had not given the matter much thought, we had casually assumed that since all the children had helped make the clothing, it was logical that they should all share the products. But from the children's point of view the entire enterprise was unreal without money. So a mint was established. A table was set aside upon which the teachers placed green paper and pairs of scissors and a sign, "U.S.

Mint." In what was admittedly a poor facsimile of reality, all the children had equal access to the mint and could go and cut themselves some money anytime they needed it. Currency, thus, was fairly nonstandardized. No one objected to our inflationary policy; the point for the children who sold was to "get" something for what they "gave."

As the children were observed "buying," one could distinguish the big spender types who would casually extract a lot of green stuff and fling it around and the cautious fiscal conservatives who would take the green paper from their pockets one piece at a time, slowly and carefully.

Although they could "make" as much money as they wanted, children handled money very differently. They already displayed a money-style. We realized how little we knew of the whole area of children and money, what ideas they had as to its need, its importance, its use. However, all through the remainder of the curriculum, when there was a health spa, Friday Flicks, a cafeteria, and so on, money or tickets were produced so the children could exchange them for goods and services. Money is a significant aspect of children's lives by ages three and four, and if they are already practicing money knowledge, attitudes, and skills, it is a safe assumption that they have learned a great deal about the ways of money in their family from observations of the adults around them.

•   •   •

Protection is one of the most basic needs of infants and children; protection against hostile persons, and malignant events, as well as protection against their own sometimes uncontrollable emotions. Parents who communicate to infants that they are powerful allow their infants to grow up believing they live in safety. Also, secure children do not have to test out their parents ability to control events by provocative behavior and so can focus on issues other than personal safety. Parents' ability to provide a secure environment is not communicated by hitting and hollering, actions that just strengthen children's belief that they live in a dangerous unpredictable world. Positive parental power is communicated when children observe their parents (a) spoken to and treated with respect by others, (b) engaged in activities valued by others, and (c) equal partners in family decisions. Children who know their parents to be powerful, respected people will not only feel safe and secure but will grow up showing their parents the same courtesy and respect they have always observed their parents give and receive.

CHAPTER 10

Talking Straight and Speaking Equal

ONE OF THE BEST THINGS parents can do to prepare the new baby's environment is to clean up the language that pervades it. Although we learn to speak at our mother's knee and our first language is called our mother tongue, written language is formalized by scholars. Scholars, until a hundred fifty years ago (and in some places still today), excluded women from their ranks, so we should not be surprised that women are excluded also from a "presence" in the formal language. As women are kept out of public space, so too are they kept out of public language. Thus we are told that "he," "his," and "him," really mean "he and she," "his and hers," and "him and her." "Man" implies "man and woman" and "men" means "men and women," but if you are a woman and go into a club that says "Men Only," you're a radical, and if you use the toilet in a room labeled "Men," you're a pervert.

If you have a difficult time with this idea, how do you think it is understood by a small child? It isn't! It is accepted, it is incorporated into speech and thought patterns, but it is not understood. To indicate its effect on thought patterns, consider the use of "man" to mean all adult human beings. If this were indeed our primary association, why don't we sometimes express the positive connection that exists among all human beings as the "sisterhood of man"? Why do we automatically associate brotherhood with man?

Because, until very recently, the public world has belonged to men, and the absence of women in the language is no accident. Whether the word "person" ought to include women has been a constant source of judicial argument.

Even clearly neutral words that refer to people are presented as applying only to men. We have sentences in school texts that begin, "Workers and their wives," or "Pioneers and their mates," or even, "Americans and their daughters." Recently when a statement out of Washington announced that women would soon be in the space program, sophisticated reporters at ease with reports of war, assassinations, and revolutions giggled and smirked as they talked about "astrowomen." Suddenly, "astronaut" had become male. This effort to change words that mean "one who" to mean "a male who" is what is at the heart of the objection to forms like actor, actress and aviator, aviatrix. Actor means one who acts, and aviator, one who pilots. (A lawyer told me he had actually heard the word "masturbatrix" used in court. Perhaps he was teasing!) If we need to know the sex of a person, we can say female or male. The words simply belong to everyone.

Until the writing of the Fifteenth Amendment in 1866, the word "male" had never appeared in the Constitution. It simply never occurred to our forefathers that women might be so bold as to believe that words like "men" in the Declaration of Independence and "citizen" or "person" in the Constitution could possibly refer to women. Not until Susan B. Anthony made her famous attempt to vote and was arrested did it become clear that some women might be uncouth enough to believe that they had been included in the phrase, "All men are created equal." Now that feminists refuse to make the same error, they are told that they are making much ado about nothing, for everyone knows how wonderfully the word "man" describes both females and males. (As a matter of fact it once did. Thanks to the linguistic sleuthing of Alma Graham we know that "man" originally meant both adult female and adult male. The word for adult female was "wif," coming down to us as "wife"; the word for adult male was correspondingly, "wir," suggestive of the Latin "vir," which comes down to us in "werewolf." The wirs grabbed "man" for themselves and when feminists say that they can keep it for themselves, men get sulky and tell bad jokes, like the one about personhole covers. While language conservatives are "amused" or "not amused" at suggested language change, they're remarkably straight-faced about the violence done to reality through our present forms. From a medical book, we get, "Man has two ovaries," or, what about, "Man suckles his young"? How about, "We hope the president will choose the best candidate, be he male or female"?

In Chapter 2, I suggested that the joking and high spirits that characterize the sex-identification initiation rites would be a lifelong accompaniment to attempts to discuss issues that deal with the relative power positions of females and males. Language is a crucial aspect of personal identification, of culture, and of thought. The language issue is a serious one, and we have many immediate instances of its power to rouse people. The French in Quebec, the blacks in South Africa, the Puerto Ricans in New York, the Irish: all are groups who have understood the political implications of language. But when feminists urge people to understand the price that girls and women pay in being excluded from their own language, it is considered a joking matter.

Language builds pictures in our minds. These pictures when repeated often enough, build expectations. These expectations affect what we do, what we aspire to, and how we treat the others who do or do not conform to our expectations. How shall we respond to the first American astronaut who fails to look like Jack Armstrong but looks like Amelia Earhart instead?

To demonstrate the picture-making quality of particular language forms, a teacher set up an experiment with her junior high school class. First she read them a sentence and then she asked each of the students to draw a picture illustrating the sentence. Each sentence used the word "man" in its generic form, much as textbooks do. "Man is a gregarious animal," "Man lives in shelters," and so on. In every case but one, the students — boys and girls as well — drew pictures of males. The one case that summoned a female picture referred to man as nurturing. It was clear that in this study, at least, the word "man" was not "meaningfully generic." The children did not draw males and females at random. Nor did half the children draw males and the other half females. What is worse, there was not even a difference in the responses of the female and male students. That is, they didn't personalize the word. Girls drew males just as boys drew males to illustrate the word "man." Boys excluded females from their drawing and so did females except in the one case. One wonders what would have occurred had the teacher asked for two pictures from each student. Would the children have brought forth a woman the second time around, as God is rumored to have done? Or would they have depicted two men?

If these junior high school students could not cross the linguistic barriers to draw pictures that included women and men, what chance does a young child have? In focusing on the sexist structure of language, we consider how thought is directed by the prevailing male language bias—which has been dubbed "Manglish." Parents must learn to speak an inclusive rather than an exclusive language ("she and he," "hers and his," "persons," "people," "one," "children") to keep their children's minds open to all kinds of alternative pictures and picturing.

Another effect of Manglish is to present the myth that the male is the real human being, the only person, as the law held him so recently to be. The female, then, is the after-thought, the biblical Eve, Freud's penisless male, de Beauvoir's Second Sex. Male becomes the norm, females are odd, mysterious, and incomprehensible because they differ from males. When the male is declared the norm, incredible flip-flops of language and reasoning take place. Thus the fact that men, in general, have a lower fat-to-muscle ratio than do women in general, is popularly presented as the fact that women have an "extra" layer of fat. In comparison to how some male language researchers mangle reality with words, that extra layer of fat just seems to melt away. In many studies of language usage both here and in England, it has been found that in general women speak closer to the standard form than do men. Good for them? No, not exactly. The way it is presented is that women are "hypercor-rect." That being the case, one has to find out why they suffer such an aberration. Well, it seems they're defensive, inclined to be prim and prissy. The less correct men stir far less interest. Actually, the general male language deficiency, of which "correct" speech is but one part, is one price males pay for sexist child-rearing practices.

There is another language fault perhaps even more dam-aging to the way we consider girls and boys, women and men, than even the Manglish phenomenon. That is the fail-ure of the language to contain a form that separates state-ments that describe unvarying qualities from statements that describe varying ones. Using the same language form, we say snakes crawl and flowers smell. One is always the case, the other generally the case. In a similar way, we have no language form that separates absolute differences from group differences. "Humans have lungs," and "Swedes are blond," are two different kinds of statements. This language fault causes our conversation to be more stereotypic than it might be had our language a built-in way to express general rather than absolute facts. A children's book that has become infamous in feminist circles uses this language fault to construct its literary content. Page after page of pictures illustrate such statements as, "Boys sell things, girls buy things." It is no surprise that someone stumbled on this form by which to compare boys and girls. Statements of this kind about women and men are as common as dirt. They result not only in restrictive thinking but demand that reality conform to our faulty language.

Let's take a close look at how just *one* of these statements of general group differences impinges on our notion of what is proper behavior in the world. The statement is: "Men are taller than women," with its corollary, "Women are shorter than men." That is clearly a statement of general group difference. The average man is somewhat taller than the average woman. But it is clearly not a difference that exists between every man and every woman. Each man you see will not be taller than each woman you see. Think of Willy Shoemaker, Abe Beame, Margaux Hemingway, and Julia Child. Well, so what? So this: the statement "Women are shorter than men, and men are taller than women," becomes an ideal, a goal, a "should."

In this way a natural group difference is twisted to mirror a societal power preference. As in most general group-sex statements, we move from a simple description, "That's the way things are," to simple prescription, "that's the way things should be." Males and females have an average height range of seven or eight inches. Men at the shorter end of this range and women at the taller end of this range are spoken of as being "too short," or "too tall," respectively. Now, except for pathological growth patterns such as dwarfism and giantism, which affect both sexes, how can one be "too short" or "too tall" for one's sex? It is an absurd idea, and like many general group sex-different statements, it does enormous damage to individuals.

Tall girls, like short boys, quickly learn that they are not quite what was expected. One is surprised by them, not always happily. So tall girls slouch and short boys jump up and down a lot. Tall girls wear their hair flat, their shoes flat, and sit a lot. Meanwhile, their shorter brothers are busily putting lifts in their shoes and piling up their hair.

If you know that daisies are white and you see a yellow one, you may be surprised, but you don't deny its yellowness. You just enlarge your view of daisies. Not so with general group statements about sex differences. Here, we insist that group differences apply to each individual. We are particularly convinced that each heterosexual couple shall contain one female shorter than one male. We insist that each couple give the "right" visual image. More marriages are probably based on being the right relative height and age than any other criteria.

Height, in our society, as in many, conveys authority. One of the major visual problems Carter's people had to solve when he debated Ford was that he not "appear" shorter than Ford, though he is so. The people at the camera were able to adjust for this fact, and we were presented with the fiction that we were seeing two men of about the same size. So much for honesty in government. How about those "total" women who wish to look up to their husbands? An interesting, but incomplete idea, for if they are looking up at their husbands, their husbands — if they look at them at all — must be looking down at them. It's a real downer. Think of our up and down associations. When you feel up, you experience a high. When you feel low, you are down. Better yet, how about "big" and "small" — what about a really "big man in his field," "real big of you," a "big deal," as opposed to a real "small person," "small-minded."

Research on voice indicates that the difference between female and male pitch as heard in their speech is much greater than an examination of their respective vocal cords would suggest. How does this happen? We make it happen by pitching our own voices differently as we begin to speak to children. Thus, when we see an infant in blue, we deepen our voices and say, "Look at the great big buster!" When we see a pink infant, we raise our pitch and say, "Isn't she the sweetest thing?" Recently reported research indicates that infants pitch their own voices differently depending on whether they are speaking to their mothers or their fathers. When women are upset or excited, their already unnaturally high voices go higher. Women are then denigrated because they are shrill. Shrill voices are not only judged to be unpleasant but weak as well. Thus, first boys and girls are patterned to accentuate a difference that is relatively slight, and then this exaggerated difference is decreed to be important. The deeper, typically male, voice, we are taught, is the one voice that conveys authority. When women in television commercials are pictured scrubbing, rubbing, and tubbing, a male voice off-camera will do the sales pitch. If a male voice did not urge one forward to buy, it is believed, you might skip the whole thing. What a shame!

Authority is also conveyed by style of speaking. A special style particularly associated with women, called the "tag ending," is a style that diminishes authority. The tag ending speech pattern follows a statement of fact with a question: "It's a fine day today, don't you agree?" or, "I find bird-watching boring, don't you?" It's a style that is integrative and incorporative, that is, it gets other people engaged in conversation by giving them an opening. It is a poor style when your aim is to have another person comply. If your aim is compliance you should drop your voice and say, "Stop that at once," instead of raising it and saying, "Stop that at once, okay?"

Parents who feel themselves liberated, or at least conscious of the need to become so, often concern themselves with the effect other sexist adults have on their children. In the acquisition and initial development of language, it is

almost always the parents and the parents alone whose influence is crucial. If your language includes women as well
as men within its structure, if it is free of false generalities
about girls and boys, men and women, you are off to a good
start. But you still have other language clean-up activities
to get on with! For if the language in its structure and form
invariably suggests sexist thinking, its content is no better.

In an elegant piece of linguistic scholarship called the
"Semantic Derogation of Women," Muriel Schulz has documented the history of words associated with women.
Schulz demonstrates how neutral and positive words associated with women tend over time to become both negative
and sexualized. "Tart" is an example she uses. Originally, it
was used as a term of endearment, as other confections often
are; cookie, cupcake, candy, and sugar. A bit cutesy-poo,
but it certainly had a sweeter beginning than ending. "Tart"
became, like an amazing host of other words, a synonym for
a prostitute. Complementary words like "master" and "mistress" have had very unequal histories. At one time, both
signaled a particular power relationship to servants and
other help. Consider how "master" has retained its thought-
associations of power and control, and what fate has
awarded the word "mistress." For those of us interested in
both women and children, the fate of the word "governess"
as detailed by Schulz is worth noting: When Elizabeth I
was queen, she was acknowledged to be "the supreme
majesty and governess of all persons." It conveyed at that
time the same power that the word "governor" still does
today. I thought of Schulz' paper in connection with the
bumper-sticker printed when Ella Grasso ran for governor:
"Does Connecticut Need a Governess?" We were all supposed to laugh; perhaps some did. But why has the word
"governess" lost its sense of power and control? Because
now it refers to a woman who deals "only" with children.

Once you as a parent have cleaned up your language environment, its structure, its forms, and its content, you just have to complete the straightening by talking straight. Say what you mean and mean what you say. Sarcasm, put-downs, ironies, and mimicry are bad language devices at home. The young simply cannot make sense out of mixed messages. "You think you're so smart, eh?" "Just let me see you do that one more time!" These kinds of statements really blow children's minds and they don't do adult communication much good either. Loving, respectful, and neutral square talk is about the best language model you can set for children.

CHAPTER 11

"Good" Girls — "Bad" Boys

THE POPULAR, but quite wrong-headed, idea that elementary schools are hospitable to girls and hostile to boys is based on two indisputable facts. In reading, the elementary school's single most significant subject, boys don't do as well as girls. Similarly, when it comes to behavior, boys are quite regularly judged to be "bad," and girls to be "good." As it happens, although these facts don't justify interpretation that schools are hospitable to girls and hostile to boys, they do tell us some important things.

First, they implicitly reveal that boys and girls arrive at school prepared differently for the intellectual and behavioral demands placed upon them. This has been the continuing theme of this book. From birth on, girls and boys live different lives; as a result, by preschool age, they have developed different skills, abilities, and kinds of knowledge. More important, however, is the converse, which is that both girls and boys have *failed* to develop certain skills, abilities, and kinds of knowledge necessary to school and "worldly success."

Schools, therefore, have a choice. They can either ignore these gaps or fill them. In practice, schools have generally elected to do both. They have chosen to ignore the gaps in the girls' background and to fill the gaps in the boys' experience. Ignoring the girls' problems means that their problems remain hidden. It's comparable to our not having "had" an environmental problem until we formally decided to have one. The bumper sticker that reads, "Remember when water and air were clean and sex was dirty?" tells us a lot about how we define and attend to problems. The most oppressive and difficult conditions are accepted as normal until a shift in people's attitudes allows them to perceive these conditions as "problems." Plagues, infant and mother mortality rates, slums, child labor, and oppressed people were all at one time accepted as "acts of God," or natural. Only after scientific knowledge was developed and public consciousness raised did these once acceptable evils become social problems.

Boys and girls have quite different kinds of behavioral problems. By the simple expedient of labeling the difficulties girls experience as "good" behavior and the difficulties boys exhibit as "bad" behavior, schools can ignore the girls' problems and can concentrate on correcting the behavioral problems of boys. But both "too good" girls and "too bad" boys will be less effective learners than children with good flexible control of their impulses. Indeed, there is evidence that extreme passivity is a more serious impediment to learning than mild forms of hyperactivity. Effective behavior strategies, like other effective strategies for learning, are found among the children raised more, rather than less, equally. These girls and boys have a wide repertoire of behaviors that they can use appropriately. They can be quiet when the classroom situation requires attentive, focused behavior. They can be uninhibitedly active when such behavior is acceptable. Boys often have too little control of internal impulses. Without this self-control, they have difficulty in focusing, attending, screening, receiving, and participating in the learning process. Concentrated, focused attention is necessary for the development of competent physical and mechanical skills as well as for the development of competent intellectual skills. Girls often have impulse con-

trol that is so great, so inflexible, and that uses up so much of
their energies, that little is left for questioning, for seeking,
for asserting. Girls therefore have great difficulty participating in the instructional process as well as in all processes
requiring vigor and vitality.

The fact that schools do not intervene in the behavioral
problems of girls, but act only to help resolve the boys' problems results in a quite fascinating mental health phenomenon. Boys are brought to the attention of psychologists,
psychiatrists, and social workers in disproportionate numbers during their early years. At age eighteen there is a
complete flip-flop, and overwhelming numbers of females
seek therapy. Many explanations have been offered for this
phenomenon. Not the least persuasive is the suggestion that
the traditional formulation of the adult male role contains so
much choice and opportunity that it can absorb an enormous continuum of behavior. There is room for the prize
fighter, judo expert, and mercenary, as well as for gossip
columnists, artists, and saints. Nonetheless, the massive
societal efforts to help boys deal with their behavioral problems, coupled with the massive societal denial of girls' behavioral problems, must also be reflected in this therapeutic
flip-flop. Girls' problems are ignored until they become so
incapacitating that care simply must be given. Unfortunately, that extreme passivity that characterizes the very
"good" girl's behavior has already prevented her enthusiastic, energetic participation in her basic schooling. No therapy, effective or not, will return those lost years, those lost
opportunities.

When Lucy Peck and I worked with nursery school children in a series of studies on the issue of sexism, we gave
"Interaction Parties." There were six: two all-girl parties,
two all-boy parties, and two girl-and-boy parties. We
wished to study the children's "natural" behavior in an un-
structured setting. At the party table each child had a place

setting with a paper plate and cup and a plastic knife, fork, and spoon. On each plate was a blower and some balloons. In the center of the table were food, drink, and candies. The parties, which were scheduled for thirty minutes, were recorded on a videotape machine. The children's regular teachers were not in the room. Lucy and I were the only adults present. It was our plan to do no more than distribute the food and drink and see what happened. We established no rules for behavior, gave no directions, but simply helped each child into a seat as she came into the party room. With one exception the girls in both all-girl groups barely spoke to each other and sat very still. If they wanted more refreshments, they asked for them, although additional food was left within reach. One little girl in the afternoon group, a child designated as difficult, ran around the tables and talked a lot. Her behavior stimulated no responsive behavior from the other girls. One girl said aloud, "I am having a very nice time." It was then that Lucy and I began to suspect that what we were seeing was quite stylized "partying" behavior rather than the "natural" behavior we had hoped to observe. One of the children's teachers came in, noted the girl who was whirring about, and whispered to us that the child had problems. The other girls — the ones who sat quietly, did not leave their seats, did not even stand in place, and who asked for assistance to get things clearly in their reach — were not assumed to have "problems."

The boys' behavior was quite different and much more varied. Some boys were quite still, others were quite sociable with each other. Some left their seats when bored to find something else in the room to do. Some of them began to handle objects and toys around the room roughly and carelessly. At one of the all-boy parties, although Lucy and I had committed ourselves to remaining neutral for the agreed-upon half hour, after twenty minutes we tried casually to prevent two boys from wreaking havoc in the room. After five more minutes we simply could not continue to pretend we were just observing. We terminated the party because we weren't quite sure the objects in the room could withstand another five minutes of unrestricted use. Interestingly enough, there was little rough play between the children at this time.

When we had our girl-and-boy parties, with these same children, their behavior seemed to modify each other. Many of the little girls were more active than they had been at the all-girls party, and there was less destructive behavior from the boys.

In considering everything we had learned from the experience we felt convinced of only one point. Just as we had responded to the few boys whose behavior was "out of control," so too would all the teachers with whom they would have contact. But what of those quiet, good little girls, the ones who behave in a totally conforming pattern in all circumstances? Who will notice their needs? Although we had noted their behavior we did not respond to it because passive behavior demands no response. Moreover, passive behavior does not interfere with the adult's plans. While "out of control" behavior must be dealt with, overcontrolled behavior can be and often is ignored. However, we did attempt to deal with this problem the next time we met with the children's teachers. We discussed the passivity problems of many young girls and proposed to the teachers that they set up a reinforcement program that would help the young girls to learn more assertive behavior.

We suggested that each time the teacher observed a girl make an assertive move, or what would be an assertive move for her, the teacher should reinforce the child by saying something positive like, "You gave us a good idea, Wendy," or, "Good, you took charge of that activity, Joan." Though the teachers agreed with our view that this kind of passive behavior was destructive, they found the idea of reinforcing girls for assertive behavior both forced and difficult. This is because the language teachers and parents use in talking to children about behavior is almost always the language of control — "Don't do that!" "Stop doing that!" — rather than the language of release — "Good, you did that," "Fine, you tried that!" When either young girls or young boys are too inhibited, too passive in their behavior, it becomes necessary for the adults around them to shore up their attempts to be assertive.

For parents who wish to help both girls and boys gain good, flexible control of their behavior, to achieve good self-discipline perhaps nothing is more useful than the idea that when it comes to discipline less is more. In almost every aspect of the discipline issue, to do less than comes naturally is to be most effective — few rules, few exceptions, few criticisms, few compliments, few punishments — not only few, but short and infrequent. My approach is the Ten Commandment–approach. You may find it useful. Like the production of the Ten Commandments, it requires the clarification of priorities, brevity, and some writing.

At some time early on, perhaps even before the child is born, parents should sit down together to establish the family commandments. Each parent should have a paper divided into three columns, the right one labeled plus ($+$), the middle unlabeled, and the left labeled minus ($-$). In the plus column, list those children's behaviors that you would always find exemplary. You then skip the next column, and in the last, or minus, column list those children's behaviors that you would always find unacceptable. When you are finished, compare your lists, discuss, debate, argue, but come to some agreement. Remember, when in doubt, leave it out. You will probably be surprised to see that what you find good or bad in children is what you find good or bad in adults. If your combined list has short "minus" and "plus" columns you are in good shape and ready to continue. If you have a long list, especially beneath the minus sign, you should rethink it. Remember, God only gave the world five prohibitions. You should also remember that the list is your teaching obligation. So keep it short!

What about the middle column? Forget it for a while and stick with the plus and minus columns. Once you have your plus column, you can ask yourself how often you exhibit those qualities. Next you must be sure to identify those behaviors when they occur in sight and sound of your children as they move through the world. "Wasn't it kind?" "Wasn't that brave?" "Wasn't that extraordinary?" Finally, when your children demonstrate those behaviors, you might wish to comment upon them. Similarly, when anyone in sight of the child violates a family prohibition it should be identified and labeled as breaking a prohibition. "That was cruel," "That was unthinkable!" (I tend to be big on moral outrage.) If you break a family prohibition you must also identify and apologize for it. If a spouse breaks a family prohibition, if it is not self-corrected (and each should give the other a hint: "Don't you think you were wrong then?"), the other parent should say *in front of the child*, "I believe that was wrong!" The sticking together act suggested to parents is a Nixonian view of the law that suggests that it's not what you do but who you are that counts in moral issues.

Parents are often told, and quite correctly, that consistency is crucial in helping children develop self-control. Consistency is crucial in many ways but it's a lot easier to pursue when you have a minimal code of laws. It is helpful to think of children learning controls, rules, and laws, just as all of us had to learn controls, rules, and laws when we learned to drive. We should also think of those conditions that will make that learning quick, easy, and secure. The first step is to have the behavioral learning as clear and as unchanging as one plus one is two. Think what would happen to learning arithmetic if one plus one was only sometimes two, if it was two only for some people or only in some places. It would be enormously difficult to learn. Prohibitions are easiest to learn when they have the reliability of the number system. Spitting at someone is bad, it was bad yesterday, it will be bad tomorrow; it is bad if mother does it, if father does it, if baby does it. Sometimes it is justified, as when someone has you by the throat, but spitting in someone's face is never good.

The first time the child commits a prohibited act, just identify it as such and then issue a warning, "Spitting at someone is bad. In our family we don't do it." No more, and if you can get it down to fewer words, do so. When a child breaks a prohibition a second time, the less said the better, the less done the better. But something must be said and must be done. You can say something like, "That was a dangerous (or bad) thing to do. You must be alone till you get better control." Now here comes the most important move. Do not allow the child to remain alone for more than *three* minutes. A child will vaguely understand something momentous has happened if you move the action along quickly. But if you allow children to remain alone for any length of time, their minds will wander, they'll find something else to do, and you can never move to the resolution of the conflict. After a child has been alone for a few moments, return to the child and say, "You seem to have regained control now." Say no more! Begin a new action or activity with the child free of rancor or residual hostility. The child's debt to society has been paid.

As you can see, this kind of discipline requires that the adults have good control or at least be able to recognize and become responsible for their own absence of control.

The importance of keeping comments about discipline to a minimum has two dimensions. First, rules are easiest remembered if short — again remember the Decalogue. Second, the verbal environment becomes polluted when family talk is generally about behavior. Save extensive talk for reporting, observing, joking, and enjoyment.

Now to return to the empty middle column. All behaviors

that are neither "too bad" nor "too good" are to be seen as belonging in the middle. Since the "too bad" and "too good" columns are best when brief, the middle column, which always remains empty, theoretically contains all other behaviors too numerous to list. These are the behaviors, which are sometimes annoying for parents or sometimes difficult to live with but not totally unacceptable. These are the behaviors that parents and children rightly negotiate. These acts must not receive punishment, nor must the parent always be the victor in negotiations. Also, parents must realize that things that often upset them terribly are not necessarily the result of children's bad behavior. A toddler who accidentally breaks something of great value has upset the parents though no crime has been committed. Parents can freely express their anguish and pain. "I'm upset — I really liked that." That is different from seeing the child's action as a crime. If your anger at the child is uncontrollable, say so and leave the scene. "I'm upset, I'd better go and lie down." This time when you return you must also be prepared to go on to another activity.

Successful discipline is based on a generally happy, active environment, where dramatic and interesting events occur. This kind of atmosphere precludes the need for children to behave badly to get action and attention. Also, children find it easy to behave well in home environments that offer a lot of payoff.

All people, little as well as big, find the public space a particularly painful one in which to experience correction and punishment. Try mightily to correct children only in private. They will grow up to return that sensitivity and only correct you in private.

The idea that "good" and "bad" behavior are both learned behaviors is a difficult one for many of us to appreciate. We tend to waver between believing that the child is naturally good or naturally bad. This is one of our cultural limitations. Not so to the Chinese, whose understanding of children's behavioral development is more sophisticated than ours and whose children (girls and boys alike) model the most exemplary kind of behavior. Public punishment and admonishing of children is so rare in China that Agnes Smedley, a China-watcher of the 1930s and 1940s, wrote a whole article detailing one incident in which a Chinese parent mistreated her child. The incident occurred on a train. The other passengers were so startled that one man quickly rose, walked over to the woman, and gently removed the child from her. The passengers easily assumed that the woman was either ill or not the child's real mother.

The average Chinese naturally believes good behavior is learned — an idea difficult for many Americans to absorb. We expect children to be born good, or to fall into good behavior as a consequence of being yelled at or spanked. When I visited China with a group of early childhood educators, we were so overwhelmed by the large number of children who exhibited good, self-confident behavior that even we, who should have known better, asked questions like: "What do you do when a child is naughty? What if there is a 'bad boy' in the group?" (No one asked about bad girls; even though we never saw any evidence in China that the girls' and boys' behavior differed.) The answer was always something like: "It takes some children longer than others to learn," or, "The other children help them." No Chinese ever picked-up our words "naughty" or "bad" in responding to our questions. They were even good at disciplining us! Once one understands and accepts the idea that good behavior is learned behavior, then one knows it is most easily achieved when it is well taught. Discipline, as I have mentioned, is well taught when it is always defined the same: two plus two is always four. Discipline is also easier to learn when a lot of rewards accompany getting things done right. In studying teachers' classroom behavior, for instance, it was found that while children get a lot of praise for giving good answers they receive no praise for good behavior. They are, of course, criticized for poor behavior.

The Chinese are gentle, loving, and supportive of their young. In the nineteen days we spent in China visiting large and small centers for very young children (newborn to five-year-olds) and observing them with their parents on the street, we saw no adult hitting a child, no frozen stares or harsh looks, and heard no raised voices. Surely, I felt, we could learn from their approaches. I thus chose to combine the fact of the children's extraordinary body training with their ability to be still and quiet when appropriate. Chinese children cared for in group settings spend a large part of their day in doing regular structured, increasingly difficult exercises, dances, and games. This I saw as the Chinese way of preventing "disorder" and promoting good development. American parents and teachers alike have been sold, and have bought, the idea that, in varying degrees, the normal state for children is to be almost continually jumpy, or semijumpy. It is only when the child's jumpiness becomes intolerable to adults trained to an amazing amount of tolerance that the adults give the overly jumpy child a label — "hyperkinetic" —and dose the child with drugs. Perhaps we, and the youngsters, might be better off if we were less tolerant of the constant discharge of small amounts of energy and instead helped structure children's lives so that their energies are used positively, as the Chinese do.

CHAPTER 12

The Toy Curriculum

IN SCHOOL academic differences are dealt with in exactly the same way as behavioral differences. That is, schools ignore the academic gaps of females and fill the academic gaps of males. Many aspects of our girl-rearing patterns prepare her well for reading and writing. Adults talk more to girls. One consequence of being a "clinger" is that girls listen to and participate more in adult and children's talk than do boys. Play activities directed at a girl also stimulate her conversational abilities. The more she hears speech and practices speech, the more familiar she becomes with the form as well as the context of her language. At a young age she "knows" a lot of words and she knows how words work.

Knowing the way language works is an enormous aid to early reading success. That is why children who come from homes where a nonstandard English dialect is spoken are at such a great disadvantage in reading written standard English. A large speaking vocabulary will aid later reading achievement, as knowing how language works aids earlier achievement. It is far more difficult to read words like "heft," "wry," and "chaos" if you have never heard them spoken than if their sounds are familiar to you. Because a young girl's play is often more sedentary, more inside-based, her play more frequently involves her small muscles. She dresses and undresses dolls, strings beads, colors, paints, cuts, and pours tea. She, more likely than her brothers, develops good finger and hand dexterity, which make writing and drawing easier and more enjoyable. All her life she will continue to explore and develop this skill by knitting, sewing, and doing needlepoint. Her small-muscle development also includes an ability to focus on small, tiny things. Thus when she first is asked to focus on a letter or letters, this does not appear as a novel experience — her play has always included attending to smaller rather than larger objects. So the traditionally raised girl will be ready for school instruction in reading and writing. Verbal play and practice, small-muscle activities, attention to details, all will blend together to make the little girl a "natural" reader and writer. Because little boys have been deprived of these same experiences, schools will have to provide the remedial help that is the core of the elementary curriculum. But what price does the girl pay in other areas of knowledge for her sedentary lifestyle, her "sex-appropriate" identification, and her inside-focusing?

In the 1960s, the British novelist C. P. Snow wrote an essay on "The Two Cultures," deploring the scientific ignorance of Britain's most intellectual citizens. Because the education of Britons used to be either completely scientific or completely classical and literary, two cultures had been created that were unable to communicate with or understand each other. One reason this isn't so much the case in America, Snow pointed out, is because American children receive their scientific orientation from their toys.

Snow's assessment of the crucial role toys play in developing intellectual skills was unusually astute. Since his focus was on Britain, however, he failed to press on with his observation of the education of Americans. Had he done so, and had he been a feminist, he might have seen some striking parallels between what he was saying of educated Britons (by that one suspects he meant educated British men) and educated Americans. Americans, too, live in two different cultures. Ours, though, is not based on interest, or class, or choice, but on gender. The toys Snow so clearly understood to be the teaching aids for early math and science education are not the toys of all young Americans. They are the toys of half of America's children: They are the boys' toys.

The nursery school curriculum not only helps fill in the educational gaps of stereotypically raised boys, but it acts to broaden the accepted definition of the male role. In the nursery school and kindergarten, boys' small-muscle development is stimulated through the many activities loosely labeled as "seat work": cutting, pasting, puzzle-doing, lotto games, and arranging small objects on paper. Storytelling, show and tell, word games, and singing all stimulate the verbal development that young boys may desperately need for later school success. But the curriculum is not simply remedial. Its thrust is much more positive for boys.

It is hard to believe that once it was considered unmanly and sissyish for American males to participate in the arts. Since painting, drawing, acting, dancing, and even singing were not quite acceptable activities for grown men, boys' education typically excluded the arts. The leaders of the early childhood education movement took a dim view of this. As far back as the 1920s, kindergarten and nursery school teachers bent every effort to encourage boys to act, to dance, to paint, to sing. This determined effort to promote opportunities, to open avenues of participation in a hostile environment had profound effects. Not only did these opportunities enhance the lives of the individual males, but eventually the general hostility of society toward males in the arts was neutralized. Cooking is another area that society has coded as "female," but early childhood educators have recoded as "not for females only." So cooking, like the arts, has been made available to boys because teachers have chosen, quite consciously, to reject a narrow stereotypic view of the male role.

Except for some simple carpentry activities that some

nursery schools and kindergartens provide all students, no
similar serious commitment for the remedial education of
females exists. Early childhood educational environments
neither help fill educational gaps nor act to broaden the accepted definition of the female role. There is no vigorous
determination to insure that young girls have experiences
with blocks, erector sets, motorized vehicles, or, indeed,
vehicles at all. Nor are there any planned physical educational activities to insure large-muscle development, good
coordination, speed, and agility for girls.

As teachers now begin to consider the whole area of
school sexism, ironically, but perhaps not unexpectedly, they
again tend to focus on experiences that are absent in the
lives of males. Playing with dolls has long been the play
area most linked to young girls. Teachers have attempted to
raise nursery school children's consciousnesses on this issue,
by reading Charlotte Zolotow's *William's Doll* to them.
This book, ostensibly about a little boy who wants a doll, is
really about his father and brother. They are loving males
who try everything to distract his interest from a doll to
some more "appropriate" toy. William's desire to have a doll
remains undiminished and in the end his grandmother buys
him one. After all, suggests grandma, he will someday have
children of his own.

The behavior of William's father and brother during the
course of the conflict is fascinating. Since they both are
loving and well intentioned, they don't try to shame, humili-
ate, or frighten him out of his wish (unlike the real-life pediatrician in Chapter 9 who didn't mind doing all three).
However, their grim determination to move his interest only
by friendly means makes the story particularly poignant.
Although they will do anything for William, they cannot
bring themselves to break the sex-stereotyped taboo. Only
Grandma the outsider can break the taboo. The only part of
the story that seems unreal is William's ability to hold out

against the clear wishes of his obviously kind family. In real life, few children hold out against the sex-stereotyping messages of their families, and a little bit of message goes a long way.

Teachers who have worked with me on projects to reduce sexism have reported surprising reactions from their children when they read to them from *William's Doll*. Many of the boys object to the story's ending. They think William should not have been given the doll by his grandmother! They believe she should not have "given in." The children who object to the grandmother giving in to William's request are like those children identified by Woodruff as "high commitment" children. They have bought into sex-role stereotyping hook, line, and sinker and believe nonstereotypical play to be wrong. Researchers find, incidentally, that strict sex-role stereotyping appeals more to boys than to girls. Do girls learn very early that the system disadvantages them, while boys understand that it gives them greater advantages? If they both already understand this, have we already taught boys to wish to maintain an unfair advantage? Or, perhaps, activities coded for boys are intrinsically more interesting than those coded for girls. When I was interviewing nursery school children on this issue, I always asked, "Who has more fun, girls or boys?" and "Why?" One respondent was a blind child whose answer was particularly memorable. She said boys had more fun because they could run and they could swing up very high. Girls, she said, only played with dolls.

While society may be tolerant of tomboys who briefly try on the male role, support is rarely given to girls who wish to broaden their options. Toy companies stay in business by knowing their market. The Mattel Corporation, which makes the Barbie Doll (the most widely sold toy item in the world!), has exploited both the parents' refusal to buy toys for their daughters that help them explore space, speed, and motors and the daughters' desire to have them. Mattel has simply placed on the market vehicles expressly designed for Barbie — a ten-speed bike, a motorboat, a motorcycle. Associating these toys with America's teen-age sweetheart permits parents to purchase them un-self-consciously and girls to want them un-self-consciously.

Let's pause for a moment to consider the real-life parents' reluctance to buy vehicles for their daughters, a reluctance similar to that expressed by William's fictional family when he requested a doll. While the first group is being "tricked" into these purchases by a clever merchandizing ploy, the fictional parents change because of the support of a friendly, understanding grandparent. But how are parents, who wish neither to be tricked nor uncomfortable, to deal with these issues? Perhaps the answer is to think of toys for children instead of toys for girls and toys for boys.

We have already discussed the fact that "female" toys and "male" toys direct children to either inside- or outside-play with negative consequences for the intellectual development of girls. Girls are also adversely affected by their lack of experience in exploration of the dimensions of physical space. Our actual experiences in the world are, for all of us, our first introduction to height, depth, area — all basic mathematical and scientific concepts. This is why the free uninhibited exploration of space is so important in building a child's inner sense of the physical world. It will be reflected in later scientific and mathematical aptitude.

"Number is space," is one of Marshall McLuhan's less mysterious aphorisms. Number is the tool with which we get our bearings in the physical world. It is also a tool of discovery. McLuhan might have also said, "Number is time." Perhaps he did. Ease and familiarity in the physical world is one of the necessary ingredients of a good spatial sense and thus a good forerunner to mathematical and scientific understanding. But if the actual free experience of space is one aspect of good preparation for math and science, other aspects of "male" play further enhance that preparation. Even indoor male play is oriented to exploration, to finding things out, and to feeling at ease in space. Boys, because they are encouraged to move away, to try things out, are also given toys that both move them away (trucks, cars), and stimulate their curiosity and inquiry (erector sets, chemistry sets, Lincoln Logs, blocks — how many? how much?). Their earliest experiences lead to an intellectual security and what becomes, in some, a quick intuitive grasp of early mathematical and scientific concepts. The importance of these experiences is underscored by the research finding that girls who have had the play experiences stereotyped as male (block and construction play, opportunities to manipulate three-dimensional objects) score higher than other girls on block design and embedded figure perception, two subtests of the intelligence tests researchers use with preschool children. In a similar way, boys who play with a wide range of toys, whose play is not limited to stereotypic male activities have higher vocabulary scores than other boys.

Learning and teaching styles are different for girls and boys in part as a result of the girls' being encouraged to stay close; the boys, to move out. Girls learn well from behavior that is modeled by adults. They learn to observe adults well and can imitate what adults do. Boys, because they are out more, because their play encourages inventiveness, do not observe adults as closely and do not learn as well from tasks that are modeled by adults. They are not as good at imitation as girls, and this may cause them difficulty in school, particularly in the early years. On the other hand, boys receive a great deal of step-by-step instruction. (Boys receive eight times the amount of step-by-step instruction from teachers than do girls.) This type of instruction may also be tied to their more scientifically oriented toys as well as to their greater experience in being taught how things work. In any case, boys become much more efficient than girls at learning through step-by-step instruction. This ability is related to greater skill in problem-solving tasks. For just as the typical little girl's earlier experiences will lead her to be a "natural" reader and writer, boys' earliest experiences with exploration and discovery with step-by-step instruction will prepare them for mathematical and scientific inquiry. They will be "natural" mathematicians and scientists by ten.

Not only does male play take boys out, it takes them beyond. When boys — and it is almost always boys — are about four, five, or six, they often tie a piece of cloth around their necks. They then fling the cloth behind them, so that it covers their backs, and begin to run around yelling that they're Superman, or Batman, or the Six Million Dollar Man (some three-year-olds, unable to handle millions, call him the "Six-Dollar Man"), or someone else supernaturally strong and powerful. Adults are often very unsympathetic to this activity, but a few educators are beginning to give more serious thought to it. When boys play Superman, they are playing at extending themselves, at "flying." Games and discussions that ask children to think about breaking barriers — "If I were as tall as the house," "If I could talk to animals" — help all children to think about breaking barriers, being inventive and creative.

Since much of girls' play is stereotypic and confines them in limited roles, parents and teachers both have to work hard to move girls beyond the kinds of activities that confine them physically, mentally, and/or emotionally. Play that encourages imitation and reenactment, while just one aspect of play, is often the only significant kind of play girls do and the only kind boys do not do!

From early years on, parents' talk with children should to some extent focus on that baby's accomplishments. Parents are urged to speak to babies to help stimulate the babies' own speech and thought. One set of good, positive comments can center on already achieved accomplishments: "You stand up so straight and tall, John," "Susie, look how far you have walked." Other comments can focus on anticipated accomplishments: "You'll be able to do that all by yourself soon." Still others can support attempts to engage in new activities: "Isn't it good that you could try something new at Leslie's house today?"

In general one of the most efficient, least anxiety-arousing ways out of the toy issue is to construct toys and toy experiences yourself. The toys that a child will especially enjoy can easily be made by parents. Crib gyms, mobiles, push-and-pull toys, grabbing and holding toys, bath toys, shaking toys, and rhythm instruments are all easily produced at home. There are numerous advantages to this approach and whatever the family's overall decision on toys might be, a few should be produced through home industry. For one thing, toy making is an excellent way for the children's parents to teach each other skills that have not been a part of their own development. Simple mechanics, carpentry, sewing, embroidery, can be taught and learned through the toy-making process. To insure that teaching never takes on a power and/or sexist dimension within the family, the parents by their own behavior must establish a positive learning environment. That we can learn from each other regardless of sex, race, and age is as important a message to give children as is the idea that teaching something to someone is a fine kind of gift; it enriches both the giver and the receiver. Unfortunately, it is often at home that children early get the idea that learning is a demeaning rather than an enhancing experience ("How many times do I have to tell you? . . . "If only you'd pay attention," and so on).

•   •   •

As soon as you discover you're going to have a baby, you should begin to save everything that looks interesting. But what is interesting to a newborn, a young toddler, a young child? Here we cannot possibly have an exhaustive discussion on toys. In discovering what toys children enjoy, however, what toys are particularly useful in skill development, and what toys can easily be devised first by parents, then by parents and children together, a whole world of interest opens for parents. For example, it is thought that very young babies are attracted more to line than to color. So a black bull's eye painted on a white cardboard circle, suspended over the crib (especially one that moves with a slight breeze), will attract a young infant for hours. Someone once suggested flinging the front page of the *Daily News,* with its bold headlines, into the child's crib each day. Except for the fact that the print will come off on the baby, it would be a fine idea.

One friend of mine used to put up pictures along the base board when her child started to crawl, to keep the crawler interested and to stimulate more crawling. Parents often find that crawlers head for open sockets and wires (the former should be covered, the latter removed). Few parents think of putting safe, fun things along the bottom of the wall for the child to touch (a piece of fur, or a fat sponge, for example) or to look at.

A major contribution to creative play is a family dress-up box. The box is great if it's an old trunk, but a heavy cardboard box large enough for a four-year-old to stand in has advantages too. As the children get older, a window can be cut out of the box near the top and a puppet stage can be created. In any case, begin saving lengths of fabric of all kinds, torn sheets, especially if they're patterned, all kinds of bathrobes, and T-shirts. Add in berets, caps, small pieces of luggage, badges; whatever looks or feels interesting. Begin soon — a good collection takes years and can be a valued family possession.

In planning a dress-up box, whether for school or home, I

urge parents to provide only those items of clothing that both girls and boys can use without increasing adult anxiety. This is important just because girls in men's fedoras, ties, and suits do not stimulate the same adult anxiety as do boys in high heels, stiffened petticoats, and flowery female hats. This difference in adult anxiety helps build the unfortunate idea that the actions of boys (even when negative) have more social importance than the actions of girls.

A mother of a six-year-old boy was summoned to school by the principal, who told her that the boy should be wearing fly-front trousers to school rather than the pull-on Danskin pants he typically wore. The mother, a very gentle woman, was quite taken aback by the principal's interest. She said that her son liked the feel of the knit pants he wore and found it easy to dress and undress himself with them. The principal became angered, saying he thought no good would come to all this unisex dressing, and she was doing her son a great disservice by her attitude.

A combination of materials that lend themselves to all kinds of interpretation, mixed well with some props of great specificity — a lanyard with a whistle, painter's gloves, a stethoscope, and some badges — moves dress-up from simply role-rehearsal play to creative and inventive dramatics. Most of the play experiences of very young girls are mired in role-rehearsal activities: dollhouses, tea sets, stoves, refrigerators, grooming kits, dolls, as well as dress-ups. This is because adults believe they know what a girl's life will be when she grows up: a good wife and mother. One way to ready her for it is through her play, which is why her play has little encouragement for invention or to be an extension of self. While boys even in play are encouraged to construct, to invent, to expand, to extend their minds, bodies, and spirits, girls' play is clearly defined and closely confined. Traditional sexist play reflects the insistence on male expansion and female restriction.

If children are to grow up with a wide range of well-developed interests, abilities, and skills they will need play activities and toys that allow for: (a) small- and large-muscle development, (b) indoor and outdoor play, (c) quiet and vigorous action, (d) imitative role-modeling opportunities well mixed with opportunities for invention, expansion, and problem solving, and (e) play that is sometimes highly verbal and at other times predominantly physical. Experiencing a full range of play opportunities when young not only helps to build children's academic, social, and physical skills but allows them to retain a wide choice of interests and activities as they grow up.

CHAPTER 13

Dolls, Dolls, Dolls

BECAUSE DOLLS are the props through which so much of girls' confining and stereotypic play is channeled, because they have so dominated girls' play and have taught such wrong-headed notions of mothering, the temptation to say, "Be done with those sexist objects!" is great and close to irresistible. But before we throw out the baby doll with the bath water, I think we should give the subject some careful consideration. Parents then can determine for themselves how much or how little doll play they wish to stimulate for sons or for daughters.

On the doll issue, as on other issues, some feminists lean toward a paranoid interpretation such as, "Why do adults give girls a doll? To immobilize one arm." It does sound extreme, but we do live in a world that has bound women's feet, cinched their waists, flattened their breasts, and put them in chastity belts. On the issue of sexism, the paranoid interpretation is often the only one that could conceivably fit the facts. A paranoid reaction to dolls would be to ask, "Who benefits from the fact that dolls have been so pervasive in our young girls' environment and typically so absent in the young boys'?" However, there is also the counter-paranoid interpretation that goes like this: Just because doll play has been trivialized, seen as fit for girls and women only, and viewed as unimportant or actually nega-tive in the boy's development doesn't make that view correct. Almost all "properly" female areas of life have been similarly trivialized: birthing, cooking, caring, clothing. That is a part of the oppression of women. First, females are restricted to limited areas of participation, then those areas are deemed fit only for women and trivialized. The doll in our culture might be seen as a perfect metaphor for this process.

If we think of all the ways in which dolls have been used, we can see why they have been so encouraged in girls' play and so discouraged, in our culture, in boys' play. Dolls have been used to give comfort, to scare off devils, and girls are permitted to show fear, to require comforting and protection. Even "fearless" Nadia Comaneci was seen clutching a huge doll after her gold-medal-winning gymnastic performance — and she was fourteen at the time. Boys, even the littlest ones, are only recently being permitted to clutch a blanket or a soft toy. Ideally, from birth on they could tough it out. Dolls have been used to practice care giving. Girls are supposed to know how to soothe and comfort, but boys are thought to be appropriately ignorant of these skills. Dolls are used as fashion miniatures. Much sewing, dressing, and undressing takes place in doll play. Girls are permitted and encouraged in this interest, boys are not. Dolls are thought to stimulate the expression and articulation of emotions, especially those "proper" to females (not passion or rage). (A breakthrough doll was one that could cry "real" tears — a proper little girl could really get into crying.) Girls are allowed much emotional release whereas boys are supposed to exhibit inner controls. Our all-American heroes are the strong silent types. This also accounts perhaps for the absence of talk in most boys' play.

All these activities indicate positive or at least semipositive opportunities for girls' development and an area of neglected opportunities for boys. So what is wrong with doll play? Surely nothing if it is well mixed with a host of other play opportunities and if doll play itself is broadened. In my work with nursery school teachers and children, one unit was devoted to "caring." One day the children were told they were going to learn to bathe and change a baby. Each child stood by the water trough, wearing a plastic apron, with a doll in hand, a washcloth, and soap. Before beginning the actual wash, the teacher and children began a discussion of bathing, which continued during the washing itself. How would you hold the baby to make the baby comfortable? What part of the body could stay in the water? How would you know if the water was the right temperature, neither too hot nor too cold? How could you help the baby enjoy a bath? Why is it important to help the baby enjoy bathing? All the children were talking, bathing, scrubbing, powdering, and diapering — having a terrific time.

What we tried to do with the doll was to give it "public dignity," we refused to trivialize doll play. In this case, we did it by building problem-solving issues around a doll-baby bath. There are other ways to enrich doll play. Parents and teachers alike can extend doll play using baby dolls to stimulate discussions of babies' needs for food, clothing, shelter, attention, novelty, and interaction.

Parents and children should play with dolls together. A girl alone with a doll is an all-too-good model for our alienated family structure. It is a somewhat surprising research finding that both mothers and fathers join in less with girls' play than boys'. Clearly, that is an area that needs equalization. Parents and children playing with dolls set a good model of many adults being involved with babies. After all, should not a doll have an extended family too? Dolls do an excellent job playing audience for family productions; they are fine schoolchildren when school is being played; excellent guests for play parties, patiently suffering patients for hospital and clinic play; and wonderful customers for playing store. Placed in vehicles made of cartons or blocks, they are also excellent at waiting in line for playing carwash, fast-food service, toll-paying, gas-getting, or just for simulating traffic jams.

There are yet other ways for parents and children to enjoy doll play. When doll play is informally reserved for those days when you simply cannot go out, it helps make doll play special and being indoors an event.

An effective way to maximize the experience of a real outing is to reenact the episodes using dolls and construction materials to make models of interesting structures one sees or visits. John Dewey, a giant of progressive education, saw experience as the basis of all learning. But experience alone, he believed, was not educative. While we cannot learn without experience, we don't necessarily learn from experience. As logicians would say, experience is a necessary but not a sufficient condition for learning. This idea is contained in the old observation: "Have you had ten years of experience, or have you had one year of experience ten times?" Dewey taught that experience only becomes educative when it is discussed, analyzed, reconstructed or reorganized after the fact. For the young child, as for all of us, discussion, writing, reenactment or any artistic transformation (painting a picture, making up a song, making a collage, a sculpture) give both meaning and understanding to an event already experienced. It is the way to make these events uniquely personal.

The use of doll play or construction materials in reenactment for intellectual and emotional purposes, while good, educative, and fun, has its limitations. First, we have to insure the child a wide range of experiences so that reenactments are not limited to a small number of domestic scenes. Next, we have to be careful of stimulating an excessive amount of what I call retrojective play, that is, play that only looks back, for that play is often imitative and repetitive. Girls often have too much of that kind of play, boys too little. Girls often miss the kind of wide open, future-oriented play more common to little boys, like Superman. But dolls can be incorporated into future-oriented play. They can assist in exploration and invention, be passengers in travel aboard boats, planes, and spaceships. Doll play as well as role play can help ready a child for a new event: a camping trip, a visit, a wedding, an eye examination, a religious celebration.

However, constant and exclusive doll play is both limiting and confining. The idea that doll play is an appropriate preparation for motherhood is both miseducative and fraught with future peril. Constant and exclusive doll play gives girls poor notions about control and mastery and equally poor strategies for dealing with these issues. Consider for a moment the tamed little girl, obedient and respectful to adults, who accepts the tight restrictions placed on her. In playing with her dolls, she lays down the law, she admonishes, she spanks. She has early internalized the power hierarchy and is acting it out on the dolls. But is she learning anything helpful or useful about mastery and control? Is she learning anything she can use as she grows older? Indeed, is she learning anything about children that will truly aid her if she elects to have and to raise her own children?

While learning to master skills is appropriately done with inanimate objects, managing and maintaining control of oneself and managing and maintaining control of others is not. That is why individual and team sports are considered so important in a boy's life and so unnecessary for a girl. It is often through athletics and sports that boys learn self and other control and mastery.

It is surely not through doll play that real control techniques are taught. Rather, it is through doll play that these techniques are thoroughly mistaught. It is one thing for a child occasionally to whack a doll when overwrought and

enraged at something or someone too threatening or powerful to confront: It is better to use dolls as scapegoats than
people or animals. There is nothing new about having dolls
stand for a hated person: People have been sticking pins in
dolls for years. But if whacking dolls is the only strategy one
has developed for confrontation, mastery, and control, the
real world of people and events will loom frightening,
threatening, and uncontrollable. Good, effective strategies
for dealing with confrontation, conflict, and competition are
all absent from doll play as they are absent from much of the
rest of girls' stereotypic play. Even the small control girls
exercise in their doll world will often be absent in their
stereotypic adult female role.

It is difficult for girls to grow up for many reasons. The
adult woman's role is often too narrow and confining, women
are thought to lose power and attractiveness as they age,
often even "adult person" and "woman" are thought to be
contradictory terms, so that it is difficult for young girls to
know exactly what an adult woman is. Moreover, one of the
greatest difficulties for young girls is their inadequacy in the
one narrow activity society urges upon them. For in the
area of child rearing they suffer educational deprivation as
they do in many others. Typical doll play is simply the
wrong preparation for child rearing.

Perhaps what is wrong with doll play is mostly the expectation adults have concerning its effects — expectation
clearly communicated to the children. Compare the differences in a parent's mind when giving a girl a doll and giving
a boy a football: The doll will position the child inside, the
football will position the child outside. The doll will evoke
sedentary play, the football vigorous, active play. The doll
will encourage interaction, the football competition. The
doll will encourage verbal activity, the football motor activity. Perhaps even more important, the doll will be a private activity and will remain so, but football play may lead a

child to public rewards: money, acclaim, education. The private nature of doll play is perhaps the single characteristic in which it most mirrors child rearing itself. No one ever won either a doll or child-rearing scholarship to college!

While girls are thought to control dolls, constant and exclusive doll play will actually control them. It will confine them, limit their physical development, and remove them from access to public rewards. In addition, it will give them little opportunity to develop skills for managing conflict, competition, and confrontation. Lastly, the doll as constant companion, a constant source of comfort, may preclude the emotional ability to tough it out and go it alone.

CHAPTER 14

Co-Ed. Phys. Ed.

IF WE THINK about the expectations adults have when they hand a child a football or other piece of athletic equipment, we can begin to understand what human potential remains undeveloped when exercise, physical education and/or sports are neglected during a child's early years. If schools have generally failed to "remediate" females' problems in behavior, in math, in the social and physical sciences, this neglect pales next to the total failure to deal with girls' and women's deficiencies in physical education. This lack of commitment to female physical education has not been a misunderstanding, but rather a clear and conscious decision. As recently as 1971, a report out of the New York State Department of Education stated that the personal qualities built by the athletic experience were deemed unnecessary in "our young girls." (In that same year the department also announced that it was still socially unacceptable for a girl to beat a boy in athletics!) The studies of school athletic expenditure throughout the country reveal that ten times as much money is spent on boys' physical education and sports as on girls'.

Although recent state and federal legislation will begin to change this enormous discrepancy, it is important for parents of a daughter to understand that it is likely that any really good, early, basic physical education she may get will be entirely up to them. If parents leave their girls' physical education to chance and to schools, it will probably be too late and then be too little.

In this connection, it is important to understand the attitudes of early childhood educators on the issue of physical education. These attitudes reveal in part the general intellectual devaluing of physical development. They have also deeply influenced child-rearing experts and parents, and are pervasive in almost all educational settings in which young children are placed.

Although vigorous play outdoors is viewed as positive, little is done to promote it. Children are taken outside and left to choose their own play. Some run, jump, climb, and ride bicycles and wagons. Others sit in sandboxes and pour sand from one cup into another. Still others stand by the teacher listening to her as she speaks to other children or adults. The teacher rarely organizes an activity or participates in any. Her behavior is not unlike parents' who take their children to the park for an "airing." That is the extent of their physical education, and for many children it is very little; for some it is none at all.

A few years back a wonderfully energetic, fairly muscular female gym teacher told the following story at a workshop I was leading. She was responsible for the physical education and athletic program in a rather large elementary school. Dissatisfied with the traditional programs, she was eager to develop a real commitment to physical education among the girls she taught, as well as among the boys. Since she was determined, energetic, and creative, she developed many strategies to promote this goal. Older girl and boy athletes, fifth and sixth graders, would have their pictures posted on the bulletin boards. Younger children of both sexes, first, second, third, and fourth graders, would be cheerleaders for the older children. Co-ed teams and activities at all levels of ability and interest were developed. A newsletter was circulated throughout the school reporting on past events and achievements and announcing future ones. Everyone seemed to be having a wonderful time. She, herself, was becoming quite a popular figure in the school, and the young girls especially, she blushed to tell us, adored her. Well done, one would think! But one day she was called into the principal's office. He was very embarrassed, he didn't know quite how to tell her, but he felt it his responsibility to overcome his hesitation and share his discomfort with her. It seemed her program was indeed successful, perhaps, he suggested, if she got his meaning, too successful. The young girls were becoming too like her, and while he personally liked the gym teacher a lot, he was not eager to produce a school full of female jocks! It just didn't seem right to him. He was sure she would understand if he asked her to cool it with all this athletic business. Had she greater sensitivity, the principal suggested, she would never have started this whole thing in the first place. They all would have been spared a great deal of unnecessary embarrassment. A school, it seems, is a place for not learning as well as learning.

While early childhood educators vaguely consider vigorous play to be healthy, although they do little to encourage it, they view regular, structured exercise as insufficiently free and creative, and frown on sports as leading to competitiveness — a word that often carries very negative connotations among these experts. Though sports training can lead to competitiveness, it doesn't have to be cast as training for war, as it often has been in the past. The idea that you only have to get your body in top-flight condition in order to kill or be killed is rather bizarre. While forced, mindless, ruthless competition can be both personally and socially damaging, voluntary competition has great emotional satisfaction for those who willingly commit themselves to it. Females have often been actively denied the right to compete. This has been as true in the past of highly-trained female athletes as it has been of all females. Several years ago, there was a conference on women and sports. In the group I led, a female coach described how she was threatened with expulsion from the physical education teacher training program in which she was enrolled because she had been "caught" competing in a track meet. Can you believe it? She knew she was good but she wanted to know just how good she was. Her desire to compete in athletic competition was never fulfilled. It remained the greatest frustration of her life.

Boys, of course, have frustrations too, but often of exactly the opposite kind. In a macho culture, the need to prove themselves continually grows as they reach adolescence, and the arena in which they must prove themselves is often athletics. They are often forced to compete, to go public, to test themselves against others when they would never have chosen to do so had they really enjoyed "free choice." While good physical education is good for everyone, and a wide choice of sports opportunities should be available for everyone, competitive athletics is only good for those who are ready, willing, and able to commit themselves to it in a non-pressured environment.

A few years ago a young female high school student wrote an advice-seeking letter to *Co-ed Magazine,* which used to be distributed to junior and senior high school female students by their Home Ec. teachers. The young woman explained that she had been asked to play tennis by a boy she liked a lot. She was an excellent player, he an only fair one. Her problem: Should she play to win? The reply: Play as best you can, but when you leave the court, allow him to carry your racket. In this way, she could display symbolic weakness to compensate for her "lack" of real weakness. Otherwise, she would risk losing the boy. The young woman's fear, early taught her, was that she would lose by winning.

Clearly, exercise itself is not a creative task. It is only

through exercise, however, that we can develop the kind of agile, strong, graceful body that not only makes athletic competition possible, but also enables us to dance — surely one of the most exciting and exacting creative experiences. It is ironic that the same people who watch with equanimity while girls engage in continually repetitive household play, find exercise insufficiently creative for these same youngsters. Exercise also offers both release of tension and relaxation for those who engage in it systematically. Further, strong bodies promote a general feeling of strength and well-being often absent in people with little or no confidence in their own physical strength.

Many people who work with children having learning disabilities claim great benefits accrue to these children through physical activities that stress crawling, balancing, eye-hand coordination, and sensing the body in space. (Remember angels in the snow? You fall backwards in the snow, move your arms up and down, and when you get up, you have the outline of an angel. Lying down in damp sand also allows for the making of a body picture.) While critics argue that some claims for exercise as a way to solve learning disabilities are exaggerated, no one has established a good case for physical inactivity for either children or adults. Perhaps one of the most marvelous facts connected with exercise is that the more you do it, the more you can do it. When young children and parents can keep graphs of the growing distances they can walk, jump, or hop, as well as the increasing number of specific exercises they can do, it is a marvelous experience in both ego and number development. It is also proof of their ability to go and grow beyond previous limitations.

When I visited China, I, like other visitors, was astounded at the children's prowess in acrobatics, gymnastics, and dance, abilities already evident by the age of three. These abilities were based on a regular exercise program built gradually and starting only a short while after the children began to walk. The Chinese child rearers never confused this activity with recess and free play, which the children also enjoyed. As a result, their very young children can sit and stand absolutely still. They neither fidget nor do they appear to daydream. Rather, they appear both alert and focused on the classroom activity. These children were not frightened or scared still. They showed great poise, friendliness, and hospitality with us, their strange-looking Western visitors. They simply had a life that balanced vigorous activity with quiet time in a well-ordered pattern.

If children's schedules from their second year on, both at home and at school, were composed of activities that similarly mixed high-energy with low-energy activities, the children would profit in all areas of development. Après-ski activities are somewhat of a joke in ski areas for they exist for the nonskiers. After skiing, real skiers flop into bed exhausted, hoping someone will have enough energy to get them some food and drink. Similarly, children sleep well, too, when they are tired from a day with a great deal of enjoyable high-energy activities, and when they can look forward to others in the morning. Except for those rare times when excitement so keys us up that sleep is momentarily impossible, sleeping problems occur when one low-energy day follows another in unending tedium. Strategies for "coming down" from excitement can also be modeled and taught by parents and learned by quite young children: a long, slow, warm bath — no matter how late the hour — a warm drink, low-volume music, an often-read story, a talk about the cause of the excitement, a huddle, and a cuddle.

•   •   •

Social permission to show emotion, which is given to girls and withheld from boys, is clearly an advantage girls have in a sexist society. Yet crying and the un-self-conscious show of fear are not the only ways to deal with emotional upsets and tensions. Enormous emotional release is found in physical activities. Physical activities not only build strong, healthy bodies, self-confidence, and control, they are also a positive way of dealing with tensions, depressions, and anxieties. Few aspects of sexist child rearing and education have been as damaging to females as the absence of opportunities in physical education. Equal opportunities for physical education is thus one of the greatest contributions we can make to our daughters' development.

CHAPTER 15

What Will You Be When You Grow Up?

LET US RETURN for a moment to the young woman whose problem was to win or not to win that game of tennis. Her dilemma reflects a whole range of problems that girls and women have with winning and losing: their aspirations. Aspirations have always been reserved for boys — even when girls can express aspirations their expressions are often little more than formalized responses. Several years ago, Lynne Iglitzin, a political scientist, asked fifth-grade students, both male and female, to write down what they thought they would "be" when they grew up. To her surprise, girls as well as boys responded with a large variety of jobs and occupations; the previously reported research had indicated that girls typically respond with just a few commonly stereotypic "women's jobs" and occupations. Next, Iglitzin asked these same students to describe a day in their lives as adults. The girls, who had just enumerated all kinds of jobs and professions that they intended to pursue when grown, described a typical day of housework and housekeeping.

The question, "What would you like to be when you grow up?" has in the past been generally reserved for little boys. We didn't have to ask little girls because we assumed that we and they both knew what their future occupation would be. In moving toward equality of opportunity for girls, we've encouraged parents and teachers to ask little girls the same question. Aware women are often distressed when their daughters answer, "a mommy," rather than answer by giving a job, an occupation, or a profession. "A mommy" answer seems to indicate that the girl is ambitionless, perhaps has a low self-concept, and certainly has a low aspiration level. However, if a boy answered the same question by saying, "a daddy," we might very well consider his answer as a liberated one. Since this is the case, perhaps we might rethink our attitude toward aspirations.

The only reason we expect an occupation as an answer to that question is because in the past it has been a question directed at males, and males in the past have been summed up by their jobs. Do we really want to teach this idea to either our daughters or our sons? When researchers question children and they wish as complete an answer as the child can give, they often say, "Can you tell me more?" or "Anything else?" Perhaps instead of training young girls to respond as young boys now do, we might better move boys away from conceptualizing themselves only as future paid workers. We might even change the question to, "What are some of the things you'd like to do when you grow up?" and then say, "Anything else?" "Anything more?" Indeed, when you reconsider the question, "What would you like to be when you grow up?" one can wonder how the expected answer ever became associated with an occupation at all. Characteristics seem to answer the question more logically than job categories: words like "courageous," "rich," "brave," "kind," "famous," "respected," "newsworthy," and "trustworthy." It is quite clear, however, that boys answer with occupations because we have boxed males into thinking of themselves as defined by their jobs. "What are you?" A waiter, a boxer, a lawyer . . . Do we really wish to train girls to a similar limited definition of the adult self?

One gets a remarkably different set of responses to this question from Chinese youngsters, leading one to believe that kids sure can psyche out adults. In China, at present, it is a virtue for children to express what we might consider a "low aspiration" or a "selfless aspiration." Thus, to the question, "What would you like to be when you grow up?" quite young children will answer, "I will be what the Party needs," or, "I shall go where I can be useful," or, "I'd like to be a soldier, a peasant, or a factory worker." In China I viewed a particularly spectacular children's musical performance, and talked with the children afterward. One American said, "You are all so talented; would any of you like to be professional entertainers when you grow up?" The answer was prompt: "If that is what the Party wants, that is what I will do." So in China, it is thought that children have the best aspirations if they have no private aspirations at all.

Few parents in our society would wish their children to grow up feeling bound as adults to the wishes of the government or ruling party. It was not so long ago, however, that children grew up, even in our culture, believing that they would repeat the lives of their parents. It is no more natural to believe this than to believe your life will be different. Think a moment about Amish families where it is still expected that both male and female will repeat the lives of the respective male and female parents. The Amish parents view the schools as their enemy. They see the schools as a force for integrating their children into a society they despise and as a vehicle for motivating children to want a future different from the present they know.

Modern American parents have supported both these school functions. But the schools, like parents, have been quite selective about who they give the message to: "You can be anything you want to be when you grow up," has been, like "Any American boy can grow up to be president," directed till quite recently only at white boys. That minority group males were entitled to the same message from their school has been continually argued by civil rights leaders since the 1960s. It was not until just yesterday, however, that the issue of the right of girls to aspirations other than wife and mother, coupled with the notion that girls need not aspire to wifehood and motherhood at all, has been raised.

It is also the right of both girls and boys to have aspirations beyond that of "fitting" into a preformed working hierarchy (at whatever level). Although feminists are most eager to have girls grow up to feel both competent and welcomed in the world of work, the women we all most admire were often free-enterprise spirits who worked to restructure their world. When Lucy Stone read of the legal restriction placed on women, her rage and sadness were enormous and she decided on her life's work. She decided to change religion, the law, social customs, males' attitudes toward females, and females' attitudes toward themselves. Now that sounds like a set of aspirations worthy of any free spirit!

Unlike female revolutionaries and Olympic athletes whose aspiration is to win, to be the best in the world, most young girls and women have great trouble with these issues. The average little girl's aspiration level is quite low and the closer she comes to possessing the traits of stereotypic femininity, the lower her aspiration level will be. Like male minority group members, girls learn early in life to expect to have jobs where societal rewards are few. They expect little money and little prestige. Even young women less thoroughly socialized into "female" traits often have great conflict about achieving social or professional prestige by themselves for themselves. This "fear of success" is an idea based on the research of Matina Horner, a psychologist, now president of Radcliffe, who found that white male college students generally could accept and enjoy success, expecting that it would lead to future success: being first in the class would lead to good professional opportunities, good social opportunities, money, and so on. Female college students generally showed no similar enthusiasm for success nor any expectation that one area of success would lead to another: being first in the class might lead to dropping out, loss of social success, unhappiness, and anxiety. Now this difference between the female and male responses, while correctly labeled as females' fear of success, masks the real problem. The problem is that both young girls and women believe that winning in one area leads to losing in others. Success does not unfold into successive successes as it does for little boys and men. Winning and losing are complex, involved issues for women and girls. This is especially true for a stereotypically raised little girl, who will sometimes be rewarded for succeeding in the same area as her brothers, sometimes punished for succeeding in these same areas. When she learns to stand, to walk, and to run, she will be rewarded by the same adult enthusiasm as her brother will. But if she risks walking and running faster and further than her brothers, she will risk social disapproval. And what form will this social disapproval take? She will jeopardize her chances of gaining the affection and protection of males.

The threat of the loss of male protection is particularly serious if girls are raised to believe they are weak and incapable of protecting themselves. Moreover, they are raised to feel weak and incapable, or feign weakness and incapacity, so that they can "get" someone to protect them. To risk the "loss" of male protection or affection is too high a price to pay for "winning." Thus girls' fantasies are often not about struggle, competition, and victory, but about rescue. The rescue fantasy is stimulated in young girls — Sleeping Beauty, Snow White, and Cinderella. If the girls are only good enough, docile enough, conforming enough (in the case of Sleeping Beauty and Snow White, comatose enough), someone will come and rescue them. Not only rescue them, but provide them with the money, prestige, and adventure they are taught to believe they cannot provide for themselves. From the song "Some Day My Prince Will Come," to Segal's *Love Story* the message is the same. Females are taught that the primary victory for them is the winning of male protection and affection. When competition is freed from this threat of loss, girls and women seem to be quite enthusiastic competitors. The thousands of competitions sponsored by agricultural societies throughout the country in the acknowledged women's fields of sewing, cooking, preserving, and floral arrangements are all quite enthusiastically pursued — as are local, state, and national beauty contests.

But girls and women do not misperceive the hostility males often feel toward women who "beat" them in fields that they are taught to believe are the special province of males. That is perhaps the most depressing aspect of the Horner findings on attitudes toward female success. While the male college students viewed their own academic success as predictive of continued success in other areas, they saw female academic success as growing out of past problems or leading to future ones. Thus a girl described as "first in her class" was thought by the male subjects to be ugly, a grind, and sexually and socially undesirable, or even a male in disguise! While a male is able to say, "Let the best man win!" many are incapable of saying, "Let the best person win!" That males feel more hostile to a female winner than to a male reveals a contempt for women that has been allowed to develop since earliest childhood.

If female ambitions and aspirations are to be liberated, then the beliefs both females and males hold about the origins and the consequences of female success must change. But it is not only notions of female success that must change but notions of male success as well. If the attitudes toward female success have been too complex in the past, attitudes toward male success have been too simplistic. If girls grow up believing themselves capable of worldly success, competent to care for themselves and others, the male success pattern will become far more complex because the traditional bargain between females and males will break down. While this bargain has been unequal, unfair, and unsatisfactory, it has been remarkably stable over time. The bargain exchanges male support and protection for female love and affection, female sexual access and service. This bargain is acceptable to women only when they are trained from infancy to believe that their only hope for survival in a dangerous and fierce world is to gain the protection and support of one man. What happens then when girls and women come to believe that the exchange is no longer necessary? What happens when girls and women believe they can take care of themselves? Then females may demand a more equal exchange. That is, they may only be willing to give love, affection, and sexual access to someone who gives love, affection, and sexual access in return. Unlike the heroines in fairy tales they may be unwilling to marry frogs and beasts with the hope that through loving service they will turn into shining knights. Girls and women may simply refuse to be the prize that goes along with their father's real estate to the fastest runner, biggest money maker, or most successful politician. Remember, "You can have my daughter and half my kingdom": daughters, like serfs, were once tied to the land. Some daughters may wish to compete for the real estate themselves.

This refusal to be the reward, the prize, the insistence that women who so wish have the opportunity to "go for" the prize themselves, will revolutionize the traditional relationship between men and women. It is this revolution that feminists seek and that reactionaries and conservatives fear. It is what leads antifeminists to assert that feminists threaten the structure of the family. They are quite right!

Feminists are working to break the unequal structures that have held both males and females enthralled not only in the family but also in the marketplace. Not only do feminists wish to make available opportunities for women who want them, they wish to reduce the incredible inappropriate rewards that successful men have always achieved. Free women, capable of taking care of themselves, will not have to seek in their partners influence, prestige, strength, and power.

CHAPTER 16

Subliminal Sex Education

AT THE HEART of sex-role stereotyping is stereotypic sex. Whether access to sex and control of reproduction is *the* central or just *one* of the central motivating forces behind societal sexism is a hotly argued issue. In any case, sex is as central to sexism as are money and power. And as we shall see, all our ideas of appropriate "female" and "male" behavior are embedded in what we consider both positive as well as negative sex practices. By raising a boy to be a "real" boy (and to grow up to be his own man) and a girl to be a "real" girl (and to grow up to be someone's little woman), we prepare children to play their "appropriate" sex role in sexual interactions. For sex education, in a sexist society, has little to do with knowing how to make love or with a knowledge of anatomy. It has much to do with remembering your proper part even in bed. It's similar to the way we teach ballroom dancing: the emphasis is not on rhythm and movement, but in teaching men to lead, women to follow.

Nowhere is stereotypic sex-role programming more clearly traceable than in the area of sexual upbringing, and in the sexual upbringing of girls particularly. A girl's education from cradle on is incredibly and depressingly centered on preparing her for her "proper" sexual relationship: One that depends on her being evaluated and chosen as a suitable sexual partner by the more powerful male. Motherhood, her other claim to social importance, can only be second to being first chosen as a sexual partner. Beauty contests are female and not male because the traditional sex-stereotyped life for females is a constant preparation for an actual beauty contest (unless of course her family does have a kingdom).

Beauty contests not only prepare girls for the process of evaluation that females have to endure, but they identify the major area in which the judgments are to be made: facial and bodily beauty. Females, too, should be good. But female goodness is a particular kind of goodness consisting of two aspects: goodness as being compliant, and goodness as being sexually controlled. Not only compliant and controlled, but contained, as well. Only think for a moment: while the good man is out and around, the good woman is in. But bad men, if caught, go "inside" — they are "put away." Bad women are bad, though, often just because they have been out and around. They are loose women. Think about witches — the only women in fairy tales who move about freely — no fear of flying there!

But inner goodness is best when connected to outer goodness. "She was as good as she was beautiful." Ugliness is often correlated with ugly or bad behavior. "She was as bad as she was ugly." But the women most damaging to men are those beautiful on the outside, but noncompliant and knowledgeable: the beautiful witches. The demand that girls be pretty, women be beautiful, is perhaps the most persistent and oppressive of all demands made on women. While it is clear that meeting the cultural beauty standard is better than not meeting it, why is it an issue of such high priority? Perhaps because it is so convenient for males and inconvenient for females. Beautiful females become just another reward for high status men. Beauty is highly visible and fits amazingly well with the notion of woman as possession or adjunct to man. To competitive, status-conscious men, the possession of a beautiful woman, like any other possession of high aesthetic value, enhances the possessor. Men with beautiful women are elevated in their standing among other men. Beauty is also marvelously superficial and requires no output of energy to discern. For men who are eager to treat women as "other," lesser beings, the use of beauty as their only evaluation permits them to relate to women in the most minimal way.

While beauty in a woman enhances a man, it is no threat to male power interests. It differs in that respect from skills, knowledge, political acumen, or cold cash. It is not a good source of power because it is thought to peak early and after that it only lessens. Unlike other virtues, it is not a developing one; it is noncontinuing, and nontransferable. Although legends and tales are written of the power beautiful women wield, it is in fact, the rarest of all occurrences: privilege, yes; influence, maybe; but real power, almost never. Beauty as a focus for women's interest not only enhances the men women belong to, but when seen as the vehicle for achieving male protection, separates women from each other and often leads to female isolation, loss of support, and further vulnerability — the beautiful damsel in distress theme. Beauty in a woman when combined with vulnerability and/or compliance is a big sexual turn-on for males trained in sexist notions of sexuality.

The fact that beauty contests are now held for tots as young as three should make us aware of how much early childhood training for little girls is preparation for this later male evaluation, preparation for their supporting role in sexual intercourse. Similarly, much of male attitudes built from birth reflect the anticipated starring role males will have in sexual as well as other worldly activities. For parents to understand the program into which they set their infants and children, they must have some opportunities to consider the sexual notions about females and males programmed deep inside themselves. The basic sex-role idea suggesting that what females and males are, know, and do is opposite one to the other has been nowhere so heightened as in the area of sex. So much so that for at least a hundred years it was thought that women were totally disinterested in sex. Why? Because men seemed to be totally interested in it. As sexual enlightenment spread, women were then permitted to be just a bit interested in sex so that there might still be an enormous difference between them. A woman who was as openly interested in sex as her male peers was held to be suffering from an illness — a mental illness, or mania — nymphomania. Till but yesterday, nothing could bring greater shame on a family, nothing could more demean a young woman than the hint that she had a vigorous, active sex life. Since, as it turns out, the female of the species does indeed naturally enjoy a vigorous sex drive, many believe the oppression of the young girl, the taming of her energies and her movements, derive from the basic attempt to neutralize her sex drive. Thus for all the talk of boys' behavior, it is girls' behavior that is quickly and effectively brought into line.

The belief that only males have sexual instincts or that only the male's sexual instincts are strong not only fits the myth of opposite sex but is part of the whole process of maximizing the male and minimizing the female. The selling of the male's great and greater sexual energies was a project as enthusiastically taken on by our learned community as it was by purveyors of pornography. People, mainly men, wove intricate tales explaining why nature gave males an almost uncontrollable sex drive and gave women little or no sex drive at all. This, it turns out, simply isn't true. Not only is it thoroughly untrue that the male's sex drive is greater, it appears that even sexual response patterns of males and females are not opposite. Remarkably similar response patterns characterize female and male sexuality. The nature of the female sexual response has been so hidden, however,

that women themselves are unaware of what constitutes
their own sexual response: incredibly, many females in the
midst of sexual arousal report themselves to be unaroused.
They have either been taught not to recognize sexual
arousal, or not to admit it to themselves or to others. Although since birth they have been capable, like their
brothers, of sexual arousal, they know not what they feel.
Talk about a different education! Just as many hold that
the biblical prohibition against the acquisition of knowledge
was basically a prohibition against the acquisition of sexual
knowledge, the serenity with which the knowledge deficiencies of women are accepted is a simple extension of the traditional determination to keep women sexually ignorant.

Now one must think about this commitment to female
sexual ignorance for a while. For in its own awful way it is
fascinating. In other areas where women's access to knowledge has been barred, the motivation has been to keep them
from participating in those fields. But female participation
in sex in a society committed to heterosexuality is seemingly
basic. So why is there such a high premium on sexually
dumb or semidumb women? Because knowledge is not only
access — it is power. But in its own cock-eyed way, de-
priving people of education in a field where their participation is not only desired but demanded is to give them the
most profound kind of education of all. It teaches girls that
in this area their participation is not to be informed by open-
ness, enthusiasm, and knowledge, but by furtiveness, fear,
and ignorance. In keeping girls and women ignorant of their
own sexuality, in discouraging women from investigating,
analyzing and discussing their own sexuality, sex has been
presented through the male experience, coupled with a
complete misunderstanding of the experiences of females.
Since males are posited as aggressive, intrusive, active,
slightly out of control, or barely in control, it should surprise
no one that our view of sex is barely separated from aggres-

sion, violence, and war. Think of the language of sex: "pene-tration," "defloration." Consider the "correct" or missionary posture for sexual intercourse: male on top, looking down, female on the bottom looking up. In the nineteenth century, missionaries actually instructed people who used other posi-tions in the biblically correct, properly hierarchical one. Someone once suggested that from the woman's sexual point of view, this war metaphor could be turned around, result-ing in seeing sexual congress as engulfment. But we do not see, think, or act sexually from the woman's point of view or from a heterosexual point of view, but only from the male's. If seeing sexual intimacy as aggression, violence, and war, the process by which men do something to women, is bad, its corollary is even worse. This is the idea that male sex-uality (the only sexuality we are focused on), is heightened when the woman is weakest, most passive, and least active. We have mired sexuality in these three notions: sex as basi-cally male, males as most male when aggressive, and females as most attractive when passive and victimlike. In so doing, we have turned love to war and rape. These notions, which form the basis of our sex education, must be exorcised if sanity is to attend sexuality.

We have already discussed the effect fairy tales have on our fantasies. But think of the sex education they contain. Think back to Little Red Riding Hood, who would be "eaten up" by a wolf (always assumed to be male) just be-cause she ventured out alone and even with the permission of her mother. But perhaps more to the point, think of Sleeping Beauty and Snow White. They are not simply pas-sive, they are presumed dead. But how attractively they are laid out: one on a bed, the other on a bier. Princes fall madly in love with their totally inert beings. This then is romance, the male overcoming distance and other obstacles to reach a "laid-out" female. Consider also the welcome reception that awaits these unknown males who kiss laid-out females. They neither get belted in the mouth nor do they get arrested. Presumably, defenseless females are grateful for the attention of any stranger who climbs in through the window.

That any male's attentions are welcome and acceptable is even more graphically presented in the innumerable Beauty and Beast themes that run from fairy tales of long ago to King Kong. It is almost beyond our capacity to consider that one might play these tales with female beasts and male beauties. Although Masters and Johnson may tell us women have equal or greater sexual capacity than males, our minds are not yet prepared to deal with this idea. We cannot go beyond the myth of the male as the sexual beast endowed with enormous sexual energy, which requires release and which he must make great efforts to control. Since females, unlike males, have little or only a tasteful amount of these energies and therefore have little trouble controlling them-selves, they are responsible for aiding in male sexual control. If females flash an ankle, an eye, an elbow, they are not helping males to control themselves but rather they are stimulating the release of these sexual energies. For if the male is the sexual being, the female is the sexual object. While all of this should sound like nonsense, these ideas are transmitted through religion and psychiatry. The laws on rape until about a year or two ago were based on this reason-ing. So of course a male would kiss a laid-out female vulner-able to him. Who could expect control when he was so clearly provoked? Recently, a judge in Madison, Wisconsin, suspended the sentence of a young man convicted of rape on the grounds that in our permissive society it was to be ex-pected that a young man would lose control of his sexual feeings and become a rapist.

Rape is an issue that feminists believe is inseparable from our ideas about sex role and sex. Teach boys at their youngest ages that the world is theirs, that they can defy rules with impunity, that it is difficult for them to exercise control, that girls are produced to be in service to male needs, that girls are too weak and timid to protect themselves, that male sexual longings demand, indeed require, release, that the sex act is most stimulating when the female is ignorant, weak, or unwilling, and what you have is training for rape. Teach girls to be frightened of being alone, to view weakness as a virtue, convince them of the necessity to be compliant, and you'll teach them that rape is not only inevitable, but an expected, accepted "female" problem.

Sex as violence has done enormous violence to girls and women, but it has dehumanized males as well. Just as we have made sex violent, we have sexualized violence, giving it heightened excitement.

Control is the business of the female, not the male. Inhibition is the female task, exhibition the male (only bad girls exhibit!). Because the female must not only control herself but assist male control, she is seen as appropriately limited. She may not be in a certain places, so she is limited spatially. She is not supposed to be out at certain hours, presumably when male control is weakest, so she is subject to curfews and is limited temporally. She is not supposed to utter provocative words, so her expressiveness is limited.

The proper female role is even more complex than simply being the supporter of male sexual control. This is the first sexual paradox: She must combine simultaneously nonprovocative and sexually controlled behavior with overt sexual attractiveness, beauty, and signals of suitable sexual submissiveness. The earliest lessons taught to the female are that she must be attractive to men. Since her survival depends on the protection of a male, she must be pleasing to men. The judges of appropriate female beauty will be men, as the judges of the ideal male will be men. It is equally good to be a man's woman as it is to be a man's man. To be a woman's man (or ladies' man) carries with it no societal approval and to be a woman's woman is not even a familiar notion. Since pleasing males is important, what then pleases males? What they have been taught to find pleasing in females: service, subservience, submission, and the kind of physical attractiveness that stimulates male aggressive sexuality.

Though the idea that boys will be boys with irrepressible energy and mischief, sexual and otherwise, runs deep, it is coupled with a notion equally widely accepted but almost totally contradictory, which forms our second sexual paradox. This is that male sexuality is fragile and capable of an easy "turn-off." Any threat to male prerogative, any tactless refusal, any unsympathetic comment concerning male genitals or male sexual performance, may render him temporarily or permanently impotent. Both sexual paradoxes are seen as the female's responsibility to resolve. The young girl must learn how to negotiate a social life that combines the correct amount of sexual interest with a prudent leavening of sexual restraint. Again, the young girl must affirm the male need for sexual mastery while simultaneously inhibiting the onset of a sexual attack. No wonder women are thought to be good at human relations.

The necessity for girls' greater sensitivity to people, excellent though the quality may be, derives from their second-class status and explains why this quality is so often missing in males. It has been missing because it has been thought unnecessary. It is not the powerful whose survival depends on "handling" or "responding," to the less powerful correctly, but always the other way around. In unequal situations, the persons lower in the hierarchy use up enormous amounts of energies watching for and reading the signs of pleasure or displeasure on the faces of the ones above.

Training young girls to "closeness" helps ready them for coupled relationships. Training young boys to roam, to make free with space, to be on their own, trains them in independence. This is often why we observe between girls and boys and women and men an unequal need for "meaningful relationships," greater on the part of females, lesser on the part of males. It is also what leads to the common greater insecurity of women in heterosexual relationships. Both shes and hes often believe he can more easily go it alone. This inequality of need puts a great stress on heterosexual relationships. While we may think of our present sexist child-rearing practices as developing girls to be the people who need people too much, we can also think of developing boys to be the people who need people too little.

Only when we break our sex-violence connection with the male as inevitable and proper predator, the female as inevitable and proper prey, will we be able to free sexual expression from the sexual havoc this combination has wrought. It has been said that the primary sex organ is the brain. That is, how you think about sex is more important to sexuality than genitalia and technique. As we stop thinking of sex as violence, and return to sex as "knowing" another, a way to communicate, a way to be in touch with one's own and another's being, many sexual problems will cease to be.

CHAPTER 17

Parent Support Systems

CHILDREN WHO LIVE in a disapproving environment fail to develop self-confidence, competence, and joy, but so do mothers and fathers. Often how good you feel about yourself as a parent does not depend on how good your children feel, or how much you enjoy the day-to-day child-rearing experience, or even how enriched you feel from the association with your children, but rather on how the wider society evaluates your actions. For example, at some time or other in our history, parents who beat their children quite unmercifully were hailed as producing "God-fearing" children. Mothers and fathers who raised sons eager to kill and maim have been hailed as parents of patriots. When frigid women were viewed as proper wives and mothers, the parents who had raised them were called "moral." In a segregated South, for white children to feel superior to blacks, for blacks to fear whites, was for both white and black children a consequence of proper, socially approved child-rearing practices.

At the same time, then, parents who raised children lovingly, whose sons were pacifists, whose daughters enjoyed sexuality, whose children believed all people to be equal, were, by social definition, bad parents. Unless they lived isolated from the opinions of others, or were immunized by their own strength and greater moral sense from the judgments of others, these "bad" parents probably suffered from feelings of guilt and doubt. To be out of step with one's society is not necessarily wrong, but it often creates feelings of doubt, isolation, and unhappiness. Except for the moral giants among us, liberation requires the development of a supportive environment in which persons who share or are sympathetic to your methods and goals give you a hearing, help you to work out your thoughts and strategies, and throw in some love and affection as a bonus.

To achieve a child-rearing environment that is continually supportive, expanding, and empowering, parents as well as those who are prospective parents will do best if they make connections with like-minded people to form mutual-support groups. A group of young parents should gather together each week, or more often if needed, to discuss a child-rearing issue. In hearing each other's views, in just being given the opportunity to share ideas in a supportive atmosphere, in suggesting books and magazines to each other for additional help, in offering closeness and warmth at a time when adults often feel separated from their peers, many participants are helped to clarify their values and translate them into workable procedures and strategies. Some groups of parents work alone, others with a leader trained in early childhood education or child-development theories. The leader, if present at all, is most helpful when offering the group information, bringing to the group's attention topics for their consideration. It is crucial that parents understand that pediatricians are not child-development experts. Most of their specific pediatric training deals with the diseases, illnesses, and accidents of childhood. Therefore, pediatricians' opinions on issues such as feeding, playing, intellectual or emotional development, are no better and no worse than those of any other interested, intelligent adults.

One or two individuals can start a group. To reach others, place a small ad in a local newspaper or civic, religious, or hospital newsletters, or ask your local radio station to make an announcement, or seek sponsorship from a women's or other service group. Although it is possible for a single individual or one couple to experience parenting as liberating, parents grouping with others will find the whole experience much more positive, more joyful, and more enhancing. It is difficult to stress this point enough. Modern nuclear parenting, especially in rural and suburban centers and, unfortunately, even in alienated urban neighborhoods, can be an enormously isolating experience if connections are not made.

An interesting observation made by an early childhood educator is that group environments for young children directed by loving, caring, stimulating, interested and interesting adults can serve the young child as a selected "extended family." Wouldn't it be fine if parents could find themselves loving, caring, stimulating, interested and interesting adults with whom to form their selected extended family?

People who do infant and child care not only need an active, interesting life among other adults as well as children, they need to have regular and frequent conversations with others doing the same job. They need to relate to others both informally and formally. The responsibility for caring for an infant is indeed great and often appears enormous particularly for those who are inexperienced. To share one's concerns with others and to hear strategies and techniques for coping with short- and long-term difficulties are basic needs of a primary or the primary child rearers. I once casually observed that satisfying mothering was, I was sure, positively related to a high phone bill. The reaction to that observation was amazing. I had hit a sensitive topic! A topic that was the focus of much mother-father squabbling.

For the mother, the telephone is often the life line to sanity, the connection to others, especially during severe winters and extended periods with sick children. However, no societal notice is taken of this problem, and the strategies

women have devised to mitigate their isolation are seen as
extravagant and a waste of time. The income-producing
husband feels few qualms about telling the non-income-pro-
ducing wife that the telephone bill is too high. The denigration of the need for women to be in contact and communication with other women is so continual and pervasive that
almost all reference to women speaking to women is deroga-
tory: idle chatter, gabbing, gossiping, clucking.

Scientists once believed the earth was flat, that the Mediterranean was the center of the world, that the earth was the
center of the universe. Doctors used to attempt to cure
people by bleeding them. Dentists removed teeth to cure
headaches, backaches, and stomach aches. Yet no one considers that the advice of today's scientists, doctors, and dentists, is tainted because of past error. Indeed, no one has the
temerity to speak sneeringly of "old scientists' tales," or of
"old doctors' tales," or "old dentists' tales"; only "old wives'
tales" carries with it the taint of prejudice, superstition, and
ignorance.

Learning who is an authority (and thus whose advice
should guide your behavior) is one of the things people are
taught as they go through school. The idea that the people
who know best about a subject are those who have done it
least has to be learned, for it does not immediately leap to
mind as common sense. Doctors write books on child rearing, and they often announce that most of what they know
they've learned from the mothers whose children they have
treated. They are not being humble. Mothers are the only
significant group of child rearers in our whole society. The
questions this raises for other mothers and fathers is why do
they need to get their advice through an intermediary? If
mothers are the source of the pediatrician's knowledge, why
shouldn't other mothers and fathers go directly to the
source? People do not go directly to mothers for advice
because they are women, and even on issues that affect only

women, men are authorities. Just as milk deliverers and repair people are typically men moving from one encased
woman to the next, male psychiatrists, gynecologists, obste-
tricians, and pediatricians move from woman to woman explaining the nature of femininity, child bearing, and child
rearing. It is one of the great contributions of the women's
movement to have worked to put women in touch with each
other, and in doing so, to get in touch with themselves.

Many people have little direct experience with theories
until they become parents. It is at that time, when they
want advice and need help, that they find many answers to
the same question. After getting different answers, they are
then told that the reason they get different answers is because people have different theories — about the nature of
childhood, the relative importance they give to the notions
of heredity and environment, the basic nature of humanity,
and their value structure. How are parents to decide which
ideas make sense in terms of what they believe? How do
they know what to believe? How do they know what other
sets of beliefs are possible? Dealing with this and other aspects of parenting requires an education in its broadest
formulation. We have to learn what theories deserve our
attention, which can be easily dismissed, which are supported by hard data, which by little more than intelligent or
not so intelligent speculation. What parents must learn is
the lesson all feminists have had to learn: No matter how
objective we think our research and theories are, no matter
how logical our conceptual framework, they derive from
minds prepared by a social reality to consider certain data
significant, certain data insignificant, certain issues trivial.
Indeed, sometimes our popular theories have us suspend the
need for data. Ideas such as penis envy and sibling rivalry
rest on no data at all, and some of our popular theories
disregard data altogether. Thus, the evidence that women
who score high on scales of "femininity" are more, rather

than less, likely to suffer mid-life depressions just isn't spread around much.

In addition to sharing information and feelings, prospective parents and parent groups can assist each other in more immediate material ways. Pregnant women and babies and children often have quickly changing clothing needs. Babies have equipment needs that change rapidly also. A clothing and furniture exchange will greatly ease some of the financial burdens of parenthood. Parent groups can also share information on low-cost, high-quality drugs and medical care. Some groups organize to provide members with free free-time, or exchange needed household and personal services with each other. Parent groups are in a position to advocate local, state, and national policy that positively affects parents and children. Having a child can involve you more, rather than less, with local facilities and policies; through experiences with hospitals, schools, libraries; with state policy on education, insurance, welfare, employment; and with national policies on budget allocation for health, education, and welfare, jobs, and prices. In this way, children can stimulate your continued or renewed entrance into the world, rather than your retirement from it.

Interestingly enough, this has been a common conception of the male parent, but never the female parent. Fathers are generally seen to be more interested, involved, responsible, stable, citizens than the unmarried, childless male, yet this concept is not applied to women at all. Women are thought of as losing interest in the world when they bear and raise young children. They are helped to lose interest in the world by assigning to them and them alone the family's care responsibilities and by focusing them on the trivia of child rearing. By working in concert, parent groups can help mothers, particularly, to work out issues of direct concern to them, as well as local, state, and national policies that affect all young parents. Working to broaden parent support systems through the existence of parents' groups, hot lines (a communication system for young parents in critical and immediate need), flying squads (groups of people set to go into homes and hospitals to support parents and children in need of assistance), is one kind of necessary development.

Strategies for dealing with the people who deal with parents will also have to be built by parents' groups. One way is to set up interview procedures in local communities to assess how knowledgeable and helpful political candidates, doctors, teachers, and librarians are on those issues parents deem critical. One thing that has surfaced when women began to meet with one another to discuss their mutual problems was the problem of dealing with problems. For generations women had accepted a male-dominated culture's evaluation of who, where, and how their needs could best be serviced — even what their needs were. Although as individuals women had often garnered little help from these services, they had often assumed it was just their own poor luck. Until women began seeing their problems as a result of a system that had defined them unfairly and unjustly, concerted action was impossible.

Mothers and fathers can benefit from this same realization. One of the conclusions women easily came to was that when in trouble they could not automatically depend on people for assistance just because they had the proper licenses, accreditation, degrees, or other designation of merit. Thus, many groups of women worked to discover ways to solve this problem. First, they had to define their own problems. Next, they established self-help groups to offer women information, knowledge, and skills so they might de-mystify and de-professionalize much of the needlessly formalized care procedures. Another strategy was to invite professional members of the community to meet with groups of women to explain practices and procedures and to listen to their clients' ideas and views of what would be most helpful to the person requiring services.

In developing the idea of sisterhood, and now perhaps the

sisterhood of motherhood and fatherhood, women have been reminded of the strength they can bring to each other and gain for themselves through association.

In the past women were sold the notion that they are basically in competition with other women: Snow White and her stepmother, Cinderella and her stepsisters. They were further taught that their natural grouping was with "their man" and "their children." A competitive society that encourages women to gauge their success by their association with their husband or children's competitive success is often a rather negative environment for the stimulation of cooperative support systems. It often results too in females being unable to recognize their mutual needs. Nonetheless, the women's movement has been successful in urging women to join with others to pursue mutual goals in a cooperative fashion. Similarly, mothers alone and mothers and fathers together can join with others to make their own child-rearing experience as positive as possible and to help establish more satisfactory and cooperative ways to benefit future babies, children, and parents.

CHAPTER 18

The Problem with Myths

IF A MOTHER has one apple and four children who want it, the only way that she can divide it, without having to offer explanations and rationalizations, is to cut it into four equal parts. This example is often used to show how basically satisfying the idea of equality is. Because unequal treatment of females and males has been so oppressive and so irrational, an entire way of thinking about women and men — bearing little relation to reality — has had to be painstakingly developed to justify this inequity.

Sexism is based on three major myths: the myth of the opposite sex, the myth of male as the real human being, and the myth of male as the sexual being. Having made myths the basis for our thinking about females and males, it is not surprising that myths also haunt our child-development theories. Symptoms of unequal, unjust child-rearing environments are termed penis envy, Oedipal conflicts, sibling rivalry, and adolescent rebellion. Since they are assumed to be natural, unalterable events in a child's life, there is no need to make efforts to correct their causes.

Elizabeth Janeway has observed that Freud, in his theory of penis envy, confused symbol with reality. Instead of reading female envy of males as the natural consequence of their unequal treatment, Freud's view was that females couldn't accept their second-class status because they had never accepted their lesser bodies. Freud believed that the female body was deficient because it did not have a penis, and he also believed all women shared his negative evaluation of their bodies. By the age of three, girls would already feel deprived because their bodies were penis-less. Although we have evidence that three-year-olds do not identify gender by genitalia, it is true that girls of this age have already experienced three years of lesser or unequal treatment. That girls envy boys their prerogatives and not their penises, is, for some reason, harder for Freudians to understand. Perhaps because the cure would have to be equal treatment, rather than convincing females to accept their basic "lack." The outrageousness of the penis-envy notion can perhaps best be understood if one considers some research done with black children on skin color preference. Many years ago, experimenters found that black children preferred white dolls to black. To interpret that finding as evidence of the inherently greater attractiveness of white skin, rather than the clear social advantage of having a white skin in a racist society, would be considered shockingly biased and ignorant today.

It is an astounding idea that your body, female or male, would fail to delight, amaze, and fascinate you, unless you were carefully taught otherwise. For while penises do pretty fancy things (though clearly less so at three than later), the female body, too, is a source of incredible wonder. It manufactures and delivers both food and babies. The entire pregnancy process in woman is so magical that it has fascinated people for millions of years. The female body is a problem for a little girl only if it makes her less attractive to her parents and deprives her of the activities and access the male body would have brought her.

Sibling rivalry is another myth that flourishes in sexist child rearing. When sisters and brothers are raised differently, are given different opportunities, differing amounts of affection, and held to different standards, jealousies and rivalries are inevitable. These jealousies are heightened when parents promote different relationships with female and male children in the belief that girls should be close to their mothers, boys should be close to their fathers, or that mothers have a special feeling for sons, fathers a special feeling for daughters. Sibling rivalry, however, is also tied to several other aspects of sexist upbringing. Remember our discussion of the problems encountered when children's positive interactions with parents diminish as they grow in independence? When parents fail to replace no-longer-needed direct infant care with other loving and stimulating activities, the child suffers a real loss, which accounts for the terribleness of the two-year-old. The void is never so dramatically obvious as when a new infant arrives and receives all the loving attention the other child once received. This inability to view the toddler as requiring direct interaction with an adult is a consequence of seeing the mother only as a body servant and of wedding motherhood to housework. Children raised in a sexist family, who have never developed strong emotional ties to fathers, are particularly deprived when a new baby arrives and the single source of attention, mother, has new demands made on her already overburdened time and energy. It is at times like these that the value to a family of a father who cares and shares housework will be most pronounced.

Sibling rivalry derives in its early stages not from some mysterious psychological source, but from the minute-to-minute, day-to-day life of toddlers, who, having outgrown their own infancy, are deprived of good, positive human interaction and contact — interaction and contact they now observe going to another. It is frequently suggested that when a new baby arrives, older children be encouraged to participate in the infant's care as a way of reducing sibling rivalry. This is a first-rate idea, but only under certain conditions. If parents argue about, or actually refuse, care responsibilities, then offering these responsibilities to a small child is going to increase rather than decrease anger. But if care of others has been demonstrated by all family members as a responsibility in which they gladly participate, a young child given an important role in this sharing will experience genuine feelings of self-actualization and accomplishment. The usual psychological interpretations of children's jealousies and rivalries avoid the one explanation that seems most logical. Children become jealous and envious when they are treated unequally and unjustly. Envy is bred into children when parents' attention and affection is either unfairly distributed, undependable, or grudgingly given.

The creation of affection "shortages" to enhance the power of the adult has been closely studied in classrooms. Parents can profit from some of the observations of teacher and pupil watchers. In some classrooms, envy, jealousies, and rivalries run high; in others, these problems are barely discernible. In the first instance, the teachers enhance their own power by establishing personal standards that often change, are barely understood by the children, and are impossible for all the children to meet. These teachers establish themselves primarily as the children's evaluators, both judge and jury, in a Kafkaesque situation where only the teacher knows the rules. The children who meet the standard receive the sunshine of the teacher's approval, the others are treated to stormy looks and frozen stares, or worse. These kinds of teachers have pets and goats. They use their authority to become the central classroom issue: Will the teacher be pleased? Will the teacher approve? Will the teacher holler? Neither the children nor the subject matter receive the same intense focus and interest as does the teacher. The teacher has become the classroom's star attraction.

Other teachers use their authority to establish standards the children understand and sometimes help to formulate. The standards do not shift with a shift of the teachers' moods, and all children can hope to achieve them. In addition, many areas of achievement are available to the children. All children automatically receive the friendly interest of the teacher simply because they are part of the class. For parents, the most important consequence of the second kind of classroom environment is its effect on the children and its effect on the children's relationships with each other.

First, the children are normally relaxed about the teachers' response, living as they do in an environment dependably secure in affection. Next, they live in a lawful environment, where known rules operate. Lastly, they can choose alternative routes to satisfaction and accomplishment. If some tasks are wearisome and difficult, they are balanced by those that are easy and pleasurable. What are children like who grow up in a school and, what is more important, in a home environment like this? They are self-assured, self-confident, and powerful. They are also very good to one another.

Perhaps no area of family life is as damaged by mythical thinking and sexist attitudes and behavior as the area of discipline. Mothers' and fathers' discipline difficulties are magnified when they believe adulthood is different for female and male children. A particularly oppressive aspect of sexist upbringing is often the parents' relaxed acceptance of their daughter's overly controlled behavior as a sign that she is good and well disciplined. The need for a heterosexual set of behavioral standards is crucial if girls are to be able to energetically enjoy and profit from their early years and grow to maturity as joyful, high-functioning women. When girls cannot, because of real danger, be permitted the same freedom as their brothers, they must understand this to be the consequence of an unjust society, a wrong that must be put right. Boys, no less than girls, need to meet a heterosexual set of behavioral standards that allow them freedom to grow and at the same time insure that their participation in present and future family and school life will be cooperative and productive.

We have already discussed the discipline difficulties that derive from mothers being unsure of how much control is appropriately exercised over sons. Mothers have been led to believe that a boy's indifference to family rules is a sign of "real" boyishness, good aggressive male development. However, other strains are put on mother-son relationships in sexist families. These begin to appear as soon as sons realize that while they are destined for first-class citizenship, females, including their mothers, are second class. And so are the activities assigned to females. One response is to view the behavior modeled by their mothers as inappropriate for them to copy. If the mother is the only available parent, then male children are forced to seek behavioral direction from their peers at a young age. Boys' failure to use their mothers as models is suggested by the finding that shows boys in general do not learn well from adult-modeled behavior.

When mothers support the myth of the opposite sex, each with its own peculiar abilities, boys will often be unwilling to accept household assignments because they have been taught it demeans them. This simply does not happen in a family where mother and father have cooperatively tended the house, the children, and each other. It happens regularly in houses where fathers are clearly exempted from household tasks and children, girls and boys, are expected to accept these tasks. This then becomes an issue between mothers who need help and are doubtlessly angry at the whole system, and sons who wish to claim what they believe to be their rightful "male" prerogatives. It is also the various incidents in this continuing struggle that are laid on the dinner table each night. For the mother, unable to engender the respect she deserves in a hierarchy that positions her lower than the father and only temporarily higher than her sons and daughters, often uses the dinner hour as a time to seek backing from the more powerful father. A day's worth of anger and complaint are disgorged at dinner. It is the mother's hope that the father will bring the kids into line and shore up her authority at least through the next day. It never works! The father as top authority not only undermines the mother's authority, but the existence of a hierarchical power system stimulates the need for an adolescent rebellion. Boys spend their early years planning and getting ready, and their adolescent years staging it. They must, in hierarchical systems, seize their manhood (used synonymously with adulthood) or remain dependent. Because girls rarely see the possibility of seizing power in hierarchical familes where papa rules the roost and mama has never achieved adulthood, the daughter's dreams are of rescue, not liberation.

Family life has a different scenario when it is seen as a joint trusteeship exercised with continually diminishing supervision and control. Supervision and control that ends as each child reaches adulthood, and the relationship becomes one of mutual love, affection, and respect between consenting adults. Family life for children thus moves from trusteeship to commonwealth status. Growing older for children brings with it the continually automatic assumption of privilege and responsibility for themselves and others. If the family is not run like a banana republic, constant palace revolutions are no longer inevitable.

Sexist family structures result in problems, and mythical thinking is of little help in solving them. Family structures that are equitable, just, and joyful reduce conflict between parents and children.

•   •   •

When parents are asked if they believe in sex-role socialization, in bringing up their daughters to be truly feminine and their sons to be truly masculine, they often reply with an enthusiastic Yes. The yeses become less enthusiastic and finally disappear altogether when parents become conscious of the price that is paid for the dubious advantages of sex-role stereotyping. When I ask parents how many academic and behavioral problems they would be willing to accept in order to produce a stereotypic male child, or how much of their daughters' futures they would be willing to mortgage by encouraging her to remain in her dollhouse, I find that they are quite willing to reconsider the entire issue of sexist child rearing. Parents not only want their children to have a happy childhood, they wish to insure, to the extent they can, a satisfying future. Anything that limits children's interests, abilities, and knowledge is hardly the way to prepare them for an eighty-year life span: a life span that will reach into the middle of the twenty-first century. The constant acceleration of change, the constant flux of political, social, economic, and psychological structures, the deepening involvement of all the world's citizens with the problems of global survival, are realities with which today's children will have to cope with as adults. For this they will need great physical, emotional, intellectual, and moral strength. Parents who move beyond sexist child rearing are taking the first step toward helping their children become all they are capable of being.

Notes

Notes

Chapter 2 / Redefining Motherhood

18   "claiming" by human mothers. M. H. Klaus, J. H. Kennell, N. Plumb, and S. Zuehlke, "Human Maternal Behavior at the First Contact with Her Young," *Pediatrics* 46 (1970): 187–192.

21   boys and girls clearly perceive that their lives are different. Eleanor E. Maccoby and Carol N. Jacklin, *The Psychology of Sex Differences.* Stanford: Stanford University Press, 1974, p. 279.

26   women lose ego strength. Norma Haan, "Personality Development from Adolescence to Adulthood in the Oakland Growth and Guidance Studies," *Seminars in Psychiatry* 4, no. 4 (Nov. 1972): 339–414.

Chapter 3 / The Pink and Blue Blues

36   Babies more interested in strong line than color. Robert L. Fantz and Sonia Nevis, "Pattern Preferences and Perceptual Cognitive Development in Early Infancy," *Merrill-Palmer Quarterly* 13 (1967): 77–108.

Chapter 4 / Creating the Myth of the Opposite Sex

41–42   Serbin-Connor research project. Lisa A. Serbin, Jane M. Connor, Carol J. Burchardt, and Cheryl C. Citron, "Effects of Peer Presence on Sex Typing of Children's Play Behavior," manuscript, SUNY at Binghamton.

44   many children's books have . . . necessity to grow out of tomboyhood as central crisis. Myra Pollack Sadker and

David Miller Sadker, *Now Upon A Time—A Contemporary View of Children's Literature.* New York: Harper and Row, 1977, pp. 238–241.

49　Geneva Woodruff study. Geneva Woodruff Puffer, "Sex Role Concept of Kindergarten: First and Second Grade Children as a Function of Their Home Environment," Ph.D. diss., Boston University, 1974, p. 88.

52　Serbin and nursery school teacher project. Lisa A. Serbin, Jane M. Connor, and Iris Lipman, "An Observational Study of Differential Attention to Males and Females During the Introduction of New Toys in the Preschool Classroom," manuscript, SUNY at Binghamton.

55　dynamic nature of the human brain. Jean Piaget, *The Origins of Intelligence in Children.* New York: Norton, 1963.

Chapter 5 / A Girl for You, a Boy for Me

59　women who seek abortions for the wrong-sex child. Dr. Park Gerald's lecture in course on Medical Genetics at Jackson Laboratories, Bar Harbor, Maine, August 1976; reported in *Boston Globe,* August 19, 1976.

Chapter 6 / Redefining Fatherhood

75　quick, efficient, silent processing of the baby's needs is not particularly good for the baby. Margaret A. Ribble, *The Rights of Infants: Early Psychological Needs and Their Satisfaction,* 2nd ed. New York: Columbia University Press, 1965, pp. 2–3; also Sylvia Brody et al., *Patterns of Mothering: Maternal Influence During Infancy.* New York: International University Press, 1956, pp. 345–346.

Chapter 7 / The Inside-Out Family

83　Mary Wollstonecraft observed nearly two hundred years ago. Mary Wollstonecraft, "A Vindication of the Rights of Women," 1792, in *The Feminist Papers,* Alice Rossi, ed. New York: Norton, 1967, pp. 56–57.

84　In the earliest months of life . . . boys are observed to receive more attention than girls. Michael Lewis, "Parents and Children: Sex Role Development," *School Review* 80, no. 2 (Feb. 1972); also Howard A. Moss, "Sex, Age and State as Determinants of Mother-Infant Interaction," *Merrill-Palmer Quarterly* 13, 1 (1967): 19–36.

Sarah Sternglantz documented similar responses in nurses. Sarah Sternglantz et al., "Environmental Aspects of Sex Role Behavior"; "Studies Beyond the Nuclear Family — The Newborn Nursery"; "Innate Sex Differences in Neonatal Crying"; "Myth or Reality?", Society for Research in Child Development, 1975, abstracts.

different responses to girls' and boys' spatial explorations. Lisa A. Serbin, Daniel K. O'Leary, Ronald N. Kent, and Illene J. Tonick, "A Comparison of Teacher Response to the Preacademic Problem Behavior of Boys and Girls," *Child Development* 44 (1973): 796–804.

85   The space boys are permitted to roam continuously enlarges relative to their sisters. Susan Saegert and Roger Hart, "The Development of Environmental Competence in Girls and Boys," paper prepared for National Conference on Non-Sexist Early Childhood Education, in *Women and Society*, P. Burnett, ed. Chicago: Maaroufa Press, in press; this paper includes a discussion of a wide range of spatial issues.

87   The intellectual development of girls . . . adversely affected. Julia A. Sherman, "Problems of Sex Differences in Space Perception and Aspects of Intellectual Functioning," *Psychological Review* 74: 290–299.

girls are socialized more easily than boys. Eleanor E. Maccoby and Carol N. Jacklin, *The Psychology of Sex Differences*, p. 348.

91   females were pictured confined in space. Lenore J. Weitzman and Diane Rizzo, *Biased Textbooks: Images of Males and Females in Elementary School Textbooks in Five Subject Areas*. Washington, D.C.: National Foundation for the Improvement of Education, 1974.

Chapter 8 / Breaking the Housework Connection

107   mothers who respond to the baby's demand for attention with food raise less intelligent children. Burton White, *The First Three Years of Life*. Englewood Cliffs: Prentice-Hall, 1975, pp. 148–149.

Chapter 9 / Family Power Plays

139   the work of Leboyer. Frédérick Leboyer, *Birth Without Violence.* New York: Knopf, 1975.

Chapter 10 / Talking Straight and Speaking Equal

155   Whether "person" ought to include women. Leo Kanowitz, *Sex Roles in Law and Society: Woman as Non-Person.* Albuquerque, N.M.: University of New Mexico Press, 1973. "Workers and their wives." Janice Law Trecker, "Women in U.S. History High School Textbooks," in *And Jill Came Tumbling After: Sexism in American Education,* Judith Stacey, Susan Bereaud, and Joan Daniels, eds. New York: Dell, 1974.

156   Derivation of word "man." A discussion of this can be found in Casey Miller and Kate Swift, *Words and Women.* Garden City, N.J.: Doubleday–Anchor, 1976, p. 28. "Man has two ovaries." Mary C. Howell, "What Medical Schools Teach About Women," in Sounding Board, *New England Journal of Medicine* 291, no. 6 (August 8, 1974).

157   "Manglish." Alma Graham, "The Making of a Nonsexist Dictionary," *Ms.* 2, no. 6 (Dec. 1973): 12–16.

158   Women speak closer to the standard form than do men. William Labov, *The Social Stratification of English in New York City.* Washington, D.C.: Center for Applied Linguistics, 1966, pp. 310–314; also Peter Trudgill, "Sex, Covert Prestige, and Linguistic Change in Urban British English of Norwich," *Language in Society* 1 (Oct 1972): 179–195.

158–159   children's book that has become infamous in feminist circles. Whitney Darrow, *I'm Glad I'm a Boy! I'm Glad I'm a Girl!* New York: Simon & Schuster, 1970.

161   difference between female and male pitch. Cheris Kramer, "Women's Speech: Separate but Unequal?", *Quarterly Journal of Speech* 60, no. 1 (Feb. 1974).

161   "tag ending." Robin Lakoff, *Language and Women's Place.* New York: Harper and Row, 1975.

162   In an elegant piece of linguistic scholarship. Muriel R. Schulz, "The Semantic Derogation of Women," in *Language and Sex, Difference and Dominance,* eds. Barrie Thorne and Nancy Henley. Rowley, MA: Newbury House, 1975, p. 67.

Chapter 11 / "Good" Girls — "Bad" Boys

164 In reading . . . boys don't do as well as girls. Nancy Frazier and Myra Sadker, *Sexism in School and Society.* New York: Harper and Row, 1973, p. 92.

165 extreme passivity is a more serious impediment to learning than mild forms of hyperactivity. Eleanor E. Maccoby, "Women's Intellect," in *The Potential of Women: A symposium*, eds. Seymour M. Farber and Roger H. L. Wilson. San Francisco: McGraw-Hill, 1963, pp. 24–39.

166 At age eighteen there is a complete flip-flop. H. F. Clarizio and George P. McCoy, *Behavior Disorders in School-Age Children.* Scranton, Pa.: Chandler, 1970, pp. 83–85.

166–167 "Interaction Parties." Selma B. Greenberg and Lucy F. Peck, "A Study of Preschooler's Spontaneous Social Interaction Pattern in Three Settings: All Female, All Male and Coed." American Education Research Association Convention, Chicago, 1974.

Chapter 12 / The Toy Curriculum

175 Adults talk more to girls. H. A. Moss, K. S. Robson, and F. Pederson. "Determinants of Maternal Stimulation of Infants and Consequences of Treatment for Later Reactions to Strangers," *Developmental Psychology* 1 (1969): 239–246.

179 Sex-role stereotyping appeals more to boys than to girls. Daniel G. Brown, "Masculinity-Femininity Development in Children," *Journal of Consulting Psychology* 21, no. 3 (1957): 197–202; also Lawrence Kohlberg, "A Cognitive-Developmental Analysis of Children's Sex Role Concepts and Attitudes," in *The Development of Sex Differences,* Eleanor Maccoby, ed. Stanford: Stanford University Press, 1966, pp. 82–173.

181 girls who have had play experiences stereotyped as male score higher. Eleanor E. Maccoby, "Women's Intellect," in *The Potential of Women*, pp. 24–39; also training in embedded figures testing improves girls' performance: Lisa A. Serbin, Jane M. Connor, and Maxine Schackman, "Sex Differences in Children's Response to Training on a Visual-Spatial Test," *Developmental Psychology*, in press.
Girls learn well from behavior that is modeled by adults.

David B. Lynn, "Determinant of Intellectual Growth in Women," *School Review,* 80 (Feb. 1972): 241.

Chapter 13 / Dolls, Dolls, Dolls

189   mothers and fathers join in less with girls' play than boys'. Beverly I. Fagot, "Sex Differences in Toddlers' Behavior and Parental Reaction." *Developmental Psychology* 10, no. 4 (1974): 554.

190   Dewey . . . experience as the basis of learning. John Dewey, *Democracy and Education.* New York: Macmillan, 1916, pp. 89–90.

Chapter 15 / What Will You Be When You Grow Up?

201   Iglitzin study. Lynne Iglitzin, "Sex Typing and Politicization in Children's Attitudes," in *Sex Bias in the Schools,* eds. Pottker and Fishel. Rutherford, N.J.: Fairleigh Dickinson University Press, 1977, pp. 178–199.

204   "fear of success." Matina Horner, "The Motive to Avoid Success and Changing Aspirations of College Women," Women on Campus, 1970, a symposium, reprinted in *Readings on the Psychology of Women,* ed. Judith M. Barwick. New York: Harper and Row, 1972, pp. 62–67.

Chapter 16 / Subliminal Sex Education

212   Women have equal or greater sexual capacity. William H. Masters and Virginia E. Johnson, *Human Sexual Response.* Boston: Little, Brown, 1966.

Chapter 18 / The Problem with Myths

227   Freud . . . confused symbol with reality. Elizabeth Janeway, *Between Myth and Morning.* New York: Morrow, 1974, p. 97.

228   three-year-olds do not identify gender by genitalia. Lawrence Kohlberg, "A Cognitive-Developmental Analysis of Children's Sex-Role Concepts and Attitudes," in *The Development of Sex Differences,* Eleanor Maccoby, ed. Stanford: Stanford University Press, 1966, pp. 103–104. research done with black children on skin color preference. Kenneth B. Clark, *Prejudice and Your Child.* Boston: Beacon Press, 1955, pp. 44–45.

LEARN
ITALIAN
ITALIANO

THE FAST AND FUN WAY

SECOND EDITION

by Marcel Danesi, Ph.D.
Professor of Italian
Professor of Methodology
University of Toronto

Heywood Wald, Coordinating Editor
Chairman, Department of Foreign Languages
Martin Van Buren High School, New York

To help you pace your learning, we've included
stopwatches *like the one above* throughout
the book to mark each 15-minute interval.
You can read one of these units each day
or pace yourself according to your needs.

BARRON'S

CONTENTS

Pronunciation 2
How English and Italian Are Similar . 5

GETTING TO KNOW PEOPLE 8
1 Starting a Conversation 8

ARRIVAL 22
2 Finding a Place to Spend the Night . . 22

SEEING THE SIGHTS 36
3 Finding Your Way on Foot 36
4 Public Transportation 48
5 All About Time and Numbers 57
6 Trains 69
7 Countries and Languages 78
8 Cars and Vans/Road Signs 88
9 Camping 105
10 Weather/Seasons/Days of the
    Week/Months 113
11 Planes/Sightseeing 125

ENTERTAINMENT 133
12 Theater/Movies/Holidays 133
13 Sports 143

ORDERING FOOD 149
14 Meals/Foods 149
15 Restaurants/Tipping 158

HOW'RE WE DOING? 164

AT THE STORE 169
16 Clothing Stores/Sizes/Basic Colors . . . 169
17 Food Stores/Weights and Measures . . 178
18 Drugstores/Pharmacies 185
19 Laundry/Dry Cleaner 191
20 At the Hairdresser, Beauty Shop/
    At the Barber 196
21 Kiosk/Stationery Store 201
22 Jeweler/Watchmaker 205
23 Gift Shop/Music Store/Photography
    Shop 210
24 Repair Services: Optometrist/
    Shoemaker 216

ESSENTIAL SERVICES 219
25 Banks (Banking) 219
26 Postal Service 226
27 Telephone Service 232
28 Dentists, Doctors, Hospitals 235
29 Getting Help 245

BEFORE YOU LEAVE 250

VOCABULARY CARDS 261

Cover and Book Design Milton Glaser, Inc.
Illustrations Juan Suarez

© Copyright 1997, 1985 by Barron's Educational Series, Inc.

All inquiries should be addressed to:
Barron's Educational Series, Inc.
250 Wireless Boulevard
Hauppauge, New York 11788

Library of Congress Catalog Card No. 97-8788

International Standard Book No. 0-7641-0210-9 (bk.)
                                0-7641-7025-2 (pkg.)

PRINTED IN THE UNITED STATES OF AMERICA
987

Library of Congress Cataloging-in-Publication Data

Danesi, Marcel, 1946–
    Learn Italian (Italiano) the fast and fun way / by Marcel
Danesi ; Heywood Wald, coordinating editor. — 2nd ed.
        p.   cm.
    ISBN 0-7641-0210-9. — ISBN 0-7641-7025-2
    1. Italian language—Conversation and phrase books—
English. I. Wald, Heywood. II. Title.
PC1121.D36   1997
458.3'421—dc21   97-8788
                                              CIP

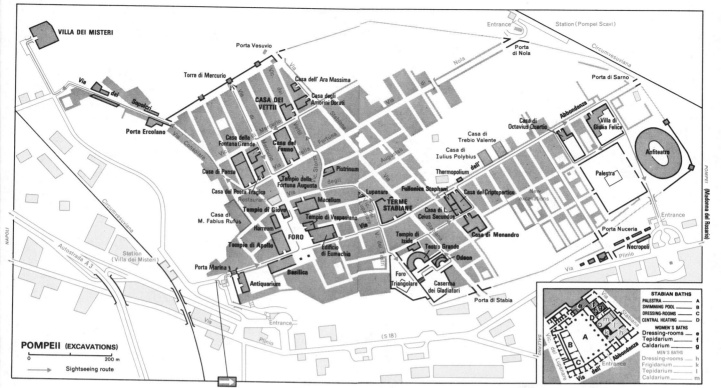

(*Courtesy of Michelin Guide*, Italy, *10th Edition—reprinted with permission*)

Italian is a "Romance" language, along with French, Spanish, Portuguese, and Rumanian, to mention the most widely spoken ones. This is because they all derive directly from the language of Rome—Latin. Most of the approximately 56 million inhabitants of Italy speak Italian. There are also many immigrants of Italian origin in North America who continue to speak Italian, especially in the home.

Italy is a peninsula in the shape of a "boot." There are also two islands on its western coast: Sardinia (**Sardegna**) and Sicily (**Sicilia**). It is surrounded by the Mediterranean Sea (**Mar Mediterraneo**), which takes on different names, as you can see on the map. The Alps (**le Alpi**) and the Apennines (**gli Appennini**) are the two main mountain chains in Italy. Politically, the country is divided into regions—each with its own dialect and local traditions. The capital of Italy is Rome (**Roma**). You will enjoy visiting many interesting spots.

You might, for example, want to see Venice's famous San Marco church and square, Florence's breathtaking Piazza del Duomo, Rome's immortal Colosseum, Naples' famous San Carlo theater. You might also want to shop in Milan's world-famous Galleria. Or, you might want to enjoy the tranquil surroundings on the island of Capri. Other famous cities you might want to visit are Trieste, Turin (**Torino**), Genoa (**Genova**), Bologna, Pisa, and Palermo—to mention but a few.

Italian painting, sculpture, literature, and music are famous all over the world. Who has not heard of the great Renaissance artist Michelangelo or of the great scientist Galileo? The names Dante, Boccaccio, Petrarch (**Petrarca**), Leonardo da Vinci, Verdi, Puccini, Rossini, Paganini, Marconi are forged into history, as, of course, is that of Christopher Columbus (**Cristoforo Colombo**). Today, Italy is famous for its artisanship and design, especially in the fields of clothing, furniture, and automobiles. Its cinematography is internationally acclaimed. Italy's cuisine also enjoys a worldwide reputation, notably with spaghetti, ravioli, lasagna (**lasagne**), gnocchi, and macaroni (**maccheroni**).

By learning the language of Italy, you will acquire a valuable key to many of its cultural treasures. Just put in 15 minutes a day at a pace comfortable for you. Some days you'll cover many pages, some not so many. Now, let's get started.

PRONUNCIATION

It is thought by many that Italian is an easy language to speak, that it is written as it is spoken. This is generally true. The following charts will help you with the troublesome letters and sounds. First we give you the vowels, then the consonants. You'll need to familiarize yourself with these sounds, even though each time a new phrase is introduced in this book, the pronunciation is also shown.

VOWELS

ITALIAN VOWELS	ENGLISH EQUIVALENT	SYMBOL
casa (house)	**f**a**ther**	**ah**
bene (well)	**b**et	**eh**
riso (rice)	**e**ase	**ee**
volo (flight)	**b**one	**oh**
sc**usi** (excuse me)	r**u**le	**oo**

NOTE: Speakers in different parts of Italy will pronounce *e* and *o* slightly differently, but not enough to make a substantial difference. The *i* and *u* may stand for "y" and "w" sounds respectively. This has to do with syllable considerations. For your own practical purposes, just follow the pronunciation aids provided throughout the book.

CONSONANTS

ITALIAN LETTERS	SYMBOLS	PRONUNCIATION/EXAMPLES
c	k	Before *a, o, u,* and all consonants, pronounce with a hard "c." Example: *come* (KOH-meh) how.
c	ch	Before *e* and *i*, use the "ch" sound, as in "church." Example: *arrivederci* (ah-rree-veh-DEHR-chee) good-bye.
ch	k	Before *e* and *i*, pronounce with a hard "k" sound. Example: *che* (keh) what.
ci	ch	Before *a, o,* and *u,* use the "ch" sound, as in "church." Example: *ciao* (CHAH-oh) hi or bye.
g	g	Before *a, o, u,* and all consonants, pronounce with a hard "g" as in "gas." Example: *gatto* (GAH-ttoh) cat.
g	j	**Before *e* and *i*, pronounce with a "j" sound as in "just." Example: *gita* (JEE-tah) trip.**
gh	g	Before *e* and *i*, use the hard "g" sound. Example: *spaghetti* (spah-GEH-ttee).
gi	j	**Before *a, o,* and *u,* pronounce with a "j" sound. Example: *giorno* (JOHR-noh) day.**
gli	lly	Pronounce like the "lli" in "million." Example: *figlia* (FEE-llyah) daughter.
gn	ny	Pronounce like the "ny" in "canyon." Example: *gnocchi* (NYOH-kkee) dumplings.

CONSONANTS (continued)

ITALIAN LETTERS	SYMBOLS	PRONUNCIATION/EXAMPLES
qu	kw	Pronounce like the English "quick." Example: *quando* (KWAHN-doh) when.
s	s, z	Might be pronounced "s" as in "sit" or "z" as in "zoo." Examples: *sorella* (soh-REH-llah) sister and *sbaglio* (ZBAH-llyoh) mistake.
sc, sch	sk	The letters "sc" before *a, o, u*, and consonants, and the letters "sch" before *e* and *i* are pronounced "sk" as in "ski." Examples: *scusi* (SKOO-see) excuse me and *scherzo* (SKEHR-tsoh) prank.
sc	sh	Before *e* and *i*, use the English "sh" sound. Example: *scendere* (SHEHN-deh-reh) to get off.
z	ts, dz	Sometimes pronounced "ts" and sometimes "dz." Examples: *zio* (TSEE-oh) uncle and *zucchero* (DZOO-kkeh-roh) sugar.

Most consonants can be doubled, and these are represented by double letters. In this book, doubled consonants are indicated with double letters ("kk," "gg," and so on). Simply double, or lengthen, your articulation.

The remaining Italian sounds and letters correspond, more or less, to English ones. For example:

(boh-LOH-nyah) **Bologna**	(sahr-DEH-nyah) **Sardegna**	(fee-REHN-tseh) **Firenze**	(pah-LEHR-moh) **Palermo**	(MAH-reh) **mare**
(NAH-poh-lee) **Napoli**	(PEE-sah) **Pisa**	(ROH-mah) **Roma** (rolled)	(toh-REE-noh) **Torino** (touching the upper teeth)	(VEE-noh) **vino**

Now write these words, along with the English translation, and pronounce them, using the pronunciation rules just given.

arrivederci _____

figlia _____

figlio _____

valige _____

volo _____

HOW ENGLISH AND ITALIAN ARE SIMILAR

Many simple Italian sentences follow the same arrangement as English ones:

The	boy	eats	the	pizza	.
Il	**ragazzo**	**mangia**	**la**	**pizza**	.

The differences that exist between the two languages will come out as you study this book. For example, you will learn that adjectives usually follow nouns in Italian:

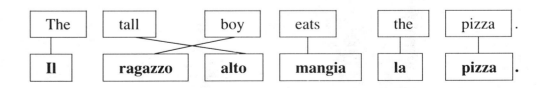

The	tall	boy	eats	the	pizza	.
Il	**ragazzo**	**alto**	**mangia**	**la**	**pizza**	.

5

Many Italian words can be learned simply by recognizing patterns such as the following:

ENGLISH WORDS ENDING IN: ITALIAN WORDS ENDING IN:

-ION	**-IONE**

correction   **correzione**
occasion   **occasione**
nation   **nazione**
station   **stazione**
function   **funzione**

-TY	**-TÀ**

city   **città**
ability   **abilità**
parity   **parità**
sociability   **sociabilità**
sincerity   **sincerità**

-IST	**-ISTA**

dentist   **dentista**
violinist   **violinista**
pianist   **pianista**
artist   **artista**

-OR	**-ORE**

actor   **attore**
sculptor   **scultore**
vigor   **vigore**
color   **colore**

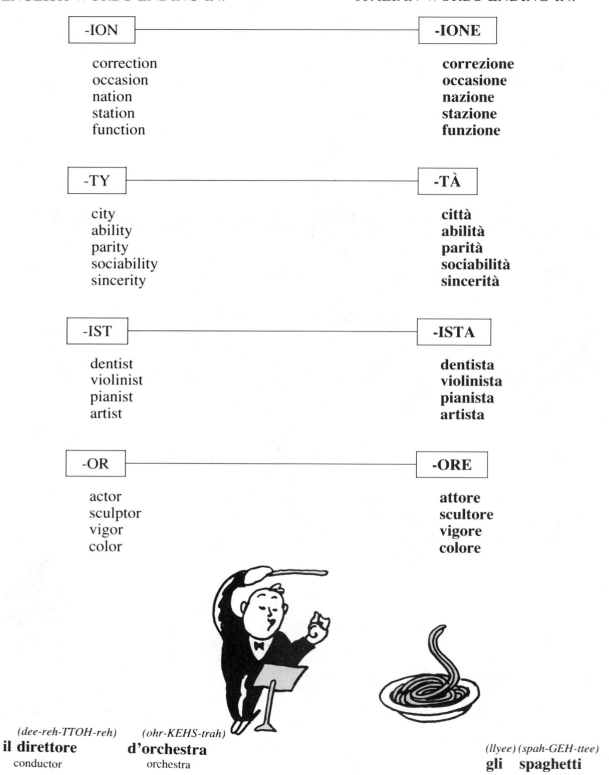

(dee-reh-TTOH-reh)   *(ohr-KEHS-trah)*
il direttore   **d'orchestra**   *(llyee) (spah-GEH-ttee)*
conductor   orchestra   **gli   spaghetti**

6

As you learn the language, you will discover many other similar patterns.

This book will attempt to make it as easy and as enjoyable as possible for you to learn to speak and understand basic Italian. For your purposes, you will need a few important grammatical skills and a basic vocabulary of about one thousand words.

(mee-keh-LAHN-jeh-loh)
il "David" di Michelangelo
Michelangelo's David

(MAH-kkee-nah)
la macchina
car

You will learn only the present and imperative tenses, which is really all you will need in order to communicate your needs and intentions. Some of the dialogues may seem to be somewhat unrealistic—this is because they are deliberately written in the present tense. All dialogues have been written with a humorous touch, so that you can enjoy them more.

You will have opportunities to check your progress throughout the book. If you forget something, or feel that you need some reinforcement, go over the appropriate parts.

By working through this book for about 15 minutes a day, you will develop the ability to ask for a hotel room, to exchange money, to order food, and so on. Do not overdo it! In the 15 minutes you will spend each day on learning Italian, work only through the pages that you can cover comfortably. Have fun!

GETTING TO KNOW PEOPLE

(FAH-reh) *(koh-noh-SHEHN-tsah)* *(JEHN-teh)*

Fare la conoscenza della gente

	(KOH-meh) *(see)* *(ee-NEE-tsee-ah)* *(kohn-vehr-sa-TSYOH-neh)*
1	**Come si inizia una conversazione** Starting a Conversation

When you go to Italy, and we hope you will soon, one of the first things you will want to do is to meet people and strike up a friendly conversation. To do this you will need some handy expressions for conversation openers. You'll find several of them you can use in these easy conversations. Underline them so you can remember them better.

Read over the following dialogue several times, pronouncing each line carefully out loud. Try to "act out" each role. The dialogue contains some basic words and expressions that will be useful to you.

(Mark and Mary Smith, their daughter Anne, and their son John have just arrived at the Rome airport and are looking for their luggage. Mark approaches an airline employee.)

	(BWOHN) (JOHR-noh) (see-NYOH-reh)	
MARK	**Buon giorno, signore.**	Hello (or Good day/Good morning), sir.
	(deh-SEE-deh-rah)	
IMPIEGATO	**Buon giorno. Desidera**	Hello. May I help you? (*literally*, do you
	(kwahl-KOH-sah)	
	qualcosa?	want something)
	(CHEHR-koh)(MEE-eh) (vah-LEE-jeh)	
MARK	**Sì. Cerco le mie valige.**	Yes. I am looking for my suitcases.
	(BEH-neh) *(KYAH-mah)*	
IMPIEGATO	**Bene. Come si chiama,**	Well (or Fine/Okay). What is your name?
	(LEH-ee)	
	lei?	(*literally*, what do you call yourself)
	(KYAH-moh)	
MARK	**Mi chiamo Mark Smith.**	My name is (Mr.) Mark Smith.
	(DOH-veh) (AH-bee-tah)	
IMPIEGATO	**Dove abita?**	Where do you live?
	(AH-bee-toh) (NEH-llyee)	
MARK	**Abito negli Stati Uniti,**	I live in the United States, in Chicago.
	a Chicago.	

8

COMMESSO	*(NOO-meh-roh) (SOO-oh)* **Il numero del suo volo?**	Your flight number?
MARK	*(treh-chehn-toh-TREH)* **Trecentotré da New York.**	303 from New York.
COMMESSO	*(moh-MEHN-toh) (fah-VOH-reh)* **Un momento, per favore.**	One moment, please.

(joh-VAH-nnee)

(As the clerk looks through some papers on his desk, Giovanni, an Italian business friend, runs into Mark.)

GIOVANNI	*(CHAH-oh) (STAH-ee)* **Ciao, Mark. Come stai?**	Hi, Mark. How are you?
MARK	**Giovanni! Sto bene, e tu?**	John! I am well, and you?
GIOVANNI	*(MOHL-toh) (SEH-ee) (kwee)* **Molto bene. Sei qui per una** *(vah-KAHN-tsah)* **vacanza?**	Very well. Are you here for a holiday?
MARK	*(preh-ZEHN-toh) (MEE-ah)* **Sì. Ti presento la mia** *(fah-MEE-llyah) (MOH-llyeh)* **famiglia. Mia moglie Mary, mia** *(FEE-llyah) (FEE-llyoh)* **figlia Anne, e mio figlio John.**	Yes. Let me introduce my family to you. My wife Mary, my daughter Anne, and my son John.
GIOVANNI	*(pyah-CHEH-reh)* **Piacere.**	A pleasure.
COMMESSO	*(SKOO-see)* **Scusi, signore, le valige** *(ah-RREE-vah-noh) (PROH-ssee-moh)* **arrivano con il prossimo volo.**	Excuse me, sir, the suitcases are arriving with the next flight.
MARK	*(ah-chee-DEHN-tee)* **Accidenti!**	Darn it!
GIOVANNI	*(pah-TSYEHN-tsah)* **Pazienza, Mark. Sei in Italia.**	Patience, Mark. You're in Italy.

9

(GRAH-tsee-eh)	
MARK *(to the clerk)* **Grazie**	Thank you and good-bye *(polite)*.
(ah-rree-veh-DEHR-lah)	
e arrivederla.	
(PREH-goh)	
IMPIEGATO **Prego, signore.**	You're welcome, sir.
MARK *(to Giovanni)* **Ciao.**	Good-bye *(familiar)*.
(TOO-ttee)	
GIOVANNI **Arrivederci a tutti.**	Good-bye to all.
(ah-rree-veh-DEHR-chee)	
TUTTI **Arrivederci.**	Good-bye *(familiar)*.

Now without looking back try to fill in the missing dialogue parts. Check your answers from the dialogue only *after* attempting to fill in the parts from memory.

Buon giorno, signore.

B_____ g_____ . Desidera qualcosa?

Sì. Cerco le mie v_____ .

Bene. Come si c_____ , lei?

M ____ c _____ Mark Smith.

Il n_____ del suo v_____ ?

Trecentotré d_____ New York.

Un momento, p_____ f_____ .

By rearranging the following words you will get sentences from the dialogue.
mia / la / presento / Ti / famiglia

_____

arrivano / valige / le / prossimo / volo / il / con / Scusi / signore

_____

tutti / a / Arrivederci

_____

10

LE PERSONE E LE COSE
(pehr-SOH-neh) *(KOH-seh)*

People and Things

One of the first things you will need to know how to do in Italian is naming people and things. Look carefully at the following:

Singolare e plurale
(seen-goh-LAH-reh) *(ploo-RAH-leh)*

singular   plural

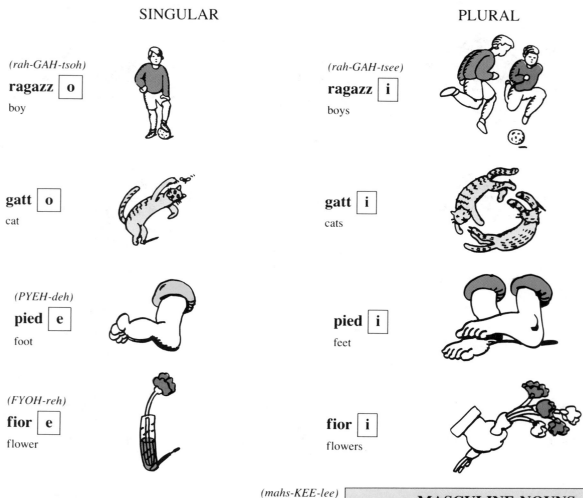

SINGULAR   PLURAL

(rah-GAH-tsoh)
ragazz | o |
boy

(rah-GAH-tsee)
ragazz | i |
boys

gatt | o |
cat

gatt | i |
cats

(PYEH-deh)
pied | e |
foot

pied | i |
feet

(FYOH-reh)
fior | e |
flower

fior | i |
flowers

These are called masculine nouns *(nomi maschili)*.
(mahs-KEE-lee)

Notice that they end in either | o | or | e |.

To form the plural, simply change the | o |

or the | e | to | i |. Got it? This diagram will help you remember.

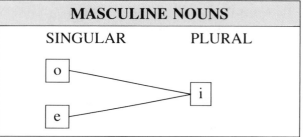

MASCULINE NOUNS

SINGULAR   PLURAL

o

e

i

11

Now look at the following additional nouns.

SINGULAR   PLURAL

cas a
house

(KAH-seh)
cas e
houses

(MEH-lah)
mel a
apple

mel e
apples

(ah-oo-toh-MOH-bee-leh)
automobil e
automobile

(ah-oo-toh-MOH-bee-lee)
automobil i
automobiles

(MAH-dreh)
madr e
mother

madr i
mothers

(feh-mmee-NEE-lee)
These are called feminine nouns *(nomi femminili)*. Notice that they end in either a or e.

To form the plural of those ending in a , simply change the a to e .

To form the plural of those ending in e ,
change the e to i (as in the case
of masculine nouns). The chart at the
right will help you remember how to form
feminine plural nouns.

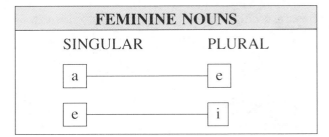

FEMININE NOUNS	
SINGULAR	PLURAL
a ———————	e
e ———————	i

12

An even easier way to remember how to form the plural of any noun is seen in this chart, which simply combines the previous two.

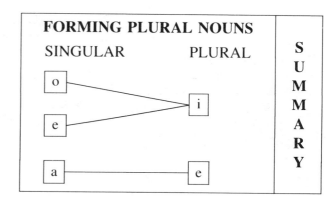

FORMING PLURAL NOUNS

SINGULAR   PLURAL

o
e —————— i

a —————— e

S U M M A R Y

Got it? Now test yourself by trying to put the following nouns into the plural.

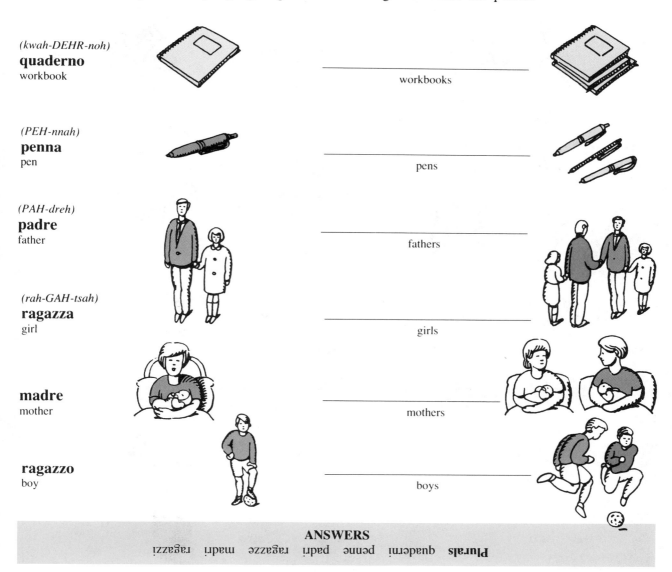

(kwah-DEHR-noh)
quaderno
workbook

_____ workbooks

(PEH-nnah)
penna
pen

_____ pens

(PAH-dreh)
padre
father

_____ fathers

(rah-GAH-tsah)
ragazza
girl

_____ girls

madre
mother

_____ mothers

ragazzo
boy

_____ boys

13

Una, un', uno, un
A and *An*

When we name something (that is, use a noun) in English, we often precede the noun with "a" or "an." The same is true in Italian. Here is how we say these words, depending on whether the noun is masculine or feminine.

WITH FEMININE NOUNS

BEFORE ANY CONSONANT	BEFORE ANY VOWEL

(OO-nah)

| una | *r*agazza |

(ah-MEE-kah)

| un' | *a*mica |
girl friend

| una | *m*adre |

| un' | *a*utomobile |

WITH MASCULINE NOUNS

BEFORE Z OR BEFORE S FOLLOWED BY A CONSONANT	BEFORE ANY OTHER CONSONANT OR ANY VOWEL

(OO-noh)

| uno | *z*io |
uncle

| un | *r*agazzo |

(stoo-DEHN-teh)

| uno | *s*tudente |
male student

| un | *p*adre |

| un | *a*mico |
male friend

(AHL-beh-roh)

| un | *a*lbero |
tree

As you can see, in front of feminine nouns, ''a'' or ''an'' is $\boxed{\text{una}}$ if the noun begins with a consonant, and $\boxed{\text{un'}}$ if it begins with a vowel. In front of masculine nouns, $\boxed{\text{uno}}$ is used if the noun begins with *z* or with *s* plus a consonant (*sp, st, sm,* etc.); otherwise $\boxed{\text{un}}$ is used. Notice that $\boxed{\text{un}}$ does not have an apostrophe in the masculine. The following chart is a handy summary to which you might refer if you run into any difficulties.

SUMMARY—HOW WE SAY ''A'' OR ''AN''	
WITH FEMININE NOUNS	**WITH MASCULINE NOUNS**
una *(before any consonant)*	**uno** *(before z or before s plus a consonant)*
un' *(before any vowel)*	**un** *(before any other consonant or any vowel)*

Now give this a try. Fill in the appropriate form of ''a'' or ''an'' in the space provided for each of the following nouns.

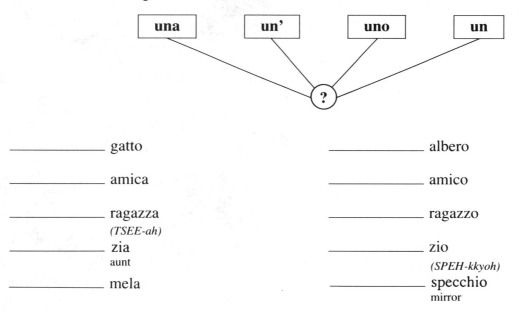

una	**un'**	**uno**	**un**

?

_____ gatto

_____ amica

_____ ragazza

(TSEE-ah)
_____ zia
aunt

_____ mela

_____ albero

_____ amico

_____ ragazzo

_____ zio

(SPEH-kkyoh)
_____ specchio
mirror

15

How did you do? Let's try another, this time filling in both the "a" or "an" and the Italian word for what is shown.

(kee)
Chi è?
Who is it?

(keh)
Che cosa è?
What is it?

a boy

_____

a cat

_____

a foot

_____

a flower

_____

a house

_____

an apple

_____

a car

_____

a pen

_____

a workbook

_____

an uncle

_____

a tree

_____

a mirror

_____

Io, tu, lei e voi
I and You

In Italian, "I" is translated as *(EE-oh)* **io** . This word is not capitalized as in English, unless it is the first word in a sentence.

"You" is represented in several ways:

tu —When addressing friends or family members in the singular (familiar address).

lei —When addressing any stranger or superior in the singular (polite address). May also be capitalized when written **(Lei)**.

voi —As the plural of both **tu** and **lei** in current spoken Italian.

(Although there is a more formal way of addressing more than one person **(loro)**, it is seldom used in the spoken language.)

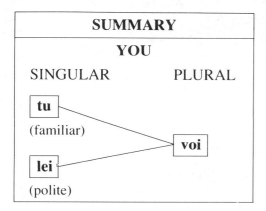

SUMMARY	
YOU	
SINGULAR	PLURAL

tu
(familiar)

voi

lei
(polite)

The chart at the left will help you remember how to say "you" in Italian.

(pahr-LYAH-moh)   *(pah-REHN-tee)*
PARLIAMO DEI PARENTI
Let's Talk About Relatives

Here is Giorgio's family.

And here is Giorgio's family tree. Fill in the blanks to practice the words that tell the different family relationships.

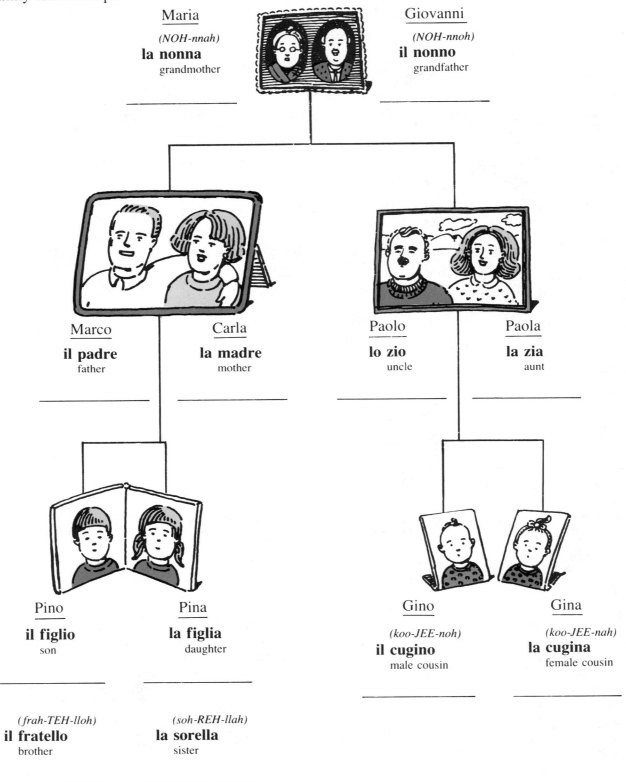

Maria
(NOH-nnah)
la nonna
grandmother

Giovanni
(NOH-nnoh)
il nonno
grandfather

Marco
il padre
father

Carla
la madre
mother

Paolo
lo zio
uncle

Paola
la zia
aunt

Pino
il figlio
son

Pina
la figlia
daughter

Gino
(koo-JEE-noh)
il cugino
male cousin

Gina
(koo-JEE-nah)
la cugina
female cousin

(frah-TEH-lloh)
il fratello
brother

(soh-REH-llah)
la sorella
sister

18

Look carefully at the family tree and then fill in the following blanks. We've done one as an example. *Be careful to copy the forms of "the"* (**il, la, lo**) *correctly.* You should know that **il marito** is the husband and **la moglie** is the wife. Good luck!

Model: Pino è ___*il figlio*___ di Marco.

1. Gino è _____ di Gina.

2. Giovanni è _____ di Carla.

3. Paola è _____ di Pino.

4. Maria è _____ di Pina.

5. Pino è _____ di Gina.

6. Giovanni è _____ di Maria.

7. Paola è _____ di Paolo.

8. Pina è _____ di Pino.

9. Giovanni è _____ di Pina.

10. Carla è _____ di Pino.

11. Gino è _____ di Paola.

12. Paolo è _____ di Pina.

13. Pina è _____ di Gina.

Not so hard, right? Practice your knowledge of family names by finding the plurals of these nouns that are hidden in the puzzle, and then writing them out for additional practice.

cugino _____

cugina _____

zio _____

zia _____

fratello _____

nonna _____

sorella _____

figlio _____

figlia _____

madre _____

padre _____

nonno _____

c	u	g	i	n	i	x	x	x	x	x	x	x	x	x	x	x	x	x	x	z
x	x	x	x	x	x	x	c	u	g	i	n	e	x	x	x	x	x	x	x	i
x	x	x	x	z	x	x	x	x	x	x	x	x	f	r	a	t	e	l	l	i
x	x	x	x	i	x	n	x	x	x	x	x	x	x	x	x	x	x	x	x	x
x	x	x	x	e	x	x	o	x	x	x	x	x	x	x	x	x	x	x	x	x
x	x	x	x	x	x	x	x	n	o	n	n	e	x	x	x	x	x	x	x	x
m	a	d	r	i	x	x	x	x	n	x	x	x	p	a	d	r	i	x	x	x
x	x	x	x	x	x	x	x	x	f	i	g	l	i	x	x	x	x	x	x	x
f	i	g	l	i	e	x	x	x	x	x	x	s	o	r	e	l	l	e	x	x

Now you're really moving! If you're a puzzle fan, give this a try—in Italian, of course.

Across

2. Grandmother
3. You're welcome
5. Something
7. Aunt
8. I live
9. Father

Down

1. Brother
4. Suitcases
6. You live

It is time to return to the Smiths, just beginning their trip to Italy. See if you understand what the following paragraph is all about. Read the selection, then answer the questions that follow.

(fah-MEE-llyah)
La famiglia Smith arriva in Italia
    family
con il volo trecentotré da New York. Il signor
      (DEE-cheh)
Smith dice «Buon giorno» all'impiegato.
   says   clerk
Il signor Smith dice «Grazie» e l'impiegato.
        (een-FEE-neh)
dice «Prego». Infine, il signor Smith dice
        finally
«Arrivederla».

ANSWERS

Crossword Across: 2. nonna 3. prego 5. qualcosa 7. zia 8. abito 9. padre
Down: 1. fratello 4. valigie 6. abita

20

(kee)
Chi arriva da New York?
Who

☐ Il commesso arriva da New York.
☐ Il signor Smith e la sua famiglia arrivano da New York.

(keh)
Che dice il signor Smith?
What

☐ Il signor Smith dice «Buon giorno».
☐ Il signor Smith dice «Ciao».

Che dice l'impiegato?

☐ L'impiegato dice «Accidenti!"»
☐ L'impiegato dice «Prego».

Now study and say aloud these parts of Giorgio's house.

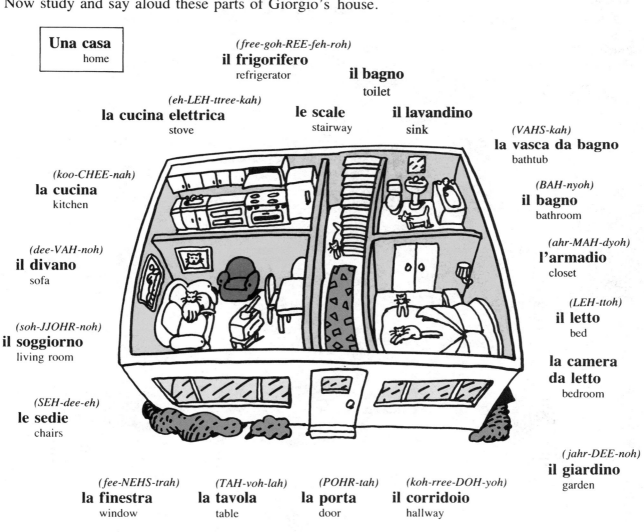

Una casa
home

(free-goh-REE-feh-roh)
il frigorifero
refrigerator

il bagno
toilet

(eh-LEH-ttree-kah)
la cucina elettrica
stove

le scale
stairway

il lavandino
sink

(VAHS-kah)
la vasca da bagno
bathtub

(koo-CHEE-nah)
la cucina
kitchen

(BAH-nyoh)
il bagno
bathroom

(dee-VAH-noh)
il divano
sofa

(ahr-MAH-dyoh)
l'armadio
closet

(soh-JJOHR-noh)
il soggiorno
living room

(LEH-ttoh)
il letto
bed

la camera da letto
bedroom

(SEH-dee-eh)
le sedie
chairs

(jahr-DEE-noh)
il giardino
garden

(fee-NEHS-trah)
la finestra
window

(TAH-voh-lah)
la tavola
table

(POHR-tah)
la porta
door

(koh-rree-DOH-yoh)
il corridoio
hallway

21

ARRIVAL
(ah-RREE-voh)
L' arrivo

| **2** | *(CHEHR-kah)* **In cerca di un posto per la** *(NOH-teh)* **notte** |

Finding a Place to Spend the Night

You'll probably book your hotel room from home—at least for your first night—but whether you have a reservation or not, you'll want to know some basic words that describe the services and facilities you expect to find at your hotel. Learn these words first, and notice how they are used in the dialogue you will read later.

(ahl-BEHR-goh)
l'albergo
hotel

(preh-noh-tah-TSYOH-neh)
la prenotazione
reservation

(PREH-tsoh)
il prezzo
price

(pah-ssah-POHR-toh)
il passaporto
passport

(KAH-meh-rah)
la camera
room

(BAH-nyoh)
il bagno
bathroom

(preh-noh-TAH-reh)
prenotare
to reserve

(eem-PEE-gah-tah)
l'impiegata
female clerk

(kah-meh-RYEH-rah)
la cameriera
maid/waitress

(POHR-tah)
la porta
door

(fee-NEHS-trah)
la finestra
window

22

I diversi modi di dire «the» in italiano
The Many Ways of Saying "The" in Italian

WITH FEMININE NOUNS

SINGULAR	PLURAL

Before Any Consonant

(lah)
la *casa*

(leh)
le *case*

la *ragazza*

le *ragazze*

la *madre*

le *madri*

Before Any Vowel

(OH-rah)
l' *ora*
hour

le *ore*

l' *amica*

(ah-MEE-keh)
le *amiche*

23

WITH MASCULINE NOUNS

SINGULAR	PLURAL

Before z or Before s Plus a Consonant

(loh)
lo *z*io

(llyee)
gli *z*ii

lo *st*udente

gli *st*udenti

Before Any Other Consonant

(eel)
il *r*agazzo

(ee)
i *r*agazzi

il *p*adre

i *p*adri

Before Any Vowel

l' *a*lbero

(llyee)
gli *a*lberi

24

Got it? This chart will help you remember.

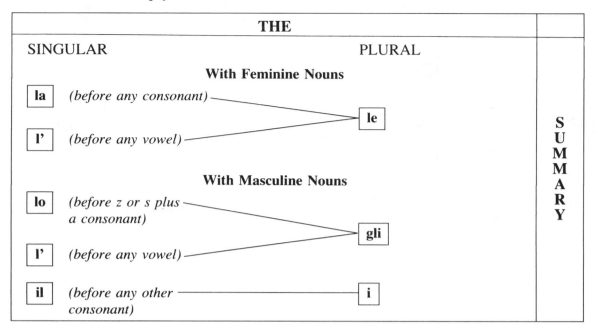

That's it! Now test your familiarity with "the." Choose the appropriate way of saying "the" in front of the following singular nouns.

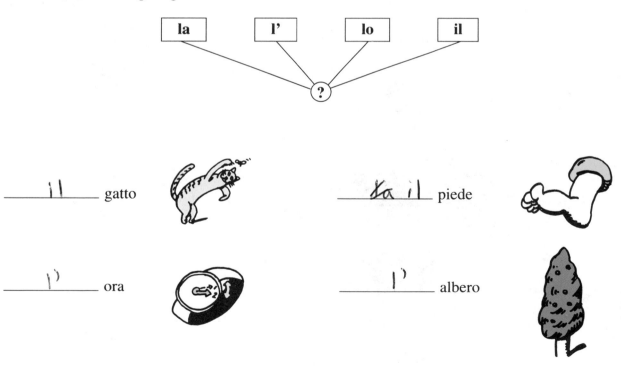

_____ il _____ gatto

_____ la̶ il _____ piede

_____ l' _____ ora

_____ l' _____ albero

25

_____il____ fiore

_____l'____ amica

_____la____ mela

_____la____ penna

Magnifico! Now choose the correct form of "the" in Italian for the same nouns in the plural.

| le | gli | i |

?

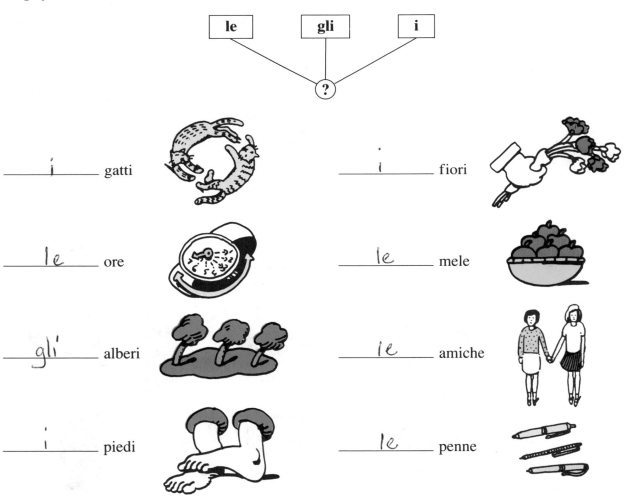

_____i____ gatti

_____i____ fiori

_____le____ ore

_____le____ mele

_____gli____ alberi

_____le____ amiche

_____i____ piedi

_____le____ penne

26

(seh) *(VWOH-EE)* *(KYEH-deh-reh)* *(kwal-KOH-zah)*

SE VUOI CHIEDERE QUALCOSA...

If You Want To Ask For Something

You'll find yourself asking questions every day of your trip—of hotel clerks, tour guides, waiters, and taxi drivers. To form a question, become familiar with these key words.

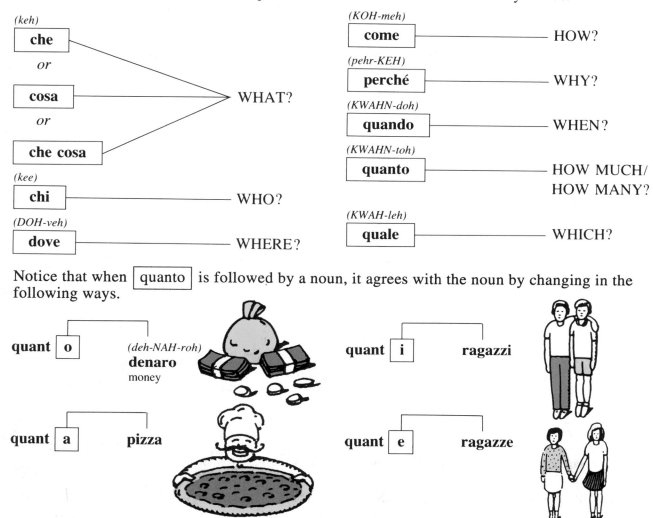

(keh)
| che |
or
| cosa |
or
| che cosa | ——— WHAT?

(kee)
| chi | ——— WHO?

(DOH-veh)
| dove | ——— WHERE?

(KOH-meh)
| come | ——— HOW?

(pehr-KEH)
| perché | ——— WHY?

(KWAHN-doh)
| quando | ——— WHEN?

(KWAHN-toh)
| quanto | ——— HOW MUCH/ HOW MANY?

(KWAH-leh)
| quale | ——— WHICH?

Notice that when | quanto | is followed by a noun, it agrees with the noun by changing in the following ways.

quant | o | *(deh-NAH-roh)* **denaro** money

quant | a | **pizza**

quant | i | **ragazzi**

quant | e | **ragazze**

There are times when you don't even need to use these words to ask a question. Often you can turn a statement into a question by either of these two methods:

(1) raise your voice intonation in the normal way for questions:

(MAHN-jah)
| Il ragazzo mangia la pizza |. ⟶ | Il ragazzo mangia la pizza |?

is eating

or

(2) put the *subject* at the end of the sentence:

| Il ragazzo | | mangia la pizza |. ⟶ | Mangia la pizza |, | il ragazzo |?

27

Now match up each question with its answer.

1. **Che cosa mangia Maria?**

2. **Parla italiano Giovanni?**
   does speak

3. **Perché canti?**
   do you sing

4. **Quando arrivano?**
   do they arrive

5. **Dove arrivano?**

6. **Dov'è la penna?**
   is

7. **Chi è?**
   Who is it?

(EH-kkoh)
a. **Ecco la penna.**
   Here is

b. **Maria mangia la pizza.**

c. **È il padre di Maria.**
   of

d. **Sì, Giovanni parla italiano**
   speaks

(PYAH-cheh)
e. **Canto perché mi piace.**
   I sing   because   I like it

f. **Arrivano domani.**
   tomorrow

(ah-eh-roh-POHR-toh)
g. **Arrivano all' aeroporto.**
   at the   airport

Now here are some more adventures of the Smith family. (We don't recommend that you go to a strange city without a reservation; but let's see how our friends make out.)

Read each line carefully several times out loud. *Role-play* the dialogue.

	(chee) (pwoh)	
MARK	**Scusi, signore, ci può dare una**	Excuse me, sir, can
	(KAH-meh-rah) *(seh-ttee-MAH-nah)* *(oh)*	
	camera per una settimana? Non ho	you give us a room for a
	una prenotazione.	week? I do not have a reservation.
	(eem-poh-SSEE-bee-leh)	
IMPIEGATO	**Impossibile, signore.**	Impossible, sir.
MARK	**Perché?**	Why?
	(ahl-BEHR-goh)	
IMPIEGATO	**Perché l'albergo è molto**	Because the hotel is very full.
	(PYEH-noh)	
	pieno.	

MARK	**Senta, io e la mia famiglia**	Listen, my family and I
	(ah-BBYAH-moh) (bee-ZOH-nyoh) (oor-JEHN-teh)	
	abbiamo bisogno urgente di	urgently need
	(SYAH-moh) (ah-meh-ree-KAH-nee)	
	una camera. Siamo americani.	a room. We are Americans.
	(cheh) (PEE-kkoh-lah)	
IMPIEGATO	**Va bene. C'è una piccola**	Okay. There is a small room on the third floor (fourth floor in North American terms).
	(TEHR-tsoh) (PYAH-noh)	
	camera al terzo piano.	
	(KOHS-tah)	
MARK	**Quanto costa?**	How much does it cost?
	(cheen-kwahn-tah-MEE-lah) (LEE-reh)	
IMPIEGATO	**Cinquantamila lire.**	50.000 lira. (*See unit 25 on banking for information on money.*)
MARK	**D'accordo.**	Okay.
IMPIEGATO	**Come si chiama?**	What's your name?
	(KWEHS-tah)	
MARK	**Sono Mark Smith. Questa è mia**	I am Mark Smith. This is my wife, Mrs. Mary
	(see-NYOH-rah)	
	moglie, la signora Mary Smith. Ecco	Smith. Here are our passports.
	i nostri passaporti.	
IMPIEGATO	**La camera numero trentacinque.**	Room number 35. Here is the key.
	(KYAH-veh)	
	Ecco la chiave.	
	(MEE-lleh)	
MARK	**Grazie mille!**	Thanks a million! (*literally*, a thousand thanks)
IMPIEGATO	**Prego.**	You're welcome.

Now, without looking back, try to complete the missing dialogue parts. Check your answers only *after* attempting to fill in the missing parts from memory.

Scusi, signore, ci può dare una c_____ per una s_____?

Non ho una p_____.

Impossibile, signore.

Perché?

P _____ è molto pieno.

Senta, io e la mia famiglia abbiamo b_____ urgente di una camera. Siamo americani.

29

Va b_____ . C'è una p_____ camera al terzo p_____ .

Q_____ costa?

Cinquantamila l_____ .

Can you make sentences found in the dialogue out of the following scrambled words?

chiave / Ecco / la

_____

signora / la / Questa / moglie / mia / è / Mary Smith

_____

chiama / si / Come

_____

Study and repeat aloud these words referring to a hotel room. Then write the Italian word and draw a line to the appropriate item in the picture.

	(LAHM-pah-dah)	*(LAH-vah-boh)*	*(ah-shoo-gah-MAH-noh)*
lo specchio mirror	**la lampada** lamp	**il lavabo** sink (for washing)	**l'asciugamano** towel

(kah-sseh-TTOH-neh)
il cassettone
chest of drawers

(DOH-chah)
la doccia
shower

la vasca
bathtub

(koo-SHEE-noh)
il cuscino
pillow

(BAH-nyoh)
il bagno
toilet

il letto
bed

il divano/il sofà
sofa

la porta
door

Pronomi e verbi

Pronouns and Verbs

You've already learned how to say "I" and "you" in Italian. Now it's time to move on to the forms for "he," "she," "we," and "they." Here are your new words:

(LOO-ee)

lui ——————————— he

lei ——————————— she (exactly the same as the polite "you")

noi ——————————— we

loro ——————————— they

Use this table to help you remember the Italian pronouns.

PRONOUNS		
io I	**noi** we	S
tu you (familiar)	**voi** you (plural)	U M
lui he	**loro** they (masculine/feminine)	M A
lei she/you (formal)		R Y

Now, here are three common Italian verbs:

(pahr-LAH-reh)	*(kahn-TAH-reh)*	*(ah-rree-VAH-reh)*
parlare	**cantare**	**arrivare**
to speak	to sing	to arrive

Notice that they end in ⬚ are ⬚. So do many other verbs. Watch how they are conjugated.

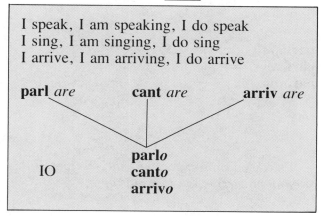

I speak, I am speaking, I do speak
I sing, I am singing, I do sing
I arrive, I am arriving, I do arrive

parl *are*   **cant** *are*   **arriv** *are*

IO   **parl***o*
       cant*o*
       arriv*o*

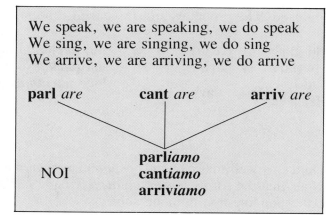

We speak, we are speaking, we do speak
We sing, we are singing, we do sing
We arrive, we are arriving, we do arrive

parl *are*   **cant** *are*   **arriv** *are*

NOI   **parl***iamo*
        cant*iamo*
        arriv*iamo*

31

You speak, you are speaking, you do speak
You sing, you are singing, you do sing
You arrive, you are arriving, you do arrive

parl *are*   **cant** *are*   **arriv** *are*

TU   **parl***i*
          cant*i*
          arriv*i*

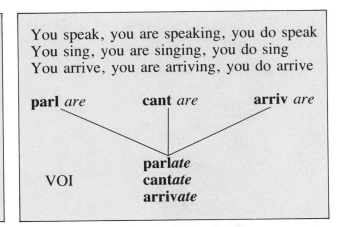

You speak, you are speaking, you do speak
You sing, you are singing, you do sing
You arrive, you are arriving, you do arrive

parl *are*   **cant** *are*   **arriv** *are*

VOI   **parl***ate*
           cant*ate*
           arriv*ate*

He/She speaks, he/she is speaking,
          he/she does speak
He/She sings, he/she is singing,
          he/she does sing
He/She arrives, he/she is arriving,
          he/she does arrive
        also
You (polite) sing, you (polite) are singing,
      you (polite) do sing

parl *are*   **cant** *are*   **arriv** *are*

LUI}
LEI} **parl***a*
       cant*a*
       arriv*a*

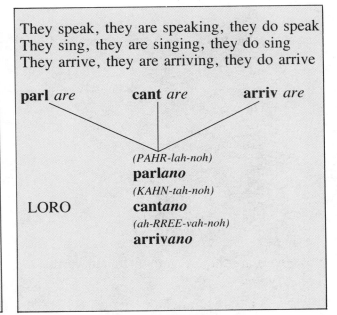

They speak, they are speaking, they do speak
They sing, they are singing, they do sing
They arrive, they are arriving, they do arrive

parl *are*   **cant** *are*   **arriv** *are*

LORO
    (PAHR-lah-noh)
    parl*ano*
    (KAHN-tah-noh)
    cant*ano*
    (ah-RREE-vah-noh)
    arriv*ano*

Got it? Note that the pronouns are not necessary because the endings specify which person is involved. The pronouns are, in general, optional.

io parl*o* or **parl***o*   **noi parl***iamo* or **parl***iamo*
tu parl*i* or **parl***i*   **voi parl***ate* or **parl***ate*
lui}   **loro parl***ano* or **parl***ano*
lei} **parl***a* or **parl***a*

Notice as well that *parlano, cantano, arrivano* are *not* stressed on the ending *-ano*. Be careful! Note that the forms *parla/canta/arriva* and *parlano/cantano/arrivano* are used with corresponding non-pronoun subjects:

| Il ragazzo | parl*a* italiano. | Le zie | cant*ano* bene. | Maria | arriv*a* domani. |

Il ragazzo parl*a* italiano.
The boy speaks Italian.

Le zie cant*ano* bene.
The aunts sing well.

Maria arriv*a* domani.
Mary is arriving tomorrow.

I ragazzi parl*ano* italiano.
The boys speak Italian.

La zia cant*a* bene.
The aunt sings well.

Maria e Carla arriv*ano* domani.
Mary and Carla are arriving tomorrow.

Here's a chart of are verb endings to help you remember.

VERB ENDINGS	
"ARE" VERBS	**S U M M A R Y**

io	-o	noi	-iamo
tu	-i	voi	-ate
lui / lei	-a	loro	-ano

Now test yourself. Add the correct endings to the verb *abitare,* which you have already encountered.
to live in a place

1. (io) abit _____
2. (tu) abit _____
3. (lui) abit _____

4. (lei) abit _____
5. (noi) abit _____
6. (voi) abit _____

7. (loro) abit _____
8. il ragazzo abit _____
9. i ragazzi abit _____

Molto bene! See if you can put the correct endings on the following verbs, and if you understand the sentence.

La ragazza parl_____ italiano.

Gli zii arriv_____ domani.

Tu parl_____ e io cant_____.

Noi cant_____ e voi parl_____.

Note: To make any verb negative, just add non before it.

parlo —I speak

cantano —they sing

non **parlo** —I do not speak

non **cantano** —they do not sing

33

Slow down! If you are getting confused, just ease up your pace and review what you've learned so far. *Capisci?* (Do you understand?) See how much Italian you already know by doing the following "verb" crossword puzzle.

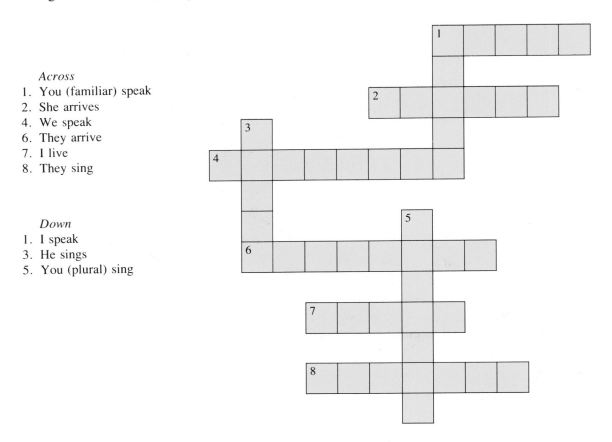

Across
1. You (familiar) speak
2. She arrives
4. We speak
6. They arrive
7. I live
8. They sing

Down
1. I speak
3. He sings
5. You (plural) sing

Now see if you remember what you have learned about forming questions by matching up the answers on the right to the questions on the left.

1. Che cosa è?
2. Chi non parla italiano?
3. Dove abita lei?
4. Come si chiama lei?
5. Quando arrivano le valige?
6. Quanto costa la camera?

a. Abito a Roma.
b. È una valigia.
c. Mi chiamo Giovanni Spina.
d. Il non parlo italiano.
e. Costa 50.000 lire.
f. Arrivano domani.

Test yourself on the many ways to say "the" by matching up the nouns on the right with the appropriate forms of "the" on the left.

1. l'   a. finestra
2. lo   b. porta
3. la   c. albergo
4. lo   d. camera
5. la   e. amica
6. la   f. amico
7. l'   g. specchio
8. il   h. zio
9. il   i. passaporto
10. l'   j. bagno

Now try to put the correct plural form (*le*, *gli*, or *i*) in front of these nouns (which are now plural).

_____ finestre   _____ amici

_____ porte   _____ specchi

_____ alberghi   _____ zii

_____ camere   _____ passaporti

_____ amiche   _____ bagni

The following brief passage will allow you to test your comprehension of what you have learned so far. Read it several times, then try to choose the correct answer to each question.

Il signor Jones non ha una prenotazione all'albergo. Non

ci sono più camere. Allora, la signora Jones dice all'impiegato

che sono americani. L'impiegato dice che c'è una piccola
that
camera al terzo piano. La camera non ha il bagno e costa

cinquantamila lire.

Chi non ha la prenotazione?
☐ Il signor Jones non ha la prenotazione.
☐ L'impiegato non ha la prenotazione.

Che cosa dice la signora Jones?
☐ Dice "Buon giorno."
☐ Dice che sono americani.

Ha il bagno?
☐ Sì.
☐ No.

Ci sono camere?
☐ Sì.
☐ No.

Dov'è la piccola camera?
☐ Al terzo piano.
☐ A Chicago.

Quanto costa?
☐ 45.000 lire.
☐ 50.000 lire.

SEEING THE SIGHTS

(POON-tee) *(een-teh-REH-sseh)*
I punti d'interesse

3	*(JEE-roh)* *(PYEH-dee)* **In giro a piedi** Finding Your Way on Foot/Getting Around on Foot

"How do I get to . . . ?" "Where is the nearest subway?" "Is the museum straight ahead?" You'll be asking directions and getting answers wherever you travel. Acquaint yourself with the words and phrases that will make getting around easier. Don't forget to read each line out loud several times to practice your pronunciation, and act out each part to be certain you understand these new words.

(John and Anne set out on their first day to visit a museum.)

(kyeh-DYAH-moh) *(VEE-jee-leh)* ANNE **John, chiediamo al vigile dove si** *(moo-ZEH-oh)* **trova il museo.**	John, let's ask the policeman how to find the museum.
JOHN *(to the policeman)* **Scusi, signore, ci sa** **dire dove si trova il museo?**	Excuse me, sir, can you tell us how to find the museum?
(CHER-toh) *(dee-REE-tee)* VIGILE **Certo. Andate diritti fino a Via** *(see-NEES-trah)* **Verdi; poi a sinistra a Via Rossini; e**	Certainly. Go straight to Verdi Street, then to the left at Rossini Street, and then to the right

36

(DEHS-trah)
poi a destra a Via Dante, dove c'è il   at Dante Street, where the traffic lights are.
(seh-MAH-foh-roh)
semaforo. Il museo si trova a due   The museum can be found two blocks after the
(ee-zoh-LAH-tee)
isolati dopo il semaforo.   traffic lights.

JOHN   **Grazie mille.**   Thanks a million.

(cheh) (keh)
VIGILE   **Non c'è di che.**   Don't mention it.

(after having followed the directions)
(KWEHS-toh)
ANNE   **Questo non è il museo.**   This is not the museum.

(oo-FFEE-choh) (pohs-TAH-leh)
È l'ufficio   postale.   It's the post office.

(TAHR-dee)
JOHN   **Pazienza. È tardi. Torniamo**   Patience. It's late. Let's

all'albergo.   go back to the hotel.

Now see if you can fill in the missing dialogue parts without looking back. Check your answers only after attempting to complete the missing parts from memory.

John, c_____ al vigile dove si trova il m_____.

Scusi, signore, ci sa d_____ dove si t_____ il museo?

C_____. Andate d_____ fino a Via Verdi; poi a s_____

a Via Rossini, e poi a d_____ a Via Dante, dove c'è il s_____.

Il museo si trova a due i_____ dopo il semaforo.

Grazie m_____.

Non c'è di c_____.

COME SI FA PER ANDARE A . . . ?

How Do I Get to . . . ?

La ragazza va | a | **Roma.**
goes

The girl goes *to* Rome.

Il signor Smith abita | in | **America.**

Mr. Smith lives *in* America.

La ragazza viene | da | **Roma.**
comes

The girl comes *from* Rome.

Odore | di | **piedi!**
smell
Smell *of* feet!

Il gatto è | su | **un tetto.**

The cat is *on* a roof.

Il museo è | lontano | **dal semaforo.**

The museum is *far* from the traffic lights.

Il gatto è | vicino a | **un fiore.**

The cat is *near* a flower.

La porta è | a destra | **e la**

finestra è | a sinistra |.

The door is *to the right* and the window is *to the left*.

La pizza è | per | **lo zio.**

The pizza is *for* the uncle.

Gli spaghetti | con | **il formaggio.**

Spaghetti *with* cheese.

Maria arriva | dopo | **sua madre.**

Mary arrives *after* her mother.

L'uomo è | su | **un tetto.**

The man is *on* a roof.

Il gatto è | accanto a | **una gatta.**

The male cat is *next to* a female cat.

38

Can you match up the following?

1. con il formaggio	a. after her mother
2. accanto a una gatta	b. with cheese
3. dopo sua madre	c. next to a female cat
4. a destra	d. to the left
5. a sinistra	e. to the right
6. a Roma	f. the smell of feet
7. da Roma	g. for the uncle
8. odore di piedi	h. from Rome
9. per lo zio	i. to Rome
10. vicino a un fiore	j. in America
11. su un tetto	k. far from the traffic lights
12. lontano dal semaforo	l. on a roof
13. in America	m. near a flower

I verbi ancora una volta
Verbs Once Again

In the previous unit you learned about "are" verbs. Now you will learn about "ere" verbs.

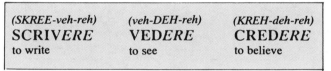

(SKREE-veh-reh) **SCRIVERE** to write	(veh-DEH-reh) **VEDERE** to see	(KREH-deh-reh) **CREDERE** to believe

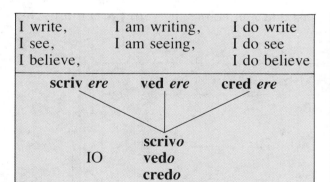

I write,   I am writing,   I do write
I see,   I am seeing,   I do see
I believe,   I do believe

scriv *ere*   **ved** *ere*   **cred** *ere*

IO   **scriv***o*
     ved*o*
     cred*o*

We write,   we are writing,   we do write
We see,   we are seeing,   we do see
We believe,   we do believe

scriv *ere*   **ved** *ere*   **cred** *ere*

NOI   **scriv***iamo*
     ved*iamo*
     cred*iamo*

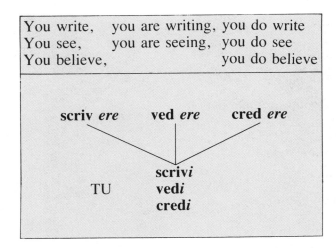

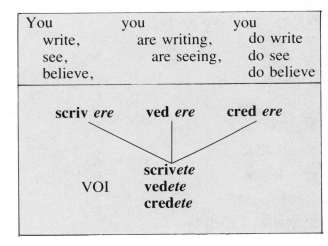

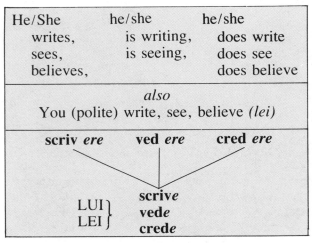

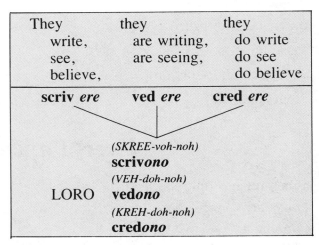

Once again, notice that the pronouns are optional and that *scrivono, vedono, credono* are not stressed on the ending *-ono*. To form the negative, just add *non* before the verb (as before). The following chart is a summary of "ere" verbs.

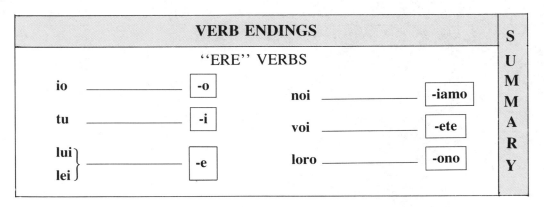

Now test your learning of these verbs in the following phrases, to get the control over an "ere" verb.

L'impiegato *scriv* _____ .   Io non *cred* _____ a Maria.   Tu non *ved* _____ il semaforo.

40

Io *scriv*_____ a Maria.

Noi *cred*_____ a Maria.

I gatti non *scriv*_____.

Voi *ved*_____ il vigile.

I ragazzi non *ved*_____
il semaforo.

Alcune parole utili
Some Useful Words

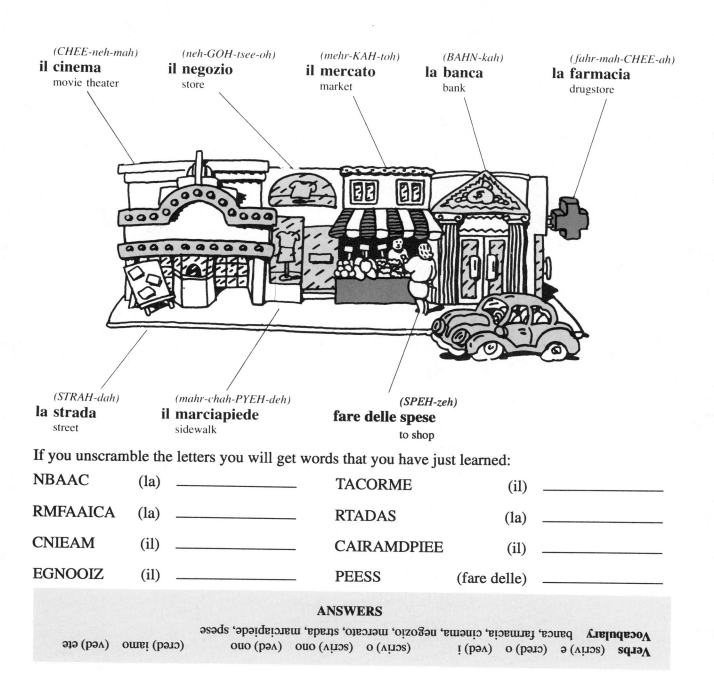

(CHEE-neh-mah)
il cinema
movie theater

(neh-GOH-tsee-oh)
il negozio
store

(mehr-KAH-toh)
il mercato
market

(BAHN-kah)
la banca
bank

(fahr-mah-CHEE-ah)
la farmacia
drugstore

(STRAH-dah)
la strada
street

(mahr-chah-PYEH-deh)
il marciapiede
sidewalk

(SPEH-zeh)
fare delle spese
to shop

If you unscramble the letters you will get words that you have just learned:

NBAAC	(la) _____		TACORME	(il) _____	
RMFAAICA	(la) _____		RTADAS	(la) _____	
CNIEAM	(il) _____		CAIRAMDPIEE	(il) _____	
EGNOOIZ	(il) _____		PEESS	(fare delle) _____	

Come si indicano le cose in italiano

How to Point Out Things in Italian

Words like "this" and "that" are important to know, particularly when you go shopping and want to buy that good-looking pair of gloves in the shop window. The Italian forms of these words vary, depending on whether the item is masculine or feminine, and whether you are pointing to one item or to many.

THIS AND THESE

WITH FEMININE NOUNS

Singular (this)
(KWEHS-tah)

| questa | ragazza |

Plural (these)
(KWEHS-teh)

| queste | ragazze |

| questa | madre |

| queste | madri |

WITH MASCULINE NOUNS

Singular
(KWEHS-toh)

| questo | ragazzo |

Plural
(KWEHS-tee)

| questi | ragazzi |

| questo | studente |

| questi | studenti |

| questo | zio |

| questi | zii |

In front of vowels, you may drop the vowel *in the singular* if you wish:

| questa amica | *or* | quest'amica |
| questo amico | *or* | quest'amico |

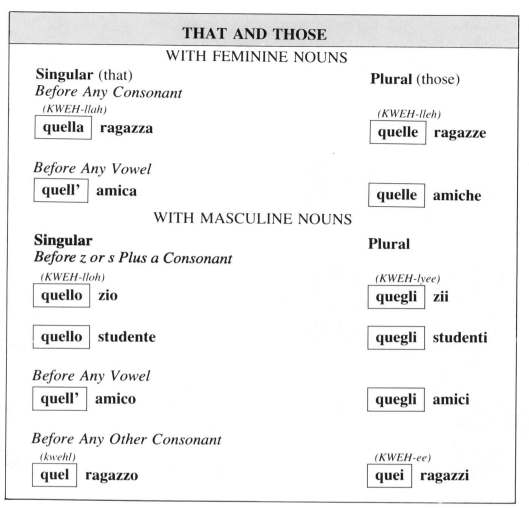

THAT AND THOSE

WITH FEMININE NOUNS

Singular (that)   **Plural** (those)
Before Any Consonant

(KWEH-llah)   *(KWEH-lleh)*

| quella | ragazza | | quelle | ragazze |

Before Any Vowel

| quell' | amica | | quelle | amiche |

WITH MASCULINE NOUNS

Singular   **Plural**
Before z or s Plus a Consonant

(KWEH-lloh)   *(KWEH-lyee)*

| quello | zio | | quegli | zii |

| quello | studente | | quegli | studenti |

Before Any Vowel

| quell' | amico | | quegli | amici |

Before Any Other Consonant

(kwehl)   *(KWEH-ee)*

| quel | ragazzo | | quei | ragazzi |

This table will help you remember these words.

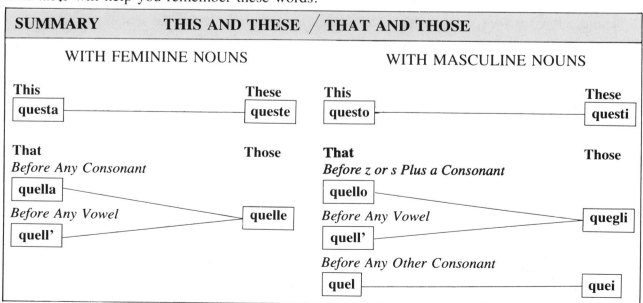

SUMMARY   THIS AND THESE / THAT AND THOSE

WITH FEMININE NOUNS   **WITH MASCULINE NOUNS**

This   **These**   **This**   **These**
| questa | | queste | | questo | | questi |

That   **Those**   **That**   **Those**
Before Any Consonant   *Before z or s Plus a Consonant*
| quella | | quello |

Before Any Vowel | quelle | *Before Any Vowel* | quegli |
| quell' | | quell' |

                                                     Before Any Other Consonant
                                                     | quel | | quei |

43

Now practice what you have learned. Fill in the appropriate form of "this" or "that" for each of these singular nouns.

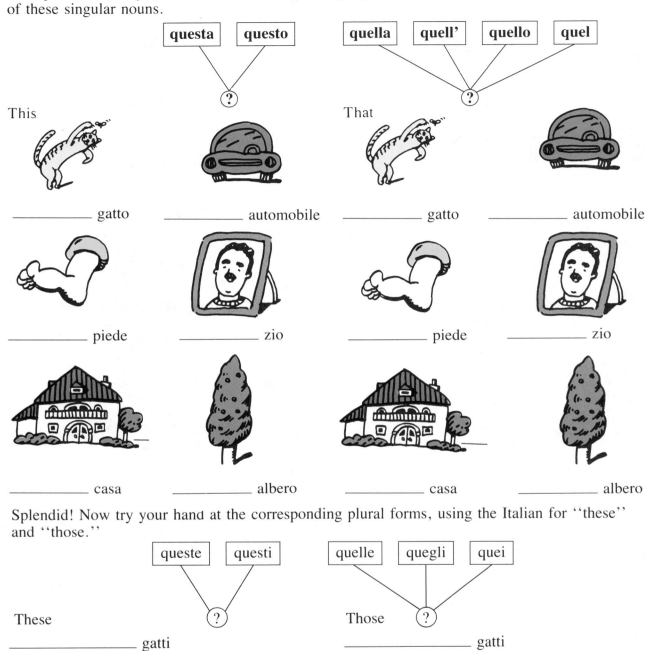

This

_____ gatto   _____ automobile

_____ piede   _____ zio

_____ casa   _____ albero

That

_____ gatto   _____ automobile

_____ piede   _____ zio

_____ casa   _____ albero

Splendid! Now try your hand at the corresponding plural forms, using the Italian for "these" and "those."

These

_____ gatti
_____ piedi

Those

_____ gatti
_____ piedi

_____ case   _____ case

_____ automobili   _____ automobili

_____ zii   _____ zii

_____ alberi   _____ alberi

Now you really have it. Can you change the following "this/these" forms to their corresponding "that/those" forms? Good luck!

questo marciapiede _____ marciapiede   questi alberghi _____ alberghi

questi marciapiedi _____ marciapiedi   quest'amica _____ amica

questa strada _____ strada   queste amiche _____ amiche

queste strade _____ strade   questo zio _____ zio

quest'albergo _____ albergo   questi zii _____ zii

For a quick refresher, complete the endings for the verb _vedere,_ too.

1. Maria non ved_____ Carlo.

2. Noi ved_____ la zia di Maria.

3. I ragazzi ved_____ i fiori.

4. Io non ved_____ i fiori.

5. Tu ved_____ lo zio di Carlo.

45

Now fill in the blanks with one of the following: | a | da | di | vicino | accanto |

Maria va _____ Roma.

Il gatto è _____ al fiore.

Pino è il cugino _____ Gina.

Io abito _____ a Maria.

La ragazza arriva _____ Firenze.

Have fun with the following crossword puzzle.

Across
2. Post office
5. Movie theater
6. Store
7. Sidewalk
8. Street

Down
1. Bank
3. Pharmacy
4. Patience
7. Market

What's happening to Maria? Read the passage to review your words for directions.

Maria chiede al vigile dove si trova la banca. Il vigile dice di andare a destra e poi a sinistra.

Maria arriva al semaforo e non vede la banca, ma vede l'ufficio postale. Allora torna
but

all'albergo.

Now, select the appropriate answers.

Chi chiede al vigile dove
si trova la banca?

☐ L'ufficio postale.
☐ Il museo.
☐ Maria.

Che cosa dice il vigile?

☐ Dice di andare a destra e poi a sinistra.
☐ Dice di tornare all'albergo.
☐ Dice «Buon giorno».

Dove arriva Maria?

☐ Maria arriva all'aeroporto.
☐ Maria arriva a Roma.
☐ Maria arriva al semaforo.

Che cosa vede?

☐ Vede l'albergo.
☐ Vede l'ufficio postale.
☐ Vede il vigile.

Dove torna?

☐ Torna in America.
☐ Torna a Roma.
☐ Torna all'albergo.

4 | (MEH-tsee) (trahs-POHR-toh) (POO-bblee-chee)
Mezzi di trasporto pubblici
Public Transportation

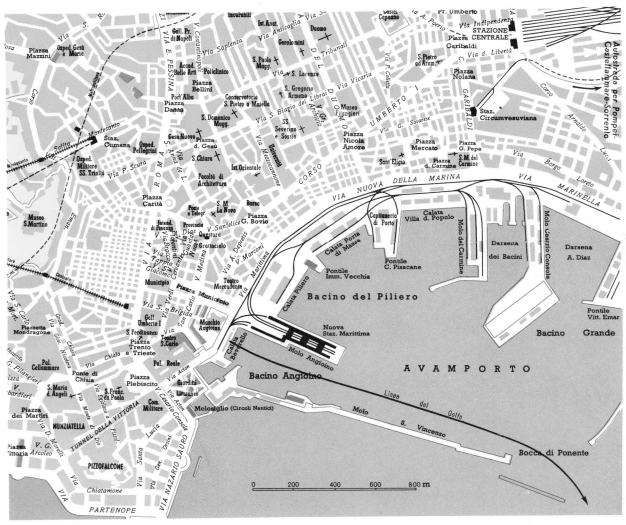

Bus Map of Naples

(Courtesy of Bonechi Publishers, Florence)

The following dialogue contains some useful words and expressions that you might find helpful when you will need to use public means of transportation.

Remember to read each line out loud several times and to act out each part.

MARY   *(prehn-DYAH-moh) (tah-SSEE)*
Prendiamo il tassì per andare   Shall we take the taxi to go to the movies?

al cinema?

MARK   **Quanto lontano è?**   How far is it?

48

MARY	**Si trova in Via Verdi.**
	It's on Verdi Street.
MARK	**No. Costa troppo.**
	No. It costs too much.
MARY	**Allora prendiamo la** *(meh-troh-poh-lee-TAH-nah)* **metropolitana.**
	Then let's take the subway.
MARK	**Penso che non ce ne sia una.**
	I don't think there is one.
MARY	**Allora prendiamo l'autobus.**
	Then let's take the bus.
MARK	**Va bene.**
	Okay.

(A while later, they get on a bus.)

MARK	**Scusi, signore, questo autobus va fino a Via Verdi?**
	Excuse me, sir, does this bus go to Verdi Street?
CONDUCENTE	**Sì, ma lei dove va?**
	Yes, but where are you going?
MARK	*(shehn-DYAH-moh)* **Scendiamo al cinema. Quanto costa** *(bee-LLYEH-ttoh)* **un biglietto?**
	We are getting off at the movie theater. How much does a ticket cost?
CONDUCENTE	**Mille lire, signore, e** *(dee-vehr-tee-MEHN-toh)* **buon divertimento.***
	1,000 lira *(see unit 25)*, sir, and enjoy yourself.
MARK	*(kohn-doo-TTOH-reh)* *(seem-PAH-tee-koh)* **Che conducente simpatico!** *(kohr-TEH-zee)* **Come sono cortesi gli italiani!**
	What a nice driver! How courteous the Italians are!

Che cosa è?

_____ _____ _____ _____

Obviously, Mark did not know that bus tickets are purchased before getting on a bus in Italy.

ANSWERS

Identification (È) un tassì (È) un autobus (È) una metropolitana (È) un'automobile

49

Altre parole che esprimono azioni
More Action Words

Now you will learn about "ire" verbs.

(dohr-MEE-reh)	*(pahr-TEE-reh)*	*(sehn-TEE-reh)*
dormire	**partire**	**sentire**
to sleep	to leave/depart	to hear

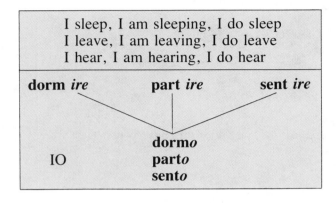

I sleep, I am sleeping, I do sleep
I leave, I am leaving, I do leave
I hear, I am hearing, I do hear

dorm *ire*　　**part** *ire*　　**sent** *ire*

IO　　**dorm***o*
　　　part*o*
　　　sent*o*

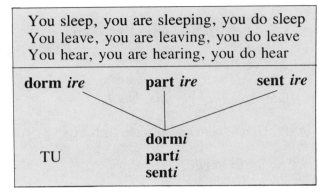

You sleep, you are sleeping, you do sleep
You leave, you are leaving, you do leave
You hear, you are hearing, you do hear

dorm *ire*　　**part** *ire*　　**sent** *ire*

TU　　**dorm***i*
　　　part*i*
　　　sent*i*

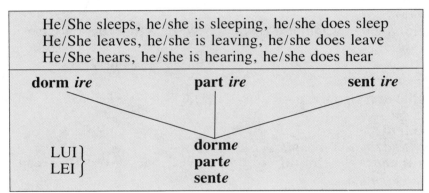

He/She sleeps, he/she is sleeping, he/she does sleep
He/She leaves, he/she is leaving, he/she does leave
He/She hears, he/she is hearing, he/she does hear

dorm *ire*　　**part** *ire*　　**sent** *ire*

LUI ⎫
LEI ⎭　　**dorm***e*
　　　part*e*
　　　sent*e*

We sleep, we are sleeping, we do sleep
We leave, we are leaving, we do leave
We hear, we are hearing, we do hear

dorm *ire*　　**part** *ire*　　**sent** *ire*

NOI　　**dorm***iamo*
　　　part*iamo*
　　　sent*iamo*

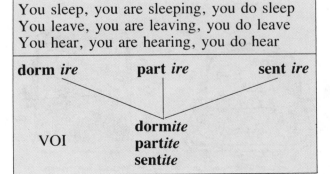

You sleep, you are sleeping, you do sleep
You leave, you are leaving, you do leave
You hear, you are hearing, you do hear

dorm *ire*　　**part** *ire*　　**sent** *ire*

VOI　　**dorm***ite*
　　　part*ite*
　　　sent*ite*

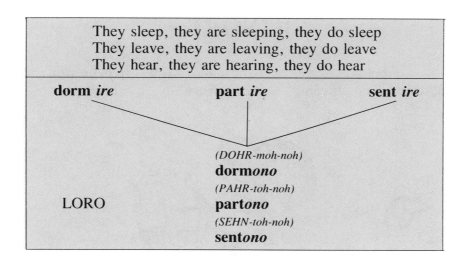

They sleep, they are sleeping, they do sleep
They leave, they are leaving, they do leave
They hear, they are hearing, they do hear

dorm *ire*   **part** *ire*   **sent** *ire*

LORO

(DOHR-moh-noh)
dorm*ono*

(PAHR-toh-noh)
part*ono*

(SEHN-toh-noh)
sent*ono*

As in the case of "are" and "ere" verbs, notice that the pronouns are optional and that *dormono, partono, sentono* are not stressed on the ending *-ono*. Remember that to form the negative you just put *non* before the verb. The following chart will help you remember the endings for "ire" verbs.

VERB ENDINGS		
"IRE" VERBS		**S U M M A R Y**

io _____	-o		**noi** _____	-iamo	
tu _____	-i		**voi** _____	-ite	
lui } **lei** } _____	-e		**loro** _____	-ono	

Practice the technique of forming "ire" verbs by adding the correct endings to the following:

(VOH-cheh)
L'autista sent_____ la voce del
voice
signor Smith.

Il signor Smith e sua moglie dorm_____
tutto il giorno.
all
Io part_____ domani.

Tu non part_____ domani.

Voi dorm_____ tutto il giorno.

Noi sent_____ la voce della signora
Smith.

51

SIGNORE . . .

How to Tell the Conductor . . .

(ah-oo-TEES-tah)
l'autista/il conducente
driver

(kohm-PRAH-reh)
comprare
to buy

(SHEHN-deh-reh)
scendere
to get off

(fehr-MAH-tah)
la fermata
stop

(bee-LLYEH-ttoh)
il biglietto
ticket

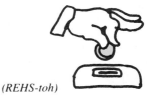

(REHS-toh)
il resto
change

Here are some verbs that don't follow the rules. You've learned how to use common verbs that end in "are," "ere," and "ire." Unfortunately, using verbs isn't that simple! *Naturalmente!* There are exceptions to the rules, and we call them "irregular verbs." Here are some common irregular verbs—notice how they take on different forms, depending upon the subject. It is hard work, but you just have to learn these well, 'cause you will want to use them often.

IRREGULAR VERBS				
ANDARE to go	**VENIRE** to come	**FARE** to do/make	**DARE** to give	**DIRE** to say/tell
IO **vado**	*(VEHN-goh)* **vengo**	*(FAH-choh)* **faccio**	**do**	*(DEE-koh)* **dico**
TU *(VAH-ee)* **vai**	*(VYEH-nee)* **vieni**	*(FAH-ee)* **fai**	*(DAH-ee)* **dai**	*(DEE-chee)* **dici**
LUI ⎫ **LEI ⎭** **va**	*(VYEH-neh)* **viene**	**fa**	**dà**	*(DEE-cheh)* **dice**
NOI **andiamo**	**veniamo**	*(fah-CHAH-moh)* **facciamo**	**diamo**	*(dee-CHAH-moh)* **diciamo**
VOI **andate**	**venite**	**fate**	**date**	**dite**
LORO **vanno**	*(VEHN-goh-noh)* **vengono**	**fanno**	**danno**	*(DEE-koh-noh)* **dicono**

Now fill in the blanks with the appropriate verb forms. How many can you complet...
looking back?

Io *vado* a Roma e tu _____ a Firenze. Il ragazzo *va* al negozio e loro _____ al c...
                                               store

Noi *andiamo* a Venezia e voi _____ a Pisa. Io *vengo* da Napoli e tu _____ da Milan...

Il signore *viene* da Bologna e loro _____ da Torino.

Voi *venite* da Palermo e noi _____ da Trieste.
         (AHN-keh)
Tu *fai* delle spese e **anche** io _____ delle spese.
      shop   also

Il ragazzo non *fa* delle spese, ma voi _____ delle spese **sempre.**
                                           always

Noi *facciamo* delle spese e anche voi _____ delle spese.

Io *dico* «buon giorno» e tu _____ **«buona sera».**
                              good evening/good afternoon

Have some fun finding the Italian translations for the following verbs in the word search puzzle.
To reinforce your memory, write each one in the space provided.

x	x	(v	a	n	n	o)	x	x	x	x	x	x	x	v	x	x	x	x	x	x	x	x	x
x	x	x	x	x	x	x	x	x	x	x	x	x	e	x	x	x	d	x	x	x	x	x	f
x	d	x	x	x	x	v	i	e	n	e	x	x	x	n	x	x	x	a	x	x	x	x	a
x	x	i	x	x	x	x	x	x	x	x	x	x	g	x	x	x	n	x	x	x	x	x	c
x	x	x	c	x	x	x	x	x	x	x	x	x	o	x	x	x	n	x	x	x	x	x	c
x	x	x	x	o	x	x	x	x	x	x	x	x	x	x	x	x	o	x	x	x	x	x	i
x	x	f	a	n	n	o	x	x	x	x	x	x	x	x	x	x	x	x	x	x	x	x	o
x	x	x	x	x	x	o	x	d	i	c	o	x	x	x	d	i	a	m	o	x	x	x	x
v	a	d	o	x	x	x	x	x	x	x	x	x	x	x	x	x	x	x	x	x	x	x	x

1. they go _____ 2. she comes _____ 3. I come _____

4. I do _____ 5. they give _____ 6. I say _____

7. they say _____ 8. we give _____ 9. they do _____

10. I go _____

ANSWERS

Word search 1. vanno 2. viene 3. vengo 4. faccio 5. danno 6. dico 7. dicono
8. diamo 9. fanno 10. vado

Irregular verbs via (a Firenze.) vanno (al cinema.) andate (a Pisa.) vieni (da Milano.)
vengono (da Torino.) veniamo (da Trieste.) faccio (delle spese.) fate (delle spese sempre.)
fate (delle spese.) dici («buona sera.»)

53

e preposizioni ancora una volta

Getting Back to Prepositions

Italian for
"," "to," and
alled
, in, di, da,
fore "the,"
they "contract"; that is, they
become one word with the various
forms of "the."

di + il	su + il
È il libro **del** ragazzo.	Il gatto è **sul** tetto.
of the	on the
(It is the book *of the* boy.)	(The cat is *on the* roof.)

The contractions are summarized for you in the following chart.

		PREPOSITIONS THAT CAN BE CONTRACTED					
+	LA	LE	L'	LO	GLI	IL	I
A	**alla**	**alle**	**all'**	**allo**	**agli**	**al**	**ai**
IN	**nella**	**nelle**	**nell'**	**nello**	**negli**	**nel**	**nei**
DI	**della**	**delle**	**dell'**	**dello**	**degli**	**del**	**dei**
DA	**dalla**	**dalle**	**dall'**	**dallo**	**dagli**	**dal**	**dai**
SU	**sulla**	**sulle**	**sull'**	**sullo**	**sugli**	**sul**	**sui**

Now try to use some of these in the following.

La ragazza arriva _____ aeroporto domani.
at the

Il gatto è _____ albero.
on the

Quei libri **sono** _____ amiche di Pino.
are of the

Quelle penne sono _____ amici di Maria.
of the

Lo zio è _____ banca.
in the

Quel signore è _____ farmacia.
in the

Maria va _____ mercato.
to the

Giovanni fa delle spese _____
in the

negozi di Roma.

Marco scende _____ autobus.
from the

Di
Some

The word "some" in Italian is expressed by using *di* plus *the* (see also the previous cha~

A

un libro

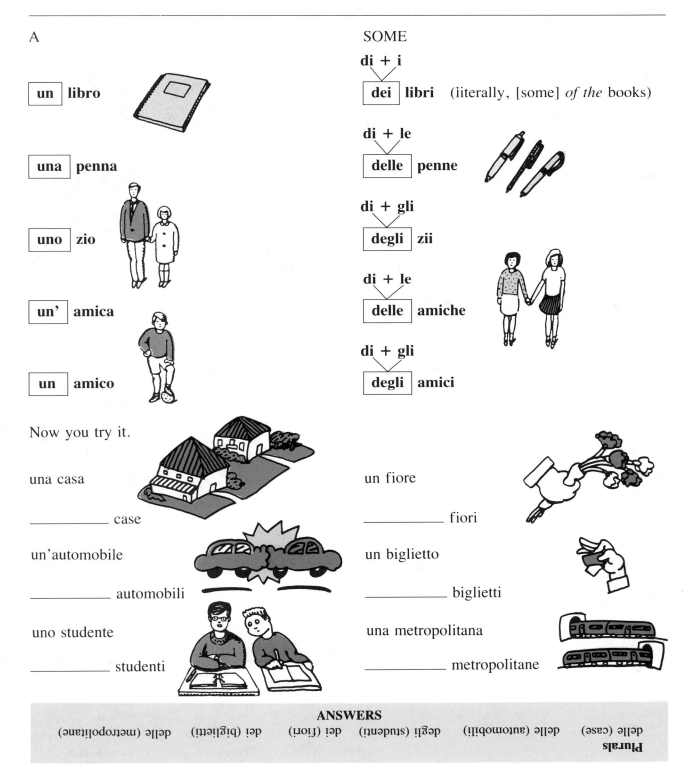

una penna

uno zio

un' amica

un amico

Now you try it.

una casa

_____ case

un'automobile

_____ automobili

uno studente

_____ studenti

SOME

di + i

dei libri (literally, [some] *of the* books)

di + le

delle penne

di + gli

degli zii

di + le

delle amiche

di + gli

degli amici

un fiore

_____ fiori

un biglietto

_____ biglietti

una metropolitana

_____ metropolitane

ANSWERS

Plurals

delle (case)   delle (automobili)   degli (studenti)   dei (fiori)   dei (biglietti)   delle (metropolitane)

55

ead the following brief passage. What you have learned will help you get where you are going. Then, select the appropriate answer to each question.

Il signor Rossi e sua moglie prendono l'autobus per due fermate. Poi prendono la

two   (KOH-zeh)

metropolitana. Loro scendono in Via Verdi. Arrivano al mercato e comprano molte cose.

things

Che cosa prendono il signor Rossi
e sua moglie per due fermate?
- ☐ Prendono la metropolitana.
- ☐ Prendono il tassì.
- ☐ Prendono l'autobus.

Poi che cosa prendono?
- ☐ Prendono la metropolitana.
- ☐ Prendono il tassì.
- ☐ Prendono l'autobus.

Dove scendono?
- ☐ Scendono in Via Rossini.
- ☐ Scendono in Via Verdi.
- ☐ Scendono in Via Dante.

Che cosa comprano?
- ☐ Comprano un libro.
- ☐ Comprano molte cose.
- ☐ Comprano una penna.

Now for review, fill in the missing verb endings.

1. Maria part_____ domani.

2. Loro dorm_____ tutto il giorno.

3. Io non dorm_____ al cinema!

4. Io part_____ domani e tu part

_____ questa **sera**.
evening

5. Tu dorm_____ sull'autobus.

6. Noi part_____ questa sera.

7. Voi non dorm_____ in quell'albergo.

Now let's see if you remember your prepositions.

Maria va _____ negozio.
to the

Io vengo _____ farmacia.
from the

Ecco la penna _____ amico di Maria.
of the

Maria **sale** _____ autobus.
gets on   the

Giovanni è _____ banca.
in the

CHE ORA È / CHE ORE SONO?

What Time Is It?

Tokio	Anchorage	New York	Parigi	Mosca
Sono le nove.	Sono le tre.	Sono le otto.	È l'una.	Sono le tre.

Expressing time is easy. Simply state the hour preceded by *le*. This is true for all hours except one o'clock, for which you use *l'*.

To add minutes, just use *e* ("and").

Sono le sei e dieci (6:10).   **Sono le sette e venti (7:20).**   **Sono le nove e trentanova (9:39).**

If the minute hand is close to the next hour, you can also tell time by quoting the next hour **meno** (minus) the number of minutes to go.

Sono le dieci e cinquanta. =
Sono le undici meno dieci (10:50).

Sono le undici e cinquantacinque. =
Sono le dodici meno cinque (11:55).

You can replace the quarter hours and the half-hours with the following expressions.

2:15 = le due e quindici = le due e	**un quarto**
3:30 = le tre e trenta = le tre e	**mezzo** / **mezza**
4:45 = le quattro e quarantacinque = le quattro e	**tre quarti** =
le cinque meno	**un quarto**

For A.M. you can use the expression | **di mattina** | ; for P.M. you can use | **di sera** | for the late afternoon and evening, and | **del pomeriggio** | for the early afternoon.

For official time, Italian uses the "24-hour clock."

> **Mario arriva al*le tredici e venti* = 13:20 = 1:20 P.M.**
> **Giovanni parte al*le diciotto e dieci* = 18:10 = 6:10 P.M.**
> **Il signor Smith arriva al*le venti e mezzo* = 20:30 = 8:30 P.M.**

COME SI CONTA IN ITALIANO
How to Count in Italian

I numeri cardinali
Cardinal Numbers

	(SEH-ee)	*(OOHN-dee-chee)*	*(SEH-dee-chee)*
1 **uno**	6 **sei**	11 **undici**	16 **sedici**
		(DOH-dee-chee)	*(dee-chah-SSEH-tteh)*
2 **due**	7 **sette**	12 **dodici**	17 **diciassette**
		(TREH-dee-chee)	*(dee-CHOH-ttoh)*
3 **tre**	8 **otto**	13 **tredici**	18 **diciotto**
(KWAH-ttroh)		*(kwah-TTOHR-dee-chee)*	*(dee-chah-NNOH-veh)*
4 **quattro**	9 **nove**	14 **quattordici**	19 **diciannove**
(CHEEN-kweh)	*(DYEH chee)*	*(KWEEN-dee-chee)*	*(VEHN-tee)*
5 **cinque**	10 **dieci**	15 **quindici**	20 **venti**

21 **ventuno**	24 **ventiquattro**	27 **ventisette**	30 **trenta**
22 **ventidue**	25 **venticinque**	28 **ventotto**	
23 **ventitré**	26 **ventisei**	29 **ventinove**	

	(cheen-KWAHN-tah)		
31 **trentuno**	50 **cinquanta**	62 **sessantadue**	81 **ottantuno**
32 **trentadue**	51 **cinquantuno**	. . .	82 **ottantadue**
. . .		70 **settanta**	. . .
(kwah-RAHN-tah)	52 **cinquantadue**	71 **settantuno**	90 **novanta**
40 **quaranta**	. . .	72 **settantadue**	91 **novantuno**
41 **quarantuno**	60 **sessanta**	. . .	92 **novantadue**
42 **quarantadue**	61 **sessantuno**	80 **ottanta**	. . .
. . .			

(CHEHN-toh) **100 cento**	**1,000 mille** **1,001 milleuno**	**1,002 milledue** **2,000 duemila**	**3,000 tremila** **10,000 diecimila**

Now try to write out in words the following:

Lui ha _____ **soldi. Lei ha** _____ **lire.**
   has   95   cents   100

Marco ha _____ **dollari. La penna costa** _____ **soldi.**
                88   67

(DOH-llah-ree)

Il biglietto costa _____ **soldi. Maria ha** _____ **dollari**
              74   has   23   dollars

americani; Marco ha _____ **dollari; Giovanni ha** _____
                               32   29

dollari. Quanti dollari? _____ **dollari.**
                          (23 + 32 + 29) 84

Che ora è? Now give the following times in words.

2:24 _____   4:12 _____

6:15 _____   8:20 _____

9:17 _____   11:01 _____

3:58 _____   5:30 _____

7:45 _____   1:10 _____

10:35 _____   12:47 _____

(meh-tsoh-JOHR-noh)	*(meh-tsah-NOH-tteh)*
mezzogiorno	**mezzanotte**
noon	midnight

The following humorous dialogue contains some useful words and expressions related to the telling of time.

Don't forget to read each line out loud several times and to act out each part.

(A stranger approaches Mark on the street.)

STRANIERO   **Scusi, signore, che ora è?**

Excuse me, sir, what time is it?

MARK **È mezzanotte.**

It's midnight.

(ahn-KOH-rah)

STRANIERO   **Ma come, è ancora giorno?**

How can that be? It is still daytime?

MARK **Scusi, allora è mezzogiorno.**

Excuse me, then it's noon.

(SKEHR-tsah)

STRANIERO   **Ma lei scherza?**

Are you joking?

(oh-roh-LOH-joh)

MARK **No. Non ho l'orologio.**

No. I don't have a watch.

(too-REES-tah)

STRANIERO   **Lei è un turista?**

Are you a tourist?

MARK **Sì.**

Yes.

(VWOH-leh)

STRANIERO   **Vuole comprare un orologio?**

Do you want to buy a watch? 500,000 lira.

   Cinquecentomila lire.

MARK **Troppo!**

That is too much!

STRANIERO   **Centomila lire.**

100,000 lira.

MARK **No, grazie.**

No, thanks.

STRANIERO   **Ecco il suo orologio.**

Here is your watch. I am an honest

(bohr-sah-YOH-loh)

   Io sono un borsaiolo onesto!

pickpocket!

Now fill in the missing dialogue parts. Check your answers only after you have attempted to fill in the parts from memory.

Scusi signore, che o_____ è?

È m_____.

Ma come, è ancora g_____.

Scusi, allora è m_____.

Ma lei s_____?

No. Non ho l'o _____.

Lei è un t_____?

Sì.

Vuole c_____un orologio?

Cinquecentomila lire.

Troppo!

Centomila l_____.

No, g_____.

Ecco il suo orologio. Io sono un

b_____ onesto!

I numeri ordinali 1–10
Ordinal Numbers 1–10

First: **primo**	Fourth: *(KWAHR-toh)* **quarto**	Seventh: *(SEH-ttee-moh)* **settimo**	Tenth: *(DEH-chee-moh)* **decimo**
Second: *(seh-KOHN-doh)* **secondo**	Fifth: *(KWEEN-toh)* **quinto**	Eighth: *(oh-TTAH-voh)* **ottavo**	
Third: *(TEHR-tsoh)* **terzo**	Sixth: **sesto**	Ninth: *(NOH-noh)* **nono**	

Repeat aloud and write the floor designations in the appropriate blanks next to this control panel.

_____

_____

_____

_____

_____

_____

_____

_____

Ricordati di . . .

Remember to . . .

(YEH-ree)
ieri Londra
yesterday

(OH-jjee) (pah-REE-jee)
oggi   Parigi
today

(doh-MAH-nee)
domani Roma
tomorrow

(AHN-keh)
anche Pisa
also/too

(DOH-poh)
dopo Madrid
after

By now, you should be able to make sense out of the following sentences.

(kwee)
Tu vieni **qui**.
here

Io vado **là (lì)**.
there

(MOHL-toh)
Mia moglie non ha **molto** denaro.
much   money

Mio marito ha **poco** denaro.
little

Adesso/ora andiamo a Bologna.
Now

Andiamo **almeno** fino a Palermo.
at least

Giovanni non sta **bene**. (John does not feel well.)
well

(MEH-lyee-oh)
Ora sta **meglio**. (Now he is better.)
better

(POH-ee)
Poi andiamo al cinema.
Then

Questo biglietto costa **troppo**.
too much

(voh-lehn-TYEH-ree)
Io vado a Milano **volentieri**.
gladly

Mia moglie **non** va **mai** al cinema.
never

Io **non** sento **niente/nulla**.
nothing

Io **non** vedo **nessuno**.
no one

See if you remember the meaning of these useful words by matching them with the equivalents.

1. nessuno		a. yesterday
2. bene		b. today
3. meglio		c. tomorrow
4. niente		d. again
5. poi		e. also/too
6. troppo		f. already
7. mai		g. here
8. volentieri		h. much
9. ieri		i. little
10. anche		j. now
11. oggi		k. at least
12. domani		l. well
13. ancora		m. better
14. già		n. then
15. adesso/ora		o. too much
16. almeno		p. gladly
17. molto		q. never
18. poco		r. nothing
19. qui		s. no one

Now put the appropriate words in the blanks below.

domani	oggi	anche	qui	molto	mai	niente	nessuno

?

Maria abita _____ a Roma.

Quando arriva Giovanni, _____ o _____?
                                          or

Domani arriva _____ la zia di Gina.

Lui non scrive _____ a suo zio.

Marisa non sa _____.
        knows

Io non vedo _____.

Luisa ha _____ denaro.
      has

Troppi verbi!

Too many verbs!

Previously, you learned about "ire" verbs. Now you will learn about a different kind of "ire" verb. These verbs take an "isc" in the *io, tu, lui / lei,* and *loro* forms. We'll show you how it is done.

(fee-NEE-reh)	*(kah-PEE-reh)*	*(preh-feh-REE-reh)*
finire	**capire**	**preferire**
to finish	to understand	to prefer

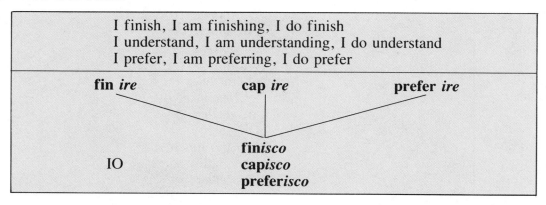

I finish, I am finishing, I do finish
I understand, I am understanding, I do understand
I prefer, I am preferring, I do prefer

fin *ire*　　　**cap** *ire*　　　**prefer** *ire*

IO

fin*isco*
cap*isco*
prefer*isco*

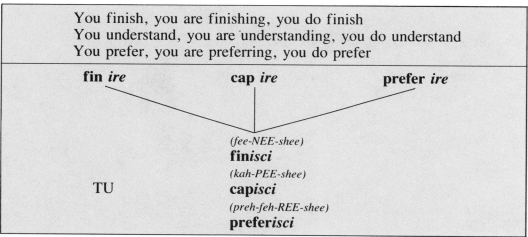

You finish, you are finishing, you do finish
You understand, you are understanding, you do understand
You prefer, you are preferring, you do prefer

fin *ire*　　　**cap** *ire*　　　**prefer** *ire*

TU

(fee-NEE-shee)
fin*isci*
(kah-PEE-shee)
cap*isci*
(preh-feh-REE-shee)
prefer*isci*

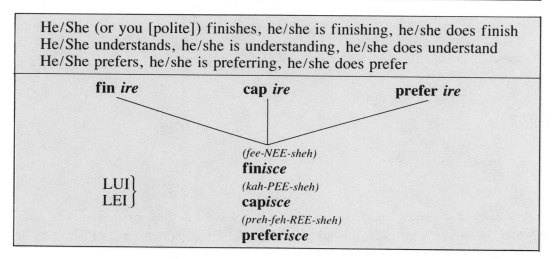

He/She (or you [polite]) finishes, he/she is finishing, he/she does finish
He/She understands, he/she is understanding, he/she does understand
He/She prefers, he/she is preferring, he/she does prefer

fin *ire*　　　**cap** *ire*　　　**prefer** *ire*

LUI
LEI

(fee-NEE-sheh)
fin*isce*
(kah-PEE-sheh)
cap*isce*
(preh-feh-REE-sheh)
prefer*isce*

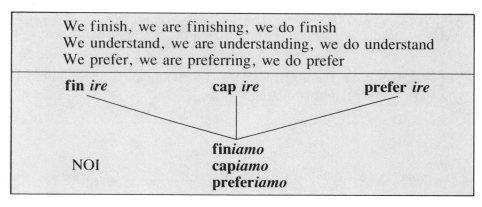

We finish, we are finishing, we do finish
We understand, we are understanding, we do understand
We prefer, we are preferring, we do prefer

fin *ire* **cap** *ire* **prefer** *ire*

NOI

fin*iamo*
cap*iamo*
prefer*iamo*

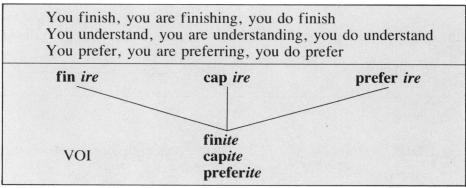

You finish, you are finishing, you do finish
You understand, you are understanding, you do understand
You prefer, you are preferring, you do prefer

fin *ire* **cap** *ire* **prefer** *ire*

VOI

fin*ite*
cap*ite*
prefer*ite*

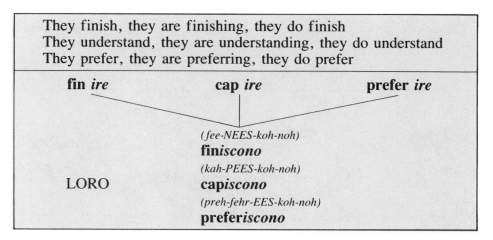

They finish, they are finishing, they do finish
They understand, they are understanding, they do understand
They prefer, they are preferring, they do prefer

fin *ire* **cap** *ire* **prefer** *ire*

LORO

(fee-NEES-koh-noh)
fin*iscono*
(kah-PEES-koh-noh)
cap*iscono*
(preh-fehr-EES-koh-noh)
prefer*iscono*

The table at the right will help you remember these "ire" verb endings.

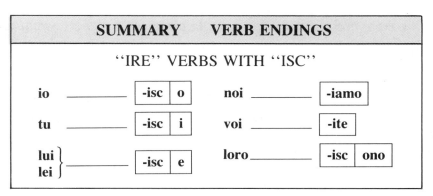

SUMMARY   VERB ENDINGS

"IRE" VERBS WITH "ISC"

io	_____	-isc	o	noi	_____	-iamo	
tu	_____	-isc	i	voi	_____	-ite	
lui } lei }	_____	-isc	e	loro	_____	-isc	ono

65

How can you recognize a special "ire" verb that takes these endings? You can't. *Mi dispiace*! (I'm sorry!) You cannot predict by yourself when to add the *isc*. You will have to learn the *isc* verbs through practice.

Let's review all the verb types! Test yourself by putting the right endings in the blanks. Look back at the charts if you have problems remembering.

io

Io cant_____ molto bene.

Io non scriv_____ mai a mio zio.

Io non dorm_____ tutto il giorno.

Io cap_____ l'italiano.

noi

Noi parl_____ l'italiano **come** gli italiani.
like

Noi ved_____ Giovanni **stasera**.
tonight

Noi fin_____ il libro domani.

Noi prefer_____ andare a Bologna.

tu

Tu parl_____ l'italiano molto bene.

Tu non ved_____ nessuno.

Tu part_____ domani per l'Italia.

Tu prefer_____ andare a Roma.

voi

Voi cant_____ molto bene.

Voi scriv_____ molto bene.

Voi dorm_____ tutto il giorno.

Voi non cap_____ l'italiano.

lui/lei

Lui arriv_____ domani.

Lei non cred_____ a Maria.

Il turista non sent_____ la voce del vigile.

Giovanni non fin_____ la pizza.

loro

Loro arriv_____ dopo le sei.

Gli studenti scriv_____ l'**esame**.
exam

Franco e Maria part_____ domani per l'Italia.

I signori Smith non cap_____ l'italiano.

ANSWERS

Verb review

	io	tu	lui / lei	noi	voi	loro
	(cant) o	(parl) i	(arriv) a	(parl) iamo	(cant) ate	(arriv) ano
	(scriv) o	(ved) i	(cred) e	(ved) iamo	(scriv) ete	(scriv) ono
	(dorm) o	(part) i	(sent) e	(fin) iamo	(dorm) ite	(part) ono
	(cap) isco	(prefer) isci	(fin) isce	(prefer) iamo	(cap) ite	(cap) iscono

Il mio e il tuo

Mine and Yours

What's mine and what's yours? Here's how to tell in Italian. Notice that the forms of these words change, depending on the noun.

WITH FEMININE NOUNS	WITH MASCULINE NOUNS		WITH FEMININE NOUNS	WITH MASCULINE NOUNS
MY			**OUR**	
(MEE-ah)	*(MEE-oh)*		*(NOHS-trah)*	*(NOHS-troh)*
la mia valigia	il mio biglietto		la nostra valigia	il nostro biglietto
(MEE-eh)	*(MYEH-ee)*		*(NOHS-treh)*	*(NOHS-tree)*
le mie valige	i miei biglietti		le nostre valige	i nostri biglietti
YOUR (FAMILIAR)			**YOUR (PLURAL)**	
(TOO-ah)	*(TOO-oh)*		*(VOHS-trah)*	*(VOHS-troh)*
la tua valigia	il tuo biglietto		la vostra valigia	il vostro biglietto
(TOO-eh)	*(TWOH-ee)*		*(VOHS-treh)*	*(VOHS-tree)*
le tue valige	i tuoi biglietti		le vostre valige	i vostri biglietti
HIS/HER *OR* YOUR (POLITE)			**THEIR**	
(SOO-ah)	*(SOO-oh)*		*(LOH-roh)*	
la sua valigia	il suo biglietto		la loro valigia	il loro biglietto
(SOO-eh)	*(SWOH-ee)*			
le sue valige	i suoi biglietti		le loro valige	i loro biglietti

Notice that "my," "your," and other possessive pronouns are preceded by the appropriate forms of "the." These are dropped only when the noun refers to a singular and unmodified family member (except for "their," which *always* retains the article "the"). For example:

mio zio	*but* **i** miei zii
tua sorella	*but* **la** tua sorella **piccola**
	small
nostro padre	*but* **il loro** padre

Notice, as well, that the forms *la sua, le sue, il suo,* and *i suoi* mean "his," "her," or "you" (polite).

Now test your knowledge by putting the appropriate possessive adjective in front of the following nouns.

_____ fiore
　　my

_____ fiori
　　my

_____ casa
　　your (familiar)

_____ case
　　your (familiar)

_____ gatto
　　his

_____ gatti
　　his

_____ gatto
　　her (be careful!)

_____ gatti
　　her

_____ amico
　　our

_____ amici
　　our

_____ zia
　　my (be careful!)

_____ zie
　　my (be careful again!)

_____ penna
　　his

_____ penne
　　his

_____ orologio
　　her

_____ orologi
　　her

_____ biglietto
　　their

_____ biglietti
　　their

_____ automobile
　　their

_____ automobili
　　their

If someone asks you, can you give the time in Italian? Read the passage and then answer the questions that follow.

Che ore sono? **chiede il padre a sua figlia.** **Sono le tre e mezzo,** **dice la figlia.**

A che ora parti per l'Italia? **chiede il padre.** **Alle cinque e venti,** *(rees-POHN-deh)* **risponde la figlia.**
answers

Ciao e buon viaggio. **Ciao papà.**
have a good trip　　dad

Che cosa chiede il padre a sua figlia?
☐ Come stai?
☐ Che ore sono?
☐ Che fai?

A che ora parte la figlia?
☐ Alle cinque e venti.
☐ Alle cinque e un quarto.
☐ A mezziogiorno.

Che ore sono?
☐ Sono le tre e un quarto.
☐ Sono le tre e venticinque.
☐ Sono le tre e mezzo.

68

If you will be taking the train, the words and expressions in the following dialogue might prove to be useful to you.

Don't forget to read each line out loud several times and to act out each part.

MARY *(EH-kkoh-chee) (stah-TSYOH-neh)*
Eccoci alla stazione   Here we are at the train station.
(feh-rroh-vee-AH-ree-ah)
ferroviaria.

ANNE *(RAH-pee-doh)*
Papà, prendiamo il rapido per   Dad, are we taking the luxury (rapid) train

andare a Firenze?   to go to Florence?

MARK **No. Costa troppo.**   No. It costs too much.

ANNE **Allora prendiamo il**   Then are we taking the fast train?
(dee-reh-TTEE-ssee-moh)
direttissimo?

MARK **Sì.** *(to a ticket clerk)* **Scusi, quanto**   Yes. Excuse me, how much does a round-trip

costa un biglietto di andata e ritorno   ticket to Florence for four persons cost?

per quattro persone a Firenze?

69

IMPIEGATA	**Il direttissimo?**	The fast train?
MARK	**Sì.**	Yes.

(skohm-pahr-tee-MEHN-toh)

IMPIEGATA	**Scompartimento per**	Smoking or no smoking compartment?

(foo-mah-TOH-ree)

fumatori o per non fumatori?

MARK	**Non fumatori.**	No smoking.
IMPIEGATA	**Duecentomila lire. Ecco i**	200,000 lira. Here are the tickets.

biglietti.

MARK	**Grazie. Quando parte il treno?**	Thank you. When does the train leave?
IMPIEGATA	**Il treno parte alle quindici e**	The train leaves at 15:30 (3:30 P M).

trenta.

Now try to complete the missing dialogue parts. Check your answers only after you have attempted to fill in the missing parts from memory.

Eccoci alla s——————— ferroviaria.

Papà, prendiamo il r——————— per andare a Firenze?

No. C——————— troppo.

Allora prendiamo il d———————?

Sì. Scusi quanto costa un biglietto di a———————

e r——————— per quattro persone a Firenze?

(oh-RAH-ree-oh)
L'orario
Train Schedule

Remember that train schedules use official time, based on a 24-hour clock:

1:00 p.m. = 13:00 hours = **le tredici**
2:00 p.m. = 14:00 hours = **le quattordici**
12:00 midnight = 24:00 hours = **le ventiquattro**

Note that the name of the city of departure *(Bologna)* is at the top of the schedule. Each city served by this line follows, with the departure time (from Bologna) for each train listed in the column on the left, followed by the arrival time on the right. Additional information regarding the type of each train is also given.

dp ab	ar an	Observations Bemerkungen		dp ab	ar an	Observations Bemerkungen

Firenze

19 04	20 32 ✕
19 33	20 55
21 13	22 39
22 01	23 20 ✕
22 23	23 30 Rapido
23 23	0 50

Milano

5 20	8 22
6 12	9 00
6 44	9 12
6 58	9 20
7 20	9 50
8 01	9 55 Rapido
8 18	1)11 24
10 36	13 00
10 54	13 40 ✕
11 00	13 50 ✕
12 00	13 55 R TEE ✕
12 30	15 20 ✕
13 12	15 25 ✕
13 23	16 00 ✕
14 05	16 40 ✕
15 02	17 10
15 42	17 30 R TEE ✕
16 07	19 00
17 15	19 05 R TEE ✕
18 20	20 30 Rapido ✕
18 49	1)21 25
19 58	22 45
20 44	23 07
21 44	23 35 R TEE ✕
21 50	23 40 R TEE ✕
22 00	0 45

1) Milano P.G.

Napoli

1 09	9 20
3 58	11 35
8 44	17 22 ✕
10 23	19 48 ✕
13 47	1)20 10 R TEE ✕
14 55	21 52 Rapido ✕
15 10	2)22 08 ✕
18 00	2) 1 46
19 24	3 01
22 01	2) 5 10
22 40	2) 5 36

1) Napoli Merg.
2) Napoli C.F.

Palermo

5 35	23 22 X Roma R ✕
13 05	8 25 R ✕ X Roma
15 10	10 58
18 15	13 20
22 01	17 35
22 40	17 57

Pisa

6 18	10 00 X Firenze
8 05	10 36 ✕ X Firenze
9 09	12 30 ✕ X Firenze
9 56	12 30 Rapido X Firenze
10 16	13 10 X Firenze
△10 30	13 10
13 05	15 32 R ✕ X Firenze
13 47	16 22 R TEE ✕ X Firenze
△14 55	17 14 Rapido ✕ X Firenze

△ 29 V - 24 IX 83

Pisa

16 24	19 02 ✕ X Firenze
17 17	19 57 ✕ X Firenze
18 53	22 10 R TEE ✕ X Firenze
19 04	22 10 ✕ X Firenze
19 33	23 23 ✕ X Firenze
21 13	23 48

Roma

1 09	1) 6 30
1 34	7 15
5 35	10 40
6 18	12 05
8 05	12 55 ✕
8 17	13 15 ✕
8 44	14 42 ✕
9 09	13 45 ✕
10 04	14 05 R TEE ✕
10 16	14 50 ✕
10 23	1)15 50 ✕
13 05	17 10 R ✕
13 12	18 50 ✕
13 47	17 45 R TEE ✕
14 10	19 48 ✕
14 55	19 13 Rapido ✕
15 10	1)19 46 ✕
15 17	20 07 ✕
16 24	17 40 ✕
17 17	22 50 ✕
18 15	1)23 09 ✕
18 53	23 00 R TEE ✕
19 04	23 50 ✕
19 24	1) 0 13 ✕

1) Roma Tib.na

Torino

3 30	8 15
4 05	8 48
6 20	10 45
15 10	19 15
18 37	22 50
19 52	0 10

Venezia

5 12	7 40
5 58	8 15
8 11	10 30
11 13	12 48 ✕
11 25	13 37 ✕
12 25	13 31 ✕
13 28	15 40
14 49	16 37 R ✕
16 35	18 54 ✕
17 22	19 14 ✕
18 13	20 28 ✕
21 01	23 08
22 01	0 04
22 25	0 38

Verona

6 21	8 06
8 19	10 00
11 14	13 14
△12 20	13 46
12 55	14 33
16 10	17 50
△16 25	18 15
17 46	19 10
18 59	20 49
22 10	23 42

△ 29 V - 24 IX 83

(courtesy of Italian State Railways)

Il rapido is a luxury train that stops only at main railway stations. *Il direttissimo* is a fast train that stops at more railway stations. *Il diretto* is a "through" train that stops at many more railway stations.

Now fill in the following blanks, writing out the numbers in words, using the timetable.

From **Bologna** to **Venezia** is less than ———— ore.

From **Bologna** to **Milano** con il **rapido** is almost ———— ore.

From **Bologna** to **Torino** is more than ———— ore.

From **Bologna** to **Pisa** con il **rapido** is about ———— ore e ————.

Voglio / Vorrei
I Want / I Would Like

(voh-LEH-reh)

"To want" is a very useful verb when requesting or asking for things. The Italian **volere** is irregular.

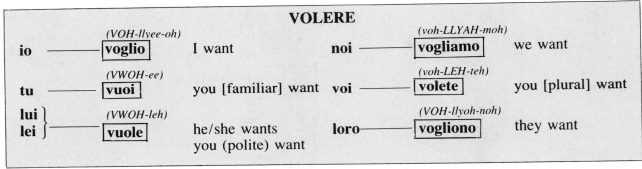

VOLERE

	(VOH-llyee-oh)			*(voh-LLYAH-moh)*	
io	**voglio**	I want	noi	**vogliamo**	we want
	(VWOH-ee)			*(voh-LEH-teh)*	
tu	**vuoi**	you [familiar] want	voi	**volete**	you [plural] want
lui }	*(VWOH-leh)*			*(VOH-llyoh-noh)*	
lei }	**vuole**	he/she wants you (polite) want	loro	**vogliono**	they want

If you want to be polite, then you should use the following form.

(voh-RREH-ee)
Vorrei ———————— I would like

Now try your hand at these. Fill in the blanks below with the appropriate forms of *volere*.

La figlia del signor Smith ___vuole___ un biglietto di andata e ritorno.
                            wants

Quelle persone ___vogliono___ andare a piedi.
                 want

Io ___voglio___ andare con il direttissimo, ma tu ___vovuoi___ andare con il rapido.
     want   want

Noi ___vogliamo___ un biglietto per lo scompartimento per non fumatori.
      want

72

Voi _volete_ due biglietti di andata e ritorno.
   want

Io _vorrei_ un orario per favore.
   would like

Io _vorrei_ anche un biglietto per Roma.
   would like

(kah-RROH-tsah)

IN CARROZZA!

All Aboard!

(vyah-JJAH-reh)
viaggiare
to travel

il treno
train

(pah-sseh-JJEH-roh)
il passeggero
passenger

(seh-DEHR-see)
sedersi
to sit down

(ahl-TSAHR-see)
alzarsi
to get up

**la
sala d'aspetto**
waiting room

(kohn-doo-TTOH-reh)
il conduttore
conductor

(kah-mmee-NAH-reh)
camminare
to walk

(fah-KKEE-noh)
il facchino
porter

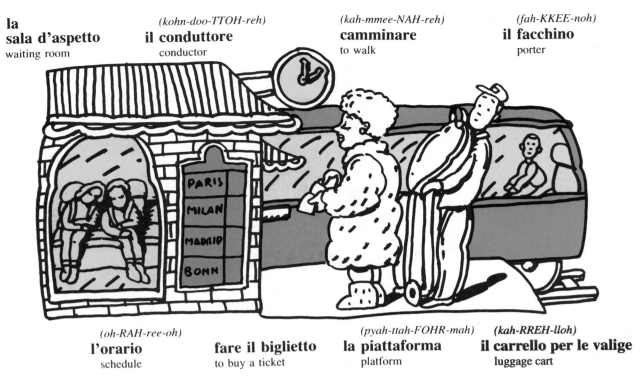

(oh-RAH-ree-oh)
l'orario
schedule

fare il biglietto
to buy a ticket

(pyah-ttah-FOHR-mah)
la piattaforma
platform

(kah-RREH-lloh)
il carrello per le valige
luggage cart

Now have fun with the following crossword puzzle.

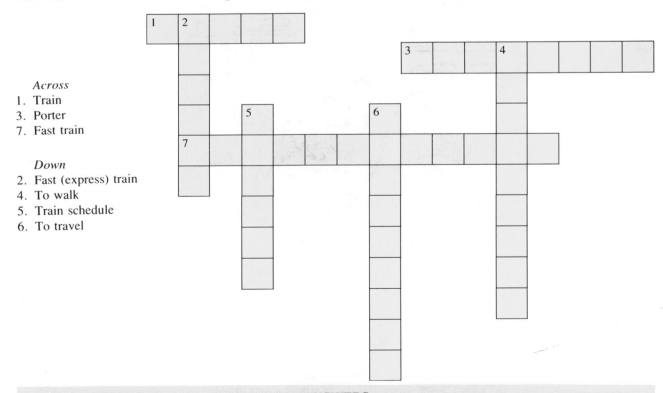

Across
1. Train
3. Porter
7. Fast train

Down
2. Fast (express) train
4. To walk
5. Train schedule
6. To travel

74

I pronomi riflessivi

Reflexive Pronouns

A reflexive verb refers or "reflects" the action back to the subject. For example, "to wash" is a reflexive verb because you wash yourself, that is "reflect back" the action of the verb upon yourself. This is done by means of reflexive pronouns, like "myself" and "yourself." Here are the reflexive pronouns in Italian.

REFLEXIVE PRONOUNS	
mi — myself	*(chee)* **ci** — ourselves
ti — yourself (familiar)	**vi** — yourselves
si — himself/herself/yourself (polite)/ itself/oneself	**si** — themselves

Now let's conjugate a reflexive verb. To do thi   just conjugate the verb as you would normally and simply put the reflexive pronouns *right before* the verb (even in the negative). For example:

io —————— **mi lavo** (I wash myself)
tu —————— **ti lavi** (you wash yourself)
lui
lei ————— **si lava** (he/she washes himself/herself)
noi —————— **ci laviamo** (we wash ourselves)
voi —————— **vi lavate** (you wash yourselves)
loro—————— **si lavano** (they wash themselves)

NEGATIVE

io _____ **non mi lavo**
tu _____ **non ti lavi**
lui/lei _____ **non si lava**
noi _____ **non ci laviamo**
voi _____ **non vi lavate**
loro _____ **non si lavano**

(lah-VAHR-see)

Notice that the reflexive form for "oneself" is attached to the infinitive form: **lavarsi**.

to wash oneself

Here are three useful reflexive verbs.

| *(ahl-TSAHR-see)* **alzarsi** to get up | *(seh-DEHR-see)* **sedersi** to sit down | *(dee-vehr-TEER-see)* **divertirsi** to enjoy oneself |

But the verb *sedersi*
is irregular, so this
is how you conjugate it.

SEDERSI	
io ———— mi siedo	noi ———— ci sediamo
tu ———— ti siedi	voi ———— vi sedete
lui } ———— si siede	loro ———— si siedono
lei }	

Now try your hand at the following. Fill in the blanks with the correct reflexive pronoun and verb form.

Il signor Smith _____ *si siede* _____ nello scompartimento.
sits down

La signora Smith _____ alle sette e mezzo.
gets up

Io _____ alle sei e tu _____ alle sette.
get up   get up

Noi _____ molto quando andiamo a Roma.
enjoy ourselves

Voi non _____ mai quando andate in Italia.
enjoy yourselves

I passeggeri _____ nello scompartimento.
sit down

Io non _____ nello scompartimento per fumatori.
sit down

Tu _____ nello scompartimento per non fumatori.
sit down

The following passage is about train travel. Read it and then answer the questions that follow.

**Marco e Maria vanno alla stazione ferroviaria.
Fanno il biglietto di andata e ritorno per Venezia.
Viaggiano con il rapido fino a Bologna. E poi da
Bologna a Venezia vanno con il direttissimo.
Arrivano alle sedici.**

Dove vanno Marco e Maria?

☐ Vanno a Roma.
☐ Vanno a Bologna.
☐ Vanno a Venezia.

Che cosa fanno?

☐ Fanno le spese.
☐ Fanno il biglietto.
☐ Non fanno niente.

Come viaggiano fino a Bologna?

☐ Viaggiano con il diretto.
☐ Viaggiano con il rapido.
☐ Viaggiano con il direttissimo.

E da Bologna a Venezia?

☐ Con il diretto.
☐ Con il rapido.
☐ Con il direttissimo.

A che ora arrivano?

☐ Arrivano alle due.
☐ Arrivano alle sedici.
☐ Arrivano alle diciotto.

Now, as a brief summary of some of the important things you have learned, talk about yourself in Italian, by answering the following questions.

Come ti chiami? _____

Come si chiama tuo marito/tua moglie? _____

Dove abiti? _____

Come stai? _____

A che ora ti alzi la mattina? _____

A che ora vai a dormire la sera?_____

7 | Paesi e lingue

(LEEN-gweh)

Countries and Languages

Parlo un po' d'italiano. (I speak a little Italian). And so quick! By now you've learned quite a bit of Italian. Take a look at the rest of the world, too, and learn how to say the names of other countries—in Italian, of course.

COUNTRY	CITY	COUNTRY	CITY
(ah-oos-TRAH-lee-ah) **l'Australia**	**Sydney**	**l'Italia**	**Roma**
il Canada	**Ottawa**	*(jah-PPOH-neh)* **il Giappone**	**Tokyo/Tokio**
(peh-KEE-noh) **la Cina** China	**Pechino** Peking	**il Messico**	*(chee-TTAH)* **la città del Messico**
		la Russia	**Mosca**
(FRAHN-chah) **la Francia**	**Parigi**	*(SPAH-nyah)* **la Spagna**	**Madrid**
(jehr-MAH-nee-ah) **la Germania**	**Berlino**	*(SVEE-tseh-rah)* **la Svizzera**	*(jee-NEH-vrah)* **Ginevra**
(een-geel-TEH-rrah) **l'Inghilterra** England	**Londra**	*(STAH-tee-oo-NEE-tee)* **gli Stati Uniti**	**Washington**

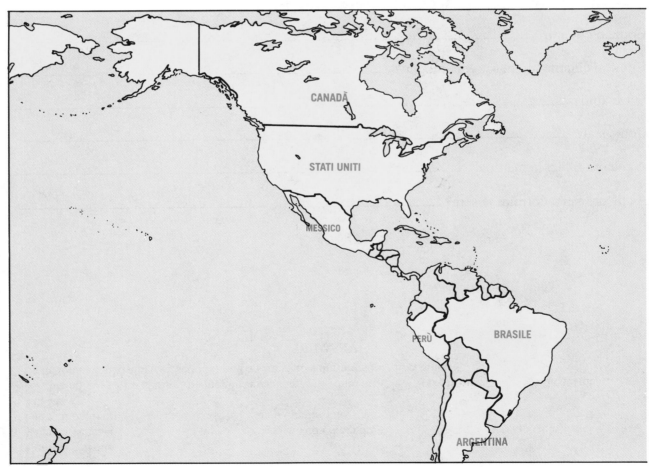

Parlo . . .
I Speak...

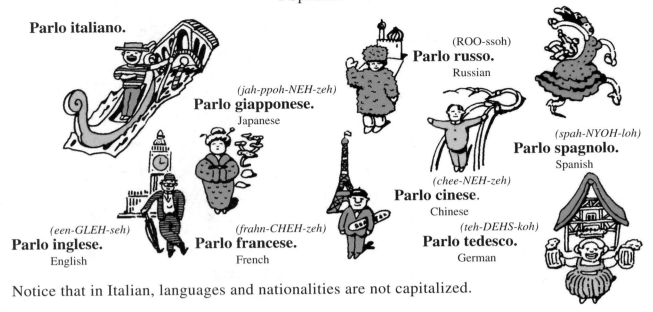

Parlo italiano.

(jah-ppoh-NEH-zeh)
Parlo giapponese.
Japanese

(ROO-ssoh)
Parlo russo.
Russian

(spah-NYOH-loh)
Parlo spagnolo.
Spanish

(chee-NEH-zeh)
Parlo cinese.
Chinese

(een-GLEH-seh)
Parlo inglese.
English

(frahn-CHEH-zeh)
Parlo francese.
French

(teh-DEHS-koh)
Parlo tedesco.
German

Notice that in Italian, languages and nationalities are not capitalized.

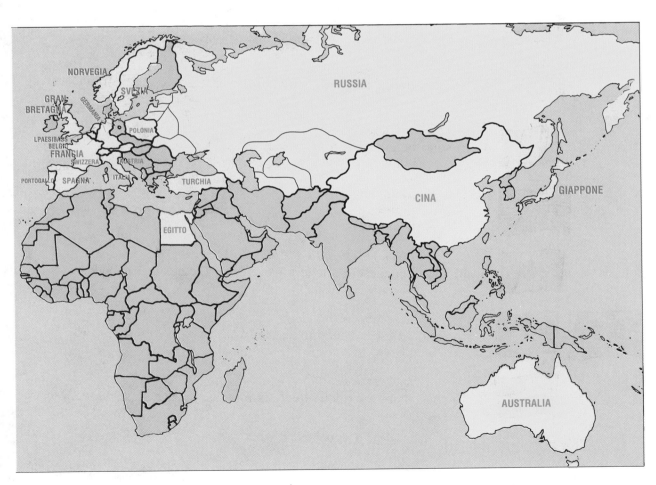

Sono
I Am

(EH-sseh-reh)
The verb *essere* is irregular.
to be

ESSERE			
io	sono	noi	siamo
tu	sei	voi	siete
lui } lei }	è	loro	sono

Now let's use this verb with nationalities.

1. Io sono americano e anche tu ___sei___ americano.

(aoos-TREE-ah-koh)
2. Io sono austriaco e anche lui ___è___ austriaco.
Austrian

(Australian)
3. Io sono australiano e anche lei ___è___ australiana.
Australian

(BEHL-gah) *(BEHL-jee)*
4. Io sono belga e anche noi ___siamo___ belgi.
Belgian

(een-GLEH-seh)
5. Io sono inglese e anche voi ___siete___ inglesi.
English

(kah-nah-DEH-zeh)
6. Io sono canadese e anche loro ___sono___ canadesi.
Canadian

(chee-NEH-zeh)
7. Io sono cinese e anche tu ___sei___ cinese.
Chinese

(dah-NEH-zeh)
8. Io sono danese e anche quel signore ___é___ danese.
Danish

ANSWERS

Verbs 1. sei **2.** è **3.** è **4.** siamo **5.** siete **6.** sono **7.** sei **8.** è

80

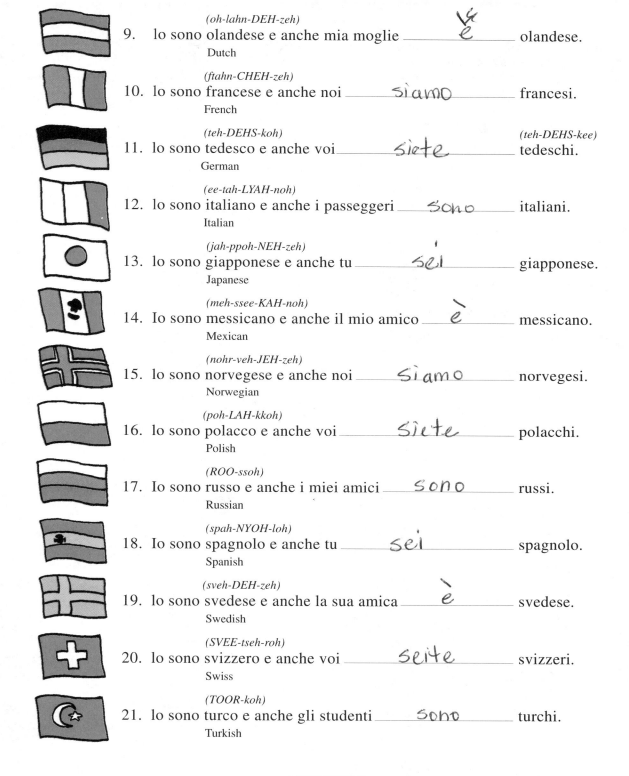

9. Io sono olandese e anche mia moglie _____ è _____ olandese.
   (oh-lahn-DEH-zeh)
   Dutch

10. Io sono francese e anche noi _____ siamo _____ francesi.
    (ftahn-CHEH-zeh)
    French

11. Io sono tedesco e anche voi _____ siete _____ tedeschi.
    (teh-DEHS-koh)   *(teh-DEHS-kee)*
    German

12. Io sono italiano e anche i passeggeri _____ sono _____ italiani.
    (ee-tah-LYAH-noh)
    Italian

13. Io sono giapponese e anche tu _____ sei _____ giapponese.
    (jah-ppoh-NEH-zeh)
    Japanese

14. Io sono messicano e anche il mio amico _____ è _____ messicano.
    (meh-ssee-KAH-noh)
    Mexican

15. Io sono norvegese e anche noi _____ siamo _____ norvegesi.
    (nohr-veh-JEH-zeh)
    Norwegian

16. Io sono polacco e anche voi _____ siete _____ polacchi.
    (poh-LAH-kkoh)
    Polish

17. Io sono russo e anche i miei amici _____ sono _____ russi.
    (ROO-ssoh)
    Russian

18. Io sono spagnolo e anche tu _____ sei _____ spagnolo.
    (spah-NYOH-loh)
    Spanish

19. Io sono svedese e anche la sua amica _____ è _____ svedese.
    (sveh-DEH-zeh)
    Swedish

20. Io sono svizzero e anche voi _____ seite _____ svizzeri.
    (SVEE-tseh-roh)
    Swiss

21. Io sono turco e anche gli studenti _____ sono _____ turchi.
    (TOOR-koh)
    Turkish

ANSWERS

Be careful with "is." Notice that is has an accent, whereas "and" does not. Also, you may recall from previous dialogues that "there is" is *c'è* with the plural form *(ci sono)* "there are." Remember that *ecco* is used to point out something. This table will help you remember these differences.

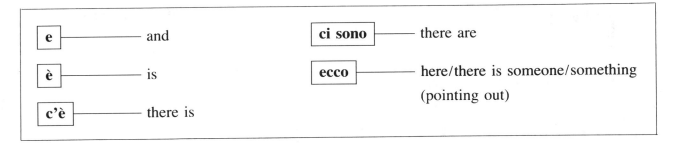

e —— and	**ci sono** —— there are
è —— is	**ecco** —— here/there is someone/something (pointing out)
c'è —— there is	

Notice that with *quale* (which) the final *e* is dropped in front of *è* ("is").

Qual è il tuo biglietto? (Which is your ticket?)

Qual è la tua chiave? (Which is your key?)

Try this now with the following questions.

_____ il tuo orologio? _____ la tua automobile? _____ il tuo passaporto?

Vado a . . .
I Am Going to . . .

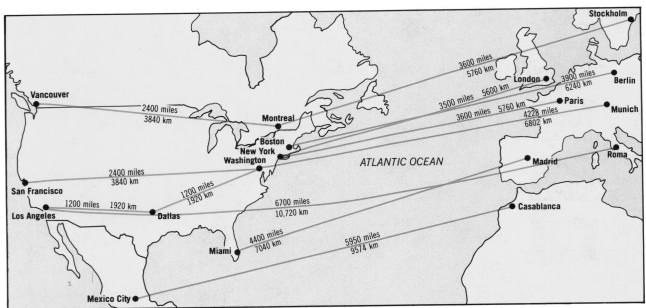

To say that something is "in" a **country**, use the corresponding preposition *in*. For example:

Dov'è Mosca? È *in* Russia. (Where is Moscow? It is in Russia.)

However, for the United States you have to use *negli Stati Uniti*. With any **city** *a* is used.

Dov'è la Statua della Libertà? È *a* New York.
       Statue   of   Liberty

You continue, using *in* or *a* in these sentences.

Dov'è la Torre Eiffel? È _____ Parigi.

Dov'è New York? È _____ Stati Uniti.

Dov'è Acapulco? È _____ Messico.

Dov'è Berlino? È _____ Germania.

Dov'è il Colosseo? È _____ Roma, _____ Italia.

Dov'è il Prado? È _____ Madrid, _____ Spagna.

Now try your skill with what you have just learned. Fill in the blanks as indicated.

_____ _____ Firenze. I fiorentini _____ molto simpatici.
  I am   in   Florentines   are

_____ Italia, si parla _____ . Roma _____ _____
   In   one   Italian   is   the

capitale d'Italia, Parigi _____ _____ capitale della _____
                    is   the   France

_____ Madrid _____ _____ capitale della _____ .
  and   is   the   Spain

Capisco
I Understand

Look back to the section on "ire" verbs, if you have forgotten how to conjugate *capire*. Now try the following.

Io *capisco* l'italiano, ma tu non *capisci* l'italiano.
                      but

You continue.

1. Io _____ il tedesco, ma tu non _____ il tedesco.

2. Lui _____ lo spagnolo, ma loro non _____ lo spagnolo.

3. Maria _____ l'inglese, ma noi non _____ l'inglese.

4. I passeggeri _____ l'italiano, ma voi non _____ l'italiano.

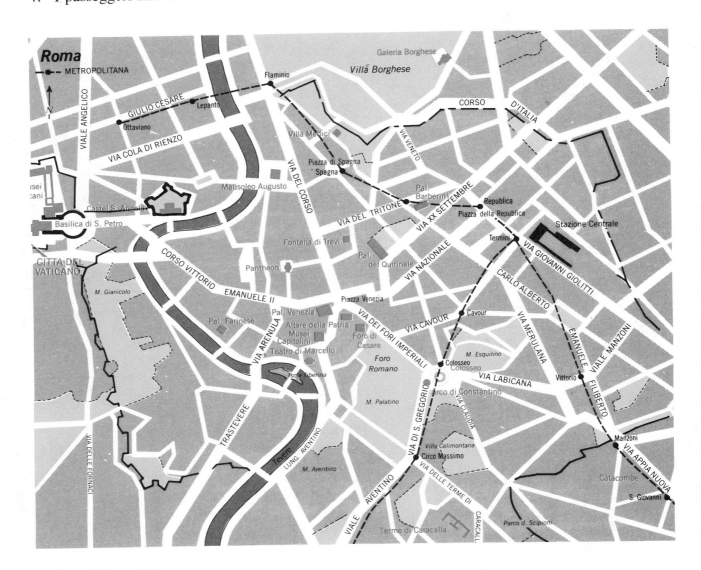

Subway Map of Rome

Read the following dialogue, repeating each line out loud several times. Don't forget to act out each part.

(Knowing the frustration of not being understood, can you imagine how Anne felt when her wallet was stolen?)

ANNE   **Scusi, signore, lei parla inglese?**   Excuse me, sir, do you speak English?

VIGILE   **No. Solo italiano.**   No. Only Italian.

ANNE   **Qualcuno ha rubato il mio**   Someone stole my wallet in the subway.
         (pohr-tah-FOH-llyoh)
         portafoglio nella metropolitana.
                     (preh-OH-kkoo-pee)
VIGILE   **Non si preoccupi, signorina!**   Don't worry, Miss! Fill out this form.

         Compili questo modulo.

ANNE   **Parli più lentamente, per favore.**   Speak more slowly, please.

VIGILE   **Va bene. Scriva il suo nome e il**   Okay. Write your name and your address, and
         (een-dee-REE-tsoh)
         suo indirizzo, e anche il numero di   also the phone number of your hotel.
         (teh-LEH-foh-noh)
         telefono del suo albergo.

ANNE   **Non ho più soldi, carte di**   I have no more money, credit cards, or passport.
         (KREH-dee-toh)   *(fah-ROH)*
         credito, o passaporto. Cosa farò?   What am I going to do?

VIGILE   **Per il passaporto, lei deve andare**   For the passport, you have to go to your
         (ahm-bah-SHAH-tah)
         alla sua ambasciata.   embassy.
                     (pwoh) (ah-yoo-TAH-reh)
ANNE   **Lei non mi può aiutare?**   Can't you help me?

         (preh-OH-koo-pee)
VIGILE   **Non si preoccupi.**   Please don't worry. I am starting the search for
         (koh-MEEN-choh) (chehr-KAH-reh)   *(SOO-bee-toh)*
         Comincio a cercare il ladro subito.   the thief right now.

ANNE   **Grazie mille.**   Thank you very much.

Now try to complete the missing dialogue parts without looking back. Check your answers after you have attempted this exercise from memory.

Scusi, signore, lei parla i _____?

No. Solo i _____.

Qualcuno ha rubato il mio p_____ nella metropolitana.

Non si preoccupi, signorina! Compili questo m_____.

Parli più l_____, per favore.

Va bene. Scriva il suo n_____ e il suo i_____, e anche il

numero di t_____ del suo albergo.

Non ho più s_____, carte di c_____, o passaporto. Cosa farò?

By rearranging the following words, you will get sentences found in the dialogue.
passaporto / Per / il / ambasciata / alla / deve / sua / lei / andare

_____

non / Lei / aiutare / può / mi

_____

The following brief passage reflects what you have learned about countries, languages, and nationalities. After you have read it, choose the appropriate completion to each sentence.

La signorina Smith è americana. Lei non parla italiano molto bene. Vuole andare in Svizzera, in Francia e in Germania, ma qualcuno ha rubato il suo portafoglio. Adesso parla a un vigile. Il vigile non parla inglese, ma capisce il francese. Allora, la signorina e il vigile parlano in francese.

La signorina Smith . . .

☐ parla italiano molto bene.
☐ non parla inglese.
☐ è americana.

Lei vuole andare . . .

☐ in Russia.
☐ in Francia.
☐ in Italia.

Qualcuno ha rubato . . .

☐ il suo portafoglio.
☐ il suo passaporto.
☐ i suoi soldi.

Adesso parla a . . .

☐ suo padre.
☐ sua madre.
☐ un vigile.

Il vigile capisce . . .

☐ il tedesco.
☐ il francese.
☐ lo spagnolo.

Now have fun with the following crossword puzzle.

Across
1. Spain
2. France
4. Germany
5. French

Down
1. Spanish
3. German

<table>
<tr><td>**8**</td><td># Automobili e pulmini / La segnaletica</td></tr>
</table>

Cars and Vans/Road Signs

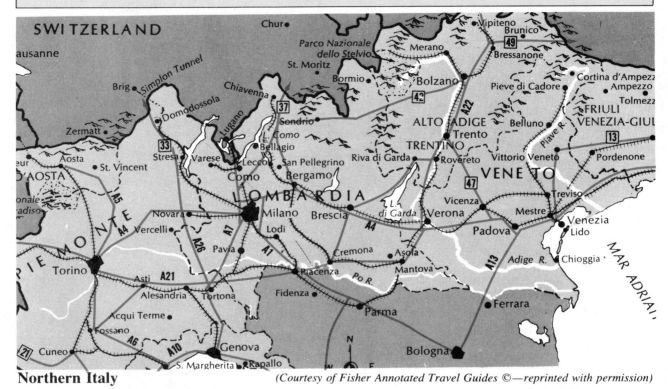

Northern Italy

(Courtesy of Fisher Annotated Travel Guides ©—reprinted with permission)

ALL'AGENZIA DI AUTOMOBILI DA NOLEGGIO

At the Car Rental Office

You may want to see the country close up. As you read the following dialogue, make sure that you repeat each line out loud several times. The words and expressions in it will prove useful if you want to rent a car.

(Mark has decided to rent a car and take his family for an excursion into the Italian countryside.)

	(noh-leh-JJAH-reh)	
MARK	**Buon giorno. Vorrei noleggiare**	Good day. I would like to rent a car.
	(MAH-kkee-nah)	
	una macchina.	
IMPIEGATA	**Per quanto tempo?**	For how long?
MARK	**Per due settimane.**	For two weeks.
IMPIEGATA	**Vediamo. Abbiamo una Lancia**	Let's see. We have a Lancia and a FIAT.
	e una FIAT.	

MARK **Prendo la FIAT. Sono incluse** (MEE-llyah) **anche le miglia nel prezzo?** (behn-DZEE-nah)	I'll take the FIAT. Is the mileage included in the price?
IMPIEGATA **Sì, ma la benzina no. La sua** (GWEE-dah) **patente di guida e la sua carta di credito,** **per favore.**	Yes, but it does not include the gas. Your driver's license and credit card, please.
MARK **Mi fa vedere come funziona il** (foon-TSYOH-nah) (MAHR-chah) **cambio di marcia e come** **funzionano i fari?**	Can you show me how the gearshift and the headlights work?
IMPIEGATA **Certo. Ecco la chiave e i** (doh-koo-MEHN-tee)(STEE-ah) **documenti. Stia attento! Gli autisti** (PAH-tsee) **italiani sono pazzi!**	Certainly. Here are the key and the papers. Be careful! Italian drivers are crazy!
MARK **Come tutti gli autisti oggi!**	Like all drivers today!

Now try to complete the missing dialogue parts without looking back. Check your answers after attempting the exercise from memory.

Buon giorno. V_____ n_____ una macchina.

Per q_____ t_____?

Per due s_____.

Vediamo. A_____ una Lancia e una FIAT.

Prendo la FIAT. Sono incluse anche le m_____ nel p_____?

Sì, ma la b_____ no. La sua p_____ di g_____

e la sua carta di credito, per favore.

Mi fa vedere come f_____ il cambio di m_____

e come funzionano i f_____?

Certo. Ecco la chiave e i d_____. S_____ a_____!

Gli a_____ italiani sono pazzi!

Alcune cose essenziali

Some Essentials

Here are some more words that you should know before you hit the road.

(ah-SSEE-koo-rah-tsyoh-neh)			
l'assicurazione	insurance	**nord-sud-est-ovest**	north-south-east-west
(ah-FFAH-reh)		*(POON-tah)*	
un buon affare	a good deal/bargain	**l'ora di punta**	rush hour
(oo-tee-lee-TAH-ree-ah)		*(stah-TSYOH-neh) (sehr-VEE-tsyoh)*	
l'utilitaria	compact car	**la stazione di servizio**	service station
		(PYEH-noh)	
una macchina grande	a large car	**fare il pieno**	to fill up
(pool-MEE-noh)		*(TRAH-ffee-koh)*	
il pulmino	van	**il traffico**	traffic
		(jee-RAH-reh)	
la multa per eccesso		**girare**	to turn
(eh-CHEH-ssoh)		*(rah-JOH-neh)*	
(veh-loh-chee-TAH)		**avere ragione**	to be right
di velocità	speeding ticket	*(TOHR-toh)*	
(pahr-KEH-jjoh)		**avere torto**	to be wrong
il parcheggio	parking		

Now choose one of the above words or expressions according to the meaning of each sentence. Don't forget to make necessary verb changes. *Buona fortuna!*

1. C'è molto t_____ durante l'ora di p_____.
   during

2. Maria ha r_____, la stazione di s_____ si trova a

   n_____, non a s_____, del semaforo.

3. Preferisco l'u_____, non la macchina g_____.

4. Alla stazione di servizio faccio sempre il p_____.

5. Hai t_____. Il p_____ costa poco. È un buon a_____.

6. Il vigile dà una m_____ per eccesso di v_____ al signor Smith.

7. Giovanni non g_____ a destra, lui g_____ a sinistra.

8. Va a est, non a o_____.

9. Qui non c'è il p_____.

LA SEGNALETICA / SEGNALI STRADALI

(seh-nyah-LEH-tee-kah)

Road Signs

If you're planning to drive while you're abroad, spend some time remembering the meanings of these signs.

Dangerous Intersection

Danger!

Stop

Speed Limit (in km/hr)

Minimum Speed

End of Limited Speed

No Entrance

Yield Right-of-way

Two-way Traffic

Dangerous Curve

Entrance to Expressway

Expressway Exit
(road narrows)

Customs

No Passing

End of No Passing Zone

One-way Street

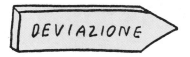

Detour

Road Closed

Parking

No Parking

No Parking
(or waiting)

Roundabout

No Cyclists

Pedestrian Crossing

Railroad Crossing
(no gate)

Guarded Railroad Crossing

92

ALLA STAZIONE DI SERVIZIO

(sehr-VEE-tsee-oh)

At the Service Station

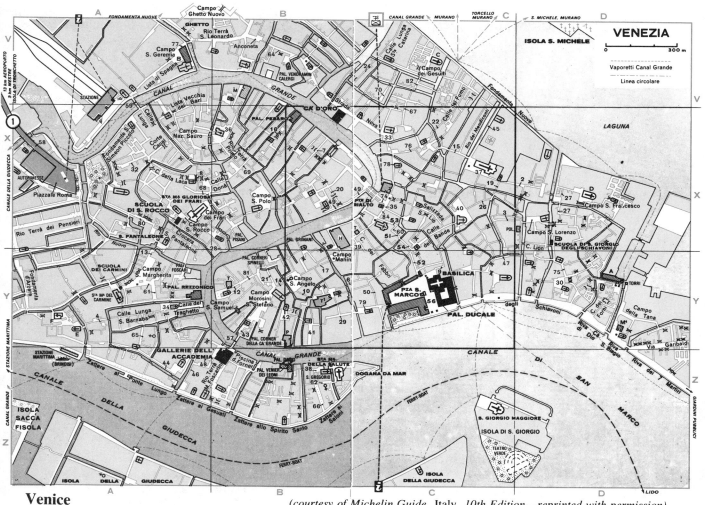

Venice

(courtesy of Michelin Guide, Italy, 10th Edition—reprinted with permission)

AUTISTA **Il pieno, per favore.**

Fill it up, please.

IMPIEGATO **Normale o super?**

Regular or super?

AUTISTA **Normale. Le**

Regular. Would you mind checking the

(dees-pyah-cher-EH-bbeh) (kohn-troh-LLAH-reh)

dispiacerebbe   controllare

(OH-lee-oh) (AH-kwah)

l'olio,   l'acqua e l'aria nelle gomme?

oil, water, and air in the tires?

IMPIEGATO **Tutto è a posto.**

Everything is okay.

AUTISTA **Voglio andare a Piazza San**

I want to go to San Marco Square. How does one

Marco. Come ci si va?

get there?

93

IMPIEGATO *(points to map)* **Guardi. Lei si** | Look. You are here at

trova qui alla Stazione di Santa Lucia. | Santa Lucia Railroad

Prenda la strada che va intorno al | Station. Take the road that goes all around the

Canal Grande. Questa strada la porta | Grand Canal. This road will take you directly to

(dee-reh-ttah-MEHN-teh)
direttamente alla piazza. | the square.

(TRAH-ffee-koh)
AUTISTA **C'è molto traffico?** | Is there a lot of traffic?

IMPIEGATO **No. Non c'è affatto traffico,** | No. There is no traffic at all, because Venice

perché Venezia non ha strade, ha | does not have roads, it has only canals!

solo canali!

Read over this dialogue several times and then test your memory by completing the missing dialogue parts. Check your answers only after you have attempted to complete the missing parts from memory.

AUTISTA _____ .

IMPIEGATO **Normale o super?**

AUTISTA _____ . **Le dispiacerebbe controllare** _____ ?

IMPIEGATO **Tutto è a posto.**

AUTISTA **Voglio andare a Piazza San Marco.** _____ ?

IMPIEGATO **Guardi. Lei si trova qui** _____

_____ . **Prenda la strada che va**

_____ . **Questa strada**

la porta _____ .

CLIENTE **C'è** _____ ?

COMMESSO **No. Non c'è** _____ **perché**

Venezia _____ !

94

L'AUTOMOBILE / LA MACCHINA
The Car

(voh-LAHN-teh)
il volante
steering wheel

(KLAHK-sohn)
il clacson
horn

(peh-DAH-leh)
il pedale del freno
brake pedal

(free-TSYOH-neh)
il pedale della frizione
clutch pedal

(tehr-jee-krees-TAH-llee)
i tergicristalli
windshield wipers

(KAHM-byoh)
la leva del cambio
gear shift

(kroos-KOH-ttoh)
il cruscotto
dashboard

(ah-cheh-leh-rah-TOH-reh)
l'acceleratore
accelerator

(bah-OO-leh)(pohr-tah-bah-GAH-llyee)
il baule / il portabagagli
trunk

(TAHR-gah)
la targa
plate

(pah-rah-OOR-tee)
il paraurti
bumper

(KOH-fah-noh)
il cofano
hood

(FAH-ree) (proh-yeh-TTOH-ree)
i fari / i proiettori
headlights

(bah-tteh-REE-ah)
la batteria
battery

(rah-dee-ah-TOH-reh)
il radiatore
radiator

(moh-TOH-reh)
il motore
motor

(pah-rah-BREH-tsah)
il parabrezza
windshield

(sehr-bah-TOH-yoh)
il serbatoio
gas tank

(kah-rroh-tseh-REE-ah)
la carrozzeria
body (of the car)

(pah-dee-LLYOH-neh)
il padiglione
roof

(pohr-TYEH-rah) (spohr-TEH-lloh)
la portiera / lo sportello
door

(POHM-pah)
la pompa
gas pump

(pah-rah-FAHN-goh)
il parafango
fender

(neh-oo-MAH-tee-chee)
i pneumatici /
tires *(GOH-mmeh)*
le gomme

Now fill in the names for the following auto parts.

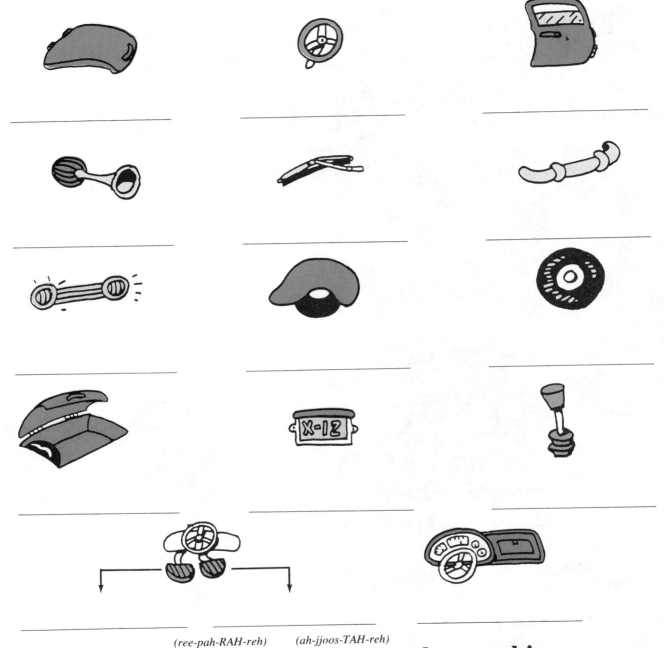

(ree-pah-RAH-reh)   (ah-jjoos-TAH-reh)

Per riparare / aggiustare la macchina
Some Essentials for Repair

The following words and expressions will be useful to you if your car breaks down in Italy.

Mi può aiutare?   Can you help me?

La mia gomma è sgonfia.   My tire is flat.

La mia macchina non parte.	My car doesn't start.
I freni non funzionano.	The brakes don't work.
Ho bisogno di benzina.	I need gas.
(Mi faccia) il pieno, per favore.	Fill 'er up, please.

Come si fa per chiedere . . .
How to Ask for . . .

In order to get people to do things for you, you will have to know how to use verbs in a "command" or "imperative" way. Look at the following chart. This shows you how to form the imperative of regular verbs.

THE IMPERATIVE			
	PARLARE *CAMMINARE*	*SCRIVERE* *RISPONDERE*	*DORMIRE* *FINIRE*
Singular *Familiar* *Command:*	**Parla!** Speak! **Cammina!** Walk!	**Scrivi!** Write! **Rispondi!** Answer!	**Dormi!** Sleep! **Finisci!** Finish!
Singular *Polite* *Command:*	**Parli!** **Cammini!**	**Scriva!** **Risponda!**	**Dorma!** **Finisca!**
Plural *Command:*	**Parlate!** **Camminate!**	**Scrivete!** **Rispondete!**	**Dormite!** **Finite!**

The command "Let's speak, walk,"
and so on, is given by a form
you already know.

Parliamo! _____	Let's speak!
Scriviamo! _____	Let's write!
Finiamo! _____	Let's finish!
Dormiamo! _____	Let's sleep!

Notice that, as in English, pronouns are not used with the imperative. Also notice that verbs like *finire,* which take the extra *isc* in the present indicative (remember?), also take it in the imperative singular command forms.

To make reflexive verbs imperative, add on the reflexive pronouns in the familiar and plural forms.

REFLEXIVE IMPERATIVES		
	ALZ*ARSI*	DIVERT*IRSI*
Singular Familiar Command:	(AHL-tsah-tee) **Alza*ti*!**	(dee-VEHR-tee-tee) **Diverti*ti*!**
Singular Polite Command:	*Si* **alzi!**	*Si* **diverta!**
Plural Command:	(ahl-TSAH-teh-vee) **Alzate*vi*!** **and** (ahl-TSYAH-moh-chee) **Alziamo*ci*!** Let's get up!	(dee-vehr-TEE-teh-vee) **Divertite*vi*!** (dee-vehr-TYAH-moh-chee) **Divertiamo*ci*!** Let's enjoy ourselves!

One more thing about imperatives: don't get discouraged! With a little practice, you will become familiar and quite proficient with these verb forms. To make any verb negative, you have learned to put *non* just before it. So too with imperative verbs. But there is one change you must make. For the singular familiar command in the negative, use the infinitive (*parlare, scrivere*).

NEGATIVE IMPERATIVES	
Singular Familiar Command:	**Non parlare!** Don't speak! **Non scrivere!** Don't write!
Other Command Forms:	**Non parli! Non scriva! Non parlate! Non scrivete!** (Just put *non* before the appropriate imperative form.)

Now try the following.

You are speaking to your friend. Tell him to do as you wish, filling in the blanks as indicated.

1. Giovanni, _____ italiano!
              speak

2. Giovanni, _____ la pizza!
              finish

3. Giovanni, _____ la **lettera**!
         (LEH-tteh-rah)
         write

4. Giovanni, non _____ lentamente!
         walk   (be careful!)

5. Giovanni, _____ domani alle sei!
         get up

Now use polite forms, because you are speaking to a stranger.

Signora Smith, _____ italiano!
speak

Signora Smith, _____ la pizza!
finish

Signora Smith, _____ la lettera!
write

Signora Smith, non _____ lentamente!
walk

Signora Smith, _____ domani alle sei!
get up

Finally, try giving commands to a group of people.

Ragazzi, _____ italiano!
speak

Ragazzi, _____ la pizza!
finish

Ragazzi, _____ la lettera!
write

Ragazzi, non _____ lentamente!
walk

Ragazzi, _____ domani alle sei!
get up

The imperatives of the irregular verbs you have learned so far are as follows.

	ANDARE	VENIRE	FARE	DARE	DIRE	SEDERSI	ESSERE
Singular Familiar Command:	Va'!	(VYEH-nee) Vieni!	Fa'!	Da'!	Di'!	(SYEH-dee-tee) Siediti!	(SEE-ee) Sii!
Singular Polite Command:	Vada!	(VEHN-gah) Venga!	(FAH-chah) Faccia!	(DEE-ah) Dia!	Dica!	Si sieda!	(SEE-ah) Sia!
Plural Command:	Andate!	Venite!	Fate!	Date!	Dite!	(seh-DEH-teh-vee) Sedetevi!	(SYAH-teh) Siate!

For the negative of an irregular verb, use the infinitive (*Non andare! Non venire!* etc.).

Now choose the familiar or polite command forms of these verbs. *Stia attento!* (Be careful!)

1. Marco, _____ a casa!
go   home

2. Anna, _____ qui!
come

3. Signor Smith, _____ a casa!
go

4. Signora Smith, _____ questo!
do

5. Signorina Rossi, _____ qui!
come

6. Maria, _____ questo!
do

ANSWERS

Familiar or polite commands 1. va' (a casa!) **2.** vieni (qui!) **3.** vada (a casa!) **4.** faccia (questo!) **5.** venga (qui!) **6.** fa' (questo!)

Plural commands parlate (italiano!) finite (la pizza!) scrivete (la lettera!) camminate (lentamente!) alzatevi (domani!)

Singular commands parli (italiano!) finisca (la pizza!) scriva (la lettera!) cammini (lentamente!) si alzi (domani!)

7. Giovanni, _____ la penna a Maria!
   give

8. Signor Verdi, _____ la penna alla signorina Smith!
   give

9. Signora Rossi, _____ la verità!   10. Gina, _____ la verità!
   say/tell   truth   say/tell

(veh-ree-TAH)

11. Pina, _____ qui!   12. Signorina Verdi, _____ qui!
    sit   sit

13. Signor Smith, _____ gentile!   14. Gino, _____ gentile!
    be   be

Using the imperative does not always mean you are giving orders. When someone asks for directions, your response will be "go to the right." That's a command, too, in a way. Giving directions in Italian is an essential communicative skill. Try your hand at giving

(ah-oo-toh-ree-MEH-ssah)

directions to the **autorimessa** in the diagram. Here are the verbs and expressions you will need.
garage

(jee-RAH-reh)
girare   **a destra**
to turn

andare diritto   **a sinistra**
straight ahead

Avere
To Have

Like "to be," *avere* is an essential verb for communicating in your new language. Notice that the "h" is not pronounced. It is always silent.

AVERE			
	to have		
io _____ *(oh)* **ho**		noi _____ *(ah-BBYAH-moh)* **abbiamo**	
tu _____ *(AH-ee)* **hai**		voi _____ *(ah-VEH-teh)* **avete**	
lui ⎱ _____ *(ah)* **ha**		loro _____ *(AH-nnoh)* **hanno**	
lei ⎰			
Singular Familiar Command: *(AH-bbee)* **Abbi!**	*Singular Polite Command:* *(AH-bbyah)* **Abbia!**	*Plural Command:* *(ah-BBYAH-teh)* **Abbiate!**	

100

Capisci? Put the right form of *avere* in the spaces provided.

Quell'uomo ___ha___ due valige.   Tu ___hai___ sempre ragione.

Io non ___ho___ la patente di guida.   Loro ___hanno___ torto.

Noi ___abbiamo___ una Lancia.   Gli autisti italiani ___hanno___
molta pazienza.

Voi ___avete___ una FIAT.

Here are two more verbs that are useful, but first, review the verb *volere* in chapter 6.

(poh-TEH-reh) POTERE to be able to		*(doh-VEH-reh)* DOVERE to have to	
(POH-ssoh) io posso	*(poh-SSYAH-moh)* noi possiamo	*(DEH-voh)* devo	*(doh-BBYAH-moh)* dobbiamo
(PWOH-ee) tu puoi	*(poh-TEH-teh)* voi potete	*(DEH-vee)* devi	*(doh-VEH-teh)* dovete
lui} lei} *(pwoh)* può	*(POH-ssoh-noh)* loro possono	*(DEH-veh)* deve	*(DEH-voh-noh)* devono

Now use the right form of *potere* or *dovere* in the following sentences.

Io non ___posso___ andare in Italia quest'**anno**.
     potere   year

I passeggeri ___devono___ scendere a Bologna.
         dovere

Voi ___dovete___ comprare l'assicurazione per la macchina!
    dovere   to buy   insurance

I turisti ___possono___ noleggiare quella macchina.
       potere

Io ___devo___ portare la mia macchina alla stazione di servizio.
  dovere

Tu ___puoi___ portare la tua macchina a quella stazione di servizio.
    potere

Il signor Smith non ___può___ guidare in Italia perché ha lasciato la sua patente in
America.
     potere   *(lah-SHAH-toh)* he left

Attenzione! (Watch out!) Driving in a foreign country means watching the road even when the scenery is breathtaking.

Che bella veduta! Yes, how beautiful! Read the passage that follows and determine what happened on this trip. Answer the questions that follow.

Un autista americano e un autista italiano hanno avuto un piccolo incidente. *(een-chee-DEHN-teh)* **L'autista**
                                                         had   Accident

(soo-CHEH-ssoh)   *(DAH-nnoh)*   *(GRAH-veh)*
italiano chiede come è successo.   **Il danno non è grave, ma la macchina dell'italiano è**
          it happened   damage   serious

(NWOH-vah)   *(deh-CHEE-deh)*   *(BREH-veh)* *(dees-koo-SYOH-neh)*
nuova. L'autista italiano decide di chiamare un vigile. Dopo una breve   **discussione, i due**
new   decided   brief   discussion

*(ah-jjoos-TAH-reh)**(oh-NYOO-noh)* *(PROH-pree-ah)*
autisti decidono di farsi aggiustare   **ognuno la**   **propria macchina. Il vigile dice ai due**
                      fix   each one   own

autisti che bisogna stare attenti quando si guida.
          be careful   one

Chi ha avuto un incidente?

☐ Due turisti americani.

☐ Un autista americano e un autista italiano.

☐ Un autista e un vigile.

Chi chiede come è successo?

☐ L'autista americano.

☐ Il vigile.

☐ L'autista italiano.

Com'è il danno?

☐ È grave.

☐ Non è grave.

☐ È molto grave.

Chi decide di chiamare il vigile?

☐ L'autista italiano.

☐ L'autista americano.

☐ Nessuno.

Che cosa decidono di fare, gli autisti?

☐ Decidono di andare insieme a Roma.

☐ Decidono di andare alla stazione di servizio.

☐ Decidono di farsi aggiustare ognuno la propria macchina.

Che cosa dice il vigile?

☐ Dice che bisogna guidare solo le macchine nuove.

☐ Dice che bisogna stare attenti quando si guida.

☐ Dice che non bisogna fare un incidente.

Now see how many of the following words and expressions you remember or can figure out by matching them up with their English meanings.

1. incidente	a. No Left Turn
2. danno	b. One-Way
3. aggiustare	c. No Parking
4. girare	d. rush hour
5. guidare	e. west
6. benzina	f. east
7. clacson	g. south
8. cruscotto	h. (car) horn
9. pneumatici	i. No Passing
10. volante	j. gas
11. Divieto di sorpasso	k. to drive
12. Divieto di svolta a sinistra	l. to turn
13. Senso unico	m. steering wheel
14. Divieto di sosta	n. dashboard
15. ora di punta	o. to fix
16. nord	p. accident
17. sud	q. tires
18. est	r. damage
19. ovest	s. north

As a quick review of those pesky imperative verbs, say the following in Italian.

Mark, get up! _____

Mrs. Smith, enjoy yourself! _____

John, don't go to the museum today! _____

Mr. Smith, don't go to the post office today! _____

Anne, John, speak Italian! _____

9   Il campeggio
(kahm-PEH-jjoh)
Camping

These words will be useful to you if you go camping to any of the many mountain spots throughout Italy. You will be able to buy equipment in most of the resort villages found in the Italian mountains.

(mah-teh-RAH-ssoh) *(pneh-oo-MAH-tee-koh)*
il materasso   pneumatico
air mattress

(KAH-pee) *(vehs-tee-AH-ree-oh)*
il capi di vestiario
articles of clothing

(pah-GAH-yeh)
le pagaie
paddles

(koh-PEHR-tah)
la coperta
blanket

(PEE-lah) *(tahs-KAH-bee-leh)*
la pila   tascabile
flashlight

(kah-NEHS-troh)
il canestro
basket

(roo-SHEH-lloh)
il ruscello
brook

(TEHN-dah)
la tenda
tent

(AHL-beh-roh)
l'albero
tree

(SOH-leh)
il sole
sun

(kah-NOH-ah)
la canoa
canoe

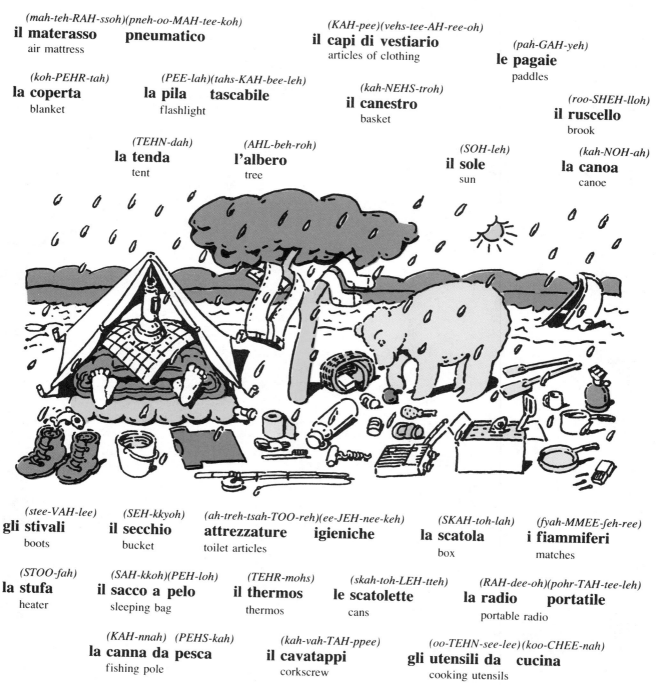

(stee-VAH-lee)
gli stivali
boots

(SEH-kkyoh)
il secchio
bucket

(ah-treh-tsah-TOO-reh) *(ee-JEH-nee-keh)*
attrezzature   igieniche
toilet articles

(SKAH-toh-lah)
la scatola
box

(fyah-MMEE-feh-ree)
i fiammiferi
matches

(STOO-fah)
la stufa
heater

(SAH-kkoh) *(PEH-loh)*
il sacco a pelo
sleeping bag

(TEHR-mohs)
il thermos
thermos

(skah-toh-LEH-tteh)
le scatolette
cans

(RAH-dee-oh) *(pohr-TAH-tee-leh)*
la radio   portatile
portable radio

(KAH-nnah) *(PEHS-kah)*
la canna da pesca
fishing pole

(kah-vah-TAH-ppee)
il cavatappi
corkscrew

(oo-TEHN-see-lee) *(koo-CHEE-nah)*
gli utensili da   cucina
cooking utensils

Practice your "outdoor" Italian. Find the camping words and expressions in the following puzzle and circle them. When you locate each one, write it down and pronounce it aloud. We've found the first one for you, as an example.

materasso pneumatico

_____   _____   _____

_____   _____   _____

_____   _____   _____

_____   _____   _____

_____   _____   _____

_____   _____   _____

```
q  m a t e r a s s o p n e u m a t i c o  a z w s p x e d c
r  f v t g b y h n u i j m k q l a s o l e p o l a i j n u
h  r b y g v t f c r l d x e s b z a p q x s w c g d e v f
r  u b g t n h y m j a u k o p e q a e z w c s x a e d c r
m  s k s c a t o l e t t e n j r i b r h u a v g i y c f t
x  c d r z s e q a z a w s x e o d c t r f p m k e i n j u
z  e a q t h e r m o s x c c a v a t a p p i d e v f r b g
t  l n h y m j u k l c o p q a z w s x e d d c r f v t y h
z  l a q x s w c d s a c c o a p e l o v f i r b g t n z a
p  o l n y q a z w x b e d r f v i j n b r v p m q z x c v
y  h n u t e n s i l i d a c u c i n a t g e b r f v f w s
q  a z w s x e d c r l f v y h n z a q x w s e c c h i o d
x  s c a n n a d a p e s c a w c d e v f s t u f a r a e w
z  a q x s w c d e b f r g h y h u n k i j i l o n q m a c
i  r a d i o p o r t a t i l e w c s d f g a h b o v m p o
m  k o n j u b h y v g t c f r x a d w x f r q w a t i e a
a  t t r e z z a t u r e i g i e n i c h e i p o u y f t r
z  x e c v b n m a s d f g h q w e e r t y o u i z x e w t
q  w n e r t y u i o p a s d f g s h j k l z x c v b r n m
p  o d i u r w q a l k s j s c a t o l a d h f g m z i b y
z  m a x n c b v l a p q o w i e r r u t y z q w e r t c p
p  z o c s t i v a l i i v u b y o d q p w o b n v m c l z
```

AL CAMPEGGIO

To the Campground

Now read the following two dialogues, which contain some useful words, expressions, and information on camping. Read them aloud, repeating each line several times, until you can pronounce them easily.

(Mark calls his friend Giovanni on the phone to ask for some camping information.)

GIOVANNI   **Pronto. Chi parla?**

Hello. Who is it?

MARK   **Ciao, Giovanni. Sono Mark. Mi**

sai dire se c'è un campeggio qui
(vee-CHEE-noh)
vicino?

Hi, Giovanni. It's Mark. Can you tell

me if there is a campground near

here?

GIOVANNI   **Sì, volentieri. Prendi**
(ah-oo-toh-STRAH-dah)   *(kee-LOH-meh-tree)*
l'autostrada per venti chilometri, e
(CHEHR-kah) *(seh-NYAH-leh)* *(strah-DAH-leh)*
cerca un segnale stradale che
(EEN-dee-kah)
indica il campeggio.

Yes, gladly. Take the

highway for 20 kilometers,

and look for a road sign that indicates where the

campground is.

(koh-NOH-shee)
MARK   **Lo conosci?**

Are you familiar with it?

(preh-oh-kkoo-PAH-reh)
GIOVANNI   **Sì. Non ti preoccupare! È**
(FAH-chee-leh)
facile trovarlo. Tutti i campeggi
(pah-EH-zee)
italiani sono vicini a piccoli paesi.

Yes. Don't worry! It's easy to find. All Italian

campgrounds are near small towns.

(BAH-nyee)
MARK   **Ci sono i bagni?**

Are there any bathrooms?

GIOVANNI   **Penso di sì.**

I think so.

(poh•TAH-bee-leh)
MARK   **C'è acqua potabile?**

Is there drinking water?

(preh-feh-REE-bee-leh)
GIOVANNI   **In Italia è preferibile bere**
(eem-boh-ttee-LLYAH-tah)
acqua imbottigliata o,
(nah-toor-ahl-MEHN-teh) *(VEE-noh)*
naturalmente, vino!

In Italy it is preferable to drink

bottled water or, naturally, wine!

(eh-leh-ttree-chee-TAH)
MARK   **C'è l'elettricità?**

Is there any electricity?

GIOVANNI   **Non credo.**

I don't believe so.

MARK   **Costa molto?**

Does it cost a lot?

GIOVANNI	**Costa molto poco.**	It costs very little.
	(fahn-TAHS-tee-koh)	
MARK	**Fantastico! Il campeggio italiano fa**	Fantastic! Italian camping is truly for me!
	(PROH-pree-oh)	
	proprio per me!	

(neh-GOH-tsee-oh) *(JEH-neh-ree)* *(ah-lee-mehn-TAH-ree)*

AL NEGOZIO DI GENERI ALIMENTARI
At the Grocery Store

(Mark Smith and his family enter a grocery store near the campground.)

	(deh-SEE-deh-rah)	
COMMESSA	**Buona sera. Desidera, signora?**	Good evening. Can I help you, madam?
	(PAH-kkoh)	
MARY	**Sì. Vorrei un pacco di spaghetti,**	Yes. I would like a package of spaghetti,
	(BOO-rroh) *(LEE-troh)*	
	cento grammi di burro, un litro di	100 grams (about ¼-pound) of butter, a liter
	(LAH-tteh) *(SAH-leh)* *(boh-TTEE-llyah)*	
	latte, un po' di sale, e una bottiglia	of milk, a bit of salt, and a bottle of wine.
	di vino.	
COMMESSA	**Trentamila lire.**	30,000 lira.
	(POH-lloh)	
MARK	**Vogliamo anche quel pollo e**	We also want that chicken and that box of
	quella scatola di fiammiferi, va bene?	matches, okay?

COMMESSA	Lei è un turista americano?	Are you an American tourist?
MARK	Sì.	Yes.
COMMESSA	Va bene. *(She takes their money.)* Dove va, al campeggio?	Okay. Where are you going, to the campground?
MARK	Sì. Grazie e arrivederla.	Yes. Thank you and good-bye.
COMMESSA	Arrivederla.	Good-bye.

Now without looking back, match the following to form lines from the first dialogue.

Pronto. Chi . . .	italiani sono vicini a piccoli paesi.
Mi sai dire se . . .	acqua potabile?
Prendi . . .	preferibile bere acqua imbottigliata o, naturalmente, vino!
Non ti . . .	di sì.
Tutti i campeggi . . .	italiano fa proprio per me!
Ci sono . . .	preoccupare!
Penso . . .	parla?
C'è . . .	c'è un campeggio qui vicino?
In Italia è . . .	l'autostrada per venti chilometri.
Il campeggio . . .	i bagni?

Check your answers only after you have attempted to match up these items from memory. Now try to complete the missing parts from the second dialogue. Check your answers only after you have attempted to do this exercise from memory.

Buona s_____. D_____, signora?

Sì. Vorrei un p_____ di spaghetti, cento g_____

di b_____, un litro di l_____, un po' di s_____,

e una b_____ di v_____.

Trentamila l_____.

Vogliamo anche quel p_____ e quella s_____ di f_____,

va bene?

Lei è un t_____ a_____?

Sì.

Va bene. Dove va, al c_____?

Sì. Grazie e a_____.

Arrivederla.

In the first dialogue above you were introduced to the verb *bere*, "to drink." This is conjugated as follows.

BERE					
					(kah-FFEH)
Io	*bevo*	**il vino.**	**Noi**	*beviamo*	**il caffè.**
					coffee
Tu	*bevi*	**il vino.**	**Voi**	*bevete*	**il caffè con latte.**
				(BEH-voh-noh	
Lei	*beve*	**il latte.**	**Loro**	*bevono*	**solo il vino.**

Come si dice . . .?
How Do You Say . . .?

Here are some expressions that might come in handy on your camping excursion.

(bee-ZOH-nyoh)			
Ho bisogno di . . .	I need	**avere fame**	to be hungry
Lo so	I know it	**avere sonno**	to be sleepy
Non lo so	I do not know it	**avere sete**	to be thirsty
		(pah-OO-rah)	
avere caldo	to be hot	**avere paura**	to be afraid
avere freddo	to be cold		

Now try to match each sentence with a picture.

1.

a. Il ragazzo ha bisogno di pane. *(PAH-neh)*
   bread

b. La donna si vergogna. *(DOH-nnah)*
   woman   is ashamed

2.

c. La donna ha caldo.

d. L'uomo ha sonno.

3.

e. I bambini hanno paura. *(bahm-BEE-nee)*
   children

f. L'uomo ha freddo.

4.

5.

6.

Camping is fun as long as the weather holds out. See how the Smith family fared on their trip. Test your readiness for camping by selecting the appropriate answers to the questions, based on the following passage.

La famiglia Smith è a un campeggio vicino a Roma.

Fa molto caldo e allora decidono di andare alla spiaggia. *(SPYAH-jjah)*
beach

Ma l'acqua è fredda e allora solo Anne va nell'acqua.

ANSWERS

Matching   1-f, 2-b, 3-d, 4-e, 5-c, 6-a

111

(jeh-LAH-toh) (KAHM-pehr)

John prende un gelato dal camper, ma la madre non vuole.
      ice cream   camper

(nahs-KOHN-deh)   (KAH-neh)

John nasconde il gelato e il cane lo mangia.
  hides   dog   eats it

Dov'è il campeggio?   ☐ È vicino a Roma.
                          ☐ È vicino a Piazza
                             San Marco.
                          ☐ È vicino a Firenze.

Dove decidono di andare?   ☐ A Roma.
                                ☐ Nel camper.
                                ☐ Alla spiaggia.

Com'è l'acqua?   ☐ È calda.
                 ☐ È fredda.
                 ☐ È piena di vino.

Chi mangia il gelato?   ☐ La madre.
                           ☐ Il cane.
                           ☐ John.

Che cosa prende, John?   ☐ Prende una bottiglia di vino.
                              ☐ Prende un gelato.
                              ☐ Prende una scatola di fiammiferi.

Now have fun with the following crossword puzzle.

Across
3. Vorrei cento grammi di . . .
4. Loro . . . solo il vino.
5. Il sacco a . . .
6. Vorrei un litro di . . .

Down
1. L'uomo non ha caldo, ha . . .
2. L'uomo va a dormire perché ha . . .
3. Vorrei una . . . di vino.
5. La canna da . . .

Italian months are very similar to English. Say them aloud a few times, until you are familiar with the Italian pronunciation.

(jeh-NNAH-yoh)
gennaio
January

(feh-BBRAH-yoh)
febbraio
February

(MAHR-tsoh)
marzo
March

(ah-PREE-leh)
aprile
April

(MAH-jjoh)
maggio
May

(JOO-nyoh)
giugno
June

(LOO-llyoh)
luglio
July

(ah-GOHS-toh)
agosto
August

(seh-TTEHM-breh)
settembre
September

(oh-TTOH-breh)
ottobre
October

(noh-VEHM-breh)
novembre
November

(dee-CHEHM-breh)
dicembre
December

113

Now do the same with these expressions relating to the seasons.

(een-VEHR-noh)
—**È inverno**
Winter

Fa molto freddo.
It's very cold.

(NEH-vee-kah)
Nevica.
It's snowing.

(JEH-lee-doh)
Fa un freddo gelido.
It's freezing.

(pree-mah-VEH-rah)
—**È primavera**
Spring

Fa fresco.
It is cool.

C'è il sole.
It is sunny.

(ehs-TAH-teh)
—**È estate**
Summer

Fa caldo.
It is hot.

(OO-mee-doh)
È umido.
It is humid.

(ah-FOH-zoh)
È afoso.
It is muggy.

(boo-rahs-KOH-soh)
Il tempo è burrascoso.
It's stormy.

(PYOH-veh)
Piove.
It's raining.

(TWOH-nah)
Tuona.
It's thundering.

(ah-oo-TOO-nnoh)
—**È autunno**
Fall

Fa fresco.
It's chilly.

(dee-ROH-ttoh)
Piove a dirotto.
It's raining cats and dogs.

(NEH-bbyah)
C'è la nebbia.
It's foggy.

CHE TEMPO FA?

How Is the Weather?

If you look carefully you will see that many expressions connected with the weather use the verb form *fa* . . .

Che tempo fa?	How is the weather?	**Fa caldo.**	It is hot.
Fa fresco.	It is cool/chilly.	**Fa molto freddo.**	It is very cold.
Fa freddo.	It is cold.	**Fa un freddo gelido.**	It is freezing.

Here are some other useful weather expressions.

C'è il sole.	It is sunny.	**Tuona.**	It is thundering.
È umido.	It is humid.	**Piove a dirotto.**	It is raining cats and dogs.
È afoso.	It is muggy.	**Nevica.**	It is snowing.
È burrascoso.	It is stormy.	**C'è la nebbia.**	It is foggy.
Piove.	It is raining.		

In general, if you want to say the weather is beautiful or bad, use the following expressions.

Fa bel tempo.	The weather is beautiful.	**Fa brutto tempo.**	The weather is bad/awful.

114

If you have learned the weather phrases well, you should be able to give the appropriate expression to describe each picture.

1. _____

2. _____

3. _____

4. _____

5. _____

6. _____

7. _____

8. _____

Look back at the calendar and read the months of the year out loud, again, and review the ordinal numbers in chapter 5. Then try the following. Be careful not to capitalize the months.

Il terzo mese _____

Il quinto mese _____

Il primo mese _____

Il quarto mese _____

Il secondo mese _____

Il sesto mese _____

Il decimo mese _____

Il settimo mese _____

Il nono mese _____

l'ottavo mese _____

Il mese dopo ottobre _____
        after
     (OOL-tee-moh)

l'ultimo mese _____
        last

ANSWERS

Identification

1. Fa bel tempo. 2. C'è il sole. 3. Fa freddo. 4. Fa caldo. 5. Piove. 6. Nevica. 7. Fa brutto tempo.
8. C'è la nebbia.

Months

(Il terzo mese) è marzo. (Il decimo mese) è ottobre. (Il quinto mese) è maggio. (Il settimo mese) è luglio.
(Il primo mese) è gennaio. (Il nono mese) è settembre. (Il quarto mese) è aprile. (L'ottavo mese) è agosto.
(Il secondo mese) è febbraio. (Il mese dopo ottobre) è novembre. (Il sesto mese) è giugno.
(L'ultimo mese) è dicembre.

115

To say a date in Italian, just use the cardinal numbers in the following formula.

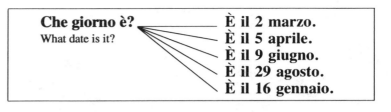

Che giorno è?	È il 2 marzo.
What date is it?	È il 5 aprile.
	È il 9 giugno.
	È il 29 agosto.
	È il 16 gennaio.

The only exception is for the first day of each month, for which you use the ordinal number.

| Che giorno è? | È il primo ottobre. |
| | È il primo luglio. |

Now you should be able to write out the following dates in Italian.

Che giorno è?

January 4	July 30
February 7	August 24
March 11	September 8
April 19	October 15
May 28	November 20
June 1 (Be careful!)	December 10

Here are the days of the week in Italian. Read them out loud several times; then see if you can figure out each of the logic puzzles that follow. Once again, notice that you do not capitalize the days of the week.

(loo-neh-DEE)
lunedì _____ Monday

(veh-nehr-DEE)
venerdì _____ Friday

(mahr-teh-DEE)
martedì _____ Tuesday

(SAH-bah-toh)
sabato _____ Saturday

(mehr-koh-leh-DEE)
mercoledì _____ Wednesday

(doh-MEH-nee-kah)
domenica _____ Sunday

(joh-veh-DEE)
giovedì _____ Thursday

1. il giorno **dopo** lunedì: _____
   after

2. il giorno dopo domenica: _____

3. il giorno **prima** di domenica: _____
   before

4. il giorno prima di venerdì: _____

5. il giorno dopo martedì: _____

6. il giorno dopo sabato: _____

7. il giorno prima di sabato: _____

(ah-jjeh-TTEE-vee)

Aggettivi
Adjectives

There are two main kinds of adjectives in Italian: one that ends in `-o` and another that ends in `-e`. Adjectives usually follow the noun they modify and agree with its gender (masculine or feminine) and its number (singular or plural). Confused? Don't worry! Just look at the following examples and then try your hand at the activities that follow.

ADJECTIVES IN `-o` : ITALIANO

WITH MASCULINE NOUNS

Singular
il ragazzo italian `o`

the Italian boy

il padre italian `o`

the Italian father

Plural
i ragazzi italian `i`

the Italian boys

i padri italian `i`

the Italian fathers

WITH FEMININE NOUNS

la ragazza italian `a`

the Italian girl

la madre italian `a`

the Italian mother

le ragazze italian `e`

the Italian girls

le madri italian `e`

the Italian mothers

ANSWERS

Days

1. martedì (Tuesday) 2. lunedì (Monday) 3. sabato (Saturday) 4. giovedì (Thursday) 5. mercoledì (Wednesday)
6. domenica (Sunday) 7. venerdì (Friday)

117

Get it? Adjectives that end in -e are even simpler. Simply use -e with any singular noun (masculine or feminine) and -i with any plural noun (masculine or feminine).

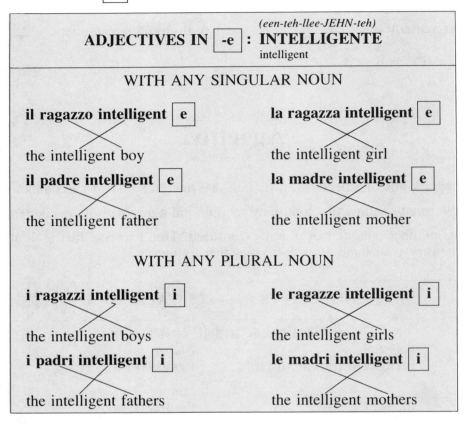

You can always refer to this chart if you forget later on.

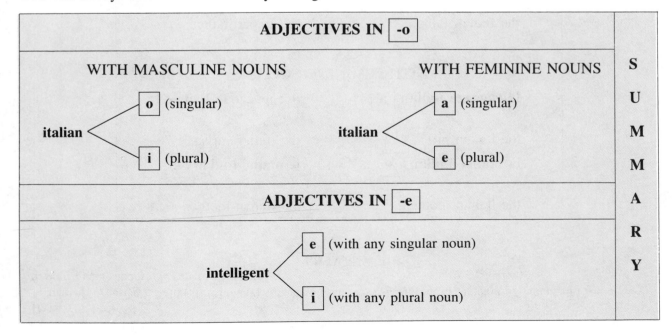

Adjectives normally follow the noun in Italian. Some are also used in front of the noun.

il ragazzo simpatico *or* **il simpatico ragazzo**

the nice boy   the nice boy

A few adjectives, like the ordinal numbers you learned in chapter 5, are used only in front of the noun.

il primo ragazzo

the first boy

As in English, an adjective can be separated from the noun by certain verbs like "to be." However, the agreement patterns in the charts still apply, as you can see in these examples.

Il ragazzo è simpatico.
The boy is nice.

La ragazza è bella.
The girl is beautiful.

I ragazzi sono simpatici.
The boys are nice.

Le ragazze sono simpatiche.
The girls are nice.

Io sono alta e tu sei bassa.
I am tall and you are short.

(joh-VAH-neh)
Io sono giovane e
I am young and
(VEH-kkyoh)
tu sei vecchio.
you are old.

(CHEH-nah) (BWOH-nah)
La cena è buona.
The dinner is good.

La cena è pronta.
The dinner is ready.

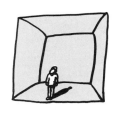

La mia stanza è grande.
My room is big.

La mia stanza è piccola.
My room is small.

(KOH-moh-dah)
La mia stanza è comoda.
My room is comfortable.

La mia stanza
My room
(roo-moh-ROH-zah)
è rumorosa.
is noisy.

119

Here is a list of the adjectives just used. Match them to their English equivalents.

1. intelligente   a. short
2. italiano   b. tall
3. simpatico   c. beautiful
4. bello   d. Italian
5. alto   e. intelligent
6. basso   f. nice
7. giovane   g. comfortable
8. vecchio   h. noisy
9. buono   i. big
10. pronto   j. small
11. grande   k. good
12. piccolo   l. ready
13. comodo   m. young
14. rumoroso   n. old

It should be easy for you to put the correct ending on each of these adjectives.

Quelle ragazze sono intelligent_____ .   Questa pizza non è buon_____ .

Il passeggero italian_____ è simpatic_____ .   La cena è pront_____ .

Quella ragazza è bell_____ , alt_____   La mia stanza è piccol_____
   e giovan_____ .   ma comod_____ .

I miei due zii sono bass_____ e vecch_____ .

The following dialogue contains various words and expressions connected with the weather.
Read it aloud several times and role-play each part.

(*Anne has made an Italian friend, Gina. Anne has spent the night at Gina's house. It is now the morning after.*)

ANNE **Buon giorno, Gina. Sono le otto.**   Good morning, Gina. It's eight o'clock. It's

    C'è un bel sole e fa bel tempo.   sunny and the weather is beautiful.

GINA **Ho ancora sonno.** *(ahn-KOH-rah)*

I'm still sleepy.

Voglio dormire ancora *(VOH-llyoh)* *(ahn-KOH-rah)*
un'altra ora.

I want to sleep another hour.

ANNE **Impossibile! Le previsioni** *(eem-poh-SEE-bee-leh)* *(preh-vee-ZYOH-nee)*
meteorologiche indicano che *(meh-teh-oh-roh-LOH-jee-keh)* *(EEN-dee-kah-noh)*
forse piove stasera. I due ragazzi con *(stah-SEH-rah)*
cui abbiamo un appuntamento ci *(KOO-ee)*
aspettano. Dobbiamo uscire *(ahs-PEH-ttah-noh)* *(doh-BBYAH-moh)* *(oo-SHEE-reh)*
questa mattina! *(mah-TTEE-nah)*

No way! (*literally*, Impossible!) The weather forecast indicates that it may rain tonight. The two boys with whom we have a date are waiting for us. We have to go out this morning!

GINA **Solo un'altra mezz'ora?**

Only another half-hour?

ANNE **No. Adesso!**

No. Now!

(She starts exercising and making noise so that Gina is forced to get up from bed.)

ANNE **Finalmente! Com'è il mio ragazzo?**

Finally! How is my date?

GINA **È molto simpatico.**

He is very nice.

ANNE **Bene!**

Good!

GINA **È anche molto ricco.** *(REE-kkoh)*

He is also very rich.

ANNE **Non importa!** *(eem-POHR-tah)*

It doesn't matter!

GINA **Su! Andiamo!** *(to herself)*
Ma ho *ancora* sonno.

Come on! Let's go!
But I'm *still* sleepy.

Now try to complete the missing dialogue parts from memory. Check your answers after you have finished.

Buon giorno, Gina. S_____ le otto. C'è un bel s_____ e fa

b_____ t_____ .

Ho ancora s_____ . Voglio dormire ancora un'altra o_____ .

Impossibile! Le p_____ m_____ indicano che forse

p_____ stasera. I due ragazzi con cui abbiamo un a_____ ci

aspettano. Dobbiamo uscire questa m_____!

Solo un'altra mezz'ora?

No. A_____! Finalmente. Com'è il mio ragazzo?

È molto s_____ .

Bene!

È anche molto r_____ .

Non i_____ .

Here are words describing the various times of the day:

(mah-TTEE-nah)	*(poh-meh-REE-jjoh)*	*(SEH-rah)*	*(NOH-tteh)*
la mattina	**il pomeriggio**	**la sera**	**la notte**
morning	afternoon	evening	night

And here are two expressions using these words:

Buona sera.	Good evening./Good afternoon.
Buona notte.	Good night.
(can be used only when departing, not arriving)	

122

Now match these words with the pictures and write them in the blanks.

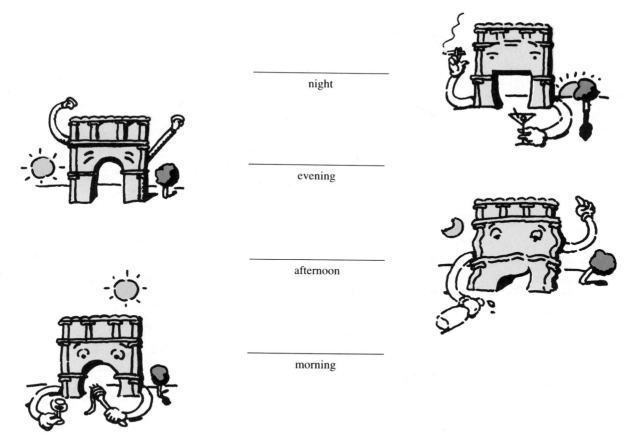

_____
night

_____
evening

_____
afternoon

_____
morning

IL LUNEDÌ
On Mondays

Il lunedì vado sempre a scuola.   (On Mondays I always go to school.)

Il martedì mangio sempre la pizza.

Il mercoledì vado sempre al cinema.

Notice that to say "on Mondays, on Tuesdays, . . ." all you have to do
is use the masculine article **il**.
The only time you use the **la** form is for Sunday.

La domenica dormo tanto.   (On Sundays I sleep a lot.)

See if you can read the following brief passage and then select the appropriate answer to each question.

Oggi è il quattro novembre.
today

(SOH-lee-toh)
Di solito il sabato faccio delle spese.
usually   I do my shopping.

Sono nato il quattordici febbraio
I was born

e ho trentadue anni.
I am thirty-two years old

(kah-lehn-DAH-ree-oh)
Oggi voglio comprare un calendario per il nuovo anno. Su questo calendario segnerò
calendar

(seh-nyeh-ROH)
I will mark down

(eem-pohr-TAHN-tee) *(nah-TAH-leh)*
tre date importanti: **Natale,**
important   Christmas

(PAHS-kwah)
Pasqua,
Easter

(kohm-pleh-AH-nnoh)
e il mio compleanno.
birthday

Che giorno è oggi?
☐ È il nove ottobre.
☐ È il quattro novembre.
☐ È il quindici febbraio.

Che cosa fai di solito il sabato?
☐ Non faccio niente.
☐ Faccio il pieno.
☐ Faccio delle spese.

Quando sei nato?
☐ Sono nato il quattordici febbraio.
☐ Sono nato a Natale.
☐ Sono nato a Pasqua.

Quanti anni hai?
☐ Ho venti anni.
☐ Ho quarantadue anni.
☐ Ho trentadue anni.

Che cosa vuoi comprare oggi?
☐ Una macchina.
☐ Un calendario.
☐ Un libro.

124

Can you find these items in the picture? Say each one aloud as you locate it.

il comandante / il pilota
(pee-LOH-tah)
captain   pilot

(oh-roh-LOH-joh)
l'orologio
clock

(LEE-neh-ah)(ah-EH-re-ah)
la linea   aerea
airline company

(koh-pee-LOH-tah)
il co-pilota
copilot

(kohn-TROH-lloh)
la torre di controllo
control tower

(MOH-bee-leh)
la scala mobile
escalator

(bee-llyeh-tteh-REE-ah)
la biglietteria
ticket counter

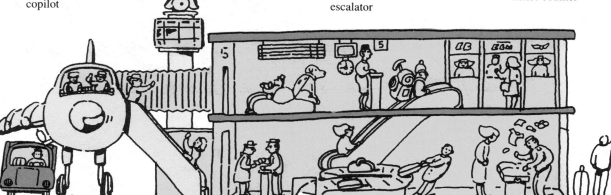

(KAH-myohn)
il camion
truck

(ah-ssees-TEHN-teh)
l'assistente di volo
flight attendant

(trahs-pohr-tah-TOH-reh)
il nastro trasportatore
conveyor/moving belt

(doh-GAH-nah)
la dogana
customs/passport control

(doh-gah-NYEH-reh)
il doganiere
customs officer

(ah-EH-reh-oh)
L'AEREO
The Plane

When you reach Italy you will probably land at either the Rome or Milan airport. Domestic flights are available to major cities within Italy.

Read the following words and expression out loud several times. They might come in handy on an Italian airplane.

(eh-kwee-PAH-jjoh)
l'equipaggio
crew

(oo-SHEE-tah) (see-koo-REH-tsah)
l'uscita di sicurezza
emergency exit

la pista
runway

(kah-BEE-nah)
la cabina
cabin

(seh-DEE-leh)
il sedile
seat

(cheen-TOO-rah)
la cintura di
seat belt

(see-koo-REH-tsah)
sicurezza

il passeggero
passenger

(vah-SSOH-yoh)
il vassoio
tray

There are certain words and expressions in this dialogue that you might hear or need on a plane. Read each line out loud several times and act out each part.

(eem-BAHR-koh)

ASSISTENTE **La carta d'imbarco, per**   Boarding pass, please.

favore.

(EH-kkoh-lah)

MARK   **Eccola.**   Here it is.

(The Smiths take their seats on the plane.)

(deh-KOH-lloh)   *(KWAHL-kelt)*

PILOTA   **Il decollo é previsto tra qualche**   The takeoff is expected in a few minutes. All

(mee-NOO-toh)   *(preh-GAH-tee)*

minato. I passeggeri sono pregati di   passengers are requested to fasten their

126

allacciare le cinture di sicurezza e di | seat belts and to refrain from smoking.

non fumare.

(pehr-FEH-ttoh)

MARY **Ah, che decollo perfetto! I piloti** | Ah, what a perfect takeoff! Italian pilots are

italiani sono proprio bravi. | really great.

MARK *(to the attendant)* **Signorina,** | Miss, when do we eat?

quando si mangia?

ASSISTENTE **Tra qualche minuto, signore.** | In a few minutes, sir.

MARK **Vorrei un cocktail, per favore.** | I would like a cocktail, please.

(SOO-bee-toh)

ASSISTENTE **Sì, subito.** | Yes, right away.

(An hour later the plane is about to land.)

(ah-tteh-RRAH-jjoh)

PILOTA **Signore e signori, l'atterraggio** | Ladies and gentlemen, we will

(preh-VEES-toh)

è previsto tra qualche minuto. | be landing in a few minutes.

MARK **Meno male! Mi fa male lo** | Thank goodness! My stomach hurts.

(STOH-mah-koh)

stomaco.

(SOH-lee-toh) (mahn-JAH-toh)

MARY **Come al solito, hai mangiato** | As usual, you ate too much!

troppo!

By matching the items in the left column to those in the right column, you will get dialogue lines. Check your answers only after you have attempted to do this exercise from memory.

La carta . . .	è previsto tra qualche minuto.
Il decollo . . .	sono proprio bravi.
I passeggeri . . .	si mangia?
I piloti italiani . . .	hai mangiato troppo!
Signorina, quando . . .	l'atterraggio è previsto tra qualche minuto.
Signore e signori . . .	male lo stomaco.
Mi fa . . .	d'imbarco, per favore.
Come al solito . . .	sono pregati di allacciare le cinture di sicurezza e di non fumare.

This word-search puzzle may be a bit tough! However, all of the words except one are part of the vocabulary you just learned.

customs _____   customs officer _____

truck _____   clock _____

seat _____   cabin _____

crew _____   runway _____

tray _____   window _____

q	a	z	w	s	x	e	d	c	r	f	v	t	s	g	b	p	l	m	o	k	n	i
y	h	n	u	j	m	i	d	o	g	a	n	i	e	r	e	q	a	z	w	s	x	e
k	o	l	p	q	a	z	o	w	s	x	e	d	d	c	r	d	c	r	f	v	t	g
g	f	o	r	o	l	o	g	i	o	v	t	g	i	b	y	b	y	h	n	i	k	o
y	h	n	u	j	m	i	a	k	l	p	o	q	l	a	f	q	a	z	w	s	x	e
d	c	a	m	i	o	n	n	r	f	v	r	t	e	q	u	i	p	a	g	g	i	o
g	a	b	y	h	n	u	a	j	m	c	k	o	p	l	s	q	a	z	w	s	x	e
q	b	a	z	w	s	x	e	d	c	r	f	v	y	h	o	n	u	j	m	k	l	o
p	i	s	t	a	q	a	z	w	x	s	e	d	i	l	e	f	v	t	g	b	y	a
h	n	n	u	j	m	i	k	l	v	a	s	s	o	i	o	p	o	q	a	z	w	r
s	a	x	e	d	c	r	f	v	t	g	b	y	h	r	n	i	k	m	l	o	p	l
q	a	z	w	s	x	e	d	f	i	n	e	s	t	r	i	n	o	c	r	f	v	q
t	g	b	y	h	n	u	j	m	q	a	z	w	s	a	x	e	d	r	t	g	b	v

Un po' di grammatica

(grah-MMAH-tee-kah)

Some Grammar

As with English, knowing how to say "me, him, her," and so on, is essential in Italian. These words are called direct object pronouns. Study the following examples.

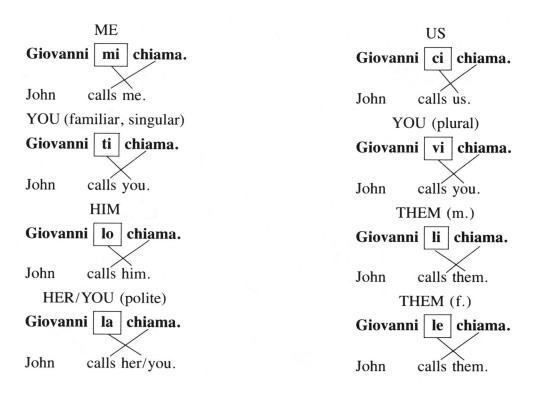

ME

Giovanni | mi | **chiama.**

John   calls me.

YOU (familiar, singular)

Giovanni | ti | **chiama.**

John   calls you.

HIM

Giovanni | lo | **chiama.**

John   calls him.

HER/YOU (polite)

Giovanni | la | **chiama.**

John   calls her/you.

US

Giovanni | ci | **chiama.**

John   calls us.

YOU (plural)

Giovanni | vi | **chiama.**

John   calls you.

THEM (m.)

Giovanni | li | **chiama.**

John   calls them.

THEM (f.)

Giovanni | le | **chiama.**

John   calls them.

Notice that these pronouns are put right before the verb, even in the negative:

Giovanni *non mi* chiama.

The forms **lo, la, li, le** also mean "it" and "them" according to gender.

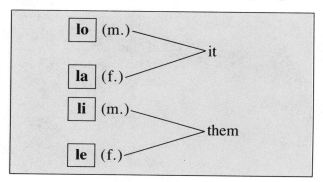

Here are some examples.

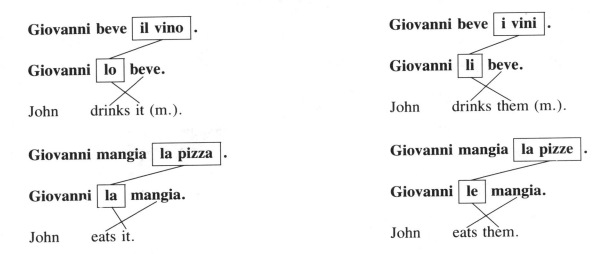

Giovanni beve | il vino | .

Giovanni | lo | **beve.**

John   drinks it (m.).

Giovanni mangia | la pizza | .

Giovanni | la | **mangia.**

John   eats it.

Giovanni beve | i vini | .

Giovanni | li | **beve.**

John   drinks them (m.).

Giovanni mangia | la pizze | .

Giovanni | le | **mangia.**

John   eats them.

Perhaps a chart will be useful to you if you forget later on.

DIRECT OBJECT PRONOUNS		
mi _____ me		**S**
ti _____ you (familiar)		**U**
lo _____ him, it (m.)		**M**
la _____ her, you (polite), it (f.)		**M**
ci _____ us		**A**
vi _____ you (plural)		**R**
li _____ them (m.)		**Y**
le _____ them (f.)		

See if you can select the right pronoun for each blank. | **lo, la, li, le ??** |

Il signor Smith chiama *la signorina*.

Maria prende *il vino rosso*.

La ragazza compra *la penna*.

La ragazza compra *le penne*.

Giovanni chiama *la sua amica*.

Il signor Smith _____ chiama.

Maria _____ prende.

La ragazza _____ compra.

La ragazza _____ compra.

Giovanni _____ chiama.

ANSWERS

Pronouns   la (chiama.)   lo (prende.)   la (compra.)   le (compra.)   la (chiama.)

130

The answers to the following questions are scrambled. Try to rearrange the words so they make sense. If you have forgotten the meaning of some of the words, look for them in the glossary.

Chiede il passaporto, il doganiere? _____
passaporto / il / doganiere / il / chiede / Sì

Porta la carta d'imbarco, l'assistente di volo? _____
la / Sì / l'assistente / porta

Compra gli stivali, il ragazzo? _____
No / non / ragazzo / il / compra / li

Chi ha la carta d'imbarco? _____
signor / Smith / Il / ha / la

Chi ci chiama? _____
vi / chiama / Giovanni

IN CITTÀ
(chee-TTAH)

On the Town

Of course, you will want to do some sightseeing on your trip, and the following passage contains some useful information. Read it carefully and then select the appropriate answers to the questions.

La famiglia Smith è a Firenze. Prima vanno a vedere la Piazza del Duomo. Hanno una
(PREE-mah)
First

macchina fotografica e fanno molte fotografie. Poi vanno a vedere il Palazzo Vecchio.
(foh-toh-GRAH-fee-kah) *(foh-toh-grah-FEE-eh)* *(pah-LAH-tsoh)(VEH-kkyoh)*
camera   photos

Comprano molte cartoline e ricordi. Vanno a vedere tanti monumenti e
(kahr-toh-LEE-neh)(ree-KOHR-dee) *(moh-noo-MEHN-tee)*
postcards   souvenirs   monuments

edifici famosi. Per andare in giro è necessario camminare molto.
(eh-dee-FEE-chee)(fah-MOH-see) *(neh-cheh-SSAH-ree-oh)*
buildings   famous   around   necessary

Dov'è la famiglia Smith?
- [ ] È a Roma.
- [ ] È a Venezia.
- [ ] È a Firenze.

Dove vanno prima?
- [ ] Vanno a vedere la Piazza del Duomo.
- [ ] Vanno a vedere il Vaticano.
- [ ] Vanno a vedere un edificio famoso.

ANSWERS

Comprehension È a Firenze. Vanno a vedere la Piazza del Duomo.

Il signor Smith la ha. Giovanni vi chiama.

Sentences Sì, il doganiere chiede il passaporto. Sì, l'assistente la porta. No, il ragazzo non li compra.

131

Con che fanno molte fotografie?

☐ Con un'aereo.
☐ Con un vassoio.
☐ Con una macchina fotografica.

Che cosa comprano?

☐ Comprano molti edifici.
☐ Comprano molte cartoline e ricordi.
☐ Comprano molti monumenti.

Che cosa vanno a vedere?

☐ Tanti monumenti e edifici famosi.
☐ La pista dell'aeroporto.
☐ La città di Firenze.

Per andare in giro, che cosa
è necessario fare?

☐ È necessario bere tanto vino.
☐ È necessario mangiare la pizza.
☐ È necessario camminare.

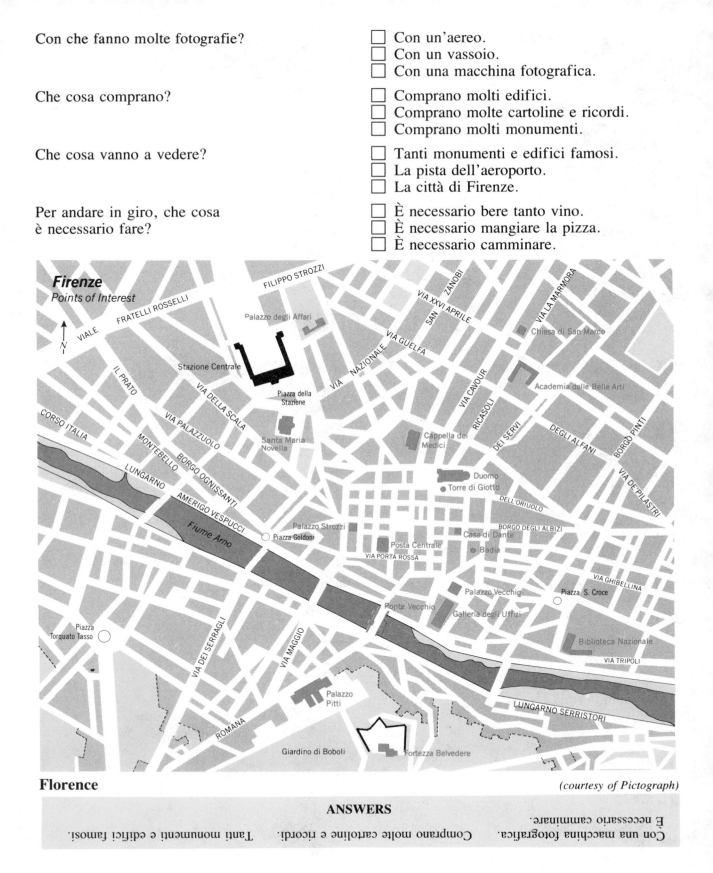

Firenze
Points of Interest

Florence

(courtesy of Pictograph)

ANSWERS

È necessario camminare.

Tanti monumenti e edifici famosi.   Comprano molte cartoline e ricordi.   Con una macchina fotografica.

132

ENTERTAINMENT
(dee-vehr-tee-MEHN-tee)
I Divertimenti

	(teh-AH-troh) *(CHEE-nee-mah)* *(FEH-steh)*
12	**Il teatro / Il cinema / Le feste** Theater / Movies / Holidays

AL TEATRO
At the Theater

Surely you will want to attend the opera
during your stay in Italy. Read the
Smith's dialogue aloud several times,
until you can reconstruct it without
looking back.

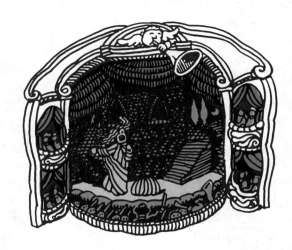

MARK **Dove andiamo stasera?**

Where are we going tonight?

              (see-KOO-rah)   *(DRAH-mmah)*
MARY **Non sono sicura. C'è un dramma**
        (een-teh-reh-SSAHN-teh)
  molto interessante di Pirandello

  al teatro.

I'm not sure. There is a very interesting

drama/play by Pirandello at the theater.

               (PYAH-cheh)
MARK **Il teatro non mi piace.**

I don't like the theater.

               (OH-peh-rah)
MARY **Allora andiamo all'opera. Stasera**

  c'è *La Traviata* di Verdi. Che
  (MOO-zee-kah)   *(meh-loh-DEE-eh)*
  musica! Che melodie!

Then let's go to the opera. Tonight there's

La Traviata by Verdi. What music!

What melodies!

133

	(NOH-yah)	
MARK	**Che noia!**	What a bore!

MARK   **Mark, se non mi porti all'opera,**   Mark, if you do not take me to the opera, I won't

domani non vengo con te al cinema,   come with you tomorrow to the movies, so you

così non puoi vedere la tua   can't see your favorite actress, Sophia Loren.

(ah-TTREE-cheh)   *(preh-feh-REE-tah)*
attrice   preferita, Sofia Loren.

(teh-SOH-roh)   *(koh-MEEN-choh)*

MARK   **Va bene, tesoro! Ma se comincio**   Okay dear! But if I start to snore don't get angry.

(roo-SSAH-reh)   *(ah-rrah-BBYAH-reh)*
a russare non ti arrabbiare.

(zbree-GYAH-moh-chee)

MARY   **Va bene. Sbrighiamoci! Sono già**   Okay. Let's hurry up! It's already 7:30 and the

(speh-TTAH-koh-loh)
le sette e mezzo e lo spettacolo comincia   show begins at 8:00.

alle otto.

MARK   **Sofia, mia bella Sofia, a domani!**   Sophia, my beautiful Sophia, see you tomorrow!

See how similar to English these words are.

il dramma
drama

la melodia
melody

il teatro
theater

Now try to complete Mary's part of the dialogue.

MARK   **Dove andiamo stasera?**

MARY   **Non** _____ . **C'è** _____

_____ .

MARK   **Il teatro non mi piace.**

MARY   **Allora** _____ .

Stasera _____. Che _____!

Che _____!

MARK   **Che noia!**

MARY   **Mark, se non mi _____, domani non _____**

_____, **così non puoi vedere** _____.

MARK   **Va bene, tesoro! Ma se comincio a russare non ti arrabbiare.**

MARY   **Va _____. Sbrighiamoci! Sono** _____.

e lo _____.

MARK   **Sofia, mia bella Sofia, a domani!**

(ree-KOHR-dee)
Ti ricordi?
Do you remember?

Do you recall how to say ''I would like''? This is a very useful expression that you will use frequently.

(johr-NAH-leh)
Vorrei **un giornale.**
newspaper

You continue.

_____   *(MEH-tsoh)*
essere nel mezzo.
in the middle

_____   **il formaggio.**

_____   *(pah-rroo-KKYEH-reh)*
andare dal parrucchiere.
to the hairdresser's

Mi dai i soldi?

Will You Give the Money to Me?

In the previous unit you learned about direct object pronouns. You will also need to know how to translate "to me, to him, to her," and the like. These are called indirect object pronouns. The following four are exactly the same as the direct object pronouns.

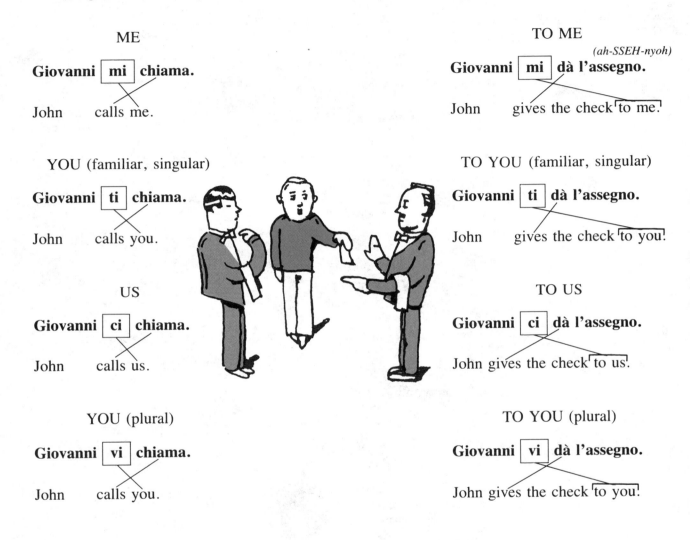

ME

Giovanni | mi | chiama.

John   calls me.

TO ME

(ah-SSEH-nyoh)

Giovanni | mi | dà l'assegno.

John   gives the check to me.

YOU (familiar, singular)

Giovanni | ti | chiama.

John   calls you.

TO YOU (familiar, singular)

Giovanni | ti | dà l'assegno.

John   gives the check to you.

US

Giovanni | ci | chiama.

John   calls us.

TO US

Giovanni | ci | dà l'assegno.

John gives the check to us.

YOU (plural)

Giovanni | vi | chiama.

John   calls you.

TO YOU (plural)

Giovanni | vi | dà l'assegno.

John gives the check to you.

This can be summarized in chart form.

mi	_____ me, to me	S
ti	_____ you, to you (familiar, singular)	U M M
ci	_____ us, to us	A
vi	_____ you, to you (plural)	R Y

Don't forget to keep these pronouns right before the verb, even in the negative.

Giovanni *non mi* chiama.
Giovanni *non mi* dà la penna.

The next examples show how to say "to him, to her, to you (polite, singular), to them."

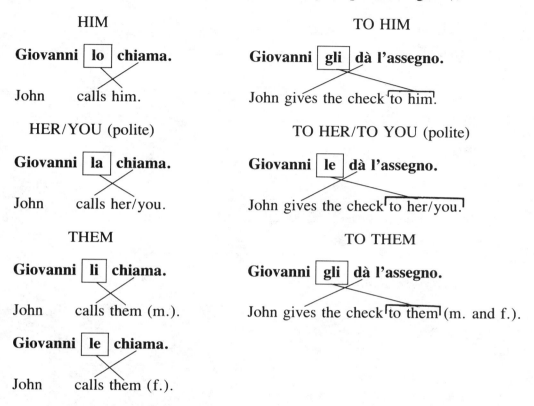

HIM

Giovanni | lo | chiama.

John   calls him.

HER/YOU (polite)

Giovanni | la | chiama.

John   calls her/you.

THEM

Giovanni | li | chiama.

John   calls them (m.).

Giovanni | le | chiama.

John   calls them (f.).

TO HIM

Giovanni | gli | dà l'assegno.

John gives the check to him.

TO HER/TO YOU (polite)

Giovanni | le | dà l'assegno.

John gives the check to her/you.

TO THEM

Giovanni | gli | dà l'assegno.

John gives the check to them (m. and f.).

Notice that there is only one form for "to them," although there is a more formal pronoun for "to them" that does not concern us here. *Gli* is the most commonly used one in spoken Italian. A summary of these pronouns might be helpful.

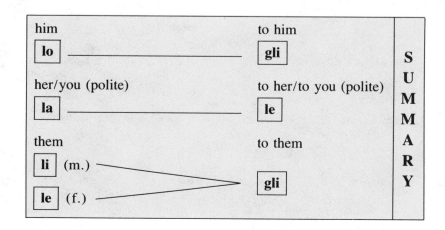

him
| lo | ——————————— | to him | gli |

her/you (polite)
| la | ——————————— | to her/to you (polite) | le |

them
| li | (m.)
| le | (f.)

to them
| gli |

S
U
M
M
A
R
Y

If you have studied these pronouns well, you should have no trouble inserting the proper one in each of the following blanks.

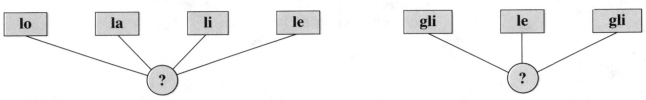

Il turista compra *l'orologio*. Il turista _____ compra.

Il turista compra *gli orologi*. Il turista _____ compra.

Il turista dà l'orologio *a suo figlio*. Il turista _____ dà l'orologio.

Il turista dà l'orologio *a sua figlia*. Il turista _____ dà l'orologio.

Il turista compra *la cartolina*. Il turista _____ compra.

Il turista compra *le cartoline*. Il turista _____ compra.

Il turista dà la cartolina *ai suoi amici*. Il turista _____ dà la cartolina.

Il turista dà la cartolina *alle sue amiche*. Il turista _____ dà la cartolina.

AL CINEMA
At the Movies

(Mark and Mary are at the movies the day after having gone to the opera. They are watching a rerun of the classic Ieri, oggi e domani.*)*

MARK **Che bel film!** *(feelm)* **E come è bella Sofia Loren!**

What a beautiful film! And is Sophia Loren ever beautiful!

MARY **Senza i sottotitoli non** *(SEHN-tsah)(soh-ttoh-TEE-toh-lee)* **capisco niente.**

Without subtitles I can't understand anything.

MARK **Non importa. Basta vedere Sofia.**

It doesn't matter. All that's important is to see Sophia.

ANSWERS

Pronouns lo (compra.)   li (compra.)   gli (dà l'orologio.)   gli (dà la)   le (dà la)
la (compra.)   le (dà l'orologio.)   le (compra.)

MARY	*(VEE-ah)* **Andiamo via. Non mi piace sedermi** *(FEE-lah)* **nella prima fila.**	Let's go. I don't like to sit in the first row.
MARK	**Ma il cinema è** *(PYEH-noh)* **pieno di gente.**	But the movie theater is full of people.
MARY	*(EHS-koh)* **Io esco!**	I'm leaving (I'm going out)!
MARK	*(SEH-gweh)* **Va bene. Tuo marito ti segue.**	Okay. Your husband will follow (*literally:* is following you).

Read the dialogue several times and then try to complete the missing parts. Check your answers after you have attempted to do so from memory.

Che bel f_____! E come è b_____ Sofia Loren!

S_____ i s_____ non capisco niente.

Non i_____. B_____ vedere Sofia.

Andiamo via. Non mi p_____ sedermi nella prima f_____.

Ma il cinema è p_____ di gente. Io e_____!

Va bene. Tuo m_____ ti segue.

Here are two more verbs that you will use often.

(oo-SHEE-reh) **USCIRE** to go out			
io _____ *(EHS-koh)* **esco**		**noi** _____ *(oo-SHAH-moh)* **usciamo**
tu _____ *(EH-shee)* **esci**		**voi** _____ *(oo-SHEE-teh)* **uscite**
lui ⎱ **lei** ⎰ _____ *(EH-sheh)* **esce**		**loro** _____ *(EHS-koh-noh)* **escono**

Now fill in each blank with the correct form of *uscire*.

La signora Smith _____ alle sei.   La moglie e il marito _____ insieme.

Io non _____ mai.   Tu _____ con Maria.

Noi _____ *(een-SYEH-meh)* **insieme** per andare together   Voi non _____ mai insieme.

al cinema.

PIACERE
to like

io	*(PYAH-choh)* **piaccio**	noi	*(pyah-CHAH-moh)* **piacciamo**
tu	*(PYAH-chee)* **piaci**	voi	*(pyah-CHEH-teh)* **piacete**
lui } lei }	*(PYAH-cheh)* **piace**	loro	*(PYAH-choh-noh)* **piacciono**

This is a troublesome verb. In order to say ''I like, you like,'' and so on, you must say ''to be pleasing to.''

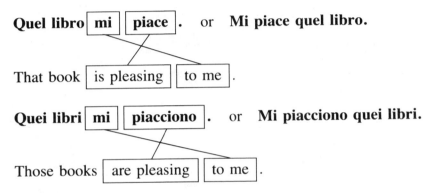

Quel libro | mi | piace |.   or   **Mi piace quel libro.**

That book | is pleasing | to me |.

Quei libri | mi | piacciono |.   or   **Mi piacciono quei libri.**

Those books | are pleasing | to me |.

Using the chart and the examples above, try to complete these sentences.

I like Mary. Mary is pleasing to me. **Mi** _____ **Maria**.

Mary likes me. I am pleasing to Mary. **Io** _____ **a Maria**.

We like the film. The film is pleasing to us. **Ci** _____ **il film**.

They like the films. The films are pleasing to them. **Gli** _____ **i film**.

I like the film. The film is pleasing to me. **Mi** _____ **il film**.

I don't like the films. The films are not pleasing to me. **Non mi** _____ **i film**.

LE FESTE
Holidays

Of course, you will want to join in the festivities, if you are in Italy during a holiday. Read this passage, and then answer the questions that follow.

(kah-poh-DAH-nnoh)

La prima festa dell'anno è il capodanno.
New Year's

(eh-pee-fah-NEE-ah)

Poi c'è l'Epifania
Epiphany

il sei gennaio. Poi a primavera c'è la Pasqua.
(PAHS-kwah)
Easter

(fehr-ah-GOHS-toh)   *(pahr-tee-koh-LAH-reh)*

Il quindici agosto c'è il Ferragosto. È una festa particolare in Italia.
Assumption   particular

Naturalmente il venticinque dicembre

(nah-TAH-leh)

c'è il Natale.

In italiano si dice «Buone feste!»

1. Qual è la prima festa dell'anno?
☐ Pasqua.
☐ Ferragosto.
☐ Capodanno.

2. Che festa c'è il sei gennaio?
☐ Ferragosto.
☐ Capodanno.
☐ Epifania.

3. Che festa c'è in primavera?
☐ Pasqua
☐ Natale.
☐ Ferragosto.

4. Che festa c'é il quindici agosto?
☐ Pasqua.
☐ Ferragosto.
☐ Natale.

5. Che festa c'è il venticinque dicembre?
☐ Pasqua.
☐ Capodanno.
☐ Natale.

6. Che vuol dire «Buone feste»?
☐ Hello.
☐ Good-bye.
☐ Happy holidays.

Let's finish this chapter with an easy one; fill in the blanks with the following words. This is Giovanni's weird dream. See what he dreamt about!

(bahn-DYEH-rah)

birra, albero, dorme, zia, bandiera, biglietti, fila
beer   flag

Giovanni e Maria comprano due _____ per andare al cinema.

Si siedono nella terza _____.

Giovanni compra e beve una _____.

(een-KOHN-trah)
Il film non è interessante. Al cinema, Maria **incontra** sua _____.
meets

Giovanni _____ durante tutto il film.

Quando Giovanni e Maria escono dal film vedono un _____ di Natale e

una _____ italiana.

ESCURSIONI A PIEDI E IL JOGGING

Hiking and Jogging

(Mark Smith is in great physical condition. He jogs every morning. This morning he is approached by a journalist who is writing an article on sports.)

GIORNALISTA   **Buon giorno, signore. Sono**   Good morning, sir. I am a journalist. Can I ask
        (johr-nah-LEES-tah)   *(ahl-KOO-neh)*   you some questions?
un giornalista. Le posso fare alcune
(doh-MAHN-deh)
domande?

MARK   **Certo. Ma parli lentamente. Sono**   Certainly. But speak slowly. I am an American

americano e non capisco tutto.   and I don't understand everything.
              (SPEH-ssoh)

GIORNALISTA   **Lei fa spesso il jogging?**   Do you jog often?

          (OH-nyee)
MARK   **Sì. Ogni mattina.**   Yes. Every morning.

Incontro sempre un gruppo   I always meet a group of tourists

di turisti che fanno il jogging con me.   who jog along with me.

Sembrano turisti spagnoli.   They look like Spanish tourists.

Portano tute sportive
(spohr-TEE-veh)

They wear sweatshirts

e scarpe da corsa.
(SKAHR-peh) (KOHR-sah)

and running shoes.

GIORNALISTA **Le piacciono altri sport?**

Do you like any other sports?

MARK **No, neanche il calcio.**
(neh-AHN-keh)(KAHL-choh)

No, not even soccer.

(They run into a group of hikers.)

GIORNALISTA **Questi signori hanno un**

These people have a sleeping bag, a backpack,

sacco a pelo, uno zaino,
(TSAH-ee-noh)

cooking utensils and a canteen.

degli utensili da cucina e

un bettolino.
(beh-ttoh-LEE-noh)

MARK **Lo so. Sono due giorni che sono**

I know. They have been here for two days.

qui. Credo che siano turisti francesi.

I think they are French tourists.

GIORNALISTA **Come lo sa?**

How do you know?

MARK **Parlano una lingua molto simile**
(SEE-mee-leh)

They speak a language very similar to Italian.

all'italiano.

(The journalist speaks to the hikers and then catches up to Mark.)

GIORNALISTA **Lei si sbaglia, signore. Quei**
(ZBAH-llyah)

You're wrong, sir. They are Italians who

signori sono italiani ma parlano un

speak a dialect similar to French.

dialetto italiano simile al francese.
(dyah-LEH-ttoh)

MARK **Ecco perché non li comprendo.**

That's why I don't understand them.

After reading the dialogue over several times, indicate if each of the following is true or false.

1. Il gruppo di turisti fa alcune domande a Mark. ☐ Vero
   True
   ☐ Falso
   False

2. Mark è americano e   ☐ Vero
   non capisce tutto.   ☐ Falso

3. Mark non fa mai il jogging.   ☐ Vero
   ☐ Falso

4. Ogni mattina Mark incontra   ☐ Vero
   un gruppo di turisti che fanno ☐ Falso
   il jogging con lui.

5. I turisti portano tute sportive   ☐ Vero
   e scarpe da corsa.   ☐ Falso

6. A Mark piacciono molti sport.   ☐ Vero
   ☐ Falso

7. I signori che incontrano hanno ☐ Vero
   un sacco a pelo, uno zaino,   ☐ Falso
   degli utensili da cucina e
   un bettolino.

8. Quei signori parlano francese.   ☐ Vero
   ☐ Falso

9. Mark vuole parlare ancora.   ☐ Vero
   ☐ Falso

Are you ready for a hiking trip now? Let's see if you can identify this gear.

Che cosa è?   È una _____.

Che cosa è?   È un _____.

Che cosa è?   È uno _____.

Che cosa sono?   Sono degli _____.

Che cosa è?   È un _____.

Ricordati . . .

Remember . . .

Nouns like *sport*, *film*, and *jogging* are all borrowed from English. The singular and plural forms are identical for these nouns.

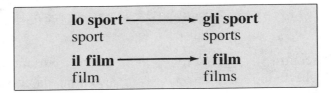

lo sport ⟶	**gli sport**
sport	sports
il film ⟶	**i film**
film	films

In the first few units you learned about the pronouns "I, you, he, she," and so forth. The pronouns **lui, lei, noi, voi, loro** can also be used as object pronouns.

John calls him.   **Giovanni** ⟨lo⟩ **chiama.**   *or*   **Giovanni chiama** ⟨lui⟩.

John calls her.   **Giovanni** ⟨la⟩ **chiama.**   *or*   **Giovanni chiama** ⟨lei⟩.

Instead of **mi** the form **me** can be used; and instead of **ti** the form **te** can be used.

John calls me.   **Giovanni** ⟨mi⟩ **chiama.**   *or*   **Giovanni chiama** ⟨me⟩.

John calls you.   **Giovanni** ⟨ti⟩ **chiama.**   *or*   **Giovanni chiama** ⟨te⟩.

Notice that these pronouns come after the verb as in English.

Before the Verb	*After the Verb*
mi	me
ti	te
lo	lui
la	lei
ci	noi
vi	voi
li	loro
le	

The type used *after* verbs is also the *only* one used after prepositions.

Giovanni viene con ⟨me⟩.   **Giovanni parla di** ⟨te⟩.   **Giovanni arriva con** ⟨loro⟩.

John is coming with me.   John is speaking of you.   John arrives with them.

See if you can replace each pronoun with an equivalent form. Don't get discouraged. These take a while to learn.

1. Il signor Smith *mi* chiama. Il signor Smith chiama _____.

2. La signora Smith chiama *te*. La signora Smith _____ chiama.

3. Io *lo* chiamo. Io chiamo _____.

4. Il giornalista chiama *lei*. Il giornalista _____ chiama.

5. Il passeggero *ci* chiama. Il passeggero chiama _____.

6. Il passeggero chiama *voi*. Il passeggero _____ chiama.

7. L'autista *li* chiama. L'autista chiama _____.

8. L'autista *le* chiama. L'autista chiama _____.

IL CICLISMO E IL NUOTO
(chee-KLEEZ-moh)   *(NWOH-toh)*

Bicycling and Swimming

As you learn these words relating to cycling and swimming, you'll see some vocabulary patterns emerging that will help in recalling them.

(oh-KKYAH-lee) *(proh-teh-TSYOH-neh)*
gli occhiali di protezione
goggles

(chee-KLEES-tah)
Il ciclista
bicyclist

(SPEEN-jeh)   *(bee-chee-KLEH-ttah)*
spinge la sua bicicletta
pushes   bicycle

(sah-LEE-tah)
in salita.
uphill

(nwoh-tah-TOH-reh)
un nuotatore
swimmer

(RAH-nah)
il nuoto a rana
breaststroke

il nuoto a crawl
crawl

(DOHR-soh)
il nuoto sul dorso
backstroke

147

Add the appropriate word or expression that describes each picture.

_____   _____   _____

_____   _____

(sehn-TYEH-ree) *(nah-too-RAH-lee)*

I SENTIERI NATURALI

Footpaths

This passage introduces some additional vocabulary. When you have
mastered it, choose the correct answer to each of the questions that follow.

(SEH-nyee)

Nei sentieri naturali ci sono tanti alberi con segni.
markings

(een-dee-kah-TOH-ree)

Ci sono anche cartelli indicatori.
signposts

(PYAHN-teh)   *(FYOH-ree)*   *(een-SEH-ttee)*   *(ah-nee-MAH-lee)*

Ci sono anche piante,   **fiori,**   **insetti**   **animali.**
plants   flowers   insects   animals

La natura italiana è molto bella.

Dove ci sono tanti
alberi?
☐ Nell'acqua.
☐ Nei sentieri naturali.
☐ Nel vino.

Che cosa altro c'è?
What else
☐ Ci sono libri.
☐ Ci sono penne.
☐ Ci sono cartelli indicatori.

Ci sono piante, fiori,
insetti e animali?
☐ Sì.
☐ No.

Com'è la natura italiana?
☐ È brutta.
☐ È bella.

ORDERING FOOD

(ohr-dee-NYAH-moh)   *(mahn-JAH-reh)*
Ordiniamo da mangiare

14	*(PAHS-tee)* *(CHEE-bee)* **I pasti /I cibi** Meals/Food

Che cosa dire quando ti *piace* qualcosa
What to Say When You *Like* Something

That troublesome verb *piacere* that you learned about
in chapter 12 is used when talking about the
things you may or may not like to eat.

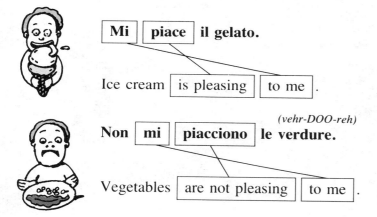

Mi | **piace** | il gelato.

Ice cream | is pleasing | to me .

(vehr-DOO-reh)

Non | **mi** | **piacciono** | le verdure.

Vegetables | are not pleasing | to me .

Now choose either *piace* or *piacciono* to complete these sentences.

Mi _____ le verdure. Non mi _____ mangiare. Mi

_____ il gelato. Mi _____ il nuoto. Non mi

_____ andare in bicicletta. Mi _____ gli sport. Mi

_____ il calcio. Mi _____ il tennis e il ciclismo.

The verb forms are the same, when used with other pronouns.

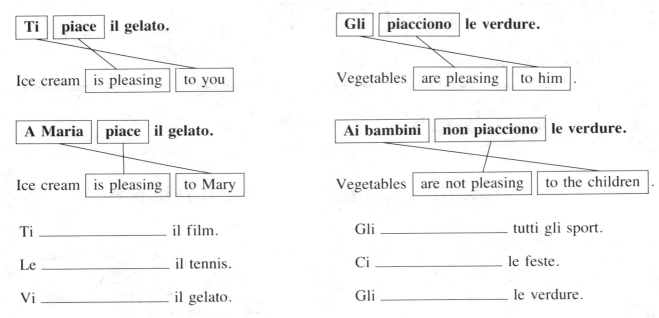

| Ti | piace | il gelato. |

Ice cream | is pleasing | to you

| Gli | piacciono | le verdure. |

Vegetables | are pleasing | to him .

| A Maria | piace | il gelato. |

Ice cream | is pleasing | to Mary

| Ai bambini | non piacciono | le verdure. |

Vegetables | are not pleasing | to the children .

Ti _____ il film.

Le _____ il tennis.

Vi _____ il gelato.

Gli _____ tutti gli sport.

Ci _____ le feste.

Gli _____ le verdure.

Now that you understand *piace* **and** *piacciono,* let's learn more about nouns.

Notice that nouns ending with an accented vowel do not change in the plural.

la città	**le città**
city	cities
il caffè	**i caffè**
coffee	coffees
il menù	**i menù**
menu	menus

Nouns ending in **-ista** can be either masculine or feminine.

il turista	**la turista**
male tourist	female tourist
il pianista	**la pianista**
male pianist	female pianist

Finally, notice this completely irregular noun.

	(WOH-mee-nee)
l'uomo	**gli uomini**
man	men

We want you to change these nouns from singular to plural. We've given you the correct article—you add the right noun form.

il gelato → i _____ , la caramella → le _____ ,

il padre → i _____ , la madre → le _____ ,

lo sport → gli _____ , il film → i _____ ,

il caffè → i _____ , la città → le _____ ,

il menù → i _____ , l'uomo → gli _____ .

(koh-lah-TSYOH-neh)
LA (PRIMA) COLAZIONE
Breakfast

(rees-toh-RAHN-teh)
un ristorante
(eh-koh-NOH-mee-koh)
economico

(The Smiths are having breakfast at a local inexpensive restaurant.)

(STRAH-noh)

MARK **Che strano! Di solito gli italiani** How strange! Italians normally do not have

non fanno la prima colazione. breakfast.

CAMERIERA **Buon giorno. Che cosa** Good morning. Can I take your orders?

prendono? (*literally,* what will you take)

(TAH-tsah) (kah-ffeh-LLAH-tteh)

MARY **Io vorrei una tazza di caffellate,** I would like a cup of coffee with milk,

ANSWERS
Nouns gelati caramelle padri madri sport film caffè città menù uomini

151

(PAH-neh) (tohs-TAH-toh)
il   pane   tostato con burro   toasted bread with

(mahr-meh-LLAH-tah)
e marmellata,   butter and marmalade,

(bee-KKYEH-reh)
e un bicchiere di   and a glass

(SOO-kkoh)(ah-RAHN-chah)
succo d'arancia.   of orange juice.

MARK **Mamma mia, che fame! Io prendo**   Good grief, what an appetite!

(pah-NEE-noh) (DOHL-cheh)
un panino   dolce, un bicchiere di   I'll take a sweet roll,

(poh-moh-DOH-roh)
succo di pomodoro e un   a glass of tomato juice,

(kah-ppoo-CHEE-noh)
cappuccino.   and a cappuccino.

ANNE **Io voglio solo una tazza di tè.**   I only want a cup of tea.

JOHN **E io solo un espresso.**   And I only an espresso coffee.

CAMERIERA **Grazie.**   Thank you.

(The Smiths finish their breakfast.)

(KOHN-toh)
MARK **Cameriera, il conto, per favore.**   Waitress, the bill please!

CAMERIERA **Ecco. Quarantamila lire in tutto.**   Here it is. 40,000 lira all together.

MARK *(to himself)* **Più una mancia.**   Plus a tip.

MARY **Va bene, signorina. Grazie.**   Okay, miss. Thank you.

After you have read the dialogue several times, try to match up the left column with the right one, to get lines from the dialogue. Check your answers.

Di solito gli italiani . . .	una tazza di caffellatte, il pane tostato con burro e marmellata e un bicchiere di succo d'arancia.
Che cosa . . .	una tazza di tè.
Io vorrei . . .	un espresso.
Io voglio solo . . .	non fanno la prima colazione.
E io solo . . .	prendono?
Io prendo . . .	il conto, per favore.
Cameriera, . . .	lire in tutto.
Quarantamila . . .	un panino dolce, un bicchiere di succo di pomodoro e un cappuccino.

(TAH-voh-lah)
LA TAVOLA
The Table

When the Smiths dine out, their place settings may look like this one. When you have read and pronounced the vocabulary, try to identify each object without referring to the Italian words.

il bicchiere da vino
wine glass

(TAH-tsah)
la tazza
cup

(SAH-leh) (PEH-peh)
il sale e il pepe
salt and pepper

(bee-KKYEH-reh)
il bicchiere
glass

(pyah-TTEE-noh)
il piattino
saucer

(TSOO-kkeh-roh)
lo zucchero
sugar

(toh-vah-LLYAH-loh)
il tovagliolo
napkin

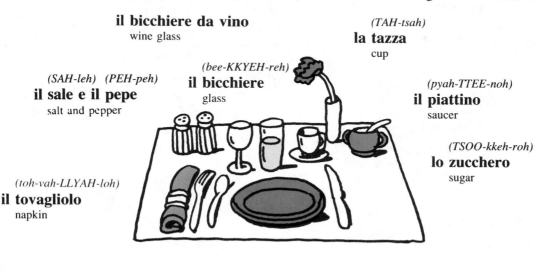

(fohr-KEH-ttah)
la forchetta
fork

(koo-KYAH-yoh)
il cucchiaio
spoon

(PYAH-ttoh)
il piatto
plate

(kohl-TEH-lloh)
il coltello
knife

How many words do you remember? Without looking at the picture, match up the two columns.

1.	il coltello	a.	wine glass
2.	il sale	b.	napkin
3.	il cucchiaio	c.	pepper
4.	il bicchiere da vino	d.	plate
5.	il pepe	e.	fork
6.	il bicchiere	f.	spoon
7.	il piatto	g.	sugar
8.	il piattino	h.	cup
9.	la forchetta	i.	saucer
10.	la tazza	j.	glass
11.	il tovagliolo	k.	knife
12.	lo zucchero	l.	salt

From the following list, choose the appropriate word for each blank.

tazza, bicchiere, forchetta, cucchiaio, cameriere, sale, pepe, zucchero, coltello

Questo panino è molto dolce. C'è molto _____.

Per mangiare la pizza, ho bisogno di una _____ e di un_____.

Ogni mattina io bevo una _____ di caffè.
    (mee-NEHS-trah)
Per mangiare la minestra, ho bisogno di un _____.
    soup
Il _____ porta il conto.

Questo è un _____ di acqua.

Mi piace il cibo con tanto _____ e _____ .

IL PASTO PRINCIPALE

(preen-chee-PAH-leh)

The Main Meal

What a feast! But to get a meal like this one, you'll have to learn how to order it.

(ahn-tee-PAHS-toh)
l'antipasto
appetizer

(proh-SHOO-ttoh)
il prosciutto
Italian ham

un piatto di minestra
bowl of soup

(meh-LOH-neh)
il melone
cantaloupe

(stoo-tsee-kah-DEHN-tee)
gli stuzzicadenti
toothpicks

un piatto di pasta
plate of pasta

(oh-LEE-veh)
le olive
olives

(een-sah-LAH-tah) (VEHR-deh)
l'insalata   verde
tossed salad

(ah-CHOO-geh)
le acciughe
anchovies

un piatto di verdure
plate of vegetables

il vino rosso / il vino bianco
red wine/   white wine

(PEH-sheh)
il pesce
fish

(FROO-ttah)
la frutta
fruit

(KAHR-neh) (MAHN-tsoh)
la carne di manzo
roast beef

By filling in the blanks and repeating each sentence several times, you will develop the ability to order the things you want.

Vorrei il _____ per antipasto.
            ham and cantaloupe

Poi, vorrei un _____ .
              bowl of soup

Mia moglie/Mio marito prende un _____ di spaghetti/ravioli/lasagne.
                                    plate

Vorrei anche un piatto di _____ .
                            vegetables

Poi, vorrei un piatto di _____ .
                          fish

Mia moglie/Mio marito prende la _____ .
                                  roast beef

Per finire, vorrei _____ e il _____ .
                    fruit   coffee

Per bere, vorrei una bottiglia di _____ .
                                    red wine

(CHEH-nah)

LA CENA

The Evening Meal

To conclude the day's dining, read the following
passage and then respond to the questions.

In Italia ci sono due pasti principali:

il pranzo nel pomeriggio e la cena di sera.
 lunch

(VEHR-soh)
Di solito la cena è verso le otto, ma c'è chi
 around   he who

mangia anche alle nove o alle dieci. Gli italiani

(ah-bahs-TAHN-tsah)
mangiano abbastanza al pranzo e alla cena.
 quite well

(mee-neh-RAH-leh) *(ah-ppeh-TEE-toh)*
Bevono di solito il vino e l'acqua minerale. «Buon appetito!» si dice prima di mangiare.
      mineral water   Good appetite   before

Quali sono i due pasti principali italiani?
☐ **Le cena e il pranzo.**
☐ Le lasagne e i ravioli.
☐ Gli spaghetti e il vino.

Quando si fa il pranzo?
☐ Alla mattina.
☐ Nel pomeriggio.
☐ A mezzanotte.

Quando si fa la cena?
☐ Alla mattina.
☐ Nel pomeriggio.
☐ Di sera.

Che cosa bevono di solito gli italiani?
☐ Niente.
☐ L'acqua.
☐ Il vino e l'acqua minerale.

Che cosa si dice prima di mangiare?
☐ Buon giorno.
☐ Buon appetito.
☐ Buona sera.

Can you find *ten* words relating to food and eating in this word-search puzzle? After you have circled them, write them on the lines provided.

z	c	b	m	j	g	f	d	w	r	t	u	s	p	i
q	e	r	u	m	a	r	m	e	l	l	a	t	a	b
m	b	c	z	f	h	u	t	i	p	w	r	a	c	m
q	t	e	t	p	a	t	d	g	j	k	m	z	v	r
f	o	r	c	h	e	t	t	a	a	n	e	z	l	p
q	v	a	z	w	s	a	x	e	d	c	s	a	l	e
r	a	f	v	c	t	g	b	y	h	n	u	j	m	p
i	g	k	m	o	l	o	p	q	a	z	w	s	x	e
e	l	d	c	l	r	f	v	t	g	b	y	h	n	i
p	i	a	t	t	o	k	m	o	p	l	q	a	z	w
s	o	x	e	e	d	c	r	f	v	t	g	b	y	h
n	l	u	j	l	m	o	k	l	p	q	a	z	w	s
x	o	e	d	l	c	r	f	v	t	g	b	y	h	n
u	j	m	i	o	l	i	v	e	k	m	p	l	j	b

_____   _____   _____

_____   _____   _____

_____

15 **I ristoranti /Dare la mancia**
(rees-toh-RAHN-tee)
Restaurants / Tipping

You will remember that to order food or drink in Italian, all you have to say is:

Vorrei un piatto di spaghetti, per favore.

Vorrei un piatto di ravioli, per favore.

Vorrei una bottiglia di vino rosso, per favore.

To say "I am going to . . ." in Italian, just use the verb in the normal way.

Tomorrow I'm going to eat pizza. —→Domani **mangio** la pizza.

Tomorrow I'm going to drink wine. —→ Domani **bevo** il vino.

You will find some Italian food selections at the back of this book. Here are some items that you might see on the menu when you dine out.

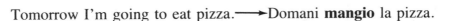

IL MENÙ

		la carne	meat
		(deh-SSEHRT)	
		il dessert / il dolce	dessert
		(beh-VAHN-deh)	
		le bevande	drinks
		le acciughe	anchovies
		(POH-lloh)	
		il pollo	chicken
		(lah-TTOO-gah)	
		la lattuga	lettuce
		(ahs-PAH-rah-jee)	
l'antipasto	appetizer	**gli asparagi**	asparagus
		(TROH-tah)	
la minestra	soup	**la trota**	trout
(een-sah-LAH-tah)		*(vee-TEH-lloh)*	
l'insalata	salad	**la carne di vitello**	veal
		(OO-vah)	
le verdure	vegetables	**l'uva**	grapes
il pesce	fish	**il vino rosso**	red wine

(The Smiths have decided to eat at an expensive restaurant.)

CAMERIERE **Buona sera. Vogliono vedere il menù?**

Good evening. Would you (formal, plural) like to see the menu?

MARK **No, grazie. Non voglio vedere i prezzi.**

No, thank you. I do not want to see the prices.

MARY *(ah-TEHN-tsyoh-neh)* **Non faccia attenzione a mio** *(SKEHR-tsah)* **marito. Lui scherza sempre.**

Don't pay any attention to my husband. He always jokes around.

CAMERIERE **Abbiamo un antipasto** *(skwee-ZEE-toh) (WOH-vah)* **squisito di uova con acciughe e** *(SPEH-tsee-eh)* **molte spezie.**

We have a delicious appetizer of deviled eggs with anchovies and many spices.

ANNE *(pee-KKAHN-teh)* **Troppo piccante!**

Too spicy!

MARK **Per il primo piatto, tutti prendiamo la minestra. Poi,** *(pah-TAH-teh)* **io prendo il pollo con le patate.**

For the first dish, we will all have soup. Then, I'll have chicken with potatoes.

MARY *(koh-toh-LEH-ttah)* **E io vorrei la cotoletta di vitello e l'insalata di lattuga con i** *(poh-moh-DOH-ree)* **pomodori.**

And I would like a veal cutlet and the lettuce and tomato salad.

ANNE **Io prendo solo un po' di formaggio** *(DYEH-tah)* **con il pane. Faccio la dieta.**

I'll have only a bit of cheese with bread. I'm on a diet.

JOHN **Io vorrei la trota con le patate.**

I would like the trout with potatoes.

MARK **Una bottiglia di vino rosso, e alla fine l'espresso per tutti e un cognac per me e mia moglie.**

A bottle of red wine, and at the end espresso coffee for everyone and a cognac for me and my wife.

CAMERIERE **Prego.**

Thank you / Fine.

(The Smiths have finished the meal and are about to leave.)

MARY   *(LAH-shah)*
Mark, lascia una mancia! Questo è   Mark, leave a tip! This is an expensive restaurant.

(LOO-ssoh)
un ristorante di lusso.

(mahn-jeh-REH-moh)
MARK   **Va bene. Non mangeremo per una**   Okay. We won't eat for a week.

settimana!

When you have read the dialogue aloud until you are familiar with it, try to complete the missing parts without looking back. Then check your answers.

Buona sera. Vogliono vedere il m_____?

No, grazie. Non v_____ vedere i p_____.

Non faccia a_____ a mio marito. Lui s_____ sempre.

Abbiamo un antipasto s_____ di uova con a_____ e molte

s_____.

Troppo p_____!

Per il primo p_____, tutti prendiamo la m_____. Poi, io prendo il

p_____ con le p_____.

E io v_____ la c_____ di v_____

e l'_____ di l_____ e p_____.

Io prendo solo un po' di f_____ con il p_____. Faccio la

d_____.

Io vorrei la t_____con le patate.

Una b_____ di vino rosso, e alla f_____ l'espresso per tutti e un

cognac per m_____ e mia m_____.

Grazie.

Il signor Smith . . .

Mr. Smith . . .

You may have noticed that the final -e of *signore* is dropped before a name, such as Smith. This is true of all masculine titles ending in -e.

il signore	**il signor Smith** Mr. Smith
il professore	**il professor Rossi** Professor Rossi
il dottore	**il dottor Verdi** Dr. Verdi

The article used with titles is dropped when speaking directly to the person.

TALKING ABOUT SOMEONE

Il signor Smith è americano.
Mr. Smith is American.

La signora Smith è intelligente.
Mrs. Smith is intelligent.

TALKING TO SOMEONE

Buon giorno, signor Smith.
Good morning, Mr. Smith.

Buona sera, signora Smith.
Good evening, Mrs. Smith.

(sehn-TEER-see)
Sentirsi (bene, male)
To Feel (Well, Sick)

(BAH-nyoh)
bagno
restroom

donne uomini
ladies gentlemen

It's easy to tell someone how you are feeling:

Mi sento bene.
Non mi sento bene. Mi sento male.

You continue. Answer the question and fill in the blanks.

Come ti senti? Mi _____ bene.

Come ti senti? Mi _____ male.

Here are some additional foods you might want to order. Say them aloud and then repeat them as you look at each picture.

Antipasti (Appetizers)

(free-TTAH-tah)
la frittata
omelet

Minestre (Soups)

(mee-nehs-TROH-neh)
il minestrone
minestrone

(pohl-peh-TTEE-neh)
le polpettine
meatballs

(TSOO-pah)
la zuppa
thick soup

Insalate (Salads)

l'insalata mista
mixed salad

Verdure (Vegetables)

gli asparagi
asparagus

l'insalata russa
Russian salad
potato salad

(spee-NAH-chee)
gli spinaci
spinach

Pesce (Fish)

(kah-lah-MAH-ree)
i calamari
squid

Carne (Meats)

(mah-YAH-leh)
la bistecca di maiale
pork steak

(gahm-beh-REH-ttee)
i gamberetti
prawns

(ah-NYEH-lloh)
la carne d' agnello
lamb

Dessert (Desserts)

il gelato
ice cream

Bevande (Drinks)

(ahl-KOH-lee-keh)
le bevande alcoliche
alcoholic beverages

i dolci
sweets

162

Now you should be able to zip right through the following brief passage and then select the appropriate answer to each question.

(trah-ttoh-REE-ah)

In Italia, si mangia al ristorante, alla trattoria, o al bar dove si mangiano i panini. I pasti
less formal restaurant   sandwiches

(kohn-SEES-toh-noh)

italiani consistono di un antipasto, un piatto di pasta o di minestra (zuppa, minestrone, e
consist

così via), e un piatto di carne o pesce, con patate, verdure, e così via. Poi c'è il dessert, la
so on

frutta e il caffè. Naturalmente si beve il vino o l'acqua minerale.

To wrap up our section on eating out, you fill in the menu; add the Italian words.

Dove si mangiano
  i panini?

☐ A casa.
☐ In Francia.
☐ Al bar.

Nei pasti italiani,
  non c'è . . .

☐ L'antipasto.
☐ La frutta.
☐ La Coca-Cola.

Che cosa si beve
  in Italia ai pasti?

☐ La Coca-Cola.
☐ Il vino e
    l'acqua minerale.
☐ Il tè.

MENU

(fish)

_____

(soup)

_____

(chicken)

_____

(salad)

_____

(sweet)

_____

(vegetable)

_____

(wine)

_____

HOW'RE WE DOING?
Vediamo quanto hai imparato!
(Let's see how much you've learned!)

It's time for a breather! This is when you should go back over those sections where you are still having problems. You should also review any vocabulary you may have forgotten and reread the dialogues and comprehension passages. After you have done all that, have some fun with the following activities. If you have forgotten the meaning of any word or expression, you can look it up in the glossary. Are you ready?

First, try unscrambling the letters of the following words. To help you reconstruct the words, English meanings are provided. Each word begins with the letter *p*.

parrimaev _____ , porzez _____ ,
      spring   price

ploita _____ , puenmaocit _____ ,
      pilot   tire

pmoeriiogg _____ , patro _____ ,
      afternoon   door

patrofgolio _____ , poien _____ ,
      wallet   full

pttiao _____ , ppee _____ ,
      plate   pepper

ptniaa _____ , pscee _____ ,
      plant   fish

pstao _____ , paaatt _____ , pozaz _____ ,
      meal   potato   crazy

praaberazz _____ , paaarfnog _____ ,
      windshield   fender

praautri _____ , prahceggoi _____ ,
      bumper   parking

pssggraeeo _____ , ppaassotro _____ ,
      passenger   passport

pomissor _____ , pgeor _____ , pean _____ ,
      next   you're welcome   bread

pdrae _____ , pasee _____ , poacc _____ .
      father   country   package

After you have reviewed your verbs, try the following "verb" crossword puzzle.

Across

2. She understands
4. They live
6. They believe
8. I help
9. I see
12. You fasten (plural)
13. I am waiting
15. I drink
16. They finish
17. Walk! (singular, familiar)
20. I call
21. You wash yourself (singular, familiar)
22. You are (plural)
24. He answers
25. They sit

Down

1. We arrive
2. I sing
3. You know (singular, familiar)
4. He fixes
5. They are sleeping
7. I say
10. I am getting up
11. You go (singular, familiar)
13. We have
14. You drive (plural)
16. I make
18. She asks
19. You are leaving (singular, familiar)
23. I come
24. He steals

This one should be a snap! Read each sentence aloud, and these words will fall right into place.

accanto, acqua, adesso, destra, aereo, albergo, alto, altro, anche, antipasto, appuntamento, autorimessa

1. Maria si siede sempre _____ alla sua amica.

2. Vorrei bere un po' di _____ .

3. L'_____ di prosciutto è molto buono.

4. La mia macchina è nell'_____ .

5. Domani, il signor Smith ha un _____ con me.

6. Gira a _____ , non a sinistra!

7. _____ Gino parla italiano molto bene.

8. Lui non è _____ ; è basso.

9. La signora vuole un _____ panino.

10. Devi mangiare _____ , non dopo.

11. **Il pilota è già nell'** _____ .

12. Non ho una prenotazione per quell'_____ .

Here we go with plurals! Transpose each "singular" phrase to a "plural" phrase, as we have done with the first one.

il mio amico alto	__i__ mie __i__ amic __i__ alt __i__		
la mia amica bella	l____ mi____ amich____ bell____		
l'autobus comodo	gl____ autobus comod____		
l'albero grande	gl____ alber____ grand____		
un bambino bravo	de____ bambin____ brav____		

166

una bandiera importante dell____ bandier____ important____

questa bicicletta nuova quest____ biciclett____ nuov____

questo caffè buono quest____ caffè buon____

quel cane intelligente que____ can____ intelligent____

quella cartolina brutta quell____ cartolin____ brutt____

l'uomo famoso gl____ uomin____ famos____

la donna gentile l____ donn____ gentil____

lo zio giovane gl____ zi____ giovan____

il suo libro interessante ____ suo____ libr____ interessant____

Find the words that mean the following in the word-search puzzle and circle them. After you find each one, write it in the proper space.

gasoline	drink	ticket
bottle	room	key
dashboard	spoon	yesterday
milk	every	

a	d	h	k	m	b	p	t	x	c	r	u	s	c	o	t	t	o
t	b	e	n	z	i	n	a	c	u	w	z	a	a	c	f	i	g
l	e	o	r	u	g	x	b	u	f	j	n	r	m	v	z	h	n
c	v	g	k	o	l	s	w	c	h	i	a	v	e	a	d	g	i
g	a	h	l	p	i	t	x	c	q	r	u	p	r	a	f	j	l
z	n	v	m	w	e	r	u	h	o	a	f	j	a	l	z	v	b
m	d	g	d	y	t	l	h	i	e	r	i	d	v	n	e	q	m
l	a	t	t	e	t	a	m	a	s	u	c	n	w	q	h	f	s
a	p	s	o	b	o	t	t	i	g	l	i	a	v	n	w	x	b
y	o	q	x	c	m	e	f	o	r	w	m	q	e	r	i	n	p

Finally, choose the appropriate answer to each question.

Buon giorno, come sta?
- ☐ Bene grazie, e lei?
- ☐ Domani mattina.

Come si chiama, lei?
- ☐ Sono americano.
- ☐ **Mi chiamo Mark Smith.**

Dove abita, lei?
- ☐ **Vado in Italia.**
- ☐ Abito negli Stati Uniti.

A che ora parte il treno?
- ☐ Parte alle diciassette.
- ☐ Parte ieri.

Che ore sono?
- ☐ È il tre marzo.
- ☐ Sono le tre e venti.

Che giorno è oggi?
- ☐ È l'una.
- ☐ È il tre novembre.

Che tempo fa?
- ☐ Piove.
- ☐ Domani.

Che cosa prende?
- ☐ Un bicchiere di vino.
- ☐ Vado in Italia.

Perché mangia i ravioli?
- ☐ Perché mi piace.
- ☐ Perché mi piacciono.

Come si sente?
- ☐ Mi sento bene.
- ☐ **Mi sento.**

How did you do? Don't worry if you made mistakes. Learning a new language is a process of trial and error. It's time to go on!

STORES
(ehn-TRYAH-moh)   *(neh-GOH-tsee)*
Entriamo nei negozi

16 | Negozi di abbigliamento /
(ah-bbee-llay-MEHN-toh)

(TAH-lyah)   *(koh-LOH-ree)*
Le taglie / I colori primari

Ti provi i vestiti?
Trying on Clothes?

You can't leave Italy without doing some shopping. Let's hope that you fare better than some of these examples!

(TOH-llyehr-see)
togliersi
to take off

(vehs-TEER-see)
vestirsi
to get dressed

(kah-MEE-chah)
L'uomo si toglie la camicia.
shirt

(MEH-ttehr-see)
mettersi
to put on

(vehs-TEE-toh)
Mi metto il vestito.
dress / suit

La donna si veste molto
(eh-leh-gahn-teh-MEHN-teh)
elegantemente.
elegantly

Si metta questa camicia.
Put on this shirt.

Troppo grande!
Too big!

Si metta questo abito
Put on this suit.

Troppo grande!
Too big!

No, è perfetto. Le sta proprio bene.
No, it's perfect. It really suits you.

Stare is a verb that you will use while shopping:

STARE			
io ——	sto *(STAH-ee)*	noi ——	stiamo
tu ——	stai	voi ——	state
lui lei } ——	sta	loro ——	stanno *(STAH-nnoh)*

to stay, to be

This verb also means "to suit someone" in the expression *stare bene a*:

Il vestito | **mi** | **sta bene** .

The dress | *suits* | *me* .

(*Literally*, the dress *stays well* on me.)

Le scarpe | **ti** | **stanno bene** .

The shoes | *suit* | *you* .

(*Literally*, the shoes *stay well* on you.)

(mahs-KEE-leh)

L'ABBIGLIAMENTO MASCHILE
Men's Clothes

(Mark and his son are at a clothing store.)

COMMESSO **I signori desiderano?**

Can I help you gentlemen?

MARK **Abbiamo bisogno di un nuovo**
(gwahr-dah-ROH-bah) *(PAH-yoh)*
guardaroba. Per mio figlio un paio
(kahl-TSEE-nee) *(pahn-tah-LOH-nee)*
di stivali, calzini, pantaloni,
(GWAHN-tee) *(moo-TAHN-deh)*
guanti, e mutande.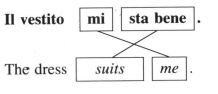

We need a new wardrobe. For my son a pair of

boots, socks, trousers,

gloves, and underwear.

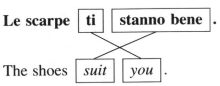

COMMESSO **Bene. E lei?**

Fine. And you?

MARK **Una camicia, una cravatta, una**
(krah-VAH-ttah)
(MAH-llyah) *(eem-pehr-meh-AH-bee-leh)*
maglia, un impermeabile,
(kah-PPEH-lloh)
e un cappello.

A shirt, a tie,

a sweater, a raincoat,

and a hat.

(The two Smiths try on their clothes.)

MARK **La camicia mi sta bene, ma il**

The shirt suits me, but not the rest.

170

resto no. A mio figlio non sta bene

niente.

Nothing suits my son.

COMMESSO   **Desiderano qualcos'altro?**

Would you like something else?

                (mah-LLYEH-ttah)
Per suo figlio abbiamo una maglietta alla
(MOH-dah)   *(cheen-TOO-rah)* *(beh-RREH-ttoh)*
moda, una cintura e un berretto.

For your son we have a fashionable

T-shirt, a belt, and a cap.

JOHN   **No, grazie.**

No, thanks.

COMMESSO   *(JAH-kkah)*
Per lei abbiamo una giacca,
   (beh-LLEE-see-moh) *(kah-POH-ttoh)*
un bellissimo   cappotto e un
(vehs-TEE-toh)   *(GREE-doh)*
vestito   all'ultimo grido.

For you we have a sports jacket, a very nice

coat, and

a suit in the latest style.

MARK   **No, grazie.**

No, thanks.

COMMESSO   *(fah-tsoh-LEH-ttoh)*
Neanche un fazzoletto
   (ohm-BREH-lloh)
o un ombrello?

Not even a handkerchief

or an umbrella?

MARK   **No.**

No.

COMMESSO   **Ma non ha detto che aveva**

bisogno di un guardaroba nuovo?

But didn't you say that

you needed a new wardrobe?

   (skehr-TSAH-voh)(voh-LEH-voh)
MARK   **Scherzavo. Volevo solo**
   (kah-PEE-vah)
vedere se lei capiva il mio italiano.

I was only kidding. I wanted to see if you

understood my Italian.

           (pah-ROH-lah) *(FWOH-ree)*
COMMESSO   **Capisce la parola   fuori?**

Do you understand the word *out*?

MARK   **Capisco. Andiamo, John.**

I understand. Let's go, John.

Ready to try your hand at completing the dialogue? Check your answers when you've finished.

I signori d_____?

Abbiamo b_____ di un n_____ guardaroba. Per mio figlio un

p_____ di stivali, c_____, p_____, g_____, e m_____.

Bene. E lei?

Una c_____, una c_____, una m_____, un i_____,

e un c_____.

La camicia mi s_____ bene, ma il r_____ no. A mio figlio non

s_____ bene niente.

Desiderano qualcos'altro? Per suo figlio abbiamo una m_____ di m_____,

una c_____ e un b_____.

No, grazie.

Per lei abbiamo una giacca, un bellissimo c_____ e un vestito all'ultimo g_____.

No, grazie.

Neanche un f_____ o un ombrello?

No.

Ma non ha detto che aveva b_____ di un guardaroba nuovo?

Il mio, il tuo . . .
Mine, Yours . . .

Remember those possessives? You can also use them to say "mine," "yours," and so on.

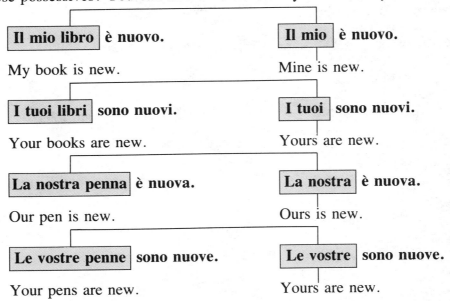

Got it? All you do is get rid of the noun and keep the corresponding form of the possessive adjective.

Questo, quello
This, This One, That, That One

Now that you know about "mine" and "yours," you can apply the same rule to "this, this one" and "these."

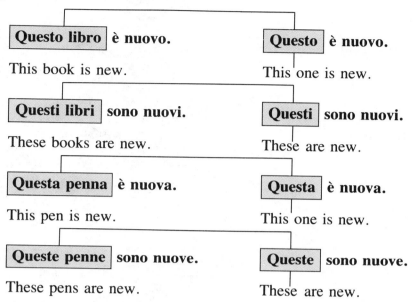

Questo libro è nuovo.	**Questo** è nuovo.
This book is new.	This one is new.
Questi libri sono nuovi.	**Questi** sono nuovi.
These books are new.	These are new.
Questa penna è nuova.	**Questa** è nuova.
This pen is new.	This one is new.
Queste penne sono nuove.	**Queste** sono nuove.
These pens are new.	These are new.

Now it gets a little trickier. For "that, that one" and "those, those ones" you have to make some adjustments.

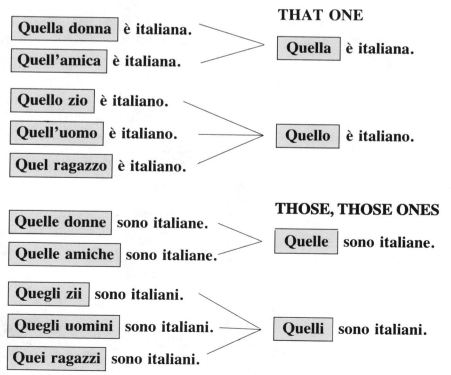

Quella donna è italiana.
Quell'amica è italiana.

THAT ONE
Quella è italiana.

Quello zio è italiano.
Quell'uomo è italiano.
Quel ragazzo è italiano.

Quello è italiano.

Quelle donne sono italiane.
Quelle amiche sono italiane.

THOSE, THOSE ONES
Quelle sono italiane.

Quegli zii sono italiani.
Quegli uomini sono italiani.
Quei ragazzi sono italiani.

Quelli sono italiani.

Do you think you've got it? Substitute the appropriate possessive pronoun for the noun in each of these sentences.

1. La mia penna è nuova.   _____ è nuova.

2. Il suo amico è francese.   _____ è francese.

3. I tuoi libri sono nuovi.   _____ sono nuovi.

4. I suoi calzini sono belli.   _____ sono belli.

5. Questi pantaloni sono belli.   _____ sono belli.

6. Queste mutande sono nuove.   _____ sono nuove.

7. Questa camicia è bianca   _____ è bianca.

8. Quella cravatta è bella.   _____ è bella.

9. Quelle maglie sono belle.   _____ sono belle.

10. Quell'impermeabile è nuovo.   _____ è nuovo.

11. Quel cappello è piccolo.   _____ è piccolo.

12. Quei vestiti sono alla moda.   _____ sono alla moda.

Taglie
Sizes

While you are shopping, you may run into some unexpected problems with sizes, because the metric system is used throughout Italy. Here are some comparisons of sizes of men's clothing.

	TAGLIA AMERICANA	TAGLIA ITALIANA
Camicie	14	36
	15	38
	16	40
	17	42
Altre cose	34	44
Other things	36	46
	38	48
	40	50
	42	52
	44	54
	46	56

174

Now can you complete these sentences? The pictures will give you the necessary clues.

1. Quando fa freddo, mi metto il _____.

2. Quando fa fresco, mi metto la _____.

3. Quando nevica, mi metto gli _____.

4. Quando piove, mi metto l'_____.

5. Quando piove, porto l'_____.

6. Quando fa caldo, mi metto i _____ corti.

L'ABBIGLIAMENTO FEMMINILE
(feh-mmee-NEE-leh)
Women's Clothes

I colori primari
Basic Colors

You'll also have to be able to identify colors on your shopping trip. When you have learned these words, answer the questions that follow.

(reh-JJEE-seh-noh)(JAH-lloh)
un reggiseno   giallo
yellow bra

(BOHR-sah)
una borsa rossa
red purse

(ah-TSOO-rroh)
un vestito azzurro
blue dress

un fazzoletto verde
green handkerchief

(moo-tahn-DEE-neh)(JAH-lloh)
le mutandine   gialle
yellow panties

(soh-ttoh-VEHS-teh)
una sottoveste bianca
white slip

(kah-mee-CHEH-ttah)
una camicetta verde
green blouse

(GOH-nnah)
una gonna rossa
red skirt

Di che colore è?

What color is it?

Di che colore è la camicetta? _____

Di che colore è il reggiseno? _____

Di che colore sono le mutandine? _____

Di che colore è il vestito? _____

Di che colore il fazzoletto? _____

Taglie

Sizes

And here are some comparisons of women's sizes.

	TAGLIA AMERICANA	TAGLIA ITALIANA
Camicette	32	40
	34	42
	36	44
	38	46
	40	48
	42	50
	44	52
Altre cose	8	36
	10	38
	12	40
	14	42
	16	44
	18	46

LE SCARPE PER UOMINI E DONNE
Shoes for Men and Women

Numeri di scarpa
Sizes

	UOMINI				
Numero americano	7	8	9	10	11
Numero italiano	39	41	43	44	45
	DONNE				
Numero americano	5	6	7	8	9
Numero italiano	35	36	38	38	40

Read the following passage about clothes and then check each statement as true or false.

Lina e Paola sono due amiche. Stasera si vestono per uscire a una festa. Lina si mette una gonna azzurra e una camicetta rossa.
(STEH-sseh)
Anche Paola si veste con le stesse cose. Alla festa Lina e Paola si
same
(POHR-tah-noh)
incontrano e vedono che portano le stesse cose. Lina decide di
they are wearing
tornare a casa per mettersi un vestito nuovo.

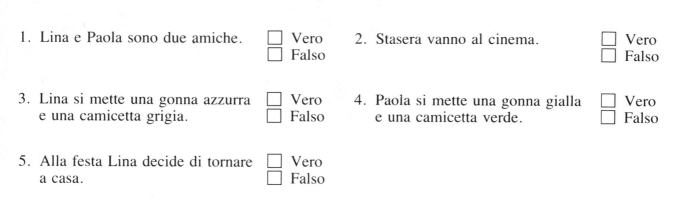

1. Lina e Paola sono due amiche. ☐ Vero ☐ Falso

2. Stasera vanno al cinema. ☐ Vero ☐ Falso

3. Lina si mette una gonna azzurra e una camicetta grigia. ☐ Vero ☐ Falso

4. Paola si mette una gonna gialla e una camicetta verde. ☐ Vero ☐ Falso

5. Alla festa Lina decide di tornare a casa. ☐ Vero ☐ Falso

ANSWERS
True/False 1. Vero **2.** Falso **3.** Falso **4.** Falso **5.** Vero

177

(oo-nee-TAH)   (PEH-zoh)

Unità di peso e di misura

Food Stores / Weights and Measures

Shopping for food can be another pleasant experience, but not unless you know what the shops are! Study the vocabulary carefully.

(lah-tteh-REE-ah)	(mah-cheh-LLAH-yoh)	(froo-ttee-VEHN-doh-loh)	(pah-nee-FEE-choh)
la latteria	**il macellaio**	**il fruttivendolo**	**il panificio**
dairy	butcher	produce market	bread bakery

il latte	**la carne**	**la verdura**	**la frutta**	**il pane**
milk	meat	vegetables	fruit	bread

(pehs-keh-REE-ah)	(kohn-feh-tteh-REE-ah)	(pahs-tee-cheh-REE-ah)	(jeh-lah-teh-REE-ah)	(eh-noh-TEH-kah)
la pescheria	**la confetteria**	**la pasticceria**	**la gelateria**	**l'enoteca**
fish shop	candy shop	pastry shop	ice cream shop	wine dealer

il pesce	**le caramelle**	**le paste**	**le torte**	**il gelato**	**il vino**
fish	candy	pastries	cakes	ice cream	wine

(doh-MAHN-dah)

Fare una domanda

To Pose a Question

Io faccio una domanda all'uomo.
I pose a question to the man.

Io *gli* faccio una domanda.

I pose a question *to him*.

178

Dal fruttivendolo
At the Produce Market

Expressions such as "at the market," "at the butcher's," "at the doctor's" or "to the market," "to the butcher's," "to the doctor's" are rendered in Italian by the preposition *da* and the appropriate noun.

Sono **dal** fruttivendolo.

I am at the market.

Vado **dal** dottore.

I am going to the doctor's.

Vado **da** Giovanni.

I am going to John's.

Troppe domande!
Too Many Questions!

(Mark Smith and his wife approach a policeman.)

MARK	**Scusi, signore, le vorrei fare una domanda.**
	Excuse me, sir, I would like to ask you a question.
VIGILE	**Faccia pure!**
	Go ahead!
MARK	**Ho bisogno di un po' di pane. Dov'è il panificio?**
	I need some bread. Where is the bread bakery?
VIGILE	**Qui vicino in Via Verdi.**
	Nearby on Verdi Street.
MARK	**Dove si compra la carne?**
	Where does one buy meat?
VIGILE	**Dal macellaio, in via Rossini.**
	At the butcher's, on Rossini Street.
MARK	**E il latte?**
	And milk?
VIGILE	**Alla latteria, in via Dante.**
	At the dairy, on Dante Street.
MARK	**Poi ho bisogno anche di verdura e frutta. Mi sa dire dov'è il fruttivendolo più vicino?**
	Then I also need vegetables and fruit. Can you tell me where the nearest market is?
VIGILE	**In Via Nazionale.**
	On National Street.

MARK	Ho anche bisogno di un po' di pesce, un pacchetto di caramelle, una torta e due bottiglie di vino. **Mi sa dire** dove si trovano la pescheria, la confetteria, la pasticceria e l'enoteca?	I also need a bit of fish, a package of candy, a cake and two bottles of wine. Can you tell me where to find a fish shop, a candy shop, a pastry shop and a wine shop?
VIGILE	Basta, basta, signore! Lei fa troppe domande!	Enough, enough, sir! You ask too many questions!
MARK	Mamma mia! Che vigile impaziente!	Heavens! (*literally*, my mom) What an impatient policeman!
MARY	*(rah-JOH-neh)* No, Mark, **il vigile ha ragione.** Tu fai troppe domande.	No, Mark, the policeman is right. You ask too many questions.

Read the dialogue aloud until you are familiar with the new vocabulary. Then check off each statement as either true or false.

1. Mark fa delle domande a una donna. ☐ Vero ☐ Falso

2. Mark non ha bisogno di pane. ☐ Vero ☐ Falso

3. La carne si compra dal macellaio. ☐ Vero ☐ Falso

4. Il latte si compra alla latteria. ☐ Vero ☐ Falso

5. La verdura si compra in una gelateria. ☐ Vero ☐ Falso

6. Il pesce si compra in una pescheria. ☐ Vero ☐ Falso

7. Il vino si compra in una confetteria. ☐ Vero ☐ Falso

8. Il vigile risponde a tutte le domande. ☐ Vero ☐ Falso

One of the following answers to each question is not correct.

Odd one out

Alla latteria si compra:
  il latte
  il burro
  il vino   _____

Dal macellaio si compra:
  la torta
  la carne
  il pollo   _____

180

Dal fruttivendolo si compra:
     la verdura
     il gelato
     la frutta   _____

Alla gelateria si compra:
     il pesce
     il gelato
     i dolci   _____

All'enoteca si compra:
     il pane
     il vino rosso
     il vino bianco   _____

Alla pasticceria si compra:
     la torta
     le paste
     la carne   _____

If you want to make a complaint, here are some suggestions.

Questo pane non è *fresco*!   This bread is not fresh!

Questo panino è *raffermo*!   This roll is stale!

(MAHR-choh)
Questo pomodoro è *marcio*!   This tomato is rotten!

Questo vino è *cattivo*!   This wine is bad tasting!

Si compra, si mangia . . .
One Buys, One Eats . . .

You might have noticed that expressions such as "one buys," and "one eats" are said in Italian by using *si* and the verb. However, be careful! The verb agrees with *what* one buys or eats.

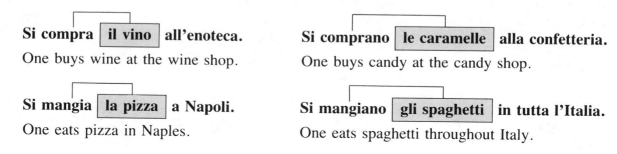

Si compra il vino **all'enoteca.**
One buys wine at the wine shop.

Si comprano le caramelle **alla confetteria.**
One buys candy at the candy shop.

Si mangia la pizza **a Napoli.**
One eats pizza in Naples.

Si mangiano gli spaghetti **in tutta l'Italia.**
One eats spaghetti throughout Italy.

When you need to compare things, use *più* before the adjective to mean "more." To say "the most," simply use the appropriate definite article before *più*.

Mario è intelligente.   Mario is intelligent.
Gino è *più* intelligente.   Gino is more intelligent.
Pino è *il più* intelligente.   Pino is the most intelligent.

Maria è alta.   Mary is tall.
Gina è *più* alta.   Gina is taller.
Lina è *la più* alta.   Lina is the tallest.

UNITÀ DI PESO E DI MISURA
Weights and Measures

(peh-ZAH-reh)
pesare
to weigh

(PEH-zoh)
il peso
weight

As we said before, the metric system is used throughout Italy. Here is a chart that gives some metric terms.

(mee-LLEE-meh-troh) **millimetro (mm)**	millimeter	= .039 inch
(chehn-TEE-meh-troh) **centimetro (cm)**	centimeter	= .39 inch
(MEH-troh) **metro (m)**	meter	= 3.28 feet
(kee-LOH-meh-troh) **chilometro (km)**	kilometer	= .62 mile
(chehn-TEE-lee-troh) **centilitro (cl)**	centiliter	= .338 fluid ounce
(LEE-troh) **litro (l)**	liter	= .26 gallon
(mee-llee-GRAH-mmoh) **milligrammo (mg)**	milligram	= .015 grain
(chehn-tee-GRAH-mmoh) **centigrammo (cg)**	centigram	= .154 grain
(GRAH-mmoh) **grammo (g)**	gram	= 15.43 grains
(eh-ttoh-GRAH-mmoh) **ettogrammo (hg)**	hectogram	= 3.52 ounces
(kee-loh-GRAH-mmoh) **chilogrammo (kg)**	kilogram	= 2.2 pounds

(boh-TTEH-gah)
ALLA BOTTEGA DI GENERI ALIMENTARI
At the Grocery Store

These questions are so easy that we haven't given you the answers! If you can't figure out the new words from the pictures, check the glossary.

(sah-poh-NEH-ttah)
Vorrei una saponetta.

Quanto costa _____?

(bah-RAH-ttoh-loh)   *(soh-LOO-bee-leh)*
Vorrei un barattolo di caffè solubile.

Quanto costa _____?

(ROH-toh-loh) *(ee-JEH-nee-kah)*
Vorrei un rotolo di carta igienica.

Quanto costa _____?

(MEH-tsoh) *(chee-LYEH-jeh)*
Vorrei mezzo chilo di ciliege.

Quanto costa _____?

Vorrei un litro di latte.

Quanto costa _____?

(doh-DZEE-nah)
Vorrei mezza dozzina di limoni.

Quanto costa _____?

Vorrei un barattolo di verdura.

Quanto costa _____?

Vorrei un pacchetto di zucchero.

Quanto costa _____?

Vorrei una dozzina di uova.

Quanto costa _____

(SKAH-toh-lah) (bees-KOH-ttee)
Vorrei una scatola di biscotti.

Quanto costa _____?

Notice that in Italian the article "the" must be used, especially at the beginning of a sentence, to express generalities.

Gli italiani mangiano gli spaghetti.
Italians eat spaghetti.

Lo zucchero costa molto.
Sugar costs a lot.

L'italiano è una bella lingua.
Italian is a beautiful language.

Il pane costa molto poco.
Bread costs very little.

This passage contains more information about shopping in Italy. Read it and then select the appropriate answer to each question.

(JEH-neh-reh)
In Italia la spesa si fa, in genere, ogni giorno.
        food shopping   generally

(soo-pehr-mehr-KAH-tee)
Ma come negli Stati Uniti, oggi ci sono anche i supermercati, dove si può comprare il cibo
                        supermarkets

(soor-jeh-LAH-toh)   *(MEH-toh-doh)* *(poh-poh-LAH-reh)*   *(mehr-KAH-toh)*
surgelato. Ma il metodo più popolare di fare la spesa è al mercato. Lì si compra sempre
frozen   method   popular   open-air market

"a buon mercato." Il cibo è fresco e buono.
    cheaply   food

Quando si fa, in genere, la spesa in Italia?
- ☐ Il sabato.
- ☐ Il venerdì.
- ☐ Ogni giorno.

Oggi ci sono anche . . .
- ☐ i supermercati.
- ☐ i negozi.
- ☐ le ciliege.

Che cosa si può comprare a un supermercato?
- ☐ Le scarpe.
- ☐ Il cibo surgelato.
- ☐ I cappotti.

Qual è il metodo più popolare di fare la spesa?
- ☐ Al supermercato.
- ☐ Alla bottega di generi alimentari.
- ☐ Al mercato.

Can you unscramble the letters to form the following words?

mrcteao _____
       open-air market

isbttooc _____
       biscuit/cookie

alotsca _____
       box

nzizaod _____
       dozen

cliiegai _____
       cherry

brttlaaoo _____
       jar/can

ettonapas _____
       soap bar

Here are some items you might find in an Italian drugstore. Say them aloud as you find them in the showcase.

(dehn-tee-FREE-choh)
il dentifricio
toothpaste

(SPAH-tsoh-lah)
la spazzola
hairbrush

(spah-tsoh-LEE-noh)
lo spazzolino da denti
toothbrush

(speh-KKYEH-ttoh)
lo specchio / lo specchietto
mirror

una scatola di fazzoletti di carta
box of tissues

(PEH-ttee-neh)
il pettine
comb

(roh-SSEH-ttoh)
il rossetto
lipstick / rouge

(LAH-kkah)
la lacca per capelli
hairspray

(KREH-mah) *(beh-LLEH-tsah)*
la crema (di bellezza)
facial cream

(SPEE-lleh)(see-koo-REH-tsah)
le spille di sicurezza
safety pins

(ZMAHL-toh) *(OON-gyeh)*
lo smalto per le unghie
nail polish

185

IN FARMACIA
At the Drugstore

(Mary Smith and Lina Rossi—an Italian friend—are at a drugstore.)

LINA **Che cosa vuoi comprare, Mary?**　　What do you want to buy, Mary?

MARY **Non sono sicura.**　　I'm not sure.

COMMESSO **Desidera, signora?**　　Can I help you, madam?

MARY **Quanto costa la crema?**　　How much does cold cream cost?

COMMESSO **Ventimila lire.**　　20.000 lira.

MARY **E quel pettine e quella spazzola?**　　And that comb and that hairbrush?

COMMESSO **Il pettine duemila e la spazzola cinquemila.**　　The comb 2.000 and the hairbrush 5.000.

LINA **Non c'è male, Mary.**　　That's not bad, Mary.

MARY **No, grazie.**　　No, thanks.

COMMESSO **Forse ha bisogno di uno spazzolino da denti e del dentifricio?**　　Maybe you need a toothbrush and some toothpaste?

MARY **No. Vorrei lo smalto per le unghie, il rossetto, il mascara, e la lacca per capelli.**　　No. I would like nail polish, lipstick, mascara, and hairspray.

(TROO-kkoh)

LINA **Ah, ti vuoi mettere il trucco?**　　Ah, you want to put on makeup?

MARY **Sì, questa sera voglio uscire.**　　Yes, tonight I want to go out.

186

After you have read the dialogue several times, check off each statement as either true or false.

1. Mary è sicura di quello che vuole comprare.
☐ Vero
☐ Falso

2. La crema costa ventimila lire.
☐ Vero
☐ Falso

3. Il pettine costa duemila lire.
☐ Vero
☐ Falso

4. La spazzola costa cinquemila lire.
☐ Vero
☐ Falso

5. Mary ha bisogno di uno spazzolino da denti.
☐ Vero
☐ Falso

6. Mary compra lo smalto per le unghie, il rossetto, il mascara, e la lacca per i capelli.
☐ Vero
☐ Falso

Some essential phrases:

Vorrei comprare . . .	*I would like* to buy . . .
Devo comprare . . .	*I have to* buy . . .
È necessario comprare . . .	*It is necessary* to buy . . .

Che, cui
That, Which, Who, Whom

The relative pronoun *che* translates as "that," "which," and "who" when used in sentences like the following.

Il libro che è rosso è interessante.

The book, which is red, is interesting.

La crema che voglio costa troppo.

The cream that I want costs too much.

Il ragazzo che mangia la pizza è mio fratello.

The boy who is eating pizza is my brother.

After a preposition, *cui* is used instead.

Ecco la borsa in cui metto il rossetto.

Here is the purse in which I put the lipstick.

Questo è il ragazzo a cui parlo italiano.

This is the boy to whom I speak italian.

ANSWERS

True/False 1. Falso 2. Vero 3. Vero 4. Vero 5. Falso 6. Vero

187

Now you choose either *che* or *cui*.

Maria compra la spazzola _____ costa cinquemila lire.

L'uomo di _____ parlo è mio marito.

Lina vuole il rossetto _____ costa molto.

Maria dice _____ la sua amica viene domani.

La donna per _____ compro la crema è mia moglie.

Sapere, conoscere
To Know

These verbs may give you some trouble, so study them well.

	(sah-PEH-reh) SAPERE	*(koh-NOH-sheh-reh)* CONOSCERE		*(sah-PEH-reh)* SAPERE	*(koh-NOH-sheh-reh)* CONOSCERE
io	so	*(koh-NOHS-koh)* conosco	noi	*(sah-PPYAH-moh)* sappiamo	*(koh-noh-SHAH-moh)* conosciamo
tu	sai	*(koh-NOH-shee)* conosci	voi	*(sah-PEH-teh)* sapete	*(koh-noh-SHEH-teh)* conoscete
lui } lei }	sa	*(koh-NOH-sheh)* conosce	loro	*(SAH-nnoh)* sanno	*(koh-NOH-skoh-noh)* conoscono

What's the difference between these two verbs? Use *conoscere* when you want to say that you know or are acquainted with "someone"; use *sapere* when you want to say you know "something" or "how to do" something. Although there is some overlapping in use, this distinction is all you will need to know for your communicative purposes.

Now choose *sapere* or *conoscere* as the case may be.

Io non _____il signor Smith.

Gina _____parlare italiano molto bene.

Quell'uomo _____ lo zio di Carlo.

Noi _____ che lui arriva domani.

Tu _____ mia moglie?

188

I signori Smith non —————————— parlare italiano molto bene.

Il signor Smith non mi —————————————————— .

(Mark Smith and his son enter a drugstore.)

MARK **Scusi, signore, lei ha**
 (see-gah-REH-tteh) *(ah-chen-DEE-noh)*
 sigarette e un accendino?

Excuse me, sir, do you have

cigarettes and a lighter?

COMMESSO **No, lei deve andare da un**
 (tah-bah-KKAH-yoh)
 tabaccaio.

No. You have to go to a tobacco shop.

MARK **Allora mi dia uno spruzzatore**
 (deh-oh-doh-RAHN-teh)(rah-ZOH-yoh)
 di deodorante e un rasoio con le
 (lah-MEH-tteh) *(eh-LEH-ttree-koh)*
 lamette. Il mio rasoio elettrico non

 funziona in questo paese!

Then give me a can of deodorant and a razor

with blades. My electric razor

doesn't work in

this country!

COMMESSO **Perché ha bisogno di un**
 (kohn-vehr-tee-TOH-reh)
 convertitore.

Because you need

a converter.

   (kohm-plee-kah-TSYOH-nee)
MARK **Quante complicazioni!**

So many complications!

COMMESSO **Senta, signore. Ho la**
 (soh-loo-TSYOH-neh) *(KREH-sheh-reh)*
 soluzione. Si faccia crescere la barba

 come me.

Listen, sir. I have the solution. Let your beard

grow like me.

(Mary and Anne now enter.)

MARY **Ciao, Mark. Cosa fai?**

Hi, Mark. What are you doing?

MARK **Compro delle cose.**

I am buying some things.

     (ahs-pee-REE-neh)
MARY **Anch'io ho bisogno di aspirine,**
 (BEHN-deh) *(tehr-MOH-meh-troh)*
 bende e un termometro.

I too need aspirins, Band-Aids,

and a thermometer.

MARK **Ti senti male?**

Do you feel sick?

MARY **Mi fa male un po' la testa, e** *(TEHS-tah)* **abbiamo bisogno di bende per il nostro viaggio.**

My head hurts a bit, and we need Band-Aids for our trip.

COMMESSO **Vuole anche delle spille di** *(TAHL-koh)* **sicurezza, un po' di talco e dei** *(pah-nnoh-LEE-nee)* **pannolini?**

Do you want safety pins, a bit of talcum powder, and some diapers?

MARY **Dei pannolini? Non ho bambini piccoli!**

Some diapers? I do not have small children!

When you are familiar with the dialogue, try to reconstruct it below.

Il / non / in / questo / mio / paese / funziona / rasoio

_____

convertitore / un / di / bisogno / Perché / ha

_____

me / come / crescere / barba / la / Si / faccia

_____

Anch'io / termometro / un / e / bende / bisogno / ho / di / aspirine

_____

spille / delle / sicurezza / di / anche / Vuole / talco / di / po' / un / e / pannolini / dei

_____

lamette / le / con / un / e / rasoio / mi / Allora / dia / spruzzatore / uno / deodorante / di

_____

190

Laundromats can be found throughout Italy in the major hotels. In general, the service in Italy for laundry and dry cleaning is quite good. However, you should always plan to bring along some wash-and-wear clothes, just in case! And remember, during the weekend of or near August 15, everything closes down in Italy.

(lah-vah-TREE-cheh)
la lavatrice
washer

(ah-shoo-gah-TREE-cheh)
l'asciugatrice
dryer

ALLA LAVANDERIA AUTOMATICA
(ah-oo-toh-MAH-tee-kah)
At the Laundromat

(Anne Smith is at the hotel laundromat where she runs into her Italian friend Lina.)

ANNE   **Ciao, Lina. Mi puoi aiutare? È la**   Hi, Lina. Can you help me? It's my first time at
        (VOHL-tah)
mia prima volta a una lavanderia italiana.   an Italian laundromat.
        (sah-POH-neh) (POHL-veh-reh)
LINA   **Certo. Hai il sapone in   polvere,**   Certainly. Do you have   soap powder,
        (CHES-tah) (FEH-rroh) (STEE-roh)
una cesta, un ferro da stiro, e   a wash basket, an iron, and
        (moh-LLEH-tteh)
delle mollette?   clothespins?

ANNE   **Sì. Ho tutto. Vedo che c'è un'**   Yes, I have everything. I see that there is a dryer

asciugatrice e un tavolo da stiro.   and an ironing board.

Meno male.   Thank goodness.

191

	(MEH-tteh-reh) *(jeh-TTOH-neh)*	
LINA	**Ora, devi mettere un gettone**	Now, you have to put a token in the washer and
	nella lavatrice e dopo nell'asciugatrice.	then in the dryer. Here. I have two tokens
	Ecco. Io ho due gettoni per te.	for you.
	(feh-SSOO-rah) *(EH-kkoh-lah)*	
ANNE	**Dov'è la fessura? Ah, eccola!**	Where is the slot? Ah, here it is!

(The machine does not start.)

	(NYEHN-teh)	
ANNE	**Perché sembra che niente**	Why does nothing seem
	(foon-TSYOH-nah)	
	funziona?	to work?
LINA	**Perché tu non sai fare.**	Because you don't know how to do things.

(Lina gives the machine a kick and the machine starts.)

	(MOH-doh)	
LINA	**Questo è il modo di fare le cose**	This is the way to do things the Italian way!
	all'italiana!	

(The machine begins to overflow with suds.)

	(soo-CHEH-deh)	
ANNE	**Mamma mia, che cosa succede?**	Oh dear! What's happening?
	(preh-oh-kkoo-PAH-reh)	
LINA	**Non ti preoccupare. C'è troppo**	Don't worry, there is too much soap. Look,
	(PAH-nnee)	
	sapone. Guarda, i tuoi panni non sono	your clothes are no longer dirty.
	(SPOHR-kee)	
	più sporchi!	

Read the dialogue several times out loud and then fill in the missing parts from memory. Afterwards, check your answers.

Ciao, Lina. Mi p_____ a_____? È la mia prima

v_____ a una l_____ italiana.

Certo. Hai il s_____ in p_____, una

c_____, un f_____ da stiro, e delle

m_____?

Sì. Ho tutto. Vedo che c'è un'a_____ e un t_____ da

stiro. Meno male.

Ora, devi m_____ un g_____ nella

l_____ e dopo nell'a_____. Ecco. Io ho due gettoni per te.

Dov'è la f_____? Ah, eccola!

Perché s_____ niente f_____?

Perché tu non s_____ fare.

Questo è il m_____ di fare le cose all'italiana!

Ci, ne
There, Some of

Notice that *ci* means "there" and that *ne* means "some of." Like the pronouns you learned earlier, these occur right before the verb.

Mark va *in Italia* domani.	**Mark *ci* va domani.**
Mark is going to Italy tomorrow.	Mark is going *there* tomorrow.

Io metto il rossetto *nella borsa*.	**Io *ci* metto il rossetto.**
I put the lipstick in the purse.	I put the lipstick *there*.

Voglio *del pane*.	***Ne* voglio.**
I want some bread.	I want *some* (of it).

Mangio *degli spaghetti*.	***Ne* mangio.**
I am eating some spaghetti.	I am eating *some* (of them).

Got it? Now it's your turn; you choose *ci* or *ne*.

Anne mette il gettone *nella fessura*. Anne _____ mette il gettone.

Lina ha *delle mollette*. Lina _____ ha.   Anne ha *cinque gettoni*. Anne _____ ha cinque.

ANSWERS

Pronouns ci (mette)   ne (ha.)   ne (ha cinque.)

193

Lina mette il sapone *nella lavatrice*. Lina _____ mette il sapone.

Anne mette un gettone *nell'asciugatrice*. Anne _____ mette un gettone.

Lina ha bisogno *di un ferro da stiro*. Lina _____ ha bisogno.

Anne non ha bisogno *di un tavolo da stiro*. Anne non _____ ha bisogno.

(sehr-VEE-tsee)

SERVIZI DI LAVANDERIA ALL'ALBERGO
Hotel Laundry Services

Here are some common expressions you may use when you use the laundry services of the hotel where you are staying.

Avete un servizio di lavanderia?	Do you have a laundry service?
(PAH-nnee)	
Devo far lavare dei panni.	I have some clothes to be washed.
(koo-CHEE-reh) *(boh-TTOH-neh)*	
Mi può cucire questo bottone?	Can you sew on this button?
(rah-mmehn-DAH-reh)	
Mi può rammendare la manica?	Can you mend the sleeve?
(stee-RAH-reh)	
Mi può stirare questa camicia?	Can you iron this shirt?
(AH-mee-doh)	
C'è troppo amido nelle mie mutande!	There's too much starch in my undershorts!
Dov'è la lavanderia a secco?	Where is the dry cleaner?
Mi può portare questo vestito alla	Can you take this suit to the cleaners?
lavanderia?	
(TOH-llyeh-reh) *(MAH-kkyah)*	
Può togliere questa macchia?	Can you take out this spot?

You might want to look over the words and expressions you have learned in this unit before you try to unscramble the following.

lvaandriea _____ lvaandriea a cceso _____
    laundry   dry cleaner

lvaartiec _____ ecirtaguiasc _____
    washer   dryer

194

spaone in plovree _____ sceta _____ tolgieer _____
soap powder   wash basket   to take out

rrfeo da stoir _____ lltteeom _____ mcchaia _____
iron   clothespins   spot

mtteere _____ ttgeone _____ fsseuar _____
to put   token   slot

pnnai _____ ccuier _____ bttnooe _____
clothes   to sew   button

rmmaenared _____ arestir _____ miado _____
to mend   to iron   starch

(lah-mehn-TEH-leh)

Lamentele
Complaints

(ree-CHEH-veh)   *(kohn-TROH-llah)*

Il signor Smith riceve i suoi panni dalla lavenderia dell'albergo. Quando li controlla, decide
checks

(lah-mehn-TAHR-see) *(dee-reh-TTOH-reh)*   *(BOO-koh)*

di andare a lamentarsi dal direttore. Nella sua camicia c'è un buco e ci hanno messo
to complain   manager   hole   they put

troppo amido. Tra i panni trova un reggiseno e mutandine da donna. Trova anche un
Among

calzino rosso e uno verde.

Wouldn't you know that Mark would have these kinds of laundry problems? Answer the true-and-false after you have read the passage.

1. Il signor Smith non ha lamentele.   ☐ Vero ☐ Falso

4. **Nella sua camicia c'è un buco.**   ☐ Vero ☐ Falso

2. Il signor Smith riceve i suoi panni dalla lavanderia a secco.   ☐ Vero ☐ Falso

5. Trova panni da donna.   ☐ Vero ☐ Falso

3. **Il signor Smith si lamenta dal direttore.**   ☐ Vero ☐ Falso

6. Trova due calzini gialli.   ☐ Vero ☐ Falso

ANSWERS
True/False 1. Falso **2.** Falso **3.** Vero **4.** Vero **5.** Vero **6.** Falso

sapone in polvere cesta togliere ferro da stiro mollette macchia mettere gettone fessura panni cucire bottone rammendare stirare amido

195

20 **Dal parrucchiere / Dal barbiere**
(pah-rroo-KKYEH-reh) *(bahr-BYEH-reh)*
At the Hairdresser, Beauty Shop / At the Barber

DAL PARRUCCHIERE

At the Beauty Shop / Hairdresser

(Mary and Anne decide to go to a beauty shop.)

PARRUCCHIERE **Desiderano?**

Can I help you?

MARY **Per mia figlia, uno shampoo, un**
(SHAHM-poh)

For my daughter, a shampoo,

(trah-ttah-MEHN-toh) *(FAH-chah)*
trattamento alla faccia,

a facial massage,

(mah-nee-KOO-reh) *(PYEH-gah)*
una manicure, e una messa in piega.

a manicure,

and a (hair) set.

Io vorrei solo una

(pehr-mah-NEHN-teh)
permanente.

I would like only a permanent.

(kah-PEH-llee)
Attenzione ai miei capelli!

Be careful with my hair!

Hanno un bel colore!

It is a beautiful color!

PARRUCCHIERE **Va bene. Prima**

Okay. First you have

(lah-VAH-reh)
bisogna lavare i capelli

to have your hair washed

(SOH-ttoh)
e poi deve andare sotto

and then you have to go

(KAHS-koh)
il casco.

under the hair dryer.

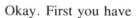

196

(after they have been under the hair dryer for a while:)

PARRUCCHIERE **Venga, signora! I capelli sono**
(ah-SHOO-ttee)   *(spah-tsoh-LAH-reh)*
asciutti. Prima le devo spazzolare

Come, madam! Your hair is dry.

First I have to brush your hair

i capelli e poi le faccio la permanente.
(SPAH-tsoh-lah)
Un momento che prendo una spazzola
(bee-goh-DEE-nee)
e alcuni bigodini.

and then I'll give you a

permanent. Hold on a moment; I'm going to get

a brush and some curlers.

(as the beautician is about to finish:)

PARRUCCHIERE **Signora, si guardi nello**
(veh-rah-MEHN-teh)
specchio! Lei è veramente bella!

Madam, you can look at yourself in the mirror.

You are truly beautiful!

MARY **Mamma mia! I miei capelli**
(BYOHN-dee)
sono biondi!

Good heavens!

My hair is blonde!

When you have the dialogue down cold, match up the phrases in the left column with those in the right column. Then, check your answers.

Per mia figlia . . .	solo una permanente.
Io vorrei . . .	lavare i capelli e poi andare sotto il casco.
Attenzione . . .	sono biondi!
Hanno un bel . . .	guardi nello specchio!
Prima bisogna . . .	spazzolare i capelli e poi le faccio la permanente.
I capelli . . .	prendo una spazzola e alcuni bigodini.
Prima le devo . . .	ai miei capelli!
Un momento che . . .	sono asciutti.
Signora, si . . .	colore!
I miei capelli . . .	uno shampoo, un trattamento alla faccia, una manicure, e una messa in piega.

Here are some more useful expressions for you.

(shah-KKWAH-reh)
Mi può sciacquare i capelli?   Can you give me a rinse?

(tah-LLYAH-reh)
Mi può tagliare i capelli?   Can you give me a haircut?

197

Non voglio la lacca, per favore.   No hair spray, please.
(frahn-JEH-ttah)
Mi fa la frangetta?   Can you give me some bangs?

One last word about those pesky object pronouns! What happens when the two types, direct and indirect (remember?), are used together? Watch!

Giovanni *mi* dà *il libro*.   **Maria *ti* dà *la penna*.**   **Lui *ci* dà *i libri*.**
John gives the book to me.   Mary gives the pen to you.   He gives the books to us.

Giovanni *me lo* dà.   **Maria *te la* dà.**   **Lui *ce li* dà.**

John gives *it to me*.   Mary gives *it to you*.   He gives *them to us*.

Confused? Don't worry. You probably won't need to know how to use the two types together. However, someone may use them when speaking to you. Just be aware that they both come before the verb and that minor changes are made: *mi* becomes *me*; *ti* becomes *te*; and so on.

DAL BARBIERE
At the Barber

Il signor Smith decide di andare

dal barbiere per farsi
to have

tagliare i capelli e la barba.
his hair cut

Al signor Smith non piace farsi la barba da solo.
to shave himself

(LOON-gah) (bah-ZEH-tteh) (BAH-ffee)
Ha la barba lunga, le basette, e i baffi.
long   sideburns   moustache

Decide di farsi tagliare tutto!
to have everything cut

Il barbiere è un uomo simpatico.

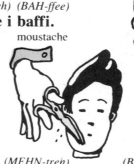

(MEHN-treh)   (BRAH-noh)
Comincia a tagliare i capelli del signor Smith, mentre canta un brano d'opera.
while   excerpt

198

(veh-LOH-cheh) *(FOHR-bee-chee)* *(mah-kkee-NEH-ttah)* *(rah-ZOH-yoh)*

È molto veloce con le forbici e la macchinetta. Con il rasoio, comincia a
quick   scissors   clippers   straight razor

(PEHN-sah)

fare la barba al signor Smith. Ma il barbiere pensa solo a cantare. Taglia la barba

del signor Smith e gli taglia anche tutti i

(KAHL-voh)

capelli! Adesso il signor Smith è calvo!
bald

Il barbiere dice al signor Smith: «Non si

(peh-ttee-NAHR-see)

preoccupi! Lei non deve più pettinarsi!»
You do not have to comb yourself anymore!

Are these passages getting easier for you? If not, go over this one again, and look up the words you don't recognize. Then select the correct answer to each question.

Dove decide di andare il signor Smith?

- ☐ Dal parrucchiere.
- ☐ Dal barbiere.
- ☐ Dal fruttivendolo.

Perché va a farsi tagliare la barba?

- ☐ Perché è calvo.
- ☐ Perché è simpatico.
- ☐ **Perché non gli piace farsi la barba da solo.**

Ha i baffi?

- ☐ Sì.
- ☐ No.

Che cosa fa il barbiere al signor Smith?

- ☐ Gli taglia tutti i capelli.
- ☐ Lo pettina.
- ☐ Gli fa la permanente.

Review the words and expressions introduced in this unit, and then give this crossword puzzle a try.

Across
2. Curlers
4. To comb oneself
6. Hair dryer
8. Hair

Down
1. Blond
2. Sideburns
3. Moustache
4. Permanent
5. Razor
7. Bald
9. To wash

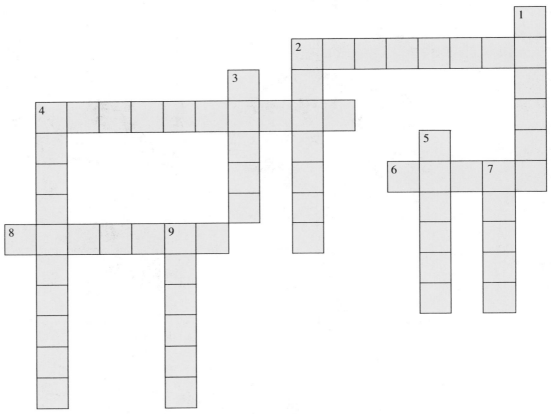

21 *(KYOHS-koh)* *(kahr-toh-leh-REE-ah)*
Il chiosco / La cartoleria
Kiosk / Stationery Store

AL CHIOSCO
At the Kiosk

Naturally by this time, you know what to do with this dialogue.

(While walking through Rome, Anne and John Smith stop at a kiosk.)

(VEHN-deh) (johr-NAH-lee)

JOHN **Scusi, lei vende i giornali in lingua inglese?**

Excuse me, do you sell English language newspapers?

PROPRIETARIO DI CHIOSCO **No signore. Lei**
(ree-VEES-teh)
è turista? Ho delle riviste americane.

No, sir. Are you a tourist? I have some American magazines.

(peh-ROH)

JOHN **No, grazie. Però vorrei comprare**
(kahr-toh-LEE-neh) (frahn-koh-BOH-llee)
delle cartoline e dei francobolli.

No, thank you. However, I would like to buy some postcards and stamps.

PROPRIETARIO DI CHIOSCO **Ecco, signore.**

Here you are, sir.

ANNE **Io vorrei comprare delle riviste per la mia amica in America e delle guide turistiche.**

I would like to buy some magazines for my friend in America and some tourist guides.

PROPRIETARIO DI CHIOSCO **Ecco, signorina.**

Here you are, miss.

ANNE **Grazie. Quanto le devo?**

Thank you. How much do I owe you?

JOHN *(looking through wallet)* **Lascia** *(LAH-shah)*   Forget it, Anne.
(PEHR-deh-reh)
      perdere, Anne.

ANNE **Perché?**   Why?

JOHN **Perché non abbiamo soldi!**   Because we do not have any money!

Now you do the dialogue. Don't forget to check your answers.

JOHN **Scusi,** _____ **?**

PROPRIETARIO DI CHIOSCO **No signore. Lei è turista? Ho delle riviste americane.**

JOHN **No,** _____ **.**

PROPRIETARIO DI CHIOSCO **Ecco, signore.**

ANNE **Io** _____ **.**

PROPRIETARIO DI CHIOSCO **Ecco, signorina.**

ANNE **Grazie.** _____ **?**

JOHN **Lascia perdere, Anne.**

ANNE **Perché?**

JOHN **Perché** _____ **!**

You may have noticed that *molto* has several meanings. Here are some of them.

Marco mangia *molti* spaghetti.	**Gina ha *molti* amici.**	**La ragazza è *molto* bella.**
Mark eats *a lot of* spaghetti.	Gina has *many* friends.	The girl is *very* beautiful.

It is usually an adjective and therefore agrees with the noun it modifies. However, when it means "very," it is *not* an adjective and it is not followed by a noun, so it does not agree with the following word.

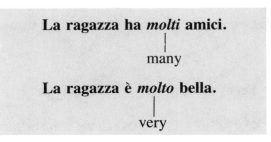

La ragazza ha *molti* amici.
|
many

La ragazza è *molto* bella.
|
very

ALLA CARTOLERIA
At the Stationery Store

You may have to visit a stationery store so you can write home. If so, you'll need to know these words.

(BEE-roh)
la biro
ballpoint pen

(mah-TEE-tah)
la matita
pencil

(LEH-tteh-reh)
la carta da lettere
stationery

(BOOS-tah)
la busta
envelope

(bloh-KKEH-ttoh)
il blocchetto
writing pad

(tah-KKWEE-noh)(ah-PPOON-tee)
il taccuino per appunti
notebook

(ah-deh-ZEE-voh)
il nastro adesivo
transparent tape

(SPAH-goh)
lo spago
string

Have you learned them well enough to recognize them all scrambled up? Try to straighten them out.

agpso (lo) _____ orib (la) _____ mttaia (la) _____

ntsroa ovisade (il) _____ btsua (la) _____

ccaniuto per ppanuit (il) _____ bolhcctteo (il) _____

tcraa da ttleeer (la) _____

You're doing so well that you should have no trouble with this passage and the questions that follow.

(EHN-trah-noh)
Due signore entrano in una cartoleria. La prima signora compra un blocchetto di carta, una
enter
paper
biro, una busta, e dei francobolli perché vuole scrivere una lettera. L'altra signora compra

un taccuino per appunti, il nastro adesivo e lo spago. La prima signora è una turista

203

americana, e l'altra è una turista francese. Le due signore fanno conoscenza e poi vanno al bar a prendere un espresso.

1. Chi entra in una cartoleria?
   - ☐ Due donne francesi.
   - ☐ Due donne americane.
   - ☐ Una francese e un'americana.

2. Chi compra la biro?
   - ☐ La donna francese.
   - ☐ La donna americana.
   - ☐ Nessuno.

3. Chi compra lo spago?
   - ☐ La donna francese.
   - ☐ La donna americana.
   - ☐ Nessuno.

4. Chi compra la matita?
   - ☐ La donna francese.
   - ☐ La donna americana.
   - ☐ Nessuno.

5. Dove vanno le due signore?
   - ☐ Al cinema.
   - ☐ Al chiosco.
   - ☐ Al bar.

You deserve an easy one, now! After reviewing the new words and expressions in this unit, you'll see some of them in the word-search puzzle. Write them out as you find them.

| _____ | _____ | _____ |
| kiosk | newspaper | magazine |

| _____ | _____ | _____ |
| stamp | ballpoint pen | pencil |

a	a	a	a	a	a	c	h	i	o	s	c	o	b	b	b	b	b	b	b
b	b	b	b	b	b	b	b	b	b	b	b	b	b	b	r	d	d	d	d
i	c	v	g	i	o	r	n	a	l	e	c	c	c	y	i	y	y	y	y
r	p	p	p	p	p	p	p	p	p	p	p	p	p	p	v	j	j	j	j
o	t	u	v	b	n	m	m	m	m	m	m	m	m	i	m	m	m	m	m
r	r	r	r	r	r	r	r	r	r	r	r	r	r	s	a	e	r	t
b	b	b	m	a	t	i	t	a	a	a	a	a	a	t	a	a	a	a
f	r	a	n	c	o	b	o	l	l	o	x	x	x	x	a	u	u	u	u

22 | **Il gioielliere / L'orologiaio**
(joh-yeh-LLYEH-reh) *(oh-roh-loh-JAH-yoh)*
Jeweler / Watchmaker

IL GIOIELLIERE

The Jeweler

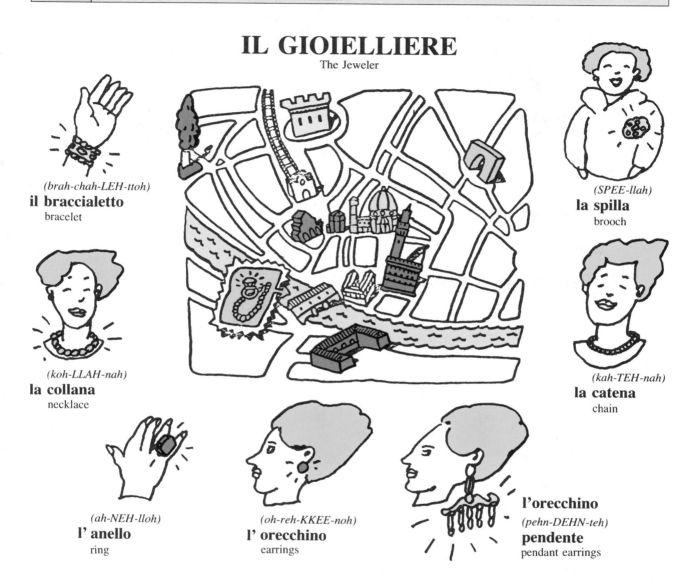

(brah-chah-LEH-ttoh)
il braccialetto
bracelet

(koh-LLAH-nah)
la collana
necklace

(SPEE-llah)
la spilla
brooch

(kah-TEH-nah)
la catena
chain

(ah-NEH-lloh)
l' anello
ring

(oh-reh-KKEE-noh)
l' orecchino
earrings

l'orecchino
(pehn-DEHN-teh)
pendente
pendant earrings

(As Mark and his wife are shopping at a jewelry store near the Ponte Vecchio in Florence, a tall, handsome man comes into the store.)

GIOIELLIERE **Desidera, signore?**

Can I help you, sir?

UOMO **Sì. Vorrei comprare qualcosa per mia moglie. Un braccialetto o un anello d'oro.**

Yes, I would like to buy something for my wife.

A bracelet or a gold ring.

205

GIOIELLIERE	**Ecco un braccialetto**	Here is a silver bracelet and a gold ring.
	(ahr-JEHN-toh)	
	d'argento e un anello d'oro.	
UOMO	**Li prendo tutti e due.**	I'll take them both.
GIOIELLIERE	**Vuole vedere qualcos'altro?**	Do you want to see something else?
UOMO	**Sì. Una spilla degli orecchini.**	Yes. A brooch and earrings.
GIOIELLIERE	**Pendenti?**	Pendants?
UOMO	**Sì. E poi vorrei anche una collana**	Yes. And then I would also like a necklace and
	e una catena.	a chain.
GIOIELLIERE	**D'oro?**	Gold?
UOMO	**Naturalmente.** *(takes out a gun)*	Naturally. And now give me all the money
	E adesso mi dia tutti i soldi che ha!	you've got!

When you're sure you have mastered this dialogue, go ahead and reconstruct it—but be sure to check it when you're finished.

Desidera, signore?

Sì. Vorrei comprare q_____ per mia moglie. Un b_____ o un

anello d'_____ .

Ecco un braccialetto d'_____ e un a_____ d'oro.

Li p_____ tutti e due.

Vuole vedere qualcos'altro?

Sì. Una s_____ e degli o_____ .

P_____?

Sì. E poi vorrei anche una c_____ e una c_____ .

D'oro?

Naturalmente. E adesso mi dia tutti i s_____ che ha!

lo smeraldo
(zmeh-RAHL-doh)

il rubino
(roo-BEE-noh)

(PYEH-treh) (preh-TSYOH-seh)
PIETRE PREZIOSE
Precious Stones

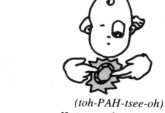

il platino
(PLAH-tee-noh)

lo zaffiro
(DZAH-ffee-roh)

il topazio
(toh-PAH-tsee-oh)

l' argento
silver

la perla
(PEHR-lah)

The English and Italian are so similar that you should be able to identify these jewels.

Can you match each stone with its color?

1. lo smeraldo
2. il rubino
3. il topazio
4. lo zaffiro
5. la perla

a. bianco
b. azzurro
c. verde
d. rosso
e. giallo

il diamante
(dyah-MAHN-teh)

l' oro
gold

Gli Avverbi
Forming Adverbs

To form adverbs from adjectives, simply do the following. If the adjective ends in *-e*, just add *-mente*.

The only adjustment to be made occurs when the adjective ends in *-le* or *-re* preceded by a vowel. In this case, you drop the *-e*.

elegante elegant	**elegante*mente*** elegant*ly*
intelligente intelligent	**intelligente*mente*** intelligent*ly*

(proh-BAH-bee-leh) **probab*ile*** probable	**probabil*mente*** probab*ly*
popol*are* popular	**popolar*mente*** popular*ly*

If the adjective ends in *-o*, change the *-o* to *-a* and add *-mente*.

sicuro **(sicura)** sure	**sicura*mente*** sure*ly*	**lento** **(lenta)** slow	**lenta*mente*** slow*ly*

ANSWERS

Matching 1-c, 2-d, 3-e, 4-b, 5-a

207

L'OROLOGIAIO
The Watchmaker

(ZVEH-llyah)
la sveglia
alarm clock

(POHL-soh)
l' orologio da polso
wrist watch

l' orologiaio
watchmaker

(oh-roh-loh-jeh-REE-ah)
l' orologeria
watchmaker's shop

If you have to get your watch fixed, here are some useful expressions.

(ah-jjoos-TAH-reh)
Mi può aggiustare il mio orologio?   Can you fix my watch?

(ah-VAHN-tee)
Il mio orologio va avanti.   My watch is fast.

(een-DYEH-troh)
Il mio orologio va indietro.   My watch is slow.

Il mio orologio non va.   My watch has stopped.

(kah-ree-KAH-reh)
Devo caricare il mio orologio.   I have to wind my watch.

Here we go with another passage; test yourself by completing the statements.

Il mio orologio non va bene. Un giorno va avanti e un altro va indietro. Oggi non va e non lo posso caricare. Allora lo porto dall'orologiaio e l'orologiaio lo aggiusta. Il giorno dopo l'orologio va ancora avanti! Forse devo comprare un orologio nuovo.

L'uomo dice che il suo orologio non _____ .

Un giorno l'orologio va _____ e un altro va _____ ,

Oggi non va e l'uomo non lo può _____ .

Allora l'uomo porta l'orologio dall'_____

e l'orologiaio lo _____ .

Ma il giorno dopo l'orologio va _____ !

L'uomo dice che deve comprare un orologio _____ .

Now, for a brief summary of several important things. How do you say the following things in Italian?

May I help you? _____

I would like to buy something. _____

My watch is fast. _____

Your watch is slow. _____

I have to buy a new watch. _____

23

Il negozio di articoli da regalo /
(ahr-TEE-koh-lee) *(reh-GAH-loh)*

Il negozio di musica /
(MOO-zee-kah)

Il negozio di fotografie
(foh-toh-grah-FEE-eh)

Gift Shop / Music Store / Photography Shop

AL NEGOZIO DI
ARTICOLI DA REGALO
At the Gift Shop

You certainly won't want to go home without some Italian presents! Here is what to look for.

(sehr-VEE-tsee-oh)
il servizio da tè
tea service

(PEH-lleh)
la pelle
leather

(reh-GAH-loh)
il regalo
present

(BOHR-sah)
la borsa
purse

(ah-NEH-lloh)
l'anello
ring

(bohr-SEH-ttah)
la borsetta
small purse

(KYAH-veh)
la chiave
key

(proh-FOO-moh)
il profumo
perfume

(pohr-tah-FOH-llyoh)
il portafoglio
wallet

(SHAHR-pah)
la sciarpa
scarf

(CHOHN-doh-loh)
il ciondolo
charm

(ree-cheh-VOO-tah)
la ricevuta
receipt

(KWAH-droh)
il quadro
painting

Are you ready for the dialogue? Follow it up with the true-false questions.

(Mary Smith and her son John go into a gift shop.)

COMMESSA **Desiderano?**	Can I help you?
MARY **Sì. Vorrei portare dei regali ai miei amici in America. Mi può aiutare?**	Yes. I would like to bring my friends in America some gifts. Can you help me?
COMMESSA **Volentieri. Forse un po' di profumo, una borsetta, o una sciarpa?**	Gladly. Maybe some perfume, a small purse, or a scarf?
MARY **No. Voglio qualcosa per uomo.**	No. I want something for men.
JOHN **Sì. Abbiamo molti zii in America.**	Yes. We have many uncles in America.
COMMESSA **Allora un portafoglio o un quadro?**	Then a wallet or a painting?
JOHN **No. Costano troppo.**	No. They cost too much.
COMMESSA **Lei può portare un regalo gratis ai suoi zii.**	You can bring a free gift to your uncles.
JOHN **Ah, sì? Che?**	Yes? What?
COMMESSA **I miei saluti!**	My greetings!

1. Mary vuole comprare dei regali per i suoi amici. ☐ Vero ☐ Falso

2. Mary compra il profumo. ☐ Vero ☐ Falso

3. Mary vuole una sciarpa. ☐ Vero ☐ Falso

4. Mary vuole qualcosa per uomo. ☐ Vero ☐ Falso

5. Il portafoglio e il quadro costano poco. ☐ Vero ☐ Falso

6. Il commesso dà un regalo gratis a John. ☐ Vero ☐ Falso

ANSWERS

True/False 1. Vero 2. Falso 3. Falso 4. Vero 5. Falso 6. Falso

AL NEGOZIO DI MUSICA
At the Music Store

We haven't given you all the translations for this new vocabulary, but you should be able to figure them out.

(RAH-dee-oh)
la radio

(teh-leh-vee-ZOH-reh)
il televisore

(náhs-troh) (mah-nyéh-tee-koh)
il nastro magnetico
tape

(reh-jees-trah-TOH-reh)
il registratore
tape recorder

(moo-zee-kah-SSEH-ttah)
la musicassetta

il compact disc

Did you get them all? Then go ahead with the following paragraph.

(KLAH-ssee-kah)

Il signor Smith ama la musica classica.
loves

Cerca un negozio di musica in tutta la città.

Finalmente ne trova uno. Ascolta i dischi
Finally

per tre ore! Suo figlio, invece, ama solo la

musica «folk». Anche il figlio entra nel negozio.

212

(kee-TAH-rrah)
Lui compra una chitarra e si mette a cantare.

(eem-bah-rah-TSAH-toh)   starts to
Imbarazzato, il signor Smith torna all'albergo.
Embarrassed

Now you can probably rearrange these sentences without even looking back.

classica / ama / Smith / Il / la / signor / musica

_____

tutta / in / città / la / Cerca / negozio / musica / di / un

_____

trova / Finalmente / uno / ne

_____

figlio / Suo / ama / solo / invece / folk / musica / la

_____

chitarra / Lui / una / compra / cantare / a / mette / e / si

_____

IL NEGOZIO DI FOTOGRAFIE
At the Photography Shop

Once again we have left out some translations—but you will recognize the words from the pictures.

(FOH-toh)
la foto

(een-grahn-dee-MEHN-toh)
l'ingrandimento

il negozio di fotografie

(dee-ah-poh-zee-TEE-veh)
le diapositive
slides

la pila
battery

(foh-toh-GRAH-fee-kah)
la macchina fotografica

(peh-LLEE-koh-lah)
la pellicola
film

213

(Mark is picking up the photos he had brought in to be developed.)

MARK **Sono pronte le mie foto?**
(EH-kkoh-leh)

COMMESSO **Sì, eccole.**

MARK **Mamma mia, come sono brutto!**

COMMESSO **No, signore. Lei ha torto.**

MARK **Lei è molto gentile. Senta, la mia macchina fotografica non funziona. La può aggiustare?**

Are my prints ready?

Yes, here they are.

Heavens, how ugly I am!

No, sir. You are wrong.

You're very kind. Listen, my camera doesn't work. Can you fix it?

COMMESSO **Certo.**

MARK **Ecco un'altra pellicola. Questa volta voglio le diapositive.**

COMMESSO **Va bene, signore. Grazie e arrivederla.**

MARK **Arrivederla.**

Certainly.

Here is another roll of film. This time I want slides.

Okay, sir. Thank you and good-bye.

Good-bye.

Be sure you thoroughly understand the dialogue before going on to the completion exercise below (and check your answers!).

Sono pronte le mie f_____?

Sì, eccole.

Mamma mia, come sono b_____!

No, signore. Lei ha t_____.

Lei è molto g_____. S_____, la mia m_____

f_____ non funziona. La può a_____?

Certo.

Ecco un'altra p_____. Questa volta voglio le d_____.

Va bene, signore. Grazie e arrivederla.

A_____.

Before you leave this chapter, go over the new vocabulary again; then practice it by unscrambling these words.

qdruao _____   grleao _____
　　　　　painting　　　　　　　　　　　　　　gift
dioar _____   chidisragi _____
　　　　　radio　　　　　　　　　　　　　　　record player
rgiestraerot _____   tlveeirose _____
　　　　　tape recorder　　　　　　　　　　　television set
msuicassatte _____   dscoi _____
　　　　　cassette　　　　　　　　　　　　　　record
plleicoal _____
　　　　　film

24	*(ree-pah-rah-TSYOH-nee)* **Riparazioni:** *(ohp-toh-meh-TREES-tah)* **L'optometrista** / *(kahl-tsoh-LAHyoh)* **Il calzolaio**

Repair Services: Optometrist / Shoemaker

This dialogue contains words and expressions that you might find helpful if you break your glasses in Italy.

DALL'OPTOMETRISTA

At the Optometrist

OPTOMETRISTA **Buon giorno, signore.**　　　　　　Good morning, sir.

(oh-KKYAH-lee) *(ROH-ttee)*

MARK **Ho gli occhiali　rotti.**　　　　　　My glasses are broken.

OPTOMETRISTA **Mi faccia**　　　　　　Let me see. Only one lens

vedere. È rotta solo una　　　　　　is broken.

(LEHN-teh) *(mohn-tah-TOO-rah)*

lente. La montatura　　　　　　The frame is intact.

(een-TAH-ttah)

è intatta.

MARK **Il prezzo?**　　　　　　The price?

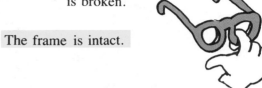

216

OPTOMETRISTA	**Cinquantamila lire.**	50.000 lira.
MARK	**Cinquantamila lire!**	50.000 lira!
	Per solo una lente?	For just one lens?
OPTOMETRISTA	**Purtroppo!**	Unfortunately!/That's the way it is!
MARK	**Li posso ritirare martedì?**	Can I get them Tuesday?
OPTOMETRISTA	**No, ma venga giovedì.**	No, but come back Thursday.
MARK	**Va bene. Grazie e arrivederla.**	OK. Thank you and good-bye.

Now here are some lines from the dialogue. Matching them won't be difficult.

Ho gli . . .	una lente?
È rotta solo . . .	venga giovedì.
La montatura . . .	occhiali rotti.
Per solo . . .	ritirare martedì?
Li posso . . .	una lente.
No, ma . . .	è intatta.

DAL CALZOLAIO
At the Shoemaker

(kahl-tsoh-LAH-yoh)
il calzolaio
shoemaker

(STREEN-geh)
le stringhe
shoelaces

(SAHN-dah-loh)
il sandalo
sandal

le scarpe
shoes

See how quickly you can read this paragraph. Then go over it until it all comes easily, and answer the questions that follow.

(SAHN-dah-lee)

La signora Smith porta le sue scarpe e i suoi sandali dal calzolaio. I sandali hanno bisogno
shoes

(TAH-kkoh)   *(STREEN-geh)*

di un tacco nuovo e le scarpe hanno bisogno di stringhe. Va dal calzolaio in Via Veneto. È un
heel   shoelaces

uomo molto simpatico. La signora Smith gli chiede se può aggiustare le sue scarpe e i suoi

(sah-RAH-nnoh)

sandali. Il calzolaio dice che saranno pronti tra due giorni. Quando la signora Smith va a
they will be

(KYOO-zoh)   *(FEH-ree-eh)*

prendere le scarpe e i sandali vede un cartello sulla porta: "Chiuso per le ferie."
sign   Closed for the holidays.

Dove va la signora Smith?
- ☐ Dall'optometrista.
- ☐ Dal gioielliere.
- ☐ Dal calzolaio.

Di che cosa hanno bisogno i sandali?
- ☐ Di un colore nuovo.
- ☐ Di un tacco nuovo.
- ☐ Di niente.

Di che cosa hanno bisogno le scarpe?
- ☐ Di stringhe.
- ☐ Di un tacco nuovo.
- ☐ Di niente.

Dov'è il calzolaio?
- ☐ In Via Nazionale.
- ☐ In Via Veneto.
- ☐ A casa.

Quando saranno pronti i sandali e le scarpe?
- ☐ Domani.
- ☐ Tra una settimana.
- ☐ Tra due giorni.

Che cosa vede sulla porta la signora Smith?
- ☐ Vede un cartello.
- ☐ Vede una foto.
- ☐ Vede una lettera.

25	**Le banche** *(BAHN-keh)* Banks (Banking)

BIGLIETTI DENARO
Denominations

Notice that Italian denominations are high in comparison to American ones. In fact, a 1,000 lira note is worth less than *one* American dollar. There are also coins for 100, 200, and 500 lira. However, if your expected change is less than 100 lira you might get a token or even a piece of candy! These are probably worth more than the actual change you would otherwise get. You can get good exchange rates at most banks and hotels. And many stores give a good exchange rate as well.

(Courtesy of Ernst Klett Verlag, Stuttgart)

LE BANCHE, IL CAMBIO, E GLI
(KAHM-byoh)

ASSEGNI TURISTICI
(ah-SSEH-nyee)

Banks, Money Exchange, and Traveler's Checks

Gente e cose
People and Things

il denaro
(deh-NAH-roh)
money

l'assegno turistico
traveler's check

i contanti
(kohn-TAHN-tee)
cash

il prestito
(PREHS-tee-toh)
loan

la banca
bank

l'impiegato di banca
(eem-pyeh-GAH-toh)
bank employee

il direttore
(dee-reh-TTOH-reh)
manager

la cassiera (f)
(kah-SSYEH-rah)

il cassiere (m)
(kah-SSYEH-reh)
teller

lo sportello
(spohr-TEH-lloh)
teller's window

il conto
account

il biglietto di banca
bank note

il libretto di assegni
(lee-BREH-ttoh)
checkbook

il modulo di versamento
(MOH-doo-loh) (vehr-sah-MEIIN-toh)
deposit slip

il modulo di prelevamento
(preh-leh-vah-MEHN-toh)
withdrawal slip

Come si fa . . .

How to . . .

(kahm-BYAH-reh)
il cambio / cambiare
to exchange

(vah-LOO-tah)
la valuta
exchange rate

(pah-GAH-reh)
pagare
to pay

(vehr-SAH-reh) *(deh-poh-zee-TAH-reh)*
versare / depositare
to deposit

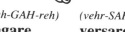

(preh-leh-VAH-reh)
prelevare
to withdraw

riscuotere un assegno
to cash a check

aprire un conto
to open an account

(feer-MAH-reh)
firmare
to sign

After all of that vocabulary, see how much of it you can remember. Match each word or expression to each picture by checking off the appropriate box.

☐ il denaro
☐ lo sportello

☐ il libretto di assegni
☐ i contanti

☐ il direttore
☐ il biglietto

☐ il cassiere
☐ il direttore

☐ il modulo di versamento
☐ il modulo di prelevamento

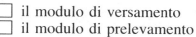

☐ i contanti
☐ l'assegno turistico

221

Did you get them all? Let's try some more:

1. Io vorrei ———————— mille dollari americani.
   <small>exchange</small>

2. Io vorrei ———————— cinquecentomila lire (500,000 lira).
   <small>withdraw</small>

3. Io vorrei ———————— un assegno.   4. Io vorrei ———————— 500,000 lire.
   <small>cash</small>   <small>deposit</small>

(Mark Smith enters a bank; there are several people ahead of him.)

CASSIERE	**Desidera?**	May I help you?
UOMO	**Vorrei riscuotere un assegno.**	I want to cash a check.
	(kohm-PEE-lee)	
CASSIERE	**Per favore compili questo modulo di prelevamento, lo firmi, e ritorni.**	Please fill out this withdrawal slip, sign it, and come back.
	(PREHS-tee-toh)	
UN GIOVANE	**Vorrei un prestito.**	I would like to apply for a loan.

CASSIERE	**Per favore, attenda là il** _(OH-koo-pah)_ **direttore. Lui si occupa** **dei prestiti.**	Please wait over there for the manager. He takes care of loans.
DONNA	**È possibile aprire un conto e fare** **un versamento?**	May I open an account and make a deposit?
CASSIERE	**Deve andare da un altro** **impiegato, al prossimo sportello.**	You must see another bank employee for that, at the next teller's window.

(Finally Mark approaches the teller.)

MARK	**Buon giorno, signore. Ho bisogno** **di cambiare questo assegno turistico** **di mille dollari americani** **in lire** **italiane.**	Good day, sir. I need to exchange this $1,000 American traveler's check for Italian lira.
CASSIERE	**Molto bene. Vuole i soldi in** **biglietti di taglio grosso o piccolo?**	Very well. Do you want the money in large or small bills?
MARK	**Grosso, per favore.**	Large, please.
CASSIERE	**Ecco, signore. Per favore firmi** _(ree-cheh-VOO-tah)_ **questa ricevuta.**	Here you are, sir. Please sign this receipt.
MARK	**Grazie e arrivederla.**	Thank you and good-bye.

After you have become familiar with the dialogue, try to complete the following sentences from it.

Vorrei riscuotere un _____ .

Vorrei un _____ .

È possibile aprire _____ _____ e fare un _____ ?

Ho bisogno di _____ questo assegno _____ di _____

_____ americani in _____ _____ . Per favore firmi questa _____ .

223

If you got all that, then this paragraph and the questions that follow will be a breeze!

Il signor Smith entra in una banca con sua moglie. Chiede al cassiere di cambiare cento dollari americani. Il cassiere gli chiede di compliare un modulo e di firmarlo (sign it). **Il signor Smith non lo vuole firmare e allora decide di non cambiare più i cento dollari.**

Chi entra in una banca?

☐ Il signor Smith e suo figlio.
☐ Il signor Smith e sua moglie.
☐ Il cassiere.

Che cosa chiede al cassiere?

☐ Gli chiede come sta.
☐ Gli chiede di versare un assegno.
☐ Gli chiede di cambiare dollari americani.

Quanti dollari vuole cambiare?

☐ Cento.
☐ Duecento.
☐ Trecento.

Che cosa gli chiede il cassiere?

☐ Di bere il caffè.
☐ Di prelevare i soldi.
☐ **Di firmare il modulo.**

Che cosa decide di fare il signor Smith?

☐ Di cambiare i soldi.
☐ Di non cambiare i soldi.
☐ Di chiamare il direttore.

ANSWERS

Comprehension Il signor Smith e sua moglie. Gli chiede di cambiare dollari americani. Cento. Di firmare il modulo. Di non cambiare i soldi.

224

This crossword puzzle is a final check on how much you have learned about money and banking.

Across

3. Exchange
4. Money
5. Checkbook
7. Teller (f.)
8. Account
9. Deposit

Down

1. Slip
2. Teller's window
3. Cash
4. Manager
6. Bank note

There are some new words in this dialogue. If you need help, check the vocabulary on the next page.

LINA **Che cosa fai?**

What are you doing?

(JOH-koh) (pohs-TEE-noh)
PINO **Gioco a postino.**

I'm playing postman.

LINA **E le lettere dove sono?**

And where are the letters?

(kah-SSEH-tteh)
PINO **Nelle cassette delle lettere delle**

In our neighbors' mailboxes.

case dei nostri vicini.

(PREH-zoh)
LINA **E dove hai preso le lettere?**

And where did you get the letters?

(bah-OO-leh)
PINO **Dal baule nella tua camera dove**

From the trunk in your room where

(TYEH-nee)
tieni quel pacchetto di lettere con un

you keep that package of letters with

(ah-TTOHR-noh)
bel nastro rosa attorno.

a beautiful pink ribbon around them.

LINA **Mamma mia! Sono le mie lettere**

Heavens! They are my love letters!

(ah-MOH-reh)
d'amore!

Are you sure you've got it? Then go ahead and fix up these sentences.

a / Gioco / postino

_____

E / dove / lettere / sono / le

_____

delle / cassette / lettere / Nelle / case / delle / dei / vicine / nostri

---

dove / E / hai preso / lettere / le

---

tieni / dove / Dal / camera / baule / tua / nella / pacchetto / quel / di / bel / lettere / un / con / attorno / nastro / rosa

---

d'amore / Sono / lettere / mie / le

la cassetta delle lettere
mailbox

il postino / il portalettere
mailman

(teh-leh-GRAH-mmah)
il telegramma
telegram

la posta / le lettere / le cartoline
mail   letters   cards

lo sportello
office window

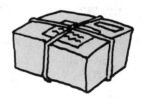

il pacco / il pacchetto
package

227

You learned the last dialogue so quickly that we have another for you!

(John wants to mail a package to the U.S. Anne goes with him to the post office.)

JOHN   **È molto lontano l'ufficio postale?**

Is the post office very far?

ANNE   **No, è vicino all'albergo,**

No, it's near the hotel,

ma c'è sempre tanta gente.

but there's always a lot of people.

Gli italiani non sempre fanno
(KOH-dah) (ohr-dee-NAH-tah)
la coda   ordinata,
(zbree-GYAH-moh-chee)
allora sbrighiamoci!

Italians don't always line up in

an orderly way, so let's hurry.

(They reach the post office and find that it isn't busy.)

JOHN   **Meno male che non c'è nessuno.**

Thank heavens that no one is here.

ANNE   **John, ecco lo sportello per i pacchi.**

John, here is the parcel post window.

(mahn-DAH-reh)
JOHN   **Ecco signore. Voglio mandare**

Here you are, sir. I want to send this package to

questo pacco negli Stati Uniti.

the U.S.

IMPIEGATA   *(weighs the package)*
(ah-ffrahn-kah-TOO-rah)
L'affrancatura per questo pacco è di

The postage for this package is 10,000 lira. Go to

diecimila lire. Vada all'altro sportello

the other window for stamps.

per i francobolli.

(John buys stamps and Anne goes to the postcard window.)

ANNE   **Quattro cartoline, per favore.**   Four postcards, please.

IMPIEGATA   **Ecco signorina.**   Here you are, miss.

ANNE   **Quanto è l'affrancatura per via**   What's the postage for airmail and for
    (ah-EH-reh-ah)   *(rah-kkoh-mahn-DAH-tah)*
    aerea e per posta raccomandata?   registered mail?

IMPIEGATA   **In tutto, ottomila lire.**   In all, 8,000 lira.

When you have read the dialogue several times, check off each statement as either true or false.

1. L'ufficio postale è molto lontano.
   ☐ Vero
   ☐ Falso

2. Gli italiani fanno sempre la coda ordinata.
   ☐ Vero
   ☐ Falso

3. Oggi non c'è tanta gente.
   ☐ Vero
   ☐ Falso

4. L'affrancatura per il pacco di John è di diecimila lire.
   ☐ Vero
   ☐ Falso

5. Anne compra tre cartoline.
   ☐ Vero
   ☐ Falso

6. L'affrancatura per Anne è di diecimila lire.
   ☐ Vero
   ☐ Falso

Ricordati . . .
Remember . . .

Here are a few useful expressions. Can you understand them?

(speh-DEE-reh)
mandare/spedire una lettera

depositare la valigia

spedire un telegramma

l'impiegata

You may have noticed that the adjective *buono* is used both before and after the noun. When it is used before the noun, you must make a few adjustments.

The form *buon* is used before a singular masculine noun beginning with any vowel or consonant, except *z* or *s* plus a consonant.

> **Buon giorno.**
> **Buon appetito.**

And in front of a feminine singular noun beginning with any vowel, the appropriate form is *buon'*.

> **Buon'amica.**

Let's take a breather and do an easy one! Fill in the blanks as suggested by the pictures.

Maria scrive una _____ .

Giovanni spedisce dei _____ in Italia.

La signora ha bisogno di un _____ .

Gina mette le lettere nella _____ .

I verbi ancora una volta!

Verbs Again!

Notice that verbs ending in -*care* and -*gare* require an *h* when the verb ending starts with an *i*.

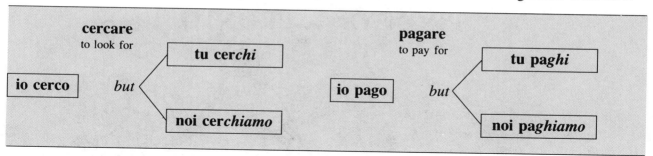

That's not so hard to remember, is it? Now let's wind up the post office chapter by adding the missing letters to the following words.

il post——no, la——assetta delle l——tter——, la post——, il t——l——gramma,

lo sportel——o, l'——ffrancatur——

Now, how do you say the following in Italian? This is a difficult exercise. So, even if you do not get the answers perfectly, you will learn considerably by trying.

I'm looking for the mailbox. Are you looking for it too, John?

_____

Who is paying for the coffee? Are you paying for it, Mary?

_____

We're looking for Dante Street. Do you know where it is, sir?

_____

They never pay for coffee at the (coffee) bar.

_____

PRONTO ... PRONTO

Hello . . . Hello

(John has become friendly with Paola, a girl he met at the bank last week. He is in a phone booth and Anne is outside.)

PAOLA	**Pronto. Chi parla?**	Hello. Who is it?
JOHN	**Ciao, Paola. Sono John.**	Hi, Paola. It's John. (*literally*, I am John)
PAOLA	**Dove sei?**	Where are you?
JOHN	*(kah-BEE-nah) (teh-leh-FOH-nee-kah)* **In una cabina telefonica vicino a casa tua. Vuoi uscire con me stasera?**	At a phone booth near your home. Do you want to come out with me tonight?
PAOLA	**Dove?**	Where?
JOHN	**Al cinema.**	To the movies.
PAOLA	**No. Non mi piace il cinema.**	No. I don't like the movies.
JOHN	*(bah-LLAH-reh)* **Allora andiamo a ballare?**	Then shall we go out dancing?
PAOLA	**No. Non so ballare.**	No. I don't know how to dance.
JOHN	**Andiamo a un ristorante?**	Shall we go to a restaurant?
PAOLA	**No. Sono a dieta.**	No. I'm on a diet.
ANNE	*(who has been waiting to use the phone)* **Ti dico io dove devi andare, John! A un'altra cabina!**	I'll tell you where to go, John! To another booth!

Are you sure you have completely mastered the dialogue? Maybe you should read it once more, before answering the true-false exercise.

1. John è in una cabina telefonica. ☐ Vero ☐ Falso

2. John chiede a Paola di andare al bar. ☐ Vero ☐ Falso

3. A Paola piace il cinema. ☐ Vero ☐ Falso

4. Paola non sa ballare. ☐ Vero ☐ Falso

5. Paola decide di andare al ristorante. ☐ Vero ☐ Falso

6. Anne ha molta pazienza. ☐ Vero ☐ Falso

(teh-leh-foh-NAH-tah)

TELEFONATA LOCALE O INTERURBANA?

(een-tehr-oor-BAH-nah)

Local or Long Distance?

The telephone system of another country always seems to have its mysteries. Here are some words and expressions that you might need.

il telefono telephone

(teh-leh-foh-NAH-reh)
telefonare to phone

formare il numero to dial

la cabina telefonica phone booth

(chehn-trah-lee-NEES-tah)
il/la centralinista operator

la carta telefonica phone card

Pronto Hello

la guida telefonica phone book

la telefonata interurbana long distance call

When you have learned them thoroughly, write the appropriate word or expression in the blanks.

In Italia, si può usare la ——————————————————————— .

Quando si risponde al telefono si dice «———————————————————» .

I numeri di telefono si trovano nella ————————————————————— .

Una telefonata "long distance": ——————————————————————— .

In una ————————————————————— si trova il telefono pubblico.

Prima di parlare al telefono, bisogna ——————————————————————— .

Lina forma il numero del macellaio. Un uomo risponde. Lina dice all'uomo che vuole

comprare un pollo. Gli dice che è molto urgente la situazione perché stasera arrivano i suoi
(preh-pah-RAH-reh)

zii dall'America. Vuole preparare una bella cena. L'uomo ascolta con pazienza. Poi dice:
to prepare
(zbah-LLYAH-toh)   *(fyoh-RAH-yoh)*

«Scusi, signora, ma lei ha sbagliato numero, Io sono un fioraio.»

You're doing great! Now prove to yourself how much you've learned by filling in the blanks:

L'uomo ascolta con ———————— .

Lina dice che è ———————— ———————— la situazione ————————

———————— ———————— i suoi zii dall'America.

L'uomo risponde. Io sono un ———————— .

(dehn-TEES-tee) *(doh-TTOH-ree)* *(ohs-peh-DAH-lee)*

Dentists, Doctors, Hospitals

UNA RAPIDA OCCHIATA

(RAH-pee-dah) *(oh-KKYAH-tah)*

A Once-Over

We're getting close to the end! But you really *should* learn the parts of the body. Mario and Gino are testing each other. Let's join in!

MARIO **Chi comincia, tu o io?** — Who'll start, you or I?

GINO **Comincia prima tu.** — You start.

MARIO **Bene. Che sono questi?** — Good. What are these?

(kah-PEH-llee)
GINO **I capelli.** — The hair(s).

MARIO **E che c'è nel mezzo agli occhi?** — And what's between the eyes?

GINO **Il naso.** — The nose.

MARIO **Tra il naso e la bocca molti uomini hanno...** — Between the nose and the mouth, many men wear...

(BAH-ffee)
GINO **i baffi.** — a moustache.

(oh-REH-kkee)
MARIO **Abbiamo due orecchi...** — We have two ears...

235

GINO *(GWAHN-cheh)* **e due guance,**

and two cheeks,

MARIO *(FAH-chah)* **ma solo una faccia**

but only one face

GINO **e una testa.**

and only one head.

MARIO **Quando si ride, si vedono…**

When one laughs, one sees…

GINO *(DEHN-tee)* **i denti**

the teeth

MARIO **e quando si va dal medico…**

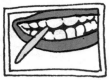

and when you go to the doctor,

GINO *(LEEN-gwah)* **gli si fa vedere la lingua, aah.**

you…show him your tongue, aah.

MARIO **Questo è…**

This is…

GINO *(MEHN-toh)* **il mento**

the chin

MARIO **e quello è…**

and that is…

GINO *(KOH-lloh)* **il collo.**

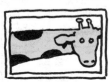

the neck.

MARIO **Ecco due…**

Here are two

GINO *(SPAH-lleh)* **spalle**

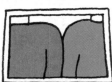

shoulders

MARIO **e due…**

and two…

GINO *(GOH-mee-tee)* **gomiti…**

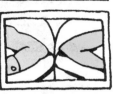

elbows…

MARIO **due…**

two…

GINO **mani**

hands

MARIO **e dieci...**   and ten...

GINO **dita.**   fingers.

MARIO **Ora tocca a te.**   Now it's your turn.

GINO **Questa è...**   This is

(SKYEH-nah)
MARIO **la schiena,**   the back,

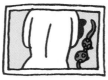

GINO **e qui davanti...**   and here in front...

(PEH-ttoh)
MARIO **c'è il petto,**   is the chest,

GINO **e lì dietro c'è...**   and there in back is...

(seh-DEH-reh)
MARIO **il sedere.**   the fanny.

GINO **E da qui a qui ci sono due...**   And from here to here you have two...

(KOH-sheh)
MARIO **cosce**   thighs

GINO **con due...**   with the two...

MARIO **ginocchia.**   knees.

GINO **E più in giù ci sono i due...**   And farther down the two...

(pohl-PAH-chee)
MARIO **polpacci,**   calves,

(kah-VEE-lyeh)
GINO **due caviglie e...**   two ankles, are

(PYEH-dee)
MARIO **i piedi**   the feet

GINO **con dieci...**   with the ten...

MARIO **dita.**   toes.

Now try this difficult association exercise. Which part of the human body would you associate with the following?

l'anello _____ , lo shampoo _____ , il mascara _____ ,

la sigaretta _____ , il profumo _____ , gli occhiali _____ ,

la radio _____ , l'intelligenza _____ , il dentifricio _____ ,
(een-teh-llee-JEHN-tsah)

la collana _____ , il guanto _____ , la scarpa _____ ,

la camicia _____ .

Ricordati
Remember

Remember that the verb *sentirsi* allows you to say that you are not feeling well.

You can also use *fare male a.*

| **Mi sento male.** | I feel bad. |

| **Mi fa male la testa.** | My head hurts. |

A list of common ailments might come in handy, just in case! Consider this a basic survival list.

(STOH-mah-koh)
Mi fa male lo stomaco. — My stomach hurts.

(GOH-lah)
Mi fa male la gola. — My throat hurts.

Mi fa male un dente. — My tooth hurts.

(rah-ffreh-DDOH-reh)
Ho il raffreddore. — I have a cold.

(FEH-bbreh)
Ho la febbre. — I have a temperature/fever.

(TOH-sseh)
Ho la tosse. — I have a cough.

(voh-mee-TAH-reh)
Mi viene da vomitare. — I feel like vomiting.

(SAHN-gweh)
Mi esce il sangue dal naso. — My nose is bleeding.

Now pretend you are at the doctor's. Write out the suggested parts. When you have finished composing your dialogue, read it out loud several times.

DOCTOR   **Buon giorno. Si sente male?**   Good day. Are you not feeling well?

YOU   _____, **dottore.**   Good day, doctor. I feel bad.

   _____ **male.**

DOCTOR   Che problema c'è?   What's the problem?

YOU   _____   I have a cough. My throat hurts, and I have

   _____   a fever.

   _____

DOCTOR   **Forse ha il raffreddore. Ha altri**   Maybe you have a cold. Do you have any
   (SEEN-toh-mee)
   sintomi?   other symptoms?

YOU   _____   Yes. My stomach hurts. I feel like vomiting,

   _____   and my nose is bleeding.

   _____

DOCTOR   **Lei ha probabilmente**   You probably have the flu.
   (een-floo-EHN-tsah)
   l'influenza.

YOU   **Che cosa devo fare?**   What should I do?

DOCTOR   **Deve andare a letto e riposarsi.**   You have to go to bed and relax.

YOU   _____?   Really?
   (KOO-rah) (mee-LLYOH-reh)
DOCTOR   **Sì. È la cura migliore.**   Yes. It's the best cure.

Splendid! We knew you could do it!

APRA LA BOCCA!

Open Wide!

You might, of course, need to go to a dentist. If so the following list may prove useful to you.

Mi fa male un dente.	My tooth hurts.
(kah-VAH-reh)	
Mi deve cavare un dente?	Do you have to take a tooth out?
(eem-pyohm-bah-TOO-rah)	
Ho bisogno di un'impiombatura?	Do I need a filling?
(dehn-TYEH-rah)	
Ho bisogno di una dentiera nuova.	I need new dentures.

You did so well with the last assignment—let's try another.

YOU _____. Doctor, my tooth hurts.

DENTISTA **Non si preoccupi. Apra** Don't worry. Open your mouth.

(kah-REE-eh)
la bocca. Lei ha una carie. You have a cavity.

YOU _____? Do you have to take a tooth out?

DENTISTA **No. Non è male.** No. It's not bad.

YOU _____? Do I need a filling?

DENTISTA **Sì. Prima le faccio un'iniezione.** Yes. First I'll give you a shot.

YOU _____. No thanks, doctor. I'll come tomorrow.

DENTISTA **Lei ha paura delle iniezioni? Non si preoccupi. Signore/Signora, dove va?**	You're afraid of needles? Don't worry. Sir/Madam, where are you going?
YOU _____, dottore. _____ volo _____ tra _____!	Good day, doctor. My flight is leaving in two hours!

APRA LA BOCCA E FACCIA AAAAAAH . . .
Say Aaaaaah . . .

You probably won't need to use these terms, but see if you can translate them.

 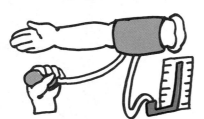  

(MEH-dee-kah)
la tessera medica

(preh-SSYOH-neh)
la pressione
(sahn-GWEE-nyah)
sanguigna

(tehr-MOH-meh-troh)
il termometro

la sigla del
(MEH-dee-koh)
dottore/medico

(Mark Smith is not feeling well, so he goes to the doctor.)

MARK	**Buon giorno, dottore. Mi sento molto male.**	Hello, doctor. I feel really bad.
DOTTORE	**Dove le fa male?**	Where does it hurt?
MARK	**In gola.**	In my throat.
DOTTORE	**Apra la bocca e faccia aaaaaah.**	Open your mouth and say aaaaaah.
MARK	**Che c'è di male, dottore?**	What's wrong, doctor?
DOTTORE	*(tohn-SEE-lleh)* **Lei ha le tonsille** *(een-fyah-MMAH-teh)* **infiammate.**	Your tonsils are inflamed.

(The doctor takes out his surgical instruments.)

MARK	**Che cosa fa, dottore?**		What are you doing, doctor?
	(TOH-lyehr-leh)		
DOTTORE	**Dobbiamo toglierle adesso.**		We should take them out now.
	È il metodo più sicuro.		It's the best way.

MARK   *(as he is running out of the office)*

Mamma mia, quel dottore è pazzo!   Heavens, that doctor is crazy!

Now wasn't that easy? You're nearly there!

1. **Mark si sente molto bene.**   ☐ Vero
                                           ☐ Falso

2. **Gli fa male la gola.**   ☐ Vero
                                           ☐ Falso

3. **Il dottore gli dice di aprire la
   bocca.**   ☐ Vero
                                           ☐ Falso

4. **Mark ha il raffreddore.**   ☐ Vero
                                           ☐ Falso

5. **Mark si fa togliere le tonsille.**   ☐ Vero
                                           ☐ Falso

(proh-toh-KOH-lloh)   *(ohs-peh-DAH-leh)*

PROTOCOLLO D'OSPEDALE
Hospital Protocol

(proh-feh-SSOH-reh)

In Italy the head physician of a hospital is called: **il professore.**

(ah-ssees-TEHN-tee)

The other doctors are called: **gli assistenti.**

Then come the nurses (male and female):

(een-fehr-MYEH-reh)   *(een-fehr-MYEH-rah)*

l'infermiere (m) / **l'infermiera** (f).

Try this paragraph—bet you get it the first time!

(een-FAHR-toh) (kahr-DEE-ah-koh)   *(SOO-bee-toh)*

Al signor Dini prende un infarto   cardiaco. Sua moglie chiama subito
                    heart attack   right away

(ah-oo-toh-ahm-boo-LAHN-tsah)

un' autoambulanza. Per strada l'autoambulanza si ferma. Non ha più benzina!
ambulance   On the way   stops

(fohr-TOO-nah)

Per fortuna passa un'altra autoambulanza che porta il signor Dini all'ospedale.
Fortunately   comes by

242

And now the questions:

Che cosa prende al signor Dini?
- ☐ Un infarto cardiaco.
- ☐ Il raffreddore.

Che cosa chiama subito sua moglie?
- ☐ Un medico.
- ☐ Un'autoambulanza.

Che cosa fa l'autoambulanza per strada?
- ☐ Va velocemente.
- ☐ Si ferma.

Perché si ferma?
- ☐ Perché non ha più benzina.
- ☐ Perché c'è troppo traffico.

Come arriva all'ospedale il signor Dini?
- ☐ A piedi.
- ☐ Con un'altra autoambulanza.

Terrific!

(bahr-tseh-LLEH-ttah)

UNA BARZELLETTA
A Joke

(JOH-vah-neh)
Un giovane va dal dottore. Il giovane dice, «Dottore, vorrei . . .»
young man

(SPOH-llyee)
«Si spogli!» dice subito il dottore.
undress

«Ma dottore . . .» dice ancora il giovane.

«Si spogli!» insiste il dottore. Il giovane si spoglia.
insists

(eh-zah-mee-NAHR-loh)
Quando il dottore va per esaminarlo, il giovane ripete,
goes to examine him

(KYEH-dehr-leh)
«Dottore, io non mi sento male! Io sono qui per chiederle,
I am here to ask you

(ah-bboh-NAHR-see)
se vuole abbonarsi alla rivista *L'Espresso*!»
subscribe

243

Do you remember the parts of the body? See how many words and expressions you can match. Don't look back until you have finished—then review those you missed.

1. il piede	a. face
2. la gamba	b. hair
3. il dito	c. eyes
4. la mano	d. mouth
5. il braccio	e. foot
6. il collo	f. leg
7. la faccia	g. finger
8. la bocca	h. ears
9. gli occhi	i. neck
10. i capelli	j. arm
11. gli orecchi	k. hand
12. Mi fa male lo stomaco.	l. I feel like vomiting.
13. Mi fa male la gola.	m. My stomach hurts.
14. Ho la febbre.	n. My head hurts.
15. Ho la tosse.	o. My throat hurts.
16. Mi viene da vomitare.	p. I have a cough.
17. Mi fa male la testa.	q. I have a fever.
18. cavare un dente	r. nurse
19. l'impiombatura	s. to take out a tooth
20. la carie	t. needle
21. la puntura	u. thermometer
22. il termometro	v. head physician
23. il professore	w. cavity
24. l'infermiere	x. ambulance
25. l'autoambulanza	y. heart attack
26. l'infarto cardiaco	z. filling

ANSWERS

Matching 1-e, 2-f, 3-g, 4-k, 5-j, 6-i, 7-a, 8-d, 9-c, 10-b, 11-h, 12-m, 13-o, 14-q, 15-p, 16-l, 17-n, 18-s, 19-z, 20-w, 21-t, 22-u, 23-v, 24-r, 25-x, 26-y

244

UNA BARZELLETTA

A Joke

GIUDICE **Allora, signora, ha rotto** *(ROH-ttoh)*

l'ombrello sulla testa di suo marito?

So, madam, you broke your umbrella

over your husband's head?

DONNA **Un errore!**

It was an accident! (*literally*, an error)

GIUDICE **Un errore?**

An accident (error)?

DONNA **Non volevo rompere** *(voh-LEH-voh)* *(ROHM-peh-reh)*

l'ombrello!

I didn't want to break the umbrella!

SE HAI BISOGNO DI UN'AUTOAMBULANZA...

If You Need an Ambulance . . .

(Mark has fallen down the stairs.
In the foyer of the hotel, Mary seeks help.)

MARY **Signore, aiuto! Mio marito ha**

rotto una gamba. Che devo fare?

Help, sir! My husband has broken a leg.

What am I to do?

IMPIEGATO **È grave, signora?**

Is it serious, madam?

MARY **Sì, penso di sì. E a pensare che la nostra partenza per l'America è domani.**	Yes, I think so. And to think that tomorrow is our departure for America.
IMPIEGATO **Non si preoccupi. Chiami l'autoambulanza.**	Don't worry. Call the ambulance.
MARY **Come si fa?**	What does one do?
IMPIEGATO **Si chiama il centralinista e si chiede aiuto.**	You call the operator and ask for help.

(At this point, Mark walks into the room.)

MARY **Mark, che fai?**	Mark, what are you doing?
MARK *(to the clerk)* **Non è necessario telefonare all'autoambulanza. Non ho niente. Scherzavo. Ora so che mia moglie mi ama ancora!**	It is not necessary to call the ambulance. I'm okay. *(literally,* I have nothing.) I was joking. Now I know that my wife still loves me.

No cheating now—complete the missing parts from memory. Afterwards, check your answers in the dialogue.

Signore, a_____! Mio marito ha rotto una g_____.

Che d_____ fare?

È g_____, signora?

Sì, penso di sì. E a pensare che la nostra p _____ per l'America è domani.

Non si preoccupi. Chiami l'a _____ .

Come si fa?

Si chiama il c_____ e si chiede aiuto.

Mark, che fai?

Non è necessario t _____ all'autoambulanza. Non ho niente. Scherzavo.

Ora so che mia moglie mi ama a_____!

CHIAMA LA POLIZIA!
Call the Police!

One last dialogue—with a few questions following it.

(The Smiths are packing their bags.)

MARK	**Mary! Non trovo il mio portafoglio!**	Mary! I can't find my wallet!
MARY	**Forse è in una valigia.**	Maybe it's in a suitcase.

(koo-SHEE-noh)

MARK	**No, non è sotto il cuscino dove lo**	No, it is not under the pillow where I
	metto ogni sera. Chiama la polizia!	put it every night. Call the police!
MARY	**Come devo fare?**	What should I do?

(teh-LEH-foh-nah)

MARK	**Telefona al centralinista!**	Phone the operator!

(A policeman arrives.)

MARK	**Signore, qualcuno**	Sir, someone stole my wallet!

(roo-BAH-toh)

	ha rubato il mio portafoglio!	
POLIZIA	**Si calmi, signore!**	Calm down, sir!
MARK	**Io lo metto sempre sotto il cuscino!**	I always put it under the pillow!
	E adesso non c'è!	And now it's not there!
POLIZIA	**C'è in una valigia?**	Is it in a suitcase?
MARK	**No.**	No.
POLIZIA	**Nella borsa di sua moglie?**	In your wife's purse?
MARY	**No, non c'è.**	No, it's not there.

(TAS-kah)

POLIZIA	**Guardi nella sua tasca.**	Look in your pocket.

(EH-kkoh-loh)

MARK	**Ah, eccolo! Meno male!**	Ah, here it is! Thank heavens!

POLIZIA *(to himself)* **I turisti sono tutti uguali!** *(oo-GWAH-lee)*   Tourists are all alike!

MARK **Grazie e arrivederla.**   Good-bye and thank you.

POLIZIA **Arrivederla.**   Good-bye.

(later at the airport)

THE SMITHS **Arrivederci, Italia, e grazie per una bella vacanza!**   Good-bye, Italy, and thanks for a great vacation!

Chi non trova il portafoglio?
- [ ] Mary.
- [ ] Mark.
- [ ] Anne.

È in una valigia, il portafoglio?
- [ ] Sì.
- [ ] No.

Dove mette il portafoglio Mark ogni sera?
- [ ] Nella valigia.
- [ ] Nella borsa.
- [ ] Sotto il cuscino.

Per chiedere l'aiuto della polizia, chi si **può chiamare?**
- [ ] Il centralinista.
- [ ] **L'impiegato**
- [ ] Il direttore dell'albergo.

Dov'è il portafoglio?
- [ ] Sotto il cuscino.
- [ ] In una valigia.
- [ ] Nella tasca di Mark.

Aren't you pleased with yourself?

IN CASO DI UN INCIDENTE/UNA DISGRAZIA
(dees-GRAH-tsyah)
Handling an Accident

Here are some common accidents.

Aiuto! Ho ricevuto una scossa elettrica!
electrical charge

Fuoco!
fire

(tah-LLYAH-tah)
Ahi! Mi sono tagliata il dito!
cut

Attenzione ai bambini!

Ahi! C'è troppa acqua!

If you have an accident follow the normal procedures for any emergency situation. Take care of first-aid needs right away. Then call for the appropriate help. Always have a phone card with you in order to be able to use the public phones in Italy. You will find Italians extremely helpful in emergency situations. So ask for anybody's help and remember the key word:

AIUTO!
Help!

Here are the expressions you might need in an emergency:

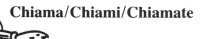

Chiam ← **a** (familiar)   **i** (polite)   **ate** (plural)   **la polizia!**   Call the police!

Chiama/Chiami/Chiamate   **il soccorso medico!**   Call for medical help!

(FWOH-koh)

Chiama/Chiami/Chiamate   **i vigili del fuoco!**   Call the fire department!

Chiama/Chiami/Chiamate   **il medico!**   Call the doctor!

Chiama/Chiami/Chiamate   **l'autoambulanza!**   Call the ambulance!

BEFORE YOU LEAVE

Prima di partire

Now we come to the final step in the learning process, and the most important one. You might view it as a final exam. What will you do and say in the following situations? You may want to look over the sections of the book that correspond to each of the following seven situations, before you get started. Ready? Then let's go!

Situazione 1: Fare la conoscenza della gente

Situation 1: Getting to Know People

A. It is daytime and you meet someone.
   What do you say in order to start a conversation?
   1. ☐ Buon giorno.
   2. ☐ Arrivederci.
   3. ☐ Prego.

B. You have just run into a friend.
   What do you say?
   1. ☐ Grazie.
   2. ☐ Ciao.
   3. ☐ Buona sera.

C. It is evening. How do you greet a stranger?
   1. ☐ Ciao.
   2. ☐ Buon giorno.
   3. ☐ Buona sera.

D. How do you say good-bye to a stranger?
   1. ☐ Arrivederci.
   2. ☐ Arrivederla.
   3. ☐ Ciao.

E. How do you say good-bye to a friend?
   1. ☐ Arrivederci/Ciao.
   2. ☐ Arrivederla.

F. Someone asks you how you are. Which of the following is *not* possible as an answer?
   1. ☐ Non c'è male, grazie.
   2. ☐ Molto bene, grazie.
   3. ☐ Buon giorno, grazie.

G. How would you ask a friend how he/she feels?
   1. ☐ Come stai?
   2. ☐ Come sta?
   3. ☐ Dove vai?

H. How would you ask a stranger how he/she feels?
   1. ☐ Come stai?
   2. ☐ Come sta?
   3. ☐ Dove vai?

I. Someone has just said "grazie." As a possible answer, you might say . . .
   1. ☐ Bene.
   2. ☐ Prego.
   3. ☐ Arrivederci.

Situazione 2: L'arrivo

Situation 2: Arrival

You do not have a reservation at the hotel. What do you say?
1. ☐ Come sta, signore?
2. ☐ Scusi, signore, non ho la prenotazione.
3. ☐ Buon giorno, signore, come si chiama?

You want to say you really need a room. You might say . . .
1. ☐ Per favore, ho bisogno urgente di una camera.
2. ☐ Per favore, mi dia il passaporto.

You want to inquire about price and what is included. So you might say . . .
1. ☐ Mi può dire come si chiama, lei?
2. ☐ Mi può dire dov'è il bagno?
3. ☐ Mi può dire quanto costa la camera e quali sono i servizi?

Under "Nome" one might find:
1. ☐ Duecentomila lire al giorno.
2. ☐ Mark Smith.
3. ☐ Tre.

Under "Indirizzo" one might find:
1. ☐ Duecentomila lire al giorno.
2. ☐ Tre.
3. ☐ Via Washington, 25, Washington, D.C., U.S.A.

Under "Numero di camera" one might find:
1. ☐ Duecentomila lire al giorno.
2. ☐ Tre.
3. ☐ Via Verdi, 3, Roma.

Under "Data" one might find:
1. ☐ Duecentomila lire al giorno.
2. ☐ Via Verdi, 3, Roma.
3. ☐ (Il) 30 luglio.

Under "Prezzo" one might find:
1. ☐ Duecentomila lire al giorno.
2. ☐ Mark Smith.
3. ☐ (Il) 3 agosto.

Under "Firma" one might find:
1. ☐ Ventidue.
2. ☐ Mark Smith.
3. ☐ (Il) 5 agosto.

Situazione 3: I punti d'interesse

Situation 3: Seeing the Sights

You are on foot and want to find a certain street. You might ask a passerby:

1. ☐ Scusi, come sta?
2. ☐ Scusi, dove si trova Via . . .?
3. ☐ Scusi, lei abita in Via . . .?

The passerby might say:

1. ☐ **A sinistra, a destra, diritto . . .**
2. ☐ Domani, ieri, oggi . . .
3. ☐ Il semaforo, l'ufficio postale, la banca . . .

You have boarded a bus. You want to ask where to get off. You might say:

1. ☐ Scusi, quanto costa il biglietto?
2. ☐ Scusi, dove devo scendere per Via Verdi?
3. ☐ Scusi, come si chiama lei?

You have flagged down a taxi; but before getting in you want to know how much it would cost to get to Via Verdi. You might say:

1. ☐ Scusi, quanto è lontana Via Verdi?
2. ☐ Scusi, lei sa dov'è Via Verdi?
3. ☐ **Scusi, quanto è per andare fino a Via Verdi?**

You have forgotten your watch. You stop a passerby to ask what time it is. You might say:

1. ☐ Scusi, mi sa dire che ora è?
2. ☐ Scusi, ha un orologio?
3. ☐ Scusi, che tempo fa?

The passerby would *not* answer:

1. ☐ Sono le due e venticinque.
2. ☐ È domani.
3. ☐ È l'una e mezzo.

You are at a train station and want to buy a ticket. You might say:

1. ☐ **Scusi, quanto è un biglietto per Firenze?**
2. ☐ Scusi, dov'è Firenze?
3. ☐ Scusi, che ore sono?

The clerk answers that there is no room left on the train. He/She might say something like:

1. ☐ Mi dispiace, ma lei è pazzo.
2. ☐ Mi dispiace, ma lei non parla italiano.
3. ☐ **Mi dispiace, ma non ci sono più posti.**

You want to say that you are an American and that you speak only a little Italian. You might say:

1. ☐ **Sono americano(a) e parlo solo un po' d'italiano.**
2. ☐ Parlo americano e non sono italiano(a).
3. ☐ Non sono italiano(a); sono americano(a).

ANSWERS

If someone were to ask what nationality you are, he/she would *not* say:
1. ☐ Lei è canadese?
2. ☐ Lei è intelligente?
3. ☐ Lei è americano(a)?

You want to rent a car cheaply. You might ask the clerk:
1. ☐ Vorrei noleggiare una macchina economica.
2. ☐ Vorrei noleggiare una macchina di lusso.
3. ☐ Vorrei noleggiare una macchina nuova.

You want to fill up your car. You might say to the attendant:
1. ☐ Per favore, pulisca il parabrezza.
2. ☐ Per favore, il pieno.
3. ☐ Per favore, controlli l'olio.

You have just been in a car accident and wish to ask how the other motorist is. You might say:
1. ☐ Buon giorno, come sta?
2. ☐ Come si sente?
3. ☐ Come si chiama?

A service station attendant might tell you that your car needs repairs. He would *not* say:
1. ☐ La sua macchina è bella.
2. ☐ La sua macchina ha bisogno di freni nuovi.
3. ☐ La sua macchina ha bisogno di un motore nuovo.

You ask an employee at a camping site if there are certain services. You would *not* say:
1. ☐ C'è l'acqua?
2. ☐ Ci sono posti per far giocare i bambini?
3. ☐ C'è il cinema?

When asked how much the charges are, a clerk might respond:
1. ☐ Duecentomila lire.
2. ☐ Duecento soldi.
3. ☐ Duecento ore.

If someone were to ask you about the weather, you would *not* say:
1. ☐ Fa bel tempo.
2. ☐ Piove sempre.
3. ☐ Nevica.
4. ☐ È vicino.

As an answer to "Che giorno è oggi?" you would *not* hear:
1. ☐ È il quindici settembre.
2. ☐ È il secondo giorno.
3. ☐ È il tre maggio.

At the airport you might hear this over the loudspeaker.
1. ☐ Il volo numero 303 per New York è interessante.
2. ☐ Il volo numero 303 per New York non arriva.
3. ☐ Il volo numero 303 per New York parte alle sedici e venti.

ANSWERS

2, 1, 2, 1, 3, 1, 4, 2, 3

253

To ask an airline employee at what time your flight leaves, you might say:

1. ☐ Scusi, a che ora parte il mio volo?
2. ☐ Scusi, quando arriva il mio volo?
3. ☐ Scusi, dov'è l'aeroporto?

Where would you find this sign?

1. ☐ All'aeroporto.
   (kah-poh-LEE-neh-ah)
2. ☐ Al capolinea.
   bus terminal
3. ☐ Alla stazione ferroviaria.

Where would you find this sign?

1. ☐ All'aeroporto.
2. ☐ Al capolinea.
3. ☐ Alla stazione ferroviaria.

Look at this plan of the city.

1. To which spot would you go to buy *aspirine*? _____

2. To which spot would you go to buy *francobolli*? _____

3. To which spot would you go to exchange *denaro*? _____

4. To which spot would you go to buy *un anello*? _____

5. To which spot would you go to buy *le sigarette*? _____

6. To which spot would you go to buy *il burro*? _____

7. To which spot would you go to get *la tua barba* shaved off? _____

8. To which spot would you go to get *una permanente*? _____

9. To which spot would you go to buy *una camicia*? _____

10. To which spot would you go to buy *un quadro*? _____

11. To which spot would you go to buy *un giornale*? _____

12. To which spot would you go to buy *delle buste*? _____

13. To which spot would you go to get *il tuo vestito* cleaned? _____

Situazione 4: I divertimenti
Situation 4: Entertainment

You are at a ticket agency. The clerk would *not* ask you:
1. ☐ Lei vuole un biglietto per l'opera?
2. ☐ Lei vuole un biglietto per il cinema?
3. ☐ Lei vuole un biglietto per l'aereo?

If someone were to ask you what your favorite sport is, you would *not* say:
1. ☐ Mi piace il tennis.
2. ☐ Mi piace il nuoto.
3. ☐ Mi piace il calcio.
4. ☐ Mi piace l'italiano.

Situazione 5: Ordiniamo da mangiare
Situation 5: Ordering Food

Use this menu to answer some of the questions.

MENÙ			
Antipasto:	Prosciutto e melone.	Dessert:	Gelato
Primo piatto:	Minestra al brodo		Torta
	Spaghetti	Bevande:	Vino rosso
	Risotto alla milanese		Vino bianco
	Tortellini alla bolognese		Acqua minerale
Secondo piatto:	Cotoletta		Caffè
	Bistecca alla fiorentina		
	Pesce		

A. You want to ask someone what kinds of restaurants are available. You might say:
1. ☐ Si mangia bene in Italia?
2. ☐ Come sono i ristoranti qui?
3. ☐ Che tipo di ristoranti ci sono?

B. As a possible answer you would *not* hear:
1. ☐ Ci sono ristoranti locali.
2. ☐ Ci sono i bar.
3. ☐ Ci sono trattorie.
4. ☐ Ci sono forchette.

255

C. When a waiter asks you to order he might say:
   1. ☐ Mangia?
   2. ☐ Desidera?
   3. ☐ Paga?

D. To see the menu you would say:
   1. ☐ Posso vedere il cucchiaio?
   2. ☐ Posso vedere il menù?
   3. ☐ Posso vedere il direttore?

E. Which of the following is not connected with eating?
   1. ☐ La colazione.
   2. ☐ Il pranzo.
   3. ☐ La benzina.
   4. ☐ La cena.

F. If you chose *Prosicutto e melone* you would *not* need:
   1. ☐ Una forchetta.
   2. ☐ Un bicchiere.
   3. ☐ Un coltello.

G. If you chose *minestra al brodo* you would need:
   1. ☐ Un cucchiaio.
   2. ☐ Un coltello.
   3. ☐ Una tazza.

H. Spaghetti, risotto, and tortellini are all types of:
   1. ☐ Zucchero.
   2. ☐ Pasta.
   3. ☐ Carne.

I. If you want to order something from the *secondo piatto* section you might say:
   1. ☐ Vorrei della frutta.
   2. ☐ Vorrei un po' di sale e pepe.
   3. ☐ Vorrei della carne o un po' di pesce.

J. To eat *torta* you would need:
   1. ☐ Un bicchiere.
   2. ☐ Una tazza.
   3. ☐ Un piatto.

K. You drink *vino* or *acqua minerale* in:
   1. ☐ Un bicchiere.
   2. ☐ Una tazza.
   3. ☐ Una bottiglia.

L. You drink *caffè* in:
   1. ☐ Un bicchiere.
   2. ☐ Una tazza.
   3. ☐ Una bottiglia.

256

Situazione 6: Entriamo nei negozi

Situation 6: At the Store

Which of the following would you *not* say in a clothing store?
1. ☐ Scusi, quanto costa questa camicia?
2. ☐ Scusi, quanto costa la benzina?
3. ☐ Vorrei dei calzini e delle cravatte.

Which of the following lists has nothing to do with clothing?
1. ☐ Un vestito azzurro, una giacca rossa, una camicia bianca.
2. ☐ Due calzini, tre cravatte, un paio di mutande.
3. ☐ L'italiano, il tedesco, lo spagnolo.

You would *not* hear which of the following in a supermarket?
1. ☐ Quanto costa la frutta?
2. ☐ Dove sono le ciliege?
3. ☐ Quanto costa la carta?
4. ☐ La carne costa molto oggi.
5. ☐ Il pesce è fresco.
6. ☐ Non abbiamo più pasta.

You would *not* say this at a pharmacy.
1. ☐ **Quanto costa la medicina?**
2. ☐ Dov'è la garza?
3. ☐ Dove sono i francobolli?

You are at the laundry. You would *not* see this there.
1. ☐ Il ferro da stiro.
2. ☐ Il casco.
3. ☐ Il sapone in polvere.

You are at a barbershop. You might say:
1. ☐ **Per favore, mi dia un compact disc.**
2. ☐ Per favore, mi tagli i capelli.
3. ☐ Per favore, mi dia un biglietto.

The hairdresser would *not* ask you:
1. ☐ Vuole la messa in piega?
2. ☐ Vuole un biscotto?
3. ☐ Vuole una permanente?
4. ☐ Vuole uno shampoo?

ANSWERS

Match up the following:

1. Quanto costa un tacco per questa scarpa?
2. Ho bisogno di un orologio nuovo.
3. Quanto costa questa rivista?
4. Quanto costano queste foto?
5. Quanto costano queste cartoline?
6. Lei ha dei ricordi d'Italia?
7. Quanto costa questo compact disc?

a. Negozio di articoli da regalo
b. Calzolaio
c. Orologiaio
d. Negozio di musica
e. Chiosco
f. Negozio di fotografic
g. Ufficio postale

Situazione 7: Servizi essenziali

Situation 7: Essential Services

You are at a bank and wish to exchange a traveler's check. You might say . . .
1. ☐ Scusi, che ore sono?
2. ☐ Scusi, mi può cambiare questo assegno turistico?
3. ☐ Scusi, devo compilare questo modulo?

Now you want to deposit some money. You might say . . .
1. ☐ Vorrei versare questo denaro.
2. ☐ Vorrei pagare il biglietto.
3. ☐ Vorrei firmare il modulo.

A bank employee would *not* ask . . .
1. ☐ Per favore, firmi questo modulo.
2. ☐ Per favore, mangi la pizza.
3. ☐ Per favore, compili questo modulo.

You want to buy stamps at a post office. You might say . . .
1. ☐ Per favore, vorrei comprare delle cartoline.
2. ☐ Per favore, vorrei comprare delle buste.
3. ☐ Per favore, vorrei comprare dei francobolli.

Which of the following would you *not* say in a post office?
1. ☐ Vorrei spedire la lettera per via aerea.
2. ☐ Vorrei spedire la lettera per via raccomandata.
3. ☐ Vorrei spedire la lettera nella valigia.

You answer a phone call with . . .
1. ☐ Pronto.
2. ☐ Buon giorno.
3. ☐ Ciao.

If you want to say "Who is it?" you would say . . .
1. ☐ Come si chiama?
2. ☐ Chi parla?
3. ☐ Perché chiama, lei?

You want to make a long distance call. You would say . . .
1. ☐ Vorrei fare una telefonata locale.
2. ☐ Vorrei fare una telefonata interurbana.
3. ☐ Vorrei il suo numero di telefono.

You want to ask someone how to dial a number. You would say . . .
1. ☐ Scusi, come si forma il numero?
2. ☐ Scusi, come si fa la telefonata?
3. ☐ Scusi, dov'è il telefono?

Which of the following would *not* be used to seek help?
1. ☐ Chiama l'autoambulanza!
2. ☐ Chiama la polizia!
3. ☐ Chiama i vigili del fuoco!
4. ☐ Chiama il soccorso medico!
5. ☐ Chiama il gatto!

You would *not* say one of the following to a doctor.
1. ☐ Dottore, mi sento male.
2. ☐ Dottore, lei è pazzo.
3. ☐ Dottore mi fa male lo stomaco.
4. ☐ Dottore, ho la febbre.

Choose the appropriate box for each of the pictures.

A. 1. ☐ È un telegramma.
    2. ☐ È una cartolina.
    3. ☐ È una lettera.

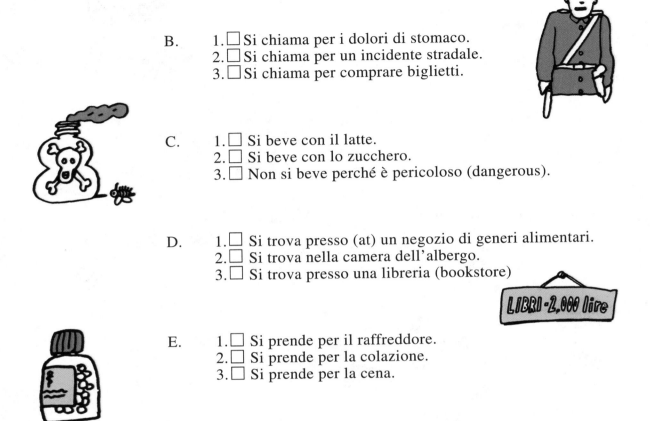

B.   1. ☐ Si chiama per i dolori di stomaco.
     2. ☐ Si chiama per un incidente stradale.
     3. ☐ Si chiama per comprare biglietti.

C.   1. ☐ Si beve con il latte.
     2. ☐ Si beve con lo zucchero.
     3. ☐ Non si beve perché è pericoloso (dangerous).

D.   1. ☐ Si trova presso (at) un negozio di generi alimentari.
     2. ☐ Si trova nella camera dell'albergo.
     3. ☐ Si trova presso una libreria (bookstore)

E.   1. ☐ Si prende per il raffreddore.
     2. ☐ Si prende per la colazione.
     3. ☐ Si prende per la cena.

to stay, to feel

How are you?
How do you feel?
I'm well/bad
not bad

to present

A pleasure!
Delighted (to know you)!
Let me introduce you to…

to eat

I eat too much!
What is there to eat?

to come

At what time are they coming?
When is he/she coming?

to live, dwell

dwelling
I live on…Street
Where do you live?

to have

I have a lot of patience!
I haven't got any time!

to go

to go away
to go out
to return, come back

to drink

alcoholic beverage
beverage
soft drink

to be

I'm American
I'm Italian
Where are you from?

stare

Come stai (fam) ?
Come sta (pol) ?
Sto bene/male
non c'è male

presentare

Piacere!
Molto lieto (m) !/Molto lieta (f) !
Ti presento (fam)/Le presento (pol)...

mangiare

Mangio troppo!
Che cosa c'è da mangiare?

venire

A che ora vengono ?
Quando viene?

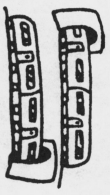

abitare

l'abitazione
Abito in via...
Dove abiti (fam) ?/Dove abita (pol) ?

avere

Ho tanta pazienza!
Non ho tempo!

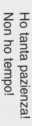

andare

andare via, andarsene
uscire
tornare, ritornare

bere

la bevanda alcolica
la bevanda
la bibita

essere

Sono americano (m)
Sono americana (f)
Sono italiano (m)
Sono italiana (f)
Di dove sei (fam) ?
Di dov'è (pol) ?

to see

I can't see
I'll see you!
See you again!/Good-bye!

to walk

to drive
to go for a walk
to go by bicycle
to go on foot
to jog
to run

to fly

airplane   airport
boarding pass by air
flight   ticket

to understand

I don't understand!
I understand a little!

to change (money)

change
exchange
to keep

to send

to mail (to put in a mail box)
to mail off

to sit (down)

armchair
chair
Where are you sitting?
sofa

to want

I would like
May I help you?

to leave

departure
to go away
to go out
to leave behind

volare

l'aeroplano
la carta d'imbarco
il volo

l'aeroporto
con l'aereo
il biglietto

camminare

guidare
fare una camminata/passeggiata
andare in bicicletta
andare a piedi
fare il footing/fare il jogging
correre

vedere

Non ci vedo
Ci vediamo!
Arrivederci!

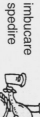

mandare

imbucare
spedire

cambiare

il cambiamento
il cambio
tenere

capire

Non capisco!
Capisco un po'!

partire

la partenza
andare via, andarsene
uscire
lasciare

volere

Vorrei
Desidera (sing) ?/Desiderano (pl) ?

sedersi

la poltrona
la sedia
Dove ti siedi (fam) ?/Dove si siede (pol)?
il divano

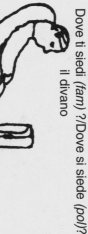

to speak

to speak poorly
to speak slowly
to speak well
to speak too fast

to know (someone)

to know something, how to
to make one's acquaintance

to sell

on sale
for sale

to give

to be on familiar speaking terms
to be on formal speaking terms

to pay

bill
debt
payment

to ask (for)

question   to request

to cost

cost
How much do they cost?/How much are they?
How much does it cost?/How much is it?

to buy

purchase
to acquire
to spend (money)

to look for

What are you looking for?
Who are you looking for?

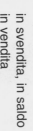
parlare

parlare male
parlare lentamente
parlare bene
parlare troppo svelto (m) / svelta (f)

dare

dare del tu   dare del Lei

costare

il costo
Quanto costano?/Quanto sono?
Quanto costa?/Quant'è?

conoscere

sapere   fare (la) conoscenza

pagare

il conto, la fattura
il debito
il pagamento

comprare

l'acquisto
acquistare
spendere (soldi)

vendere

in svendita, in saldo
in vendita

chiedere

la domanda   richiedere

cercare

Che cosa cerchi (fam) / cerca (pol)?
Chi cerchi (fam) / Chi cerca (pol)?

to receive

receipt   to send

to bring, carry

portable

to sign

first name
signature
surname, family name

to take

to have something to drink
to have something to eat

to please, to like

I like it
I like them
pleasant
please
With pleasure!

to sleep

to fall asleep
to go to sleep/to go to bed
to wake up

to be able to

Can you do it?
I can't!

to put

to put on   to take off

to say, tell

Tell me everything!
to tell the truth

ricevere

la ricevuta

mandare

portare

portatile

firmare

il nome
la firma
il cognome

prendere

prendere qualcosa da bere
prendere qualcosa da mangiare

piacere

Mi piace
Mi piacciono
piacevole
per piacere, per favore
Con piacere!

dormire

addormentarsi
andare a dormire/andare a letto
svegliarsi

potere

Puoi farlo? (*fam*) / Può farlo? (*pol*)
Non posso!

mettere

mettersi

togliersi, levarsi

dire

Dimmi tutto! (*fam*) /Mi dica tutto! (*pol*)
dire la verità

little, few

a little, a bit
several

that, which, who(m)

if
what
when
where
which (one)
who
why, because

preposition

at, to
between, among
for
from
in, to
of
on
with
without

how, as

How come?
What's your name *(fam)* ?
What's your name *(pol)* ?

much, a lot

enough   too much

to open

closed
open
to close

more

More than ever!   Never again!

how much

How much do they cost?
How much does it cost?

to answer

answer
question
to ask

poco

un poco/un po'

alcuni (m) / alcune (f)

che

se
che, che cosa, cosa
quando
dove
quale
chi
perché

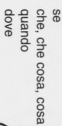

la preposizione

a
tra/fra
per
da
in
di
su
con
senza

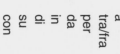

come

Come mai?
Come ti chiami (fam) ?
Come si chiama pol) ?

molto (m) / molta (f)

abbastanza   troppo

aprire

chiuso
aperto
chiudere

più

Più che mai!   Mai più!

quanto

Quanto costano?
Quanto costa?

rispondere

la risposta
la domanda
chiedere, domandare

small

short
tall

new

again, anew

hi, hello

good morning
good afternoon, evening
good night
good-bye

better

I'm feeling better
I'm well

old

old age

all

each one
each, every
everyone
no one, nobody
nothing

easy

difficult

young

adolescent, teenager
adult
to grow up

less, minus

at least
at the very least

piccolo (m) / piccola (f)

basso (m) / bassa (f)
alto (m) / alta (f)

nuovo (m) / nuova (f)

di nuovo

ciao, pronto (on the phone)

buon giorno
buona sera
buona notte
arrivederci

meglio

Sto meglio
Sto bene

vecchio (m) / vecchia (f)

la vecchiaia

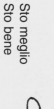

tutto

ciascuno
ogni
tutti, ognuno
nessuno
niente

facile

difficile

giovane

l'adolescente
l'adulto
crescere

meno

almeno
per lo meno

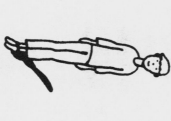

left

left hand
to the left

good

good at something
better
best

cold

I am cold
It (an object) is cold
It's cold

beautiful, handsome

ugly

bad

worse
the worst

expensive

cheap
costly

very, quite

very full
very tired

hot, warm

I am hot
It (an object) is hot
It's hot

big

fat
huge
skinny, thin
wide

sinistro

la mano sinistra
a sinistra

---

buono (m) / **buona** (f)

bravo (m) / brava (f)
migliore
il migliore

---

freddo (m) / **fredda** (f)

Ho freddo
E' freddo (m) / fredda (f)
Fa freddo

---

bello (m)/ **bella** (f)

brutto (m) / brutta (f)

---

cattivo (m) / **cattiva** (f)

peggiore
il peggiore

---

caro (m) / **cara** (f)

a buon mercato, economico
costoso (m) / costosa (f)

---

assai, molto

assai/molto pieno (m) / piena (f)
assai/molto stanco (m) / stanca (f)

---

caldo (m) / **calda** (f)

Ho caldo
E' caldo (m) / calda (f)
Fa caldo

---

grande

grasso (m) / grassa (f)
grosso (m) / grossa (f)
magro (m) / magra (f)
largo (m) / larga (f)

shop

to shop (in general)
to shop (for food)

street

block (of a city)
corner
highway
sidewalk
traffic lights

place

behind
here
on top
up
down
in front

far
near
under
there
where

country

farm
field
flower
grass
landscape, countryside
plant
tree
village

to travel

excursion, tour
map
to arrive
to leave
travel agency
trip

date

then
yesterday
after
already
always
before   never
now   often
today   tomorrow
What's the date?

city

building
city hall
downtown
movie theater
museum
office
skyscraper
square
theater

address

apartment   house, home

right

right hand
to the right

la bottega

fare delle spese
fare la spesa

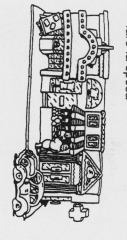

la strada, la via

l'isolato
l'angolo
l'autostrada
il marciapiede
il semaforo

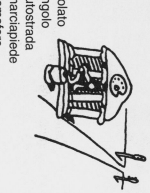

il paese

la fattoria
il prato
il fiore
l'erba
il paesaggio
la pianta
l'albero
il paese, il villaggio

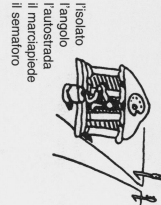

il luogo

dietro	lontano
qui/qua	vicino
sopra	sotto
su	lì/là
giù	dove
davanti	

viaggiare

il giro
la cartina geografica
arrivare
partire
l'agenzia di viaggi
il viaggio

la città

l'edificio
il municipio
il centro
il cinema
il museo
l'ufficio
il grattacielo
la piazza
il teatro

la data, il giorno

poi	
ieri	
dopo	
già	
sempre	
prima	mai
adesso, ora	spesso
oggi	domani

Che giorno è/Quanti ne abbiamo?

l'indirizzo

l'appartamento   la casa

destro (m) / destra (f)

la mano destra
a destra

ticket

round-trip ticket
to purchase a ticket

train

first class
seat
train station
schedule
track

porter

elevator
stairs
tip

hotel

boarding house
front/registration desk
key
reservation
room

church

cross
mosque
synagogue
temple

castle

bridge
tower

store

clothing store
food store
hardware store
stationery store
bookstore
department store
drugstore
music store
shoe store
smoke shop

market

merchandise
merchant
stand (of merchandise)

bank

account
bank book
check
bank employee
deposit
form (to fill out)
to deposit
travelers' checks
to withdraw
withdrawal

il facchino

l'ascensore
le scale
la mancia

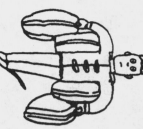

il treno

la prima classe   l'orario
il posto   il binario
la stazione ferroviaria

il biglietto

il biglietto di andata e ritorno
fare il biglietto

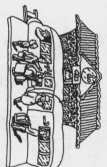

il castello

il ponte
la torre

la chiesa

la croce
la moschea
la sinagoga
il tempio

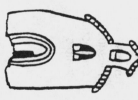

l'albergo

la pensione
il banco d'accettazione
la chiave
la prenotazione
la camera

la banca

il conto
il libretto di banca
l'assegno
l'impiegato (m) /l'impiegata (f)
il deposito, il versamento
il modulo (da compilare)
depositare, versare
gli assegni turistici
prelevare
il prelevamento

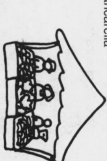

il mercato

la merce
il mercante/ la mercante
la bancarella

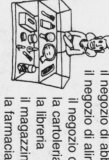

il negozio

il negozio di abbigliamento
il negozio di alimentari
il negozio di ferramenta
la cartoleria
la libreria
il magazzino
la farmacia
la discografia
la calzoleria, il calzolaio
la tabaccheria, il tabaccaio

clothes

blouse
boot
coat
jacket
pants   shirt
shoe   skirt
stocking   sweater
sock   tie

house

bathroom
bedroom
entrance   exit
garage   kitchen
living room   roof

money

bill   cash money
credit card   dollar
lira   small change

door

car door
front door (to a building)
handle

price

cheap
expensive
fixed price
How much does it cost?
sale
What's the price?

suitcase

carry-on bag
lost suitcase
luggage
to pack one's suitcases

hotel room

bathroom
bed
floor
TV set
wake-up call

customs

border
customs officer
identification (paper)
passport
to declare

baggage

heavy
light
weight

i vestiti, i capi di abbigliamento

la camicetta
lo stivale
il cappotto
la giacca
i pantaloni
la scarpa
la calza
il calzino

la camicia
la gonna
la maglia
la cravatta

la casa

il bagno
la camera da letto
l'ingresso
l'autorimessa, il garage
il soggiorno, il salotto

l'uscita
la cucina
il tetto

il denaro

la banconota
la carta di credito
la lira

i contanti
il dollaro
gli spiccioli

la porta

lo sportello
il portone
la maniglia

il prezzo

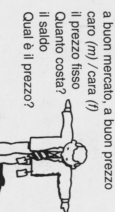

a buon mercato, a buon prezzo
caro (m) / cara (f)
il prezzo fisso
Quanto costa?
il saldo
Qual è il prezzo?

la valigia

la borsa a mano
la valigia smarrita
i bagagli
fare le valigie

la camera

il bagno
il letto
il piano
il televisore
la sveglia

la dogana

la frontiera
il doganiere
la carta d'identità
il passaporto
dichiarare

il bagaglio

pesante
leggero (m) / leggera (f)
il peso

water

alcoholic beverage
coffee
mineral water
tea

beer
juice
soft drink
wine

bread

baker
bun

bakery
sandwich (flat)

vegetables

bean
cabbage
carrot
cauliflower
eggplant
olive
pea
string bean

mushroom
onion
potato
tomato

meal

breakfast
lunch
dinner
snack
to have breakfast
to have lunch
to have dinner

meat

bacon
beef
chicken
cold cuts
ham
pork
turkey

lamb
sausage
veal

fish

clam   cod
lobster   mussels
salmon   seafood
shrimp   trout   tuna

purse

briefcase
handbag
knapsack, schoolbag
wallet

to be thirsty

I'm not very thirsty
I'm very thirsty

to be hungry

I'm not very hungry
I'm very hungry

la verdura

il fagiolo	
il cavolo	
la carota	
il cavolfiore	
la melanzana	
l'oliva	il fungo
il pisello	la cipolla
il fagiolino	la patata
	il pomodoro

il pesce

la vongola	il merluzzo
l'aragosta	le cozze
il salmone	i frutti di mare
il gambero	la trota il tonno

l'acqua

la bevanda alcolica	la birra
il caffè	il succo
l'acqua minerale	la bibita
il tè	il vino

avere fame

Ho poca fame
Ho molta fame

la carne

la pancetta	
il manzo	
il pollo	
gli affettati	
il prosciutto	l'agnello
il maiale	la salsiccia
il tacchino	il vitello

il pane

il panettiere	il panificio
il panino	il tramezzino

la borsa

la cartella
la borsa a mano
lo zaino
il portafoglio

il pasto

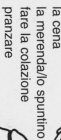

la (prima) colazione
il pranzo
la cena
la merenda/lo spuntino
fare la colazione
pranzare
cenare

avere sete

Ho poca sete
Ho molta sete

season

spring
autumn, fall

summer
winter

weather

It's cold
It's cool
It's hot, warm
It's sunny
It's raining
It's snowing
It's windy
It's beautiful (weather)
It's awful (weather)

time

What time is it?
It's one o'clock
It's two ten
It's six thirty
It's noon
It's midnight
It's five minutes to nine

month

January
February
March
April
May
June

July
August
September
October
November
December

day

morning
evening

afternoon
night

week

Monday
Tuesday
Wednesday
Thursday
Saturday

Friday
Sunday

kitchen

cup
glass
plate
table

fork
knife
spoon

food

cheese
condiments
egg
sugar

drinks, beverages
pasta
vegetables

fruit

apple
apricot
banana
cherry
grapefruit
grapes
lemon
pear
peach

orange
pineapple
strawberry

la stagione

la primavera   l'estate

l'autunno   l'inverno

il mese

gennaio	luglio
febbraio	agosto
marzo	settembre
aprile	ottobre
maggio	novembre
giugno	dicembre

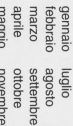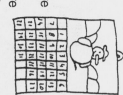

la cucina

la tazza	la forchetta
il bicchiere	il coltello
il piatto	il cucchiaio
il tavolo, la tavola	

il tempo

Fa freddo
Fa fresco
Fa caldo
C'è il sole
Piove
Nevica
Tira vento
Fa bel tempo
Fa cattivo/brutto tempo

il giorno, la giornata

la mattina, il mattino   il pomeriggio

la sera, la serata   la notte

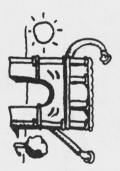

il cibo

il formaggio	le bevande
i condimenti	la pasta
l'uovo	la verdura
lo zucchero	

l'ora

Che ora è?/Che ore sono?
E' l'una
Sono le due e dieci
Sono le sei e mezzo
E' mezzogiorno
E' mezzanotte
Sono le nove meno cinque

la settimana

lunedì	
martedì	
mercoledì	
giovedì	venerdì
sabato	domenica

la frutta

la mela	l'arancia
l'albicocca	l'ananas
la banana	la fragola
la ciliegia	
il pompelmo	
l'uva	
il limone	
la pera	
la pesca	

color

orange
black
blue
brown
green
red
white
yellow
gray

hand

finger
fingernail
thumb
index
ring finger
middle finger
little finger

titles

Mr.
Mrs.
Miss
Dr.
Prof.

body

arm
chest
knee
neck

foot
leg
shoulder

child

boy
girl
teenager, adolescent

family - 2

aunt
uncle
cousin
grandfather
grandmother
relative
parents

head

ear
eye
face
hair
lip
mouth
nose
tongue
tooth

friend

enemy
friendly
friendship

family - 1

brother
daughter
father
mother
sister
son

il colore

arancione
nero (m) / nera (f)
azzurro (m) / azzurra (f)
marrone
verde
rosso (m) / rossa (f)
bianco (m) / bianca (f)
giallo (m) / gialla (f)
grigio (m) / grigia (f)

la mano

il dito
l'unghia
il pollice
l'indice
l'anulare

il dito medio
il mignolo

titoli

Signore
Signora
Signorina
Dottore (m) / Dottoressa (f)
Professore (m) / Professoressa (f)

il corpo

il braccio
il petto
il ginocchio
il collo

il piede
la gamba
la spalla

la testa

l'orecchio
l'occhio
la faccia
i capelli
il labbro
la bocca
il naso
la lingua
il dente

il bambino (m) / la bambina (f)

il ragazzo
la ragazza
l'adolescente

l'amico (m) / l'amica (f)

il nemico
amichevole
l'amicizia

la famiglia - 2

la zia
il zio
cugino (m) / la cugina (f)
il nonno
la nonna
il parente (m) / la parente (f)
i genitori

la famiglia - 1

il fratello
la figlia
il padre
la madre
la sorella
il figlio